IRVING
BERLIN

Irving Berlin writing lyrics for "Now It Can Be Told," from *Alexander's Ragtime Band* (1938).

IRVING BERLIN

A Life in Song

PHILIP FURIA

With the Assistance of Graham Wood

Irving Berlin Songography
compiled by Ken Bloom

Schirmer Books
NEW YORK

Schirmer Books
1633 Broadway
New York, New York 10019

Library of Congress Catalog Number: 98–15486
Printed in the United States of America

Printing number
  2   3   4   5   6   7   8   9   10

As this page cannot legibly accommodate all of the permissions to use previously published material, the permissions appear on page 301.

Library of Congress Cataloging-in-Publication Data

Furia, Philip, 1943–
Irving Berlin ; a life in song / Philip Furia, with the assistance of Graham Wood ; "Irving Berlin Songography" compiled by Ken Bloom.
    p. cm.
    Includes discography, filmography, bibliographical references, and index.
    ISBN 0-02-864815-3
  1. Berlin, Irving, 1888–   .
  2. Composers—United States—Biography.
  I. Wood, Graham.
  II. Title.
ML410.B499F87   1998
782.42164'092—dc21
[B]   98-15486
                                   CIP
                                   MN

This paper meets the requirements of ANSI/NISO Z39.48-1992 (Permanence of Paper).

For my sons,
Peter and Nick,
"A Couple of Swells"

Contents

Acknowledgments ix

1 RUSSIAN LULLABY 1

2 RAGGED METER MAN 25

3 I LOVE A PIANO 47

4 A PRETTY GIRL IS LIKE A MELODY 67

5 SAY IT WITH MUSIC 87

6 BLUE SKIES 109

7 THE SONG IS ENDED 125

8 HOW DEEP IS THE OCEAN? 145

9 CHEEK TO CHEEK 165

10 GOD BLESS AMERICA 191

11 ANYTHING YOU CAN DO 215

12 COUNT YOUR BLESSINGS 237

Irving Berlin Songography compiled by Ken Bloom 267

Endnotes 285

Permissions 301

Index 307

Acknowledgments

I have tried to acknowledge two of my greatest debts on the title page of this book. Graham Wood, my research assistant at the University of Minnesota, generously shared his musical expertise with me, gently refining my own rudimentary insights and graciously offering his own astute observations on how music and words consort together in song. Ken Bloom, whose impeccable scholarship I have long admired, kindly offered his own Irving Berlin Songography for inclusion in this book.

Paul Wilkes, my colleague at the University of North Carolina at Wilmington, read an early draft of this book and offered the kind of advice and encouragement only a writer of many successful books can render to an academic trying to reach a larger audience of readers. Paul also performed the gracious office of introducing me to Mary Ellin Barrett, who opened many doors—and boxes of manuscripts—for research on her father, Irving Berlin. Mary Ellin Barrett and Linda Emmet each gave the manuscript a very careful and helpful reading, sharing their observations on their father's life and work with me.

Others who have helped me include Theodore S. Chapin, Executive Director of the Rodgers and Hammerstein Organization, who manages the Irving Berlin Music Company; Raymond White, Curator of the Irving Berlin Archive of the Library of Congress; Laura Kaiser of the UCLA Film and Television Archive; Ned Comstock of the USC Doheny Memorial Cinema–Television Library; Miles Kreuger, President of the Institute of the American Musical; Maxine Fleckner Ducey and Ann Wilkens of the Wisconsin Center for Film and Theater Research; Marty Jacobs of the Museum of the City of New York; and Brigitta Kueppers of the UCLA Film Scripts Archive. Bert Fink, Maxyne Lang, Robin Walton, and Flora Griggs at the Rodgers and Hammerstein Organization helped me with photographs and song copyrights. Mark Petty provided arcane material on Irving Berlin; Tony Hill has shared his encyclopedic knowledge of Berlin with me for many years; and Les Block, who, ever since we mounted a theatrical tribute to Irving Berlin, has been an invaluable source of musical knowledge, show business lore, and the need, in writing as on stage, to "get in and get out."

Richard Carlin of Schirmer Books invited me to undertake this project and provided excellent editorial suggestions. Also at Schirmer,

Jill Lectka worked with me at the beginning of the book and guided me through the first draft, and Richard Steins copyedited the manuscript with care and insight. The Graduate School of the University of North Carolina at Wilmington supported the completion of the book with travel funding to several film and manuscript archives. My assistant, Janice Keller, made my "day job" as Chair of the Department of English manageable enough to enable me to complete this book. Finally, my wife, Laurie Patterson, has taken time from her profession, her graduate studies, and her other protean activities to edit my manuscript, discuss lyrics, music, and films, and share her house and husband with the demanding presence of Irving Berlin.

IRVING
BERLIN

Chapter 1

RUSSIAN LULLABY

I always think of my youth in the first decades of the century as the best time of my life. . . . My own existence was a struggle from one dollar to the next. But I was finding myself.

Although he had no formal musical education and could only play the piano in one key, Irving Berlin is universally acclaimed as America's greatest songwriter. That acclaim comes not only from the American people, who have embraced his songs as they have those of no other composer, but from other songwriters themselves. For George Gershwin, Irving Berlin was "the greatest American song composer," our equivalent of Franz Schubert. Cole Porter went further, calling Irving Berlin "the greatest songwriter of all time." Jerome Kern, when asked to define Irving Berlin's place in American music, replied, "Irving Berlin has no 'place' in American music—Irving Berlin IS American music." Perhaps his preeminence as a songwriter reflects the fact that—unlike these other composers, all of whom had extensive musical training—Irving Berlin never ventured beyond the strict confines of the popular song. Throughout his long life, he was content to struggle with the rigors of the thirty-two bar formula, its patterns of repetition and variation, of rhythmic surprise against metrical regularity, and of melodic richness within the range of the average singing voice.

Songwriting, moreover, is only partly a musical art; it is also an art of words, the two arts of music and poetry coalescing to produce a third, where word and sound, syllable and note, verbal phrase and musical cadence must be in accord. So difficult is that art, that most songs are written by two people, a composer and a lyricist, working in collaboration. The answer to that perennial question, "Which comes first—the music or the words?" is different for different song-writers. For Gilbert and Sullivan, the words always came first, so that their songs are actually Gilbert's poems set to music by Sullivan. In American popular song, the reverse was usually true; Lorenz Hart, for example, would not even begin to write words until Richard Rodgers gave him a completed melody. For Irving Berlin, however, the words and music came together. He was one of the few songwriters of his era to write both lyrics and music. Just as his innate musical talent overcame the absence of formal training, so his mastery of words transcended the limits of growing up in a house-hold where Yiddish was spoken and attending school only for a few years. Where other lyricists, such as Hart, Ira Gershwin, or Yip Harburg, all of whom went to college, dazzle us with their brilliant rhymes, witty imagery, and learned allusions, Irving Berlin's words are deceptively simple, casually colloquial, and always in perfect concord with his music.

Berlin's singular devotion to the art of weaving words and music together produced songs of extraordinary quality. During the course of his career, he wrote thousands of songs, sometimes at the rate of at least one each day, but only a few met his high standards. At times, he considered only one in five—sometimes only one in ten—suitable for publishing, performing, and recording. Eight hundred ninety-nine of his songs were registered for copyright, but the quali-ty of these is remarkable. Most songwriters dream of having a single hit song in a lifetime. More than half—451—of Berlin's songs became hits, and 282 of these reached that coveted circle of the "Top Ten." More amazing still is that 35 of his songs reached the pinnacle of the "Number One" most popular song of their day.

Even more indicative of the quality of his songs is that so many have become "standards"—the kind of song that transcends its own era of popularity to become a timeless part of our musical heritage. Heard today in jazz and cabaret performances, movie soundtracks, even in television commercials, these evergreens constitute the clos-est thing America has to a vital body of classical song. Each new generation of singers and musicians reinterprets this Great American Song Book, bringing out depths and nuances that make these standards sound as fresh today as when they were first written.

Still, Berlin's achievement as a songwriter goes beyond quality and quantity. The sheer range and variety of his songs are stagger-ing. Where most successful songwriters find that their success lasts only until the world of popular music takes another stylistic turn, Irving Berlin endured half a century of changes in musical fashion and wrote outstanding songs in every prevailing idiom. When America was seized by the ragtime dance craze early in the twentieth century, Irving Berlin wrote the biggest hits of the era—and the biggest hit song the world had ever seen until that time, "Alexander's Ragtime Band." When American boys went off to World War I, Irving Berlin gave them "Oh! How I Hate to Get Up in the Morning," then in World War II he concocted the sterner, "This Is the Army, Mr. Jones." In the 1920s and 1930s, when the public longed for wistful romantic ballads that could be crooned over the radio, he wrote so many—"All Alone," "What'll I Do?," "Always," "How Deep Is the Ocean?"—that another songwriter, Cole Porter, dubbed the entire genre "the Berlin Ballad." When Ziegfeld needed songs to celebrate the beauty of the American girl, Irving Berlin gave him "A Pretty Girl Is Like a Melody," then for lavish revues at his own Music Box Theatre, he provided "Say It with Music." When talking pictures came in 1927, Irving Berlin was there from the very start with "Blue Skies," sung by Al Jolson in *The Jazz Singer*. Then, for the screen's greatest singing and dancing couple, Fred Astaire and Ginger Rogers, he penned such classics as "Cheek to Cheek" and "Top Hat, White Tie, and Tails." During America's dark days of the Depression and war, Berlin lifted his country's spirit with "God Bless America." A Jewish immigrant in an increasingly multicultural society, he enabled everyone to celebrate holidays with such secular songs as "Easter Parade" and "White Christmas." In the 1940s, when the Broadway stage demanded a new kind of musical, where songs were integrated into character and dramatic situation, Irving Berlin created a score for *Annie Get Your Gun* that had such "integrated" songs as "You Can't Get a Man with a Gun" and "Anything You Can Do," almost all of which went on to become independent popular hits; this score produced more hits than any Broadway musical, before or since, has done.

Perhaps the greatest tribute to Irving Berlin's versatility throughout his career came from another songwriter, Alec Wilder. Wilder studied the songs of Gershwin, Porter, and others to find distinctive stylistic qualities, but when he came to Irving Berlin, he simply confessed his awe at the variety of songs Berlin created. While cautioning that Berlin was not necessarily "the best writer in each and every area of popular music . . . let it be said that he is the best all-round, over-all songwriter America has ever had." One of the things that can be said about an artist who has mastered his craft is that he has a distinctive, recognizable style. "Paradoxically," as William G. Hyland, another scholar of popular song, has said, Irving Berlin was the master stylist of popular song because "he had no style . . . no category of popular music eluded him. He could write love songs, waltzes, ragtime, swing, jazz, or novelties." Berlin himself might have put it more succinctly. Of such brilliant contemporaries as Porter, the Gershwins, Rodgers and Hart, arguably the greatest group of lyricists and composers in the history of song, he could have said "anything they can do, I can do too."

The enduring power of Berlin's songs is all the more surprising, because his songs, more than those of any other songwriter, summon up their historical era. His words and music capture what it felt like to be alive for much of the twentieth century: the emergence of new rhythms of life, new voices and new values, in the early years of the century; the ballyhoo of the Roaring Twenties; the sleek sophistication that defied the grim years of the Great Depression; the clinging to home and heartland during World War II; and the heady, brassy glory of the 1950s and 1960s as America found itself the most prosperous and powerful nation on earth. In 1655, a Scotsman, Andrew Fletcher, said he didn't care who made a nation's laws, so long as he could make its songs. In 1930, in "Let Me Sing and I'm Happy," Irving Berlin relished his ability to not only sing but write the songs of his country:

> What care I who makes the laws of a nation.
> Let those who will, take care of its rights and wrongs.
> What care I who cares—for the world's affairs,
> As long as I can sing its popular songs.

Berlin loved and respected the people he wrote for, he saw his art as one that "embodies the feelings of the mob," and he regarded his profession as "not much more than a mirror which reflects those feelings." In a song he always tried to "express the feeling you get about the way people feel themselves," and he judged his success by the public reaction to his songs. "The public wants anything that's good," he believed, "and the only way to learn if it is good is to try it out on them." When he succeeded, he knew his words and music had "come off as the feeling and conversation of people set to music."

It is that ability to express the feelings of Americans that his contemporaries so admired in Berlin's work. "Emotionally," Jerome Kern said, "he honestly absorbs the vibrations emanating from the people, manners, and life of his time, and, in turn, gives these impressions back to the world—simplified, clarified, glorified." And not just of his own countrymen. Berlin's songs have an international popularity, and they capture that complex and ambiguous twentieth-century feeling of being "modern." While the nineteenth century was an age that believed the heroic individual controlled the course of history, in the twentieth century people have felt caught up in vast economic, social, and cultural changes they can barely understand, much less control. Although he was born in the nineteenth century, Irving Berlin entered his teenage years at the beginning of the twen-

tieth century and experienced all the historical events and developments of his time: two world wars, the Great Depression, and technological innovations such as film and radio, which completely
transformed the character of modern life. He also experienced those
characteristically modern emotions: the bustling energy of the modern city with its ragged, staccato rhythms, the streamlined, gleaming
feel of the machine age, but also the loneliness, emptiness, and
despair amid the teeming profusion of modern life. While Berlin
could not understand or control these events and emotions any better than other individuals, he was able to express how they felt, to
the masses, in song.

In the best of these songs, he was able to anchor an historical
event or capture a universal sentiment in terms of how it felt to the
particular—yet still common—individual. Other songwriters, like
George M. Cohan, reflected the widespread patriotism that led to
America's entry into World War I in general terms:

> We'll be over—we're coming over,
> And we won't come back
> Till it's over over there!

Irving Berlin, himself a soldier, refracted the vastness of world
war through the tiny lens of the ordinary soldier facing the common-
est of challenges:

> Oh! How I hate to get up in the morning.
> Oh! How I'd love to remain in bed.

While "Over There" remains a quaint period piece, "Oh! How I
Hate to Get Up in the Morning" transcends its era and registers a
much more pervasive twentieth-century sentiment. Heard today, it is
less about army life in World War I and more about the modern
American's reluctance to embrace his own Ben Franklin work ethic
of "Early to bed and early to rise."

The man who gave voice to the masses began life as a victim of
massive historical forces. Born Israel Baline (in Russian, "Beilin")
on May 11, 1888, he was the youngest of eight children of Leah
Lipkin and Moses Baline. For more than a thousand years, Jews like
the Balines had wandered, settled, then wandered again across
Europe, Africa, and Asia. In the Middle Ages, they had found a relative degree of freedom and security in Poland, and eventually nearly
half of the world's Jews came to live there. With the expansion of the
Russian empire and the partition of Poland in the eighteenth century,
Jews were forced to live in the Pale of Settlement, a band of territory

stretching from the Baltic to the Black Sea, which served as a buffer between Russia and Eastern Europe. Throughout the nineteenth century, Russia was torn between revolutionary reform and auto-cratic suppression, but with the accession of Czar Alexander III in 1881 after the assassination of his liberal father, conditions wors-ened for Jews. They could not farm, enter civil service, or travel. Even within the Pale, they were forced to live in large cities and towns rather than the countryside. Pogroms, raids by vigilantes on Jewish settlements, were countenanced and even fomented by the government, and in 1891, 20,000 Jews were driven out of Moscow.

Irving Berlin told his first biographer, Alexander Woollcott, that his first memory was of lying with the rest of his family beside a road, wrapped in a blanket, watching as his home and village were burned in a pogrom. The first memories of most people are fraught with terror, as if fear itself begets self-consciousness, which, in turn, engenders memory. For most of us, however, those initial fears are unfounded: monsters at the window turn out to be children on Halloween. But Berlin's first-remembered terrors were real, though, like many children of immigrants, he could not be sure, in later life, where they had taken place. In his early years, Berlin believed he had been born in the village of Tolochin, near the city of Mogilev in Belorussia, since that was the family home of the Balines. Later he learned that he was probably born in the village of Tyumen, in Siberia, where his father, an itinerant cantor, had taken his family. Berlin himself pointed out that it was not impossible for Jews to live beyond the Pale ("We weren't all political prisoners there, you know"), and Moses Baline may have traveled that far to serve a Jewish congregation.

From Tyumen, the Balines returned to Tolochin, and from there, with the help of Moses' oldest brother, a jeweler, they joined other Jews in an exodus paralleled only by the great dispersion after the destruction of Jerusalem in 586 B.C. From Russia, they looked to the promised land of America, the one country, save for the dreamed-of homeland of their own, that held out economic opportunity and polit-ical freedom for Jews. Between 1881 and 1891, 135,000 Russian Jews had already emigrated to America and, according to the propa-ganda of steamship companies, the New World was ready to wel-come other refugees to share in its bounty. Following a pattern as old as history itself, the Balines trekked westward across Russia to the sea. At Antwerp, they boarded the S.S. *Rhynland*, one of the huge new steam-powered transport ships built to carry immigrants—more than 5 million in the 1880s—from European ports to America. Irving Berlin's one vivid memory of the voyage was of having his forehead gashed when another passenger accidentally dropped a knife from an upper bunk on him as he slept.

After eleven days at sea, the *Rhynland* arrived in New York on September 13, 1893. It passed by the Statue of Liberty, then a new fixture in the harbor, given by France to commemorate the American Revolution. But while Congress appropriated funds to erect the statue, nothing was provided to build the huge pedestal on which it rests, and it took newspaper chains to whip up enough public enthusiasm to complete the project. In 1949, on its fiftieth anniversary, Irving Berlin wrote a musical, *Miss Liberty*, about the hullabaloo that surrounded the statue, putting into song the words by young Emma Lazarus on the base:

> Give me your tired, your poor,
> Your huddled masses yearning to breathe free,
> The wretched refuse of your teeming shore.
> Send these, the homeless, tempest-tost to me.

The Balines were indeed part of those huddled masses, and the United States government had recently established a facility at Ellis Island to process this new wave of immigrants. A day later, a ferry boat deposited them on the island of Manhattan. "We spoke only Yiddish," recalled the songwriter who would soon master the American vernacular, "and were conspicuous in our 'Jew clothes.'"

Berlin's sense of the odd picture his family cut in America reflects the changing pattern of European immigration. Before 1860, most immigrants to America came from the British Isles, Germany, and the Scandinavian countries. In the 1890s, however, more than half of the immigrants came from southern and eastern Europe, standing apart from the more homogenous population by their clothes, their foods, and, most of all, their languages. To an older generation of Anglo-Saxon Protestants, these swarthy Italians and Poles, Greeks and Hungarians, Jews and Catholics, looked, acted, and sounded decidedly "foreign." The new immigrants were also unlike their northern European predecessors in that they congregated in the large Eastern cities, worked in factories, and lived in tenement buildings in ethnic neighborhoods. By 1890, Philadelphia, Boston, and other Eastern cities were filled with immigrants, but none more so than New York, where by the end of the century three-fourths of the city's population were immigrants or the children of immigrants. And nowhere in New York was the melting pot more teeming than in the Lower East Side where nearly 700 people per acre were living.

It was here that the Balines were taken by a relative, a *Landsman*, who met them at the dock. Their first apartment was in the basement of a tenement on Monroe Street and had only three rooms, cold water, and no windows. Although their next apartment, at 330 Cherry Street, offered little more room, it was at least on the third floor, and on sweltering summer nights young Israel found relief by sleeping on the fire escape or the roof. Stephen Crane wrote a shocking novel in 1893 called *Maggie: A Girl of the Streets* in which he exposed the horrible life of slum dwellers in Lower East Side tenements:

> From a careening building, a dozen gruesome doorways gave up loads of babies to the street and the gutter. A wind of early autumn raised yellow dust from cobbles and swirled it against an hundred windows. Long streamers of garments fluttered from fire-escapes. In all unhandy places were buckets, brooms, rags and bottles. In the street infants played or fought with other infants or sat stupidly in the way of vehicles. Formidable women, with uncombed hair and disordered dress, gossiped while leaning on railings, or screamed in frantic quarrels. Withered persons, in curious postures of submission to something, sat smoking pipes in obscure corners. A thousand odors of cooking food came forth to the street. The building quivered and creaked from the weight of humanity stamping about in its bowels.

Irving Berlin, however, refused to sensationalize the conditions under which he grew up, saying "Everyone should have a Lower East Side in their lives" and insisting he was happy as a child who knew nothing else besides poverty:

> I never felt poverty because I'd never known anything else. We had an enormous family. Eight or nine in four rooms and in the summer some of us slept on the fire escape or on the roof. I was a boy with poor parents, but let's be realistic about it. I didn't starve. I wasn't cold or hungry. There was always bread and butter and hot tea. I slept better in tenement houses and in lodging houses at 15 cents a night than I do now in a nice bed.

Among the best of his early memories were of Christmas at the home of his Irish neighbors:

> I was a little Russian-born kid, son of an Orthodox rabbi, living on the Lower East Side of New York City. I did not have a Christmas. I bounded across the street to my friendly neighbors, the O'Haras, and shared their goodies.

An early photograph of Irving Berlin, perhaps taken in 1901 when he was thirteen. It may have been taken for his Bar Mitzvah.

> Not only that, this was my first sight of a Christmas tree.
> The O'Haras were very poor and later, as I grew used to
> their annual tree, I realized they had to buy one with
> broken branches and small height, but to me that first
> tree seemed to tower to Heaven.

Perhaps Berlin brought such memories to bear on "White Christmas," with its melancholy, chromatic melody and a lyric that places the speaker outside of the youthful, Christmas-card world it evokes.

The Balines slid further and further into poverty. Moses Baline, unable to find a regular position as a cantor, went to work in a kosher slaughter house as a *schomer*, an inspector who certified that chickens had been killed in the religiously prescribed style. He augmented his meager income by giving Hebrew lessons to neighborhood boys, assisting the cantor on the Sabbath, and serving as choir master for Rosh Hashanah and Yom Kippur. Berlin later recalled, "I used to sing in a choir with my father and made my first public appearance when I was ten years old." Aside from "singing in *schul*, I had little musical education," he added. For a boy whose father had been a cantor and grandfather a rabbi, singing was, as he would later put it in a song, "doin' what comes natur'lly." "I suppose it was singing with my father that gave me my musical background," he later reflected, "It was in my blood." Still, he noted, revealing how quickly he had become "Americanized," "when I was a boy, my great ambition was to become a cartoonist."

"Izzy," as he was then called, attended public school for a few years, first at a neighborhood school on Madison Street, then at P.S. 147 at East Broadway and Montgomery Street. One teacher recalled him as a pupil who "just dreams and sings to himself," but others found him a good student, which made it all the sadder when he had to quit school, because of his father's death, in 1901. Even before Moses Baline became ill, everyone in the family had to go to work. Leah (her name now "Americanized" to "Lena") became a midwife, the daughters (except for one who married) worked in cigar factories or did bead work, and Berlin's older brother toiled in a garment "sweat-shop." When their combined earnings weren't enough to get by, the Balines turned to the pawn shop. "I used to go there selling bits and pieces of an old brass samovar that my mother had brought from Russia and kept under the bed," Berlin recalled, "I'd get five and ten cents for the pieces and kept selling them until the entire samovar had disappeared."

To contribute a few pennies to the family till, Izzy had to go to work at an early age: running errands, delivering telegrams, then sewing collars in a sweat-shop; when that proved too grueling, he sold newspapers. Beneath the Brooklyn Bridge, he peddled the *New*

York Evening Journal, a typical "yellow press" publication owned by William Randolph Hearst. It is interesting to imagine young Izzy Baline helping to rally support for such jingoistic causes as the Spanish-American War as he yelled "Paper, boss; paper, ma'am." It may even be that he learned an early lesson in appealing to mass sentiment from the newspapers he hawked. One story that has become a part of the Berlin legend is that one day, sitting on an East River pier, he was so fascinated by a ship that was bound for China he did not notice the boom of a crane nor the warning shouts of the crew. Knocked into the filthy East River, he was rescued by an Irishman and rushed to Gouvernor's Hospital. "I was scared," Berlin later recalled, "More scared than at any time till the Wall Street crash." Once the nurses had emptied a good deal of the East River from the small boy's lungs, they were amused to find that throughout the ordeal his hand had clutched the four pennies he had before he fell. When he returned home that night, Lena Baline, as she did every evening, waited with her apron spread open while her children deposited, in turn, the coins they had earned that day. Despite all he had been through, little Izzy could still drop those four pennies into his mother's lap.

Yet behind such tenacity also was shame. As Berlin later confided to his first biographer, Alexander Woollcott, in these years he was "sick with a sense of his own worthlessness," as he realized that "he contributed less than the least of his sisters and that skeptical eyes were being turned on him as his legs lengthened and his earning powers remained the same." With that paradoxical logic of adolescents, he reasoned that the best thing he could do for his family was to leave it. His only chance of escaping poverty and helping his widowed mother seemed to lie in the musical talent he had inherited from generations of cantors and rabbis. He had found that if he sang popular songs while he sold newspapers, people would sometimes toss coins to him. In the evenings, on street corners, he and his friends would sing songs, and policemen, instead of shooing them off, would hang around and listen to the boys. One night, Berlin recalled, someone said to him, "You are losing time, Berlin. Go down to the Bowery and get some change. They're looking for good singers there. Get busy and butt in."

The neighborhood along Bowery Avenue at Chatham Square had emerged in the 1880s as the entertainment district for the working classes, particularly for the new immigrants of New York's Lower East Side. Another historical change that Irving Berlin witnessed during his lifetime was the separation of American entertainment into high and low (or "popular") culture. An early nineteenth-century theater might offer anything from an Italian opera to a rowdy burlesque in the same season, and in the audience would be people

of all classes: the well-to-do in the "upper" boxes, the working classes standing in the pit, and lower classes and blacks in the gallery.
(There was even a separate section, the "third tier," for prostitutes to
distinguish them from refined ladies.) By the 1870s, however, the
upper classes established their own theaters "uptown" to feature
operatic and concert works exclusively, while the middle class gravi-
tated to Union Square to see melodrama or Gilbert and Sullivan at
the "legitimate" theater. The lower classes, in turn, stayed below
14th Street, where they might attend an array of minstrel and variety shows, "concert" saloons, and dime museums. Visitors could
view Siamese twins or living skeletons, see the hands of a famous
murderer preserved in a jar, and gawk at gory waxworks and bloody
dioramas, all overseen by a "Professor," who lectured on the freaks
and spectacles to give them legitimacy as "educational" entertainment.

Nowhere was all of this more alluring and rife than in the
Bowery, the only major neighborhood in the city that was utterly
bereft of churches. As a contemporary, John McCabe, observed:

> To see the Bowery in its glory, one must visit it at night.
> It is a blaze of light from one end to the other. . . . The
> street is the paradise of beer saloons, bar-rooms, concert
> and dance halls, cheap theatres, and low-class shows. . . .
> There is nothing in this glare of light, nothing in this
> swarming pavement, to indicate that midnight is passed.
> The windows gleam, the saloons are all aglare, a half-
> score pianos and violins send as many airs floating into
> the night. The theatres are well-filled with pleasure-seek-
> ers. The admission is cheap, and the performances
> adapted to the tastes of their patrons.

Singers, acrobats, animal acts, and dramatizations based on current news stories were especially appealing to immigrants, who
could enjoy the spectacle without having to understand the spoken
word. When words were spoken, by immigrant comedians like
Weber and Fields, they had to be hammered home with shouts and
slapstick to span the barriers of poor English and drunken sensibilities, and they were often met with hoots and catcalls from the rowdy
audience.

For an immigrant boy like Irving Berlin, the Bowery represented
an alternative to the sweat-shops. He had glimpsed that bustling
world when he sold newspapers, heard songs pouring out of saloons
and beer halls, and, with the same shrewdness that attracted other
boys like Eddie Cantor to the Bowery, saw that a flair for singing or
telling jokes could be turned into a job in a saloon or variety show.

Although he could not have known it at the time, a vast cultural transformation was taking place around him. According to social historian Lewis Erenberg:

> In the 1890s American popular culture began a larger orientation away from the confinement, restrictions, and conventions of urban industrial society and the code of gentility. In working-class, black, and immigrant cultures, new institutions of amusement and leisure were growing into general respectability, offering immigrant children and middle-class urbanites visions of a more luxurious and experiential life, one not bound by the old restrictive ways. In movies, vaudeville, ragtime, and cabarets, a popular culture was being created and transformed by new values, which by 1910, would achieve a legitimacy in urban life unheard of in the Victorian age.

Whether it was the attraction of Bowery entertainment or that gnawing sense of his own worthlessness, Irving Berlin struck out one evening after supper, determined to succeed on his own or starve. If he told his mother of his ambition, it must have been unimaginable to her that the son of a cantor—and grandson of a rabbi—wanted to earn money by singing popular songs in a saloon. Whatever transpired, Irving Berlin, at the age of thirteen, went, as he put it in later years, "on the bum."

The first night he spent away from home he slept under the stairway of a tenement house, awaking cold, hungry, homesick, and frightened. Then he began his two-year career as a street "busker," going from one saloon to the other—the Bucket of Blood, the Flea Bag, Suicide Hall—singing to the patrons in the hopes they would throw a few coins his way. If he earned fifteen cents, he could rent a bed in a flophouse with a locker for his clothes; for ten cents he got the bed without the locker; for seven cents, he could sleep on a canvas hammock; and if he had only a nickel he got a chalked-out space on the floor. If he earned nothing, he spent the night on a park bench.

As young and small as he was, Berlin sometimes was turned away from saloons by the bouncers and had to warble his songs to passersby on the streets. Even when he could gain entrance, his thin voice was sometimes drowned out by the professional singing waiters who were out for the same coins that customers threw in the sawdust. At one saloon, Callahan's, his soulful rendition of a "sob ballad" of the 1890s, "The Mansion of Aching Hearts," netted him the twenty cents it took for a "grubstake" and a room in a flophouse. When it came time to sign the register, Berlin was too ashamed to use his real name and instead, taking the name of an actress from the poster for a play called, fittingly, *From Rags to Riches*, he signed himself "Cooney."

For the next two years, Berlin lived at places like the Cobdock Hotel, which he later described as a "flophouse," then added, "it would have resented being called that. It was a place to which the gals would take their sailors." He also resided at a "lodging house" called "The Mascot." "It was a 15-cents a night joint," where "You got a cubby-hole to sleep in, one open at the top, and you were always scared that somebody would reach over and steal your pants." For a while, he attached himself to an older busker called "Blind Sol," who commanded attention in the saloons, where his rendition of sentimental ballads on the violin, together with his infirmity, garnered generous contributions. Blind Sol needed help getting from one saloon to another, and young buskers would escort him as a way of gaining admittance into saloons as well as a share of Sol's earnings. While Sol fiddled, Berlin sang ("I know I didn't sing good but I sang soft"). The youngsters also got a lesson in the tricks of the busker's trade, such as how to "put over" a song in performance so that it would move the listeners' hearts—and wallets. Berlin, who would one day put those lessons to use in writing songs, also got to know the piano players in the various saloons, with whom Sol also split his earnings. Eventually, Berlin moved out on his own again and became known not only in the Bowery but in waterfront saloons like MacAlear's, where he could earn as much as fifty cents on a Saturday night.

In 1902, after a year of busking, he landed a part in the chorus of a Broadway show called *The Show Girl*. He got to tour with the company as the show went through out-of-town "tryouts," where musical shows were "doctored"—scripts changed, cast members replaced, songs added or revised—in order to get them ready for a New York run. One of Berlin's "bits" in the production was to sneak into the audience and break into a popular song called "Sammie." In the course of tryouts, however, Berlin himself was cut from the chorus and had to return to New York from Binghamton. When *The Show Girl* reached New York, it clearly still needed "doctoring," because it closed after only a few performances.

On the strength of his brief stint with *The Show Girl*, Berlin looked for work on Tin Pan Alley, the sheet-music publishers whose offices were then crowded along 28th Street between Broadway and Sixth Avenue. There, so the story goes, the incessant din of pianos tinkling, banging, and cranking out new songs from Von Tilzer's, Shapiro and Bernstein's, Witmark's, and more than a dozen other publishing houses earned the area its mellifluous sobriquet. Many of these publishers, mostly immigrant Jews themselves, had started out as salesmen and, by the 1880s, came to believe that the public could be persuaded to buy sheet music as readily as they bought ties and corsets. With the advent of machine-made pianos, every middle-class home could boast a parlor piano, and there was a demand for songs that could be played for the family sing-along. New "department" stores like Woolworth's set up racks of sheet music, beautifully adorned with illustrated covers, right next to their candy counters. So profitable were sales that the price of sheet music steadily dropped from a dollar a song in the 1880s to forty cents in the '90s, then twenty-five cents at the turn of the century, and a mere dime by 1910.

In 1893, the year Irving Berlin came to America, Tin Pan Alley was galvanized by the sale of more than a million copies of sheet music for a single song, "After the Ball" by Charles K. Harris. Until then, no one imagined that songwriting could be such a profitable enterprise. America's greatest songwriter of the nineteenth century, Stephen Foster, had died penniless, and even at the height of his success never enjoyed anywhere near such sales. Unlike earlier sheet-music publishers, rather than waiting for a song to become popular, Tin Pan Alley publishers actively sought to create a market for their products. They sent "pluggers" directly to the public, playing and singing new songs anywhere a crowd was gathered. As publisher Edward Marks explained:

> The best songs came from the gutter. There was no surer way of starting a song off to popularity than to get it sung as loudly as possible in the city's lowest dives. If a publisher knew his business, he always launched a sales campaign by impressing his song on the happily befogged consciousness of the gang in the saloons and halls.

Some of the more enterprising pluggers mounted small pianos on trucks or bicycles and roamed around town with new songs; one leaned out of an airplane with a megaphone to warble his latest song; another put a piano in a hot-air balloon and drifted over Coney Island serenading the crowd. At its most refined, pluggers were used as "singing stooges" in vaudeville houses. When a performer sang a song from the stage, the stooge, planted in the back of the audience, would rise and, as if spontaneously carried away by the song's beauty, lead the audience in chorus after chorus.

Irving Berlin's "bit" with the song "Sammie" in *The Show Girl* was similar to that of a singing stooge, and with that experience under his belt he presented himself to Tin Pan Alley magnate, Harry Von Tilzer. Von Tilzer (whose real name was Harry Gumm, and whose niece, Frances Gumm, would later change her name to Judy

Garland) had written such tearjerkers as "The Mansion of Aching
Hearts" and "A Bird in a Gilded Cage," as well as the nostalgic evergreen, "I Want a Girl (Just Like the Girl That Married Dear Old
Dad)." Von Tilzer realized that the money in the popular song business came from publishing rather than writing songs, and he set up
his own music publishing house at 42 West 28th Street in the heart
of Tin Pan Alley.

Impressed by the young Berlin's way with a song, Von Tilzer paid
him $5 a week to be a singing stooge at Tony Pastor's Music Hall at
Union Square. Pastor, who had started with P. T. Barnum, originally
had run a variety theater in the Bowery, with the typical risqué
songs, "blued" comedy skits, and circus acts that appealed to the
rough-and-tumble, male, working-class audience. In 1881, however,
he opened his new theater further uptown at 14th Street, where he
booked no freaks or prize-fights. Instead, he offered only acts that
would appeal to families: comedians, dancers, singers, acrobats, and
animal acts. Pastor also shut down the barroom and banned smoking, hoping to appeal to the "carriage trade." He attracted ladies to
the theater by offering door prizes of dress patterns, flour, and coal.

It was at Tony Pastor's that vaudeville was born. Vaudeville not
only supplanted the rowdy variety show of the Bowery but the minstrel show as well. Compared to vaudeville's carefully orchestrated
flow of acts, minstrel shows, where all the participants were seated
in a row, seemed stiff and formulaic. While the "blackface" humor of
minstrel shows focused on a narrow band of racial stereotypes,
vaudeville expanded its "bill" to include other ethnic caricatures—
Irish, Italian, Jewish—that appealed to its melting pot audience.
Vaudeville emphasized the individual act, rather than the ensemble
of minstrelsy; consequently, acts competed for the best billing and
material. Singers went directly to Tin Pan Alley publishers in search
of their latest wares, and the publishers were eager to have vaudevil-
lians promote their songs. In 1900, vaudeville houses across the
country organized themselves into two vast "circuits"—the Keith-
Albee Company in the East and the Orpheum in the West—so that a
star could popularize a song nationwide in a matter of months. In
order to get a big-name vaudeville star like Sophie Tucker to use one
of his new songs in her act, a publisher might put her name on the
sheet music, cutting her in, along with the composer and lyricist, for
a share of the royalties.

Harry Von Tilzer put Irving Berlin to work as a singing stooge for
a "family act" at Tony Pastor's: The Three Keatons. In addition to
singing, Pa Keaton told jokes, Ma played the saxophone, and young
Buster performed acrobatics that would later help him become one
of the most eloquent comedians of silent film. Ironically, it would be
Irving Berlin's song "Blue Skies," sung by Al Jolson in the 1927

"talkie," *The Jazz Singer*, that helped precipitate the end of silent films and careers such as Keaton's. In 1905, however, it was the reverse of fortunes, because after the Keatons finished their booking at Tony Pastor's, Irving Berlin was out of a job and back on the streets as a busker.

Still another job Irving Berlin had in these years placed him directly in movie theaters or, as they were then called, "nickelodeons," after their price of admission. Movies were largely an entertainment of the lower classes and were especially popular among immigrants, who could follow silent films without the barrier of language. Still, sound was always present in the background as a piano—or in big-city theaters, an orchestra—performed music to accompany the film (and drown out the sound of the projector). There was also music in between the numerous reel changes required for early films. A popular diversion between reels was to show "song slides," hand-painted enhancements of photographs that illustrated the lyrics of a song. As the slides were shown, a singer sang the song, and the audience joined in as the words were flashed on the screen— a precursor of the "bouncing ball" songs of later films. Irving Berlin told a newspaper reporter that he had once worked in a movie house singing songs to accompany such slide presentations. For $15 a week, he worked all day long, singing three songs at each change of reels. Singing for as many as ten reel changes a day gave Berlin still more experience at putting over a lyric.

It was only after he caught the eye of Chuck Connors, a character who could have stepped out of a turn-of-the-century melodrama, that Irving Berlin finally rose above the life of a street busker. The self-proclaimed "Mayor of Chinatown," Connors, a Cockney, conducted "tours" of the area. Centered at Mott and Pell Streets, Chinatown was, like the Bowery, part of New York's "street theater," but was even more exotic. Berlin always carried with him the memory of the "Hip Sing Toy" gang and "the Chinese with their white women"—the dreaded "white slave trade" of the early century. Chinatown was also notorious for opium dens, because, even though opium was a legal drug at the time, it had the cachet of criminal activity.

Connors, sporting a blue suit with flashy buttons and a derby which he always wore sideways, shrewdly took his sensation-seeking customers to the safer "sin dens" of the area, such as Olliffe's Drugstore, supposedly the oldest drugstore in the country, where opium was sold over the counter and where the first soda fountain had been installed. From there he would escort them to a "private" boxing match or up to Jimmy Pong's opium den, where they could watch numerous Chinese lying on cots and smoking opium. Along the way he might stop to chat with his pal Teddy Roosevelt, then police commissioner of New York,

then move on to a saloon, where his customers could see actual gang-
sters. At the Pelham Café and Dance Hall at 12 Pell Street, there was a
brothel and an opium den where slumming tourists could see
Chinatown Gertie, who, for a small fee (which she would split with
Connors), would allow the gawkers a glimpse of herself, clad in a
kimono, smoking opium from a pipe. Still, the Pelham was a dangerous enough place where criminals met and where two rival gangs, the
Irish-Italian Five-Pointers and the Eastmans, a Jewish gang, had a
running territorial dispute that over the years "claimed the lives of
some twenty to thirty hoodlums."

Connors, who also fancied himself something of a talent scout,
may have put in a word for Berlin with the owner of the Pelham, a
Russian Jew known, because of his swarthy complexion, as "Nigger
Mike" Salter. Salter, who boasted of having killed ten men, could be
a friendly soul, however. His brothel was more of a refuge for the
"aging streetwalkers who no longer wished to deal with the 'little
yellow men' of the Bowery"; Chinamen were not allowed beyond the
outer bar of the Pelham. Berlin recounted how at first Salter refused
to hire him, but then, after the owner stepped out, he began singing
to the customers. When the other waiters tried to drown him out, he
sang louder and finally won the crowd over just as Salter returned.
At sixteen, he got the job he had dreamed of for years: for seven dollars a week—plus tips—Irving Berlin, with the two other waiters,
Bullhead Lawrence and Kutch Kutchinsky, would deliver beer to the
customers. When the resident piano player, "Professor" Mike "Nick"
Nicholson, struck up a tune, Berlin would regale the crowd with a
song like "A Woman Is Only a Woman But a Good Cigar Is a
Smoke," hoping they would toss coins his way. "He was a vocal
blockbuster," one customer recalled, "his voice sounded more like
gastritis in tempo."

"A waiter learns an awful lot about people," Berlin said of his
years at the Pelham, "He gets a course in advanced psychology that
it takes a lot of living to get any other way." Berlin's specialty was
making up risqué parodies of songs like "Are Ye Comin' Out Tonight,
Mary Ann?" (his salacious lyrics probably enhanced by his innocent,
youthful demeanor). Jubal Sweet, who worked in the Pelham Café at
the time, later recalled how Irving Berlin plied his trade:

> Like it was yesterday, I remember Oiving Berlin. Looked
> like a meal or two wouldn't hurt him. Wasn't strong and
> didn't look like he would get away with a nickel or a
> dime that one of the other guys claimed. . . . Now a
> singing waiter couldn't be stooping over every time a
> coin hit the floor. Spoil his song like—see? No, he'd keep
> moving around easy, singing all the time, every time a

The Pelham Café at 12 Pell Street in Chinatown.

nickel would drop he'd put his toe on it and kick it or
nurse it to a certain spot. When he was done he had all
the jack in a pile, see? Oiving got to be pretty good at
it . . . he had a neat flip of the ankle. Like you'd brush a
speck offa the table with your fingers.

Life as a singing waiter was grueling—Berlin started at eight in
the evening and worked until six the next morning—but the steady
work was much better than street busking and in the course of time
his popularity with customers grew. Berlin later told a reporter, "I
got my musical education in the Bowery, but I never mingled with
the real tough people, so-called gorillas, but attended strictly to business." Such types included "Hob-nailed Casey," who sat at his regular table and cleaned his fingernails with his knife, glowering at all
around him. One night, when Casey tried to pick a fight with the
piano player, another employee, Frisco Joe, grabbed a gun from the
icebox and shot Casey, who staggered out and died in the street.
During the scene, "Izzy" had to keep on singing the sentimental Irish
song, "Ring to the Name of Rosie." One of the older waiters, Kutch
Kutchinsky, according to Jubal Sweet, "sort of took to the kid and
seen to it that nobody stuck nothing" to him.

The reputation of the Pelham Café grew, and Chuck Connors continued to lead tourists there. Connors scored a definite coup on November 18, 1905, when his entourage included Prince Louis of Battenberg, a relative of King Edward VII of England. The Prince, a rear admiral in the British Navy, had arrived in New York on his flagship, the HMS *Drake*, and on Saturday night commissioned Connors to escort him and his friends to Chinatown. Eighteen reporters joined the party, as well as two detectives (for protection), and, after eating Chinese food and taking in a mission, the group arrived at the Pelham Café at one in the morning. Professor Nicholson saluted the royal party with "Strike Up the Band, Here Comes a Sailor" and "God Save the King." They took in the "noted singing waiters," reputed to be "the best singers in Chinatown," then, after food and drink, the prince got up to leave. When he offered to pay the bill, "Nigger Mike" magisterially waved the money away and insisted the prince's evening was "on the house." The prince then offered a tip to Irving Berlin. Depending on which account one reads, the young waiter either accepted the tip and announced he would frame it and hang it on the wall or cavalierly waved the money aside and said "No, sir, it was my honor to sing." Whichever account is true, Irving Berlin's gesture caught the attention of the reporters in the group, because it crystallized how the royal visit had touched the life of a particular common American. The papers carried stories for days about the young singing waiter in Chinatown who had indeed, looked at—and spoken to—a prince.

Competition for the tourist trade was fierce among Chinatown saloons and particularly so between the Pelham Café and Callahan's, where Irving had frequently sung in his busking days. Al Piantadosi, the piano player at Callahan's, and "Big Jerry," the gun-slinging bouncer, wrote a song called "My Mariucci Take a Steamboat," which was published by a Tin Pan Alley firm. With its catchy "Toot! Toot!" refrain that invited listeners to join in, the song enjoyed a measure of popularity in New York. Jealous of Callahan's success, "Nigger Mike" summoned Berlin and Nick Nicholson and sarcastically goaded them into emulating the feat. "To hold our job," Berlin recalled, "we got to work and because Piantadosi's song was Italian, we made our song Italian." Nicholson improvised a melody, then both he and Berlin went to work on the lyric. For all his cleverness in confecting ribald parodies of popular songs, Berlin fell back on pure imitation for "Marie from Sunny Italy." His lyric portrays a lover standing, Romeo-like, beneath a window and pleading for his "sweet Italian beauty" to come out and "listen to my serenade." Although the song invokes ethnic stereotypes, there is not a trace of dialect in the lyric, which instead relies on such archly poetic phrases as "There's not another maiden e'er could suit me." At other points, Berlin runs the gamut of the tritest clichés of popular song-writing: "the little birds" are "sweetly humming," "the Summer moon is beaming," and "the little stars are gleaming." Here and there a true vernacular phrase, such as "Please don't be so aggravating," finds its way into the lyric, but the rest is a string of platitudes. Berlin's apprentice effort is also marred by forced rhymes, "queen" with "mandolin" and "beauty" with "suit me." While such "slant" rhymes might be suitable for poetry, in song lyrics rhymes have to be true in order to chime with the music. Similarly, Berlin found that the art of matching one syllable to a note forced him to add extra syllables as padding—"how I *do* love you"—and to invert the normal order of words—"I shall happy be—" to make them fit the musical accents.

A more serious flaw in "Marie from Sunny Italy" is that Berlin does not adapt his lyric to the structure of the music. Like most nineteenth-century songs, Nicholson's melody consists of a verse followed by a chorus, or as it was sometimes called, a refrain. Traditionally, the verse was where the lyricist told a story, while the chorus consisted of a brief lyrical exclamation. In a Stephen Foster song such as "Oh! Susanna!," for example, the verses trace the story of the singer's wanderings, while the brief chorus punctuates the narrative:

> Oh! Susanna! Don't you cry for me.
> For I've come from Alabama with a banjo on my knee!

Structurally, Nicholson's song is divided into a verse of twenty-eight bars followed by a sixteen-bar chorus, and he made a musical distinction between the two sections by using a Cuban habanera rhythm in the verse, coupled with a minor-mode melody, to give it an ethnic flavor, while in the chorus he used a more American "pop" melody and a rhythm derived from ragtime. Berlin's lyric, however, is all of a piece, an extended plea by the lover for his Marie that ignores the musical contrast between verse and chorus. In a few years, largely through Berlin's example, the twentieth-century popular song would completely reverse the importance of verse and chorus, with the chorus expanding to thirty-two bars and carrying the musical and lyrical weight of the song, while the verse became merely a brief introduction to the chorus and was often omitted by singers in performances. In "Marie from Sunny Italy," however, Berlin evinces little grasp of the musical divisions of the song.

Despite all its flaws, Berlin's lyric does show that Berlin had learned some fundamentals of songwriting from his work as a singing waiter. Unlike many other lyricists who would follow him, such as Ira Gershwin and Lorenz Hart, Berlin started as a professional singer and would always bring a singer's ear to the craft of songwriting. That meant he would frequently opt for the more "singable" word over the more flashily literate or witty ones. Fundamental to the singer's craft was the disposition of long open (*o*, *a*, *u*) and closed (*e* and *i*) vowels over long notes, so a singer could, as they say, "lean on" the syllables and notes. Berlin found such long vowels replete in his title, "Mar*ie* from Sun*ny* Ital*y*," and shrewdly knew that a good song worked its title over and over again throughout the lyric, impressing itself on the listener's mind so that he remembered what song to ask for at the sheet-music counter. As Ira Gershwin (who always found the title the hardest part of a lyric to write) once quipped:

> A title
> Is vital;
> Once you've it,
> Prove it.

While Berlin had his title, however, he did not "prove it," because, instead of developing, the lyric remains a static repetition of the lover's plea for Marie to come out and, in what may have been an inadvertent play on her name, "marry me."

Their labors completed, Nicholson and Berlin sought out someone who could write down the song, because neither composer nor lyricist could read music. They appealed to Fiddler John, a Bowery cobbler who played for extra money at night, but he confessed to the same ignorance, though he did refer them to a young violinist who put "Marie to Sunny Italy" down on paper. It may seem an indication of the poor state of songwriting in 1907 that such a song was actually bought by a major Tin Pan Alley firm and published in sheet music. Nonetheless it only cost about $1,000 for a publisher to print 10,000 copies of sheet music, each of which sold for 10 cents. Of that sale, only 1 cent went to the composer and another to the lyricist as royalty payments, and the publisher pocketed the rest. In some cases, publishers purchased a melody or lyric outright from a songwriter, sometimes for as little as $10 or $15, and retained all of the royalties themselves. With such returns, publishers were willing to take a chance on a song, and by 1910 they were publishing some 25,000 songs a year. While only a handful of these were big sellers, those were enough to bring in sales of more than 5 million a year to the industry.

"Marie from Sunny Italy" was released on May 8, 1907, three days before Berlin turned nineteen. It sold only a few copies of sheet music, the first of which was purchased by Joseph Schenck, a young friend of Berlin's who worked in Olliffe's Drugstore. Schenck sold Berlin cough drops when his singing voice went hoarse and occasionally helped him with the rent. Schenck would one day become a powerful figure in Hollywood as head of United Artists and would commission Berlin to write songs for his company's films.

Despite the hopes of "Nigger Mike" and the crew of the Pelham Café, "Marie" was not even a modest success. The song earned only 75 cents in royalties, and Berlin got his first lesson in the primacy of the composer over the lyricist when the songwriters split the royalties and the odd penny went to Nicholson, leaving Berlin with only 37 cents (the next year he would receive $1.20). There was, however, a handsome cover on the sheet music. Covers for sheet music from this period were often quite beautiful, and artists as prominent as Norman Rockwell and Winslow Homer lent their talents to the Tin Pan Alley publishing firms. The cover for "Marie from Sunny Italy" shows a Venetian scene, replete with gondola and a lady serenaded by a mandolin-strumming lover. Also on the cover was the name "I. Berlin" as the lyricist. According to some accounts, the name was a fortuitous printing error, but Berlin later told Allexander Woollcott that his Bowery friends, in everyday conversation, had further Anglicized his Russian name from "Baline" to "Berlin." He also confessed that the wish to be known as Irving remained for some time "a secret of his bosom," less "solemn and Talmudic" than "Israel," but more dignified than "Izzy." Fearing derision from the Pelham crowd if the cover carried "Irving," he compromised "between an old pride and a new embarrassment" and called himself "I. Berlin." The name "Berlin" was a shrewd one that drew upon the reverence of Americans toward German composers. So deep was that awe that Czech composer Antonín Dvořák, when he visited America in the 1890s, berated Americans for slavishly following German musical models instead of looking to their own national traditions for inspiration. To demonstrate his point, Dvořák composed the *New World Symphony*, where he wove musical motifs from African-American spirituals into the symphonic texture. Berlin himself would soon adapt the rhythms of African-American ragtime into popular song, but before he was able to forge that musical alloy, he had several years of apprenticeship ahead of him.

While "Marie from Sunny Italy," as Berlin later put it, "went the way of all imitation," it nevertheless "was an important song" that "got me out of Chinatown." While the song may have helped, the actual incident that forced Berlin's exit from Chinatown was a prank by his fellow waiters. In the flush of his success as a singing waiter, he had bought a diamond ring from a traveling salesman, but when the long hours at the Pelham induced him to sleep on the job, waiters and customers would slip the ring from his finger. When he awoke, they would demand some favor of him—such as a free bottle of champagne—for its return. One night, as fellow-waiter Bullhead Lawrence recalled, the joke went too far:

> Izzy fell asleep at the bar and that's what sent him on his way. It was about two o'clock in the morning when Mike came in. We decided to have some fun with Izzy. So I took a diamond ring off his finger and Mike took all the money out of the till. Then we woke Izzy and Mike demanded what he meant by sleeping on the job and letting the place get robbed. Izzy ran to the till and saw it was empty, then he saw his ring was gone. It was all in fun, of course, but Mike got sore anyway and kicked Izzy out for good.

Berlin would always credit "Nigger Mike" with launching him on his songwriting career, saying that, until Salter bullied him into writing the lyric for "Marie from Sunny Italy," all he had ever wanted was a job that paid $25 a week.

Salter may have pushed Berlin into songwriting but the failure of the song made him determined to write more successfully. The incident sparked an ambition that would drive him the rest of his life. Another heritage he took from the Pelham was a lifelong habit: His all-night shifts as a singing waiter made Berlin an insomniac who slaved through the night, partly to perfect a song but also to tire himself out enough to fall asleep as morning dawned. Those Berlin songs that seem so effortless in their graceful simplicity are the product of white-hot intensity that burned through the lonely hours of the night. With such determination and work habits, "Irving Berlin," at the age of twenty, left the world of Chinatown, the Bowery, and the Lower East Side but would always carry their legacy with him.

Chapter 2

RAGGED METER MAN

Fourteenth Street was very swell for me. I was quite a
big shot there. I was an entertainer for about a year and
then I went uptown and before long I was writing songs
with a drawing account of $25 a week. I'd really had an
easy time as a kid, honest. My struggles didn't actually
begin until after I'd written "Alexander's Ragtime Band."
It's been a struggle ever since to keep success going.

With his name in the papers and a published song under his belt,
Irving Berlin had little trouble securing another singing waiter's job,
with shorter hours and higher wages, at Jimmy Kelly's restaurant at
Union Square. Kelly, a boxer, had been a bouncer at "Nigger
Mike's," but in establishing his own restaurant at 212 East 14th
Street he had moved into a much classier world than Chinatown or
the Bowery. Tony Pastor's vaudeville house, along with some of the
earliest sheet-music music publishers, had settled in this area at the
edge of Greenwich Village in the 1880s, and while theatrical and
musical life had moved uptown to Tin Pan Alley by 1910, enough
élan remained around Union Square for Kelly to don tails when he
stood behind the bar.

Not only did Berlin find new employment in the Union Square
area, he moved there, sharing a furnished room at East 18th Street
with a friend named Max Winslow. Winslow worked for Tin Pan
Alley publisher Harry Von Tilzer, the man who had hired Berlin to
be a singing stooge at Tony Pastor's. Winslow had heard Berlin sing
risqué parodies at the Pelham Café and had tried, unsuccessfully, to
persuade Von Tilzer to hire the singing waiter as a staff lyricist. At

Jimmy Kelly's, Berlin continued singing those "blue" parodies but also kept trying to write his own songs.

The very first song, according to copyright date, that he wrote after "Marie from Sunny Italy" was "The Best of Friends Must Part." What is remarkable about this song, completed in February of 1908, is that Berlin is credited with both words and music. While he probably had already begun picking out tunes on the saloon piano, for this song he hummed a melody to the regular piano player, who wrote it down for him to take to a music publisher. The music consists of tight, repetitive phrases, and the lyric renders in equally terse terms a practical-minded woman's decision to call off her affair with a man who can hold neither job nor money:

> Done lost your job? Where is your pay?
> Been shooting dice? That's very nice . . .
> Don't talk of love, just like a dove,
> Can't eat the stars, that shine above.
> That stuff don't go, you'd better blow,
> Can't buy a meal with that lovin' you know.

Although the woman insists, "I'm cold as ice," her restraint begins to break, musically and lyrically, but by the end of the song she regains her stoic determination that "when you find you can't make both ends meet, then the best of friends must part." Here, in the first song where he coupled words to his own music, Berlin introduced a note of realism into the hackneyed romantic formulas of Tin Pan Alley.

That Berlin was still primarily a lyricist, even when he wrote his own music, is clear from his first successful song, "Dorando." A vaudevillian in search of new material heard Berlin performing one of his risqué parodies one evening in Jimmy Kelly's, and offered the singing waiter $10 if he could come up with a poem that could serve as a recitation piece. Poetry recitations were common fare on vaudeville bills, and actors rendered such classics as "Gunga Din" and "Casey at the Bat" with tremulous intonation and vivid gesticulation. Especially popular were dialect poems, such as T. A. Daly's "Mia Carlotta," which appeared in newspapers in 1908:

> Giuseppe, da barber, he gotta da cash.
> He gotta da clo'es an' da bigga moustache,
> He gotta da seely young girls for da "mash,"
> But notta
> You bat my life, notta—

> Carlotta.
>
> I gotta!

It was this sort of poem the vaudevillian wanted Berlin to write for him. As a subject he suggested the recent uproar at the 1908 Olympics when an Italian named Dorando Pietri was about to win the marathon until excited spectators milled around him and, the judges ruled, unfairly "helped" him across the finish line. Dorando was disqualified and the medal awarded to the runner-up, an American, much to the consternation of New York's ethnic population.

Berlin, as he would so often do in his later songs, portrayed this public event as it affected the ordinary man, an immigrant Italian barber who sells his shop to bet on Dorando, only to lose everything:

> Dorando he's a drop!
>
> Good-bye, poor old barber shop.
>
> It's no fun to lose da mon,
>
> When de sun-of-a-gun no run,
>
> Dorando, he's good-a for not!

As if there wasn't enough ethnic flavor in the story, Berlin attributed the cause of Dorando's loss to the fact that he mistakenly eats "da Irish beef-a stew" instead of "da spaghett" that "make me run quick-a-quick."

At the urging of his roommate, Max Winslow, who had quit his job on Tin Pan Alley with Harry Von Tilzer, Berlin took his poem to Winslow's new boss, Henry Waterson, one of the owners of Seminary Music on Union Square. Waterson looked at Berlin's effort and offered him $25 for it—provided Berlin had an acceptable tune to go with his lyric. In an early flash of chutzpah, Berlin assured the publisher the words had a melody. When Waterson called his bluff by ordering Berlin to step across the hall and hum his melody to a staff arranger, the neophyte composer had to concoct a tune in the time it took him to reach the piano. That melody, moreover, was surprisingly intricate with shifting meters and tonalities. Following the usual practice of Alley composers of immigrant songs, Berlin casts his verse in a minor "ethnic" mode and his chorus in a more modern and "American" major key. But at the point in the chorus where the barber cries, "Please-a nunga stop!," the music shifts back to the minor key to underscore the loss of the Italian runner.

"Dorando" was a success after it was published in the spring of 1909, earning Berlin $4,000 in royalties (though he later claimed

that he made only $25 from the song while his publisher garnered
$20,000). Berlin's close call at Waterson's office may have made him
a bit more careful when it came to writing music, because for the
rest of 1909 he relied upon collaborators. He also experimented with
more ambitious songs than the ethnic fare of "Marie from Sunny
Italy" and "Dorando." With Al Piantadosi, the Chinatown waiter who
had written "My Mariucci Take a Steamboat," the song that had
goaded Berlin into trying his hand at lyrics, he wrote the arty "Just
Like the Rose," cast in the European waltz style. In the verse Berlin
weaves an extended simile that compares the loss of love to a rose's
heartbreak when its beloved lily is plucked away. Then in the chorus, he drives the comparison home:

> Just like the rose, dear, I loved you,
> Like the lily they stole you away,
> Just like the rose I adored you,
> Worshipped you night and day.

Replete with terms like "woe" and "o'er," "Just Like the Rose" took
Berlin out of his comic, vernacular vein and had the frenetic songwriter uncharacteristically "sighing for sweet repose."

With another composer, Edgar Leslie, Berlin returned to his colloquial and witty self but with a touch of greater sophistication. A well-
educated New Englander who would go on to write such hits as "For
Me and My Gal," Leslie was a great admirer of Gilbert and Sullivan
and English music-hall songs. Ever since their first great operetta,
H.M.S. Pinafore, premiered in America in 1878, Gilbert and Sullivan
were as popular in the New World as in England. Witty, literate, and
satirical, the songs of Gilbert and Sullivan were far superior to the
songs of Tin Pan Alley, a superiority attributable to the fact that
Gilbert's words took precedence over Sullivan's music—just the
opposite of Tin Pan Alley priorities, where the tune was generally
regarded as preeminent. Many of their "songs," in fact, were poems
Gilbert had written and published as "Bab Ballads" in *Fun* (a rival of
Punch), which Sullivan later set to music. This procedure seemed the
only way to get quality in songwriting, and when Sullivan was asked
that inevitable question—"Which comes first, the music or the
words?"—he invariably snapped, "The words, of course." As their collaboration developed, Gilbert, admittedly tone-deaf and unable to
carry a tune, learned to make his lyrics more "singable"—to loosen
his tongue-twisting rhythms and replace his percussively alliterative
gutturals and fricatives with liquid consonants and open vowels. Yet
Gilbert always remained wary of music's power to transcend words,
and he insisted his words come first; otherwise, as he suggested in
one of his lyrics, his words might not even need to make sense:

> His gentle spirit rolls
> In the melody of souls—
> Which is pretty, but I don't know what it means.

Trying to achieve such witty effects in American songwriting, Berlin learned, was virtually impossible, but with Leslie he wrote several lyrics that aspired to the wit of Gilbert's and English music-hall "patter" songs. "I Didn't Go Home At All" details the story of a philandering husband who explains his all-night absence to his wife by averring, "I promised I'd be home at ten, so I didn't go home at all." Similarly, "Someone's Waiting For Me" recounts the tale of two husbands out on the town, singing "What! Go home to wifey? Well, not on your lifey, we'll wait, wait, wait." These songs, like their British models, were primarily narrative songs, where the story was told in the verse and the brief chorus merely punctuated the account with lyrical outbursts. Berlin, however, was much more adept at lyrical expression than in telling a story, and he would flourish when the emphasis in song shifted from verse to chorus.

We can see how much more effectively Berlin handles a lyrical chorus in "Sadie Salome Go Home" also with music by Leslie. This song was inspired by the scandal over Richard Strauss's opera, *Salomé*, with its erotic "Dance of the Seven Veils." Again thinking in terms of how such a public event impinges upon a particular individual, Berlin focuses on an outraged "Mose," who realizes that the suggestive dancer on stage is really his girlfriend Sadie Cohen. Borrowing the line "So put some clothes on, Rosie" from the popular song "Meet Me in Rose Time, Rosie," Berlin turns it to parody as Mose pleads in Yiddish turns of phrase:

> Who put in your head such notions?
> You look sweet but jiggle with your feet.
> Who put in your back such funny motions?

Berlin even essays some off-rhymes to reflect ethnic pronunciation:

> You better go and get your *dresses*,
> Ev'ryone's got the op'ra *glasses*.

Although mild by today's standards, the suggestive allusions to the notorious dance ("We did it," Berlin recalled, "to see whether we could get away with it") made the song an enormous success. It sold 3,000 copies for Waterson & Snyder Company (the new name Max Winslow suggested for Seminary Music). The song also helped a young comic, Fanny Brice, earn a role in the then-new *Ziegfeld*

Follies, singing with a Yiddish accent (as Berlin had suggested) that soon became her trademark.

With "Dorando" and "Sadie Salome" to his credit, Berlin was hired by Waterson & Snyder as a staff lyricist at $25 a week plus royalties, leaving Jimmy Kelly's and his days as a singing waiter behind him. Once he joined the firm, most of Berlin's lyrics were written for tunes by Ted Snyder, a composer little older than Berlin. Snyder's rhythmic music kept Berlin's lyrical sights on the vernacular, finding poetic expressiveness in the commonest of catch phrases. Seizing upon just such a phrase in the summer of 1909, Berlin and Snyder turned it into an enormous hit. As Berlin recounted the story of the song's genesis, he was in John the Barber's shop on 45th Street one evening when George White, a vaudevillian who would later write such songs as "My Blue Heaven," strolled in. Berlin had known White from his busking days in the Bowery and asked his old friend if he wanted to take in a show. "Sure," White laughed, "My wife's gone to the country." Berlin recalled:

> Bing! *There* I had a common place familiar title line. It was singable, capable of humorous upbuilding, simple, and one that did not seriously offend against the *"sexless"* rule [Tin Pan Alley's efforts to write "unisex" song lyrics that could easily be sung by either male or female performers]. Wives and their offspring of both sexes, as well as their husbands, would be amused by singing it or hearing it sung.
>
> I persuaded Whiting to forget the theatre and to devote the night to developing the line with me into a song. Now, the usual, and unsuccessful, way of handling a line like that is to dash off a jumble of verses about the henpecked husband, all leading up to a chorus running, we'll say, something like this:
>
> > My wife's gone to the country,
> >   She went away last night.
> > Oh, I'm so glad! I'm so glad!
> >   I'm crazy with delight!
>
> Just wordy, obvious elaboration. No *punch*! All night I sweated to find what I knew was there, and finally I speared the lone word, just a single word, that *made* the song—and a fortune.

The secret word that came from Berlin's all-night struggle was, simply, "Hurrah!":

> That lone word gave the whole idea of the song in one
> quick wallop. It gave the singer a chance to hoot with
> sheer joy. It *invited* the roomful to join in the hilarious
> shout. It everlastingly put the catch line over. And I wasn't
> content until I had used my good thing to the limit.

Berlin not only learned the power of a catch phrase but that of a
single word, much as the brief "Toot! Toot!" had invited audiences to
join in singing "My Mariucci Take a Steamboat" back in 1907. He
learned too the importance of inspiration but also of the toil necessary to adorn natural inspiration in artful simplicity.

Finally, Berlin may also have discerned the relative importance of
the verse and chorus of a song. Until now, he had adhered to the
nineteenth-century pattern whereby the verse carried the all-important narrative of a song and the brief chorus merely punctuated that
story. Beginning with "My Wife's Gone to the Country," however, he
placed equal emphasis upon the chorus and the verse.

All of these lessons were driven home by the song's immediate success, selling 300,000 copies to become, in a matter of a few days, the
best-known song in America. The *New York Evening Journal*, the
newspaper he had once sold on the streets of the Lower East Side,
invited Berlin to supply additional lyrics, and the songwriter responded with a staggering series of 100 new verses and choruses, sporting
such other current catch phrases as "I love my wife, but oh! you kid!"
The newspaper reprinted every word, and threw in the news that
Mrs. Randolph Hearst had told a reporter she wanted to meet the boy
who had written the song that was sweeping the country.

Given such success, it is not surprising that Berlin wrote nearly
all of his songs for the rest of 1909 with Ted Snyder. Snyder had
made a name for himself as a composer of such "ragtime" instrumentals as "Wild Cherries Rag," and in Irving Berlin he found a collaborator who could set ragtime rhythms to words. The roots of ragtime are hard to trace, but it seems to have started out in the
brothels of New Orleans as a raucously swinging piano music that
combined a syncopated melody with a strict duple time accompaniment, the left hand thumping out a steady two-beat pattern while the
right hand came in slightly before or after the beat. This type of
steady accompaniment overlaid with a "ragged" melody was probably inspired by nineteenth-century black American adaptations of
European music and dances. Drawing upon the rhythmic complexi-
ty of African musical traditions, blacks embellished the steady oompah beat of the American brass band with free-swinging flourishes
that gave the music a sprightly, jagged liveliness. As ragtime migrated northward up the Mississippi in the 1880s, composers like Scott

Joplin of Missouri crafted elegant compositions structured, like the sonata and rondo, in sections that developed themes and variations.

Ragtime first came to the attention of the general public at the Chicago World's Fair of 1893, one of the great landmarks in American cultural history. Officially known as the World's Columbian Exposition, the Fair commemorated the four-hundredth anniversary of Columbus' voyage to America. It is fitting that the same year brought Irving Berlin to America and introduced Americans to ragtime. The Fair attracted 27 million people and "had a profound effect on American music, art, architecture, and mores." By the late 1890s, ragtime became a national craze as Tin Pan Alley publishers marketed so-called "coon songs"—syncopated (sometimes only barely so) comedy songs that drew upon minstrel show caricatures of blacks. As in minstrel shows, coon songs were created by whites who often borrowed and sanitized songs sung in black saloons and barrelhouses (though some ragtime coon song composers, like Ernest Hogan, were black and turned out some of the most demeaning caricatures, such as "All Coons Look Alike to Me").

Lyrically, coon songs employed a confected black dialect that was strikingly different from the elevated diction of sentimental ballads. Trying to write in slang and fit words to an even mildly syncopated melody produced a new kind of song. Few coon songs, for example, try to tell a story as lengthy and involved as the one that unfolds in the verses of "After the Ball" or "A Bird in a Gilded Cage." Most simply sketch a situation in one or two verses, then concentrate on the chorus with its simple lyrical expression. A caricatured black might plead, "I Want Yer, Ma Honey" or celebrate "My Black Baby Mine." Some coon songs are still familiar today, such as "Hello, Ma Baby" and "Bill Bailey, Won't You Please Come Home," though only by looking at the grotesque racist images on the sheet music would we be able to identify these as "coon" songs.

Musically and lyrically, ragtime coon songs were an antidote to the lachrymose waltz ballads of the turn of the century. In "Mister Johnson, Turn Me Loose," a stereotypical black in the clutches of "Mr. Johnson" (slang for the police), pleads in such vernacular phrases as "Don't Take Me to the Calaboose!" Because it was taboo on Tin Pan Alley for black characters to express serious romantic feelings, love songs were always comic and frequently sexual, employing what music historian Isaac Goldberg called, "a vocabulary of unadorned passion—a crude *ars amandi*" With a forthrightness unimaginable in a white romantic ballad, a "coon-shouter," as blackface singers were dubbed, could belt out a sentiment like "All I want is lovin'—I don't want your money," or lament, "You've been a good old wagon but you done broke down" (with a sly implication that the "wagon" was a woman who had lost her sexual attractiveness). The code words for sex in coon songs were "warm" and "hot," so that titles like "Dar's No Coon Warm Enough for Me," "A Red Hot Coon," or "The Warmest Colored Gal in Town," signaled their risqué subtext. Sometimes, the humor came from black pretensions to white ways, as in "She's Getting Mo' Like the White Folks Everyday":

> Now she can sing "The Swanee River"
> Like it was never sung before,
> But since she's worked in that hotel
> She warbles "Il Trovatore."

In these lines one can hear the seeds of Berlin's "Alexander's Ragtime Band" with its lines about "play a bugle call like you never heard before" and "if you care to hear the Swanee River played in ragtime." The very name "Alexander" was a coon song staple that mocked the pretentious names blacks supposedly chose for themselves, as in "Alexander (Don't You Love Your Black Baby No More?)."

By 1910, virtually any song with a lively rhythm, syncopated or not, was regarded as ragtime, and the music itself seemed to capture the pace of modern American life. Waterson & Snyder were one of the firms who specialized in such songs, and, as staff lyricist, Berlin found that his skill with the vernacular was suited to Snyder's rhythmic melodies. Their early ragtime songs drew upon the coon-song tradition of racial caricature, such as "Do Your Duty Doctor! (Oh, Oh, Oh, Oh, Doctor)," where an ailing "Liza" is given this diagnosis by her lecherous physician:

> You're suff'ring from a love attack,
> And if you want to bring health back,
> A loving man must love you every day.

Ragtime instrumentals, such as Snyder's "Wild Cherries Rag," could be turned into songs by making one of the original musical sections a verse, another the chorus, and discarding the other sections. Berlin could then add a lyric about "looney coons" and "spoony coons" who are aroused by ragtime music:

> I'm goin' crazy that rag's a daisy
> I just can't make my feeling behave.

The most overtly sexual equation with ragtime music came in "Alexander and His Clarinet," where Berlin makes the instrument a clear emblem of phallic prowess:

> Alexander played his clarinet with vim,
> Up to Liza's door, then played himself right in,
> When he got inside he played and played like sin, . . .

Characteristically, the aroused listener of ragtime is torn between emotions; at first angry when she sees Alexander has brought his clarinet, Liza suddenly beseeches him:

> For lawdy sake don't dare to go,
> My pet, I love you yet,
> And then besides, I love your clarinet.

The tension between emotions accorded well with the tension in ragtime itself between the irregular accents of the melody and the steady beat of the accompaniment.

Berlin had long been familiar with ragtime, which he initially knew by the name "noodles," from black pianists who sat in at the Pelham Café, such as Luckey Roberts, who played "stride" piano (a ragtime style that required the pianist to stretch his left hand over a wide range by alternating low bass notes with chords in the middle register in rapid succession, an oompah style that recalled the brass band roots of ragtime piano). Perhaps that familiarity emboldened him to try to compose his own ragtime melodies. "I know rhythm," he later explained, attributing his knowledge to his Russian heritage: "Russians make wonderful dancers" and were "great on harmony and rhythm." "Rhythm," he added, "is a big part" of the success of his songs.

By this time, Berlin also knew how to play the piano, though like other "composers" on Tin Pan Alley—such as George M. Cohan—he could only play in the key of F♯. Among songwriters, this was known as playing on the "nigger keys," since F♯, with its five sharps (F♯, G♯, A♯, C♯, and D♯), consists of almost all black keys. Playing primarily on the black keys was less daunting to neophyte composers. As Berlin himself said, "the black keys are right there under your fingers," adding "children who learn to play instinctively always learn the key of F♯," while "the key of C is for people who study music." He even speculated that his liability was secretly an asset, because by concentrating on the limited notes of the single key of F♯, he could explore nuances and subtleties that trained composers, ranging over the twenty-four diatonic keys, overlooked. Because the key of F♯ includes the pentatonic scale of folk and nonwestern music, moreover, melodies that emerged from it often exuded an exotic character from beyond the European tradition.

Berlin and other composers could transcend the limitations of F♯ by using a transposing piano. This instrument had a lever that shift-

Irving Berlin, 26 years old, at work in his office in 1914.

ed the keys so that the pianist could continue to hit the keys of F♯ but hear how a song sounded in any of the other major and minor keys. A step above the player piano, the transposing piano, which could be purchased from the Weser Company for $100, required only that a person know how to play in a single key in order to encompass the full range of the instrument. Berlin's only remaining limitation as a composer was that for many years he could not read music, but he contented himself with having a trained musician transcribe the melodies he played. Then, when they were played back to him, Berlin would, remarkably, pick out his harmonies by ear.

Berlin's musicianly ambition did not sit well with Waterson and Snyder at first. As Alexander Woollcott put it, "They were tolerant but firm, in the manner of the manager whose most profitable comedian is suddenly attacked with a ruinous ambition to play *Hamlet*." Berlin persisted, however, and shrewdly waited until he knew none of the staff composers was in the office when he showed up with a new lyric. The first ragtime song Berlin wrote completely on his own was "Yiddle on Your Fiddle, Play Some Ragtime" in November 1909. Following the practice of some of his earlier musical collaborators, he accented the tension between ethnic immigrant tradition and modern America by writing a verse in the minor mode and lacing the sweeping melody with exotic intervals and chromatic inflections in the accompaniment. The chorus, by contrast, is in the choppy style of ragtime "stride" piano, and opens with a triple rhyme on the same repeated notes: "*Yiddle* in the *middle* of your *fiddle*, play some ragtime."

The song reworks the equation between ragtime and sexual desire, but instead of a black woman aroused by the music, it is now a "Sadie" who swoons over the "modern" ragtime fiddling of Yiddle at a traditional Jewish wedding. She pleads for more ragtime but in Yiddish phrasing that also provides another triple rhyme: "if you'll *maybe play* for *Sadie*, some more ragtime." Calling him her "choc'late baby" (perhaps because he has mastered black music), Sadie follows Jewish tradition by putting "a quarter right on Yiddle's dish," as he is drinking his soup, but what she requests is another ragtime number.

As his own composer and lyricist, Berlin could make the piano imitate the sound of the fiddle and create clever matches between music and lyric, such as having the melody rise suddenly when Sadie "jumped up and looked him in the eyes" or extend the length of his chorus to underscore Sadie's plea "Yiddle, don't you stop, if you do, I'll drop."

The cultural gulf between ragtime and "serious" music often tempted composers to impudently "rag" a classical melody, and Berlin created another hit by taking the main strain of Mendelssohn's "Frühlingslied" ("Spring Song") and turning it into "That Mesmerizing Mendelssohn Tune." "I had always loved Mendelssohn and his 'Spring Song,'" Berlin explained, "and simply wanted to work it into a rag tune." Subtitled "Mendelssohn Rag," the song syncopates the classical melody and sets it to a colloquial lyric that praises rather than mocks the original:

Love me to that ever lovin' Spring song melody . . .
That tantalizin', hypnotizin', mesmerizin', Mendelssohn tune.

Berlin's song sold over 500,000 copies of sheet music and sales were only helped by newspaper critics who decried the sacrilege done to "proper" music by such "arrant nonsense."

By "writing both words and music," Berlin found, "I can compose them together and make them fit":

> I sacrifice one for the other. If I have a melody I want to use, I plug away at the lyrics until I make them fit the best parts of my music and vice versa. . . . Nearly all other writers work in teams, one writing the music and the other the words. They are either forced to fit some one's words to their music or some one's music to their words. Latitude—which begets novelty—is denied them, and in consequence both lyrics and melody suffer.

The first striking instance of Berlin's fitting words to his own music came in a song he completed in the summer of 1910, entitled, fittingly enough, "Try It on Your Piano." Berlin takes what had been his standard ragtime theme as a lyricist—the power of ragtime music to arouse sexual desire—and turns it upside down. "Lucy Brown" is impervious to the seductive charms of the piano-playing Benjamin Maner (whose last name rhymes, slangily, with "piano"); when he offers to show her "a new way to make love/ That hasn't been discovered yet," she sends him back to his beloved instrument:

> Try it on your piano grand,
> I don't care to understand
> B or I flat, C or Y flat,
> Try it hon' but not in my flat.

In the first of his many musical and lyrical "puns," the final word "flat" actually falls on a flatted note.

Once Berlin starts writing his own words and music, moreover, we find him increasingly adept at a technique songwriters call "memorability," lacing a lyric with subtle internal rhymes, sometimes back-to-back on repeated notes. In "Innocent Bessie Brown," published in October 1910, he recounts the standard tale of a country girl seduced by a city slicker but refreshes the climax with barely heard but still "memorable" rhymes:

> And when the day was breaking they were still partaking
> Of some fizzes of *gin*
> that fizzed with*in*,
> *In-*
> nocent Bessie Brown.

If "singability" helped a performer to project and sustain the words and notes of a melody, "memorability" insinuated a song into the listener's mind.

By the end of 1910, Irving Berlin had established himself as a figure on Tin Pan Alley. Newspapers hailed him as "The Man Who Is Making the Country Hum" and found good copy in his rags-to-riches journey up from Chinatown. His inability to read music, his piano-playing restrictions, and the thousands of dollars he made—"more money in royalties than the President of the United States received in salary a year ago," crowed one reporter—made him an American icon, a self-taught jack-of-all-trades who bypassed the needless tedium of classical education to produce money-making hits.

Like every American success story since Ben Franklin, Berlin freely offered "how to" tips to all who wished to emulate his success. In the *New York World* of July 10, 1910, Berlin was quoted:

> Song writing all depends on the public. The thing it likes one minute it tires of the next. . . . You must be able to switch your lyre to something else. If not, a new writer will take your place and your star, which rose so suddenly, will set as rapidly as it came up.

Shrewdly, Berlin flattered his public even as he instructed it and clearly set himself apart from the "one-hit" songwriters who lined Tin Pan Alley but who had not been able to adapt to shifting public tastes. When Berlin's first truly great song came, however, it came without effort, without calculation. One morning while he was shaving, in a burst of what he later called "simon-pure inspiration" a "melody came to me right out of the air." At the time, Berlin "was not impressed by it":

> In fact, after playing it over a few times on the piano, he did not take the trouble to note the melody on paper. He might never have completed the song had it not been for a trip to Palm Beach, Florida. . . . Just before train time he went to his offices to look over his manuscripts, in order to leave the best of them for publication during his absence.

In his papers, "he found a memorandum referring to 'Alexander,' and after considerable reflection, he recalled its strains. Largely for the lack of anything better with which to kill time, he sat at the piano and completed the song." "I wrote the whole thing in eighteen minutes, surrounded on all sides by roaring pianos and roaring vaudeville actors."

The experience enlarged his view of the creative process beyond hard work and shrewd calculation:

> Do I believe in inspiration? In having things hit you from nowhere? Big things you've never dreamed of? Occasionally—yes. I have never given Irving Berlin any credit for *Alexander*.

By entitling the song "Alexander's Ragtime Band," Berlin—or his muse—returned ragtime to its origins in the American brass band tradition, even incorporating a bugle call into the melody. In a newspaper essay he wrote at the time, "Why We Love Band Music," Berlin speculated that band music is a communal art form that, more than any other kind of music, draws Americans together. Keeping within that tradition, "'Alexander' was done originally as an instrumental number—no words," Berlin maintained, "I wrote it without words as a two-step and it was a dead failure. Six months later, I wrote words to it. . . . When the lyrics were added later, it became alive. People sang it and it became a sensation. For music to live, it must be sung." The magical alchemy of words and music produced a song that became more popular than any other song before it.

That phenomenal success was not immediate, however, and the song ran the gamut of the various forms of musical entertainment of its day. One venue where Berlin tried to feature it was Jesse Lasky's innovative *Folies Bergère*, the first of the "cabaret" shows, based on European models, that would soon change the character of New York night life by breaking down the formalism of nineteenth-century society, mingling people of different classes together, and bringing women out of their domestic world and into a public domain that had previously been dominated by men. Unlike vaudeville, cabaret was not family entertainment but a place where men and women could socialize together with an informality unimaginable in the nineteenth century.

The opening of the *Folies* stirred great public interest. "In the history of New York theatre-going," reported the *Morning Telegraph*, "there perhaps has never been an event that equaled the opening of the new *Folies Bergère*," which the newspaper described as "at once a café, a music hall, a theatre, a restaurant, a club." From the moment it opened for dining at 6:00 P.M., orchestras and singers entertained patrons as they ate, making the *Folies*, for all the ballyhoo about its novel combination of music and dining, an upscale—and uptown—version of the Bowery saloons with their piano players and singing waiters. More elaborate entertainment began at 8:15 with a series of stage shows, first *Hell*, a musical burlesque, followed by *Temptation*, a ballet with forty dancers, then another burlesque, and finally, "a cabaret show with half a dozen vaudeville acts ran from 11:15 until 1 o'clock in the morning."

Berlin, who had written some interpolated songs for the show, tried to get Lasky to use "Alexander's Ragtime Band" for his star soprano. "This is a good song," Lasky told Berlin, but pointed out his star was "a contralto and needs a song that can be sung much slower." Berlin's song did manage to squeeze into the show for one performance—another star took it upon himself to whistle it during a pantomime number—but it was cut from subsequent shows

For all of the excitement it generated, the *Folies* was an abortive experiment. Lasky later told Berlin that if he had used "Alexander's Ragtime Band," his show might have been a success, and he always liked to refer to himself as "the man who turned down 'Alexander's Ragtime Band.'" The problem with the *Folies*, however, was more fundamental. Lasky had conceived of cabaret primarily as a theatrical performance where, incidentally, food and drink would be served. By placing all the emphasis on the main show, Lasky overlooked the fact that what was truly innovative was the intimate late-night cabaret, where people dined as entertainers moved casually among them. In this informal combination of dining and performance lay the seeds for a genuinely new kind of entertainment.

Berlin himself performed "Alexander's Ragtime Band" when he made his debut as a new member of the Friars Club, the theatrical fraternity, which was staging its annual *Friars' Frolic* show on May 28, 1911. The show, a fund-raiser which featured George M. Cohan, was a huge success. "George M. Cohan was one of the first to like the song I sang," Berlin recalled. "He seemed to think the tune was all right," even though "it wasn't a hit at first." The Friars took their show on the road where it played from Boston and Philadelphia to Chicago and St. Louis, and audiences loved "Alexander's Ragtime Band" (one newspaper reported its "encores were as the sands of the sea"). Still, Berlin's music firm did little to promote it. Neither Snyder nor Waterson was enthralled with the number, perhaps, Charles Hamm speculates, because Snyder "was jealous of his younger colleague who was so suddenly outstripping him professionally."

Max Winslow, however, plugged his friend's song relentlessly. He persuaded the producer of *The Merry Whirl*, a burlesque show, to include it as the first act finale, where it was performed with a "Grizzly Bear" dance by the chorus. While burlesque in 1911 was hardly the ecdysiastic bump-and-grind of today, it did feature scantily clad chorines and off-color comedy. Nevertheless, *Variety* described *The Merry Whirl* as "classy as burlesque ever held—classier even," and "Alexander's Ragtime Band" was "the big song hit of the evening."

While the song was successful in these theatrical venues, it really caught on in vaudeville. After starting "in only a mild pale-pink way for the first three months," as Berlin recalled, " it took heart and went like hot-cakes." The big push came when coon-shouter Emma Carus (who always opened her act with, "I'm not pretty but I'm good to my folks") sang it in Chicago. It is fitting that the city that introduced Americans to ragtime at the 1893 World's Fair should launch "Alexander's Ragtime Band" into an international success. Chicago had remained a center for ragtime and took up Berlin's song in theaters, saloons, dance halls, nickelodeons, and restaurants. From Chicago, "Alexander's Ragtime Band" spread across the country on the vaudeville circuit. Soon vaudeville managers were besieged with acts that wanted to use the song, and one had to instruct four of the five acts on his bill to "cut that band song out."

By the end of the year, "Alexander's Ragtime Band" had sold a million copies, then another million in 1912 as it spread across England and Europe. Tin Pan Alley hailed it, first, as an even bigger hit than Charles Harris's "After the Ball," then "as the biggest song hit ever known." What was the magic in Berlin's inspired creation? The music has little of the syncopation we now define as the basis of true ragtime, though in 1911 virtually any lilting melody was dubbed "ragtime." It differed from most songs of its day—and most songs Berlin himself had written to this point—by placing far greater emphasis upon the chorus rather than the verse. The chorus was thirty-two bars long, twice the length of the chorus of nineteenth-century songs, and, as Berlin himself pointed out, "went beyond" the range of "an octave and maybe a note" that confined "most songs." He may have been following a precedent set by several songs of recent years, such as "I Wonder Who's Kissing Her Now" (1909) and "Some of These Days" (1910). The greater emphasis upon the chorus suited Berlin's working temperament; as an interviewer reported, "the second verse of a song is Berlin's bugbear. With the melody and the first verse and refrain written, Berlin's interest cools and he is eager to get to work on a new idea." Berlin's interest in the chorus also reflected his talent for lyrical, rather than narrative, songwriting. Instead of having to tell a story through a sequence of several verses, the verse of "Alexander's Ragtime Band" is merely an introduction to the chorus. (Initially he had written a second verse for the song, but soon eliminated it from published sheet music.) Exploiting the possibilities of his transposing piano, Berlin further demarcated the new structural priorities of his song by changing keys between the verse, which was in the key of C, and the chorus in F—a rare shift for a Tin Pan Alley song.

As has been remarked many times, the music has few traces of ragtime syncopation and those are mostly confined to the verse, where the first three measures begin on the off beat. While the verse is catchy, the real power of the song lies in the chorus, which has a subtly melancholy character. The G♯ that opens the chorus sounds the kind of chromatic strain that Berlin himself said derived from "Slavonic and Semitic folk tunes." That mournful quality can be heard in the film *Alexander's Ragtime Band* where Tyrone Power, playing the violinist whose orchestra popularizes the new song, first tries to play it as a soulful dirge until he swings into its sprightly rhythm. That rhythm, along with the jaunty lyric, was at odds with the chromatic strain of the melody, and such a tension was one of the secrets of the song's success. In an essay he wrote later, called "Song and Sorrow Are Playmates," Berlin remarked upon the contrast between the "rollicking" words and the mournful melody, defying "any composer of standard ballads to produce melodies more intrinsically sad."

Although Berlin himself dismissed the words he added to his ragtime instrumental as "simply terrible" and "silly in the matter of common sense," another secret of the song's success was his clever matching of words to music. When the bugle-call melody descends to middle C in the phrase,

Let me take you by the hand,

then rises up more than a full octave, Berlin makes the lyrical thought rise "up" as well:

Up to the man, up to the man.

More subtle than his matches of words and music are his innovative mismatches. In a kind of "ragging" of verbal against musical accents, Berlin uses the musical beat to distort the emphasis on the word "natural" (normally, "*na*tural") that forces it to rhyme with "call":

They can play a bugle *call*
like you never heard before,
So natur*al*
that you want to go to war.

Further, he makes the two syllables, "*na-tu*," subtly rhyme with "*that you*." At another musical leap near the end of the chorus, Berlin plants a similarly "ragged" lyrical climax:

And if you care to hear the Swanee River played in ragtime.

While not syncopated musically, the octave jump gives the normally unaccented word "in" a powerful emphasis with the highest note of the chorus in a kind of verbal syncopation.

For all of these clever manipulations of music against words, Berlin continued to maintain that the real secret to lyric writing lay in simplicity of phrase:

> Three-fourths of that quality which brings success to popular songs is the phrasing. I make a study of it—ease, naturalness, every-day-ness—and it is my first considera-tion when I start on lyrics. "Easy to sing, easy to say, easy to remember and applicable to everyday events" is a good rule for a phrase.

Such artful simplicity is apparent from the short phrases of the verse that effortlessly fit the syncopated music with jagged rhymes and fragmented but perfectly conversational syntax:

> Ain't you goin', Ain't you goin'.
> To the *leader* man,
> Ragged *meter* man? . . .
> Let me take you to Alex*ander*'s
> gr*and* st*and*, brass *band*,
> Ain't you comin' along?

Here again, the deft interplay between words and notes puts the packed rhymes and alliteration of "grand stand, brass band" on four equal half notes.

Neither Berlin's simplicity nor his ingenuity, however, can fully account for the phenomenal success of "Alexander's Ragtime Band"—not just in America but in England and Europe as well. As musicologist Edward Jablonski has observed:

> What *Alexander* succeeded in doing was to take a style already in vogue and make it a national passion. *Alexander* sold one million copies within a few months; before the end of the year it was the most frequently heard popular song in the country. A success of such formidable proportions had inevitable repercussions. For one thing, the ragtime song displaced the sentimen-tal ballad, dialect song, or vaudeville ditty in populari-ty. With everybody in tin-pan alley writing ragtime songs, the former emphasis upon formal, stilted melodies was now placed on comparatively less formal

and less stilted rhythms. This change of emphasis made
it possible for a new vitality to enter the writing for
American popular songs.

Not only did "Alexander's Ragtime Band" appear at a critical
juncture in the history of American song, it crystallized a crucial
cultural moment as well, one when people fully realized that they
were living in a truly modern age. The British novelist Virginia
Woolf tried to capture that sense of "modernity" in a calculatedly
hyperbolic declaration: "On or about December, 1910, human
nature changed." Woolf was wryly trying to define that sense of
newness, of a total break with the traditional past, of the deluge of
radical ideas that struck people after the first decade of the twentieth century. The impression of change was especially strong in
America, where the effects of urbanization, industrialization, and
immigration made people feel they were living in a vastly different
world from that of the nineteenth century: a world of cities and factories instead of towns and farms, of suffragettes and strikes, of skyscrapers and subways, Freud and Einstein, of telephones and automobiles and airplanes.

Much of this sense of cultural transformation, both for those who
embraced and those who resisted it, centered on the world of popular entertainment. *The Report on the Social Evil of 1910*, for example,
warned that "Youth is gravitating toward the city, away from home,
religious and personal ideals, breaking the moorings of the past."
The report pointed its finger at "those ungoverned, unlicensed,
unregulated amusement resorts," such as "movies, vaudeville, ragtime, and cabarets." Ragtime, above all, came under attack from the
white establishment as a sign of the "the rising tide of immigrant
and black-inspired culture." A prominent psychiatrist reported the
alarming findings that mental patients showed a marked preference
for ragtime over classical music and concluded, "Ragtime isn't
music, it's a disease."

Into this tense cultural situation, "Alexander's Ragtime Band"
came as a palliative rather than an explosion, making ragtime seem
ingratiating, not threatening. "Come on along," the chorus urged
and offered to "take you by the hand." Berlin himself observed how

its opening words, emphasized by immediate repetition—"Come on and hear! Come on and hear!"—were an
invitation to "come," to join in, and "hear" the singer and
his song. And that idea of *inviting* every receptive auditor
within shouting distance became a part of the happy ruc-
tion—an idea pounded in again and again throughout

the song in various ways—was the secret of the song's tremendous success.

Like a pied piper or a camp meeting revivalist, the singer invited everyone to come forward and embrace the music of the new age.

The figure of Alexander himself, while derived from the coon song tradition, is heard but never really seen in the song, and he purveys not a disconcertingly new music but the traditional "Swanee River" in a different form, bridging, rather than breaking from, the past. Instead of railing against it, newspapers could satirize it affectionately. Headlines asked "Has It Got You Going Too?," and cartoons showed people driven mad by the song's ubiquity. In the London *Times*, another British novelist, Arnold Bennett, reached out an olive branch to the new age and its music. Ragtime, he wrote, "is the music of the hustler, of the feverishly active speculator; of the 'skyscraper' and the 'grain-elevator.'" While Bennett deplored it as "empty sometimes and meaningless," he concluded there can be no "doubt about its vigor," which is "brimming over with life."

On one occasion, "Alexander's Ragtime Band" even helped save lives. When a fire broke out in the projection booth of a Philadelphia theater, the pianist, who had been playing "Hearts and Flowers," suddenly switched to "Alexander's Ragtime Band" and induced the crowd, which otherwise might have panicked, to join in singing the refrain until the fire was extinguished. What Berlin's song did in that auditorium, it managed to do for all of America, making the world safe for ragtime and for modernism.

Chapter 3

I LOVE A PIANO

I confess that my knowledge of music is almost nothing. I never had any musical education, and I cannot even play the piano. Furthermore, I have no desire to study music—at least not for the present—because it would completely change my method of work, and composing, even such as mine, I assure you is work, and mighty hard work.

When Irving Berlin turned twenty-three on May 11, 1911, he already had what many people would consider a lifetime of achievements. He had written some 200 songs, most of which were successful and some spectacularly so, earning him more than $100,000 in royalties. He had also established himself as a performer on Broadway, singing his own compositions while his "musical secretary," Clifford Hess, accompanied him on the piano. In the spring of 1911, he sang his songs in the Friars Club's annual revue and, the next year, together with other show business luminaries, paraded up Broadway. Newspaper photographers captured a grinning young Irving Berlin, donned in a top hat, and proclaimed him the "King of Ragtime." On Berlin's copy of the photo, he wrote "This is the life."

In September 1911, Berlin starred in a vaudeville revue at the elegant Hammerstein Victoria Theatre on Times Square. Founded by the father of the lyricist Oscar Hammerstein II, the Victoria was one of the premiere vaudeville houses. For this occasion, its marquee carried Irving Berlin's name in lights, while a life-sized poster of him in the lobby labeled him "The Composer of a Hundred Hits." "To see this slim little kid on stage," one reviewer wrote, "going through a list that sounded like all the hits in the world, is something to think about." During his run, a crowd of 200 old friends from the Bowery showed up for a matinee, led by Chuck Connors. Berlin was so touched by their vociferous ovation for "one of their own" that he broke down on stage. Tears turned to laughter, however, when he showed up for the evening performance to find some of his old cronies still lingering in the lobby. "Gee, Izzy," they complained, "We've been hanging around this bum joint for three hours trying to get a chance to pinch that swell picture of you."

These attainments, however, only drove Berlin to maintain and even extend his success. He dreaded fading into oblivion, as had so many songwriters before him, remembered, if at all, as the composer of one or two hits. In newspaper interviews he even spoke with some disparagement about "popular" songs that, by their very nature, were soon forgotten, to be replaced by other ditties of the day. In a light verse poem he composed for a gathering of songwriters, he contrasted himself and his contemporaries to "Chopin, Verdi, Beethoven and Liszt," who "live on with each generation," while "popular song" is "never missed once" the "composer has ceased to exist." "Alexander's Ragtime Band," he felt, was destined to be an enduring song, one that would be remembered for generations to come, but he longed to write more of such classic works.

The songwriter Berlin most admired was Stephen Foster, whose picture hung in his office. Foster's "Old Folks at Home" and "Massa's in de Cold Ground," were in what was then termed the "minstrel" or "Ethiopian" style, a forerunner of the "coon" songs of the turn of the century. Berlin had shown his own mastery of this genre with "Alexander's Ragtime Band" and many other ragtime numbers. What he had not mastered, however, were Foster's great ballads, such as "Jeannie With the Light Brown Hair" and "Beautiful Dreamer." Although Foster termed these his "English" songs, they clearly stem from his own Irish heritage, marked by pentatonic melodies and wistfully melancholy lyrics, very similar to the songs of Thomas Moore, such as "Believe Me, If All Those Endearing Young Charms." Written in the early nineteenth century, these songs still sound fresh and lovely today, and it was this kind of simple yet sophisticated ballad that Berlin aspired to write.

While Berlin admired Foster's artistry, however, he was wary of Foster's notorious end: dying in poverty, at the age of thirty-seven. Although his songs earned millions of dollars, Foster received only the royalties from them, because, like most songwriters, he sold his songs to music publishers, and they held the copyrights and reaped the greatest profits. Irving Berlin was determined to own his own songs and began buying up the rights to his creations, so that, alone among the great songwriters of his era, he would own and could

therefore control his own songs. An important step toward control-
ling his own work came at the end of 1911, when Berlin was made a
partner in the publishing firm for which he had long worked. The
company now was named Waterson, Berlin & Snyder and relocated
at 112 West 38th Street, close to the heart of the theater district.

To celebrate the occasion, Waterson threw a champagne party for
his young partner. But, when he stood to make a speech, he said
something that revealed Berlin's success had also bred some jealous
rumors:

> You know, Irvy, there's a story circulating on Broadway—
> that the reason you can turn out so much golden ragtime
> is because you got your own colored pickaninny tucked
> away in a closet.

Unable to fathom Berlin's phenomenal success, given his musical
illiteracy and limited piano abilities, other songwriters concocted the
myth that he secretly paid a black ragtime pianist to create his
melodies. To be sure, it was common for a Tin Pan Alley publisher
or even an established songwriter to purchase a song outright for a
lump sum payment and give the creator no credit, a practice particularly harmful to black songwriters, such as Fats Waller and Andy
Razaf.

Yet Berlin defended himself against these rumors by affirming
that "Songwriters don't steal, at least those of reputation don't" and
complaining that "the public, by some freak of mind, would rather
believe that the fellow who is getting the credit isn't the one who is
doing the work":

> I asked them to tell me from whom I had bought my suc-
> cesses—twenty-five or thirty of them. And I wanted to
> know, if a negro could write "Alexander," why couldn't
> I? Then I told them if they could produce the negro and
> he had another hit like "Alexander" in his system, I
> would choke it out of him and give him twenty thousand
> dollars in the bargain.

Within a few years, as Berlin kept producing hit song after hit
song, he could joke about such rumors, noting, for example, that
instead of one he must now have a secret Harlem office with an
entire staff of ghostwriters. At this point in his career, however,
these rumors soured his hard-won success and strengthened his in-
born determination to create more great songs.

The rumors also may have prompted his unfortunate denials that
ragtime was the indigenous music of African-Americans:

> The syncopated, shoulder-shaking type of vocal and instrumental melody, which has now been dignified internationally as "typical American music" is not wholly, or even largely, of African origin as is popularly supposed. Our popular songwriters and composers are not negroes. Many of them are of Russian birth and ancestry. All of them are of pure white blood. As in the case of everything else American, their universally popular music is the product of a sort of musical melting pot. Their distinctive school is a combination of the influences of Southern plantation songs, of European music from almost countless countries and of the syncopation that is found in the music of innumerable nationalities.

The best antidote to these rumors was to write another song, one that built on the success of "Alexander's Ragtime Band." By the end of 1911, America's revolutionary transformation in culture, manners, and entertainment had entered the "dance craze." Just as a century before, the waltz had shocked society by inviting dancers to touch one another in a manner never permitted in the more courtly minuets and gavottes of the eighteenth century, so twentieth-century ragtime spawned a series of new dances where couples grasped—nearly hugged—each other firmly about the neck and waist. With such "barbaric" names as the turkey trot, the bunny hug, the grizzly bear, the chicken scratch, the buzzard lope, and the monkey glide, these new dances emanated from black dives and red-light districts, and relied upon ragtime syncopation for their frenzied and suggestive steps. These steps were based on a walk or shuffle that was much more informal than traditional dance steps, and the dances also placed more emphasis on bodily movement than did traditional ones, which concentrated on patterns for the feet. Even as late as 1910, it was considered unseemly for refined adults to be seen dancing in public, but between 1912 and 1914 more than 100 new dances were introduced that had young and old dancing on practically a daily basis. Lamenting "The Revolt of Decency," the *New York Sun* echoed the common assumption that all of the dances were originated by blacks and pointed out that they were not "new" at all but "are based on the primitive motive of orgies enjoyed by the aboriginal inhabitants of every uncivilized land."

This dance craze flourished in the new, fashionable cabarets. As F. Scott Fitzgerald, chronicler of the Jazz Age, observed, the dance craze "brought the nice girl into the café, thus beginning a profound revolution in American life." Restaurant owners, eager to bolster business in the economically depressed days of 1911, took note of Jesse Lasky's attempt to mingle dining and entertainment at the

Folies Bergère. Julius Keller, who owned the exclusive Maxim's, had once run a saloon in the Lower East Side, where the rowdy crowds had always loved singing waiters, such as Irving Berlin had once been. "If customers of that joint could derive the utmost enjoyment from hearing waiters sing," he reasoned, "the more cultured people of 38th Street would do the same." Amid the plush decor of his new restaurant, he had singers and dancers entertain his patrons as they dined. The performers developed a new, more informal and intimate style of delivery, mingling with the customers and even including them in their acts, blurring the line between audience and performer. Because city regulations required restaurant owners to purchase a theatrical license if they had a stage or scenery, the "show" emanated from the "floor," and it was not long before diners took to the floor themselves to dance. As the orchestra played, patrons tried out the new dances on the same floor where professional singers and dancers had performed. As Jesse Lasky reflected on the failure of his pioneering cabaret, "it seems to me now that the *Folies Bergère* probably had all the ingredients for a smashing success, save one—a little two-by-four square of hardwood."

When the city cracked down on cabarets by imposing a 2:00 A.M. curfew, patrons simply signed membership cards to join a private "night club" that enabled them to go on dancing. What was even more shocking to the guardians of morality was that people could dance during the day at the *thé dansants* or "tea dances" that cabarets and hotels started as early as 2:00 P.M. and extended into the once-sacred tea hour. (Tea was hardly the potable at such affairs; as one waiter remarked, "we seldom serve tea; they wiggle much better on whiskey.") At such afternoon dances, one editorial moaned, "the young simply take advantage of the dance to embrace." Particularly offensive were such Latin imports as the tango, where dancers pressed their bodies, upper *and* lower, together and even did a shocking "dip." Unescorted society ladies, married and unmarried, could learn these new steps from professional dancers who were barely a step above gigolos. In place of the traditional gypsy violins that played for listening, black bands now played raucous ragtime music for the dances that had emerged from their own red-light districts. "From the slum to the stage," intoned the *New York World* under the headline, "The City of Dreadful Dance," "from the stage to the restaurant, from restaurant to home, the dive dances have clutched and taken hold upon the young who know no better and the old who should." So alarming was the trend that, in 1913, a New York grand jury found "a presentment condemning the turkey trot and kindred dances and laying particular stress upon the fact that the hotels and cafes allow such dances in their establishments."

As with every new popular craze, Tin Pan Alley was quick to exploit dance's new-found popularity. The dance craze dovetailed with the ragtime revival to make rhythm uppermost in songwriting. Music was conceived as an adjunct to dancing, rather than something merely to listen to, and lyrics and vocal performance were overshadowed by the musical beat. Many of the popular songs of the day had lyrics that simply "instructed" listeners in the new step, frequently with suggestive overtones. It was Irving Berlin who crystallized the whole dance craze—and the sexual energy and license it evoked—in a single song he wrote at the end of 1911, "Everybody's Doin' It Now." Setting the slangy catch phrase title to a sprightly syncopated melody, Berlin once again had an infectious invitation for all to join in a joyous collective celebration. But where such an invitation in "Alexander's Ragtime Band" made the ragtime craze seem almost wholesome, in "Everybody's Doin' It" the singer urged an erotic abandon. Berlin's years of singing risqué parodies in Chinatown saloons may have inspired him to insert the spoken repetition of "Doin' it, Doin' it" to underscore the suggestive power of simple verbs and pronouns. The imagery of the lyric also depicts the collective loss of decorum on the dance floor and the new emphasis on bodily expression: a "ragtime couple" throw "their shoulders in the air," "snap their fingers," and exult, "It's a bear, it's a bear, it's a bear."

The same breakdown of propriety is mirrored in the grammar:

> Ain't that music touching your heart?
> Hear that trombone bustin' apart?

Such vernacular touches may have their roots in the black dialect of "coon" songs, but here they are the new lingua franca of proper society casting off its genteel traditions. As "Everybody's Doin' It" became yet another of Berlin's phenomenally successful hits, the songwriter reflected on his uncanny ability to capture an historical moment in song: "It was the dance craze put to music and words."

The song—and Berlin—also became a lightning rod for the defenders of morality, one of whom lamented of the whole dance craze, "Everybody's Overdoing It." The New York Commission on Amusements and Vacation Resources for Working Girls, founded in 1910, reported that "reckless and uncontrolled dances" were only "an opportunity for license and debauch," and by 1912 the mayor of New York was pressured into imposing curfews on "so-called respectable places" that had been turned by the dance craze "into places of vulgarity if not infamy." The mayor also promised an investigation of Tin Pan Alley firms like Waterson, Berlin & Snyder that fueled the dance craze with such risqué songs as "Everybody's Doin'

It." The firm's pluggers were banned from some department stores, but still the song and the dance craze rolled on. When Berlin himself performed his hit at Hammerstein's Victoria Theatre, a newspaper reviewer described the kind of pandemonium that foreshadowed Sinatra's bobby-soxers and rock concerts:

> Everybody is doing it or doing something when this popular song writer sings this ragtime classic. . . . The musicians in the orchestra begin swaying while playing their instruments, the curtain is raised and behind the scenes stage hands are discovered "doing it" with chairs, brooms or whatever they may be handling when the strains of his contagious tune strikes them.

His capacity to turn out such hit songs seemed fathomless, yet it was a turn in his personal, rather than professional, life that temporarily silenced Irving Berlin's muse.

Tin Pan Alley publishers regularly sought out noted vaudeville and Broadway stars to sing their firm's songs, while lesser-known singers, in turn, beseeched publishers for the opportunity to introduce a new song on stage. No Alley firm was more besieged by aspiring singers than Waterson, Berlin & Snyder and no songwriter's wares were more prized than Irving Berlin's. The opportunity to introduce Irving Berlin's latest song could be the break of a lifetime for young singers, and the zeal with which they pursued that chance amazed Berlin himself. One day, two women literally came to blows in his office. The first was Dorothy Goetz, the beautiful sister of composer Ray Goetz, one of Berlin's early collaborators. Just as Dorothy began to plead for his latest song, Berlin recalled:

> another Broadway adorable swept into the room. As soon as she heard what the first girl was asking, she rushed across to the desk, pulling her away, shouting: "No! I want it." Dorothy was a woman of spirit. She swung a haymaking left and slapped the newcomer across the face. The two closed, swapping punches like a couple of prize-ring veterans, and I was powerless to separate them. They were scratching, tearing hair and shouting in lovely voices that they wanted to sing my song. Well, I had dreamed of people fighting for the right to sing my stuff—but this was the first time I saw that dream come true.

While the second girl got the song, Dorothy got Irving Berlin. Smitten by her feisty energy that seemed to match his own, Berlin

conducted a whirlwind courtship, and the two were married in
February 1912.

The couple gave reporters all they could wish for in a romantic
story. Dorothy told them she was "a convent bred girl with high
ideals of marriage" and that one of the first promises she demanded
of her intended husband "was that he write no more songs on the
order of 'My Wife's Gone to the Country.'" Berlin, in his turn, made
an even more revealing comment about the meaning the marriage
had for him:

> Well, she's just the finest, sweetest little girl in the world,
> and I can tell you this is the most wonderful thing that
> ever happened to me. Why up to two months ago I was
> all wrapped up in my musical work and on the fair way
> to becoming a nervous wreck. My work and my songs
> made up my life, from night to morning and morning to
> night. It was all music, all songs, all the hope of song
> hits. Two months have worked a marvelous change, and
> I seem to see life from a different side. Mind you, I'm not
> giving up my music, indeed no, but I'm giving it a saner
> attention than I did before, and I'm beginning to realize
> that there is something in life besides success.

The demonic drive for perfection that had possessed him since the
success of "Alexander's Ragtime Band" now seemed to relax its grip.

Death, however, struck almost as rapidly as love. On their honeymoon in Cuba, Dorothy contracted typhoid fever, became ill shortly
after they moved into their new apartment on New York's Upper
West Side, and died on July 17, barely five months after she and
Berlin had met. Berlin was inconsolable. He had always been an
intensely private man, opening himself to no one. As a performer on
stage or as a songwriter giving interviews to the press, he was jovial
and gregarious, but if a personal rather than professional chord were
touched, he instantly turned shy and awkward. He does not seem to
have known women before Dorothy, though critics characterized him
as a darling to female audiences, so what may have been his first genuine relationship ended suddenly and tragically. Years later, a florist
in Buffalo, where Dorothy was buried near her family's home, told
reporters that Berlin had quietly paid him to place a white rose on
her grave every other day. The order was carried out for thirteen
years until Berlin rescinded it after he remarried in 1926.

Berlin was seldom seen over the remainder of the summer, and
composed very few songs, none of them distinguished. Dorothy's
brother tried to lift the songwriter out of his depression by suggest-
ing that he turn his sorrow into song. "You're a man who writes

from your emotions," Goetz said, "Let your emotions work for you."
At first, Berlin demurred, partly out of his intense privacy, partly
because of the commercial nature of his craft. Goetz pointed out that
all great poets and composers had created art—often commercially
successful art—from their personal tragedies, but Berlin steadfastly
regarded the writing of popular songs as business, one that involved
gauging public taste, manipulating formulas, and hammering out a
salable technical fusion of words and music. Now, however, he was
being urged to follow Sir Philip Sidney's advice to all poets: "Look in
thy heart and write."

Near the end of the year, he studied an earlier song he had been
working on. It had a pedestrian lyric filled with standard Alley
clichés ("I love the flowers that bloom in the spring / I love the birds
in the treetops that sing"), but the melody was enriched with subtle
chromatic intervals and chords. Substituting a more straightforward lyric about loss he created a more moving song, even though
it was nowhere near as powerful as his great ballads of the 1920s
and 1930s. The chorus begins in the key of C with a simple melodic
pattern:

> I lost the sunshine and ros-es.

Between the two syllables of "ros-es," however, while the melody
drops only one interval, the harmony obtrudes with a wrenchingly
dissonant chord that mirrors the sudden, inexplicable loss. In the
next phrase,

> I lost the heavens of blue,

there is another chromatic intrusion at the word "of," both melodi-
cally and harmonically, that gives a more melancholy meaning to
the word "blue," a kind of musical and lyrical pun that he would use
again later in his classic "Blue Skies."

Such effects build throughout the song, turning the normally gay
waltz dark and haunting:

> I lost the gladness
> that turned into sadness,
> when I lost you.

As songwriter Alec Wilder observes of "When I Lost You," "none
of the hundred and thirty songs published up to this point in Berlin's
career revealed this aspect of his talent, the ability to write with
moving sentiment about personal trouble and pain."

What makes "When I Lost You" even more unique in Berlin's
early work is that he did not try to write another ballad for several
years. Instead, he returned to his ragtime style in numbers like
"When the Midnight Choo-Choo Leaves for Alabam'" and "At the
Devil's Ball." The comic novelty songs he wrote at this time, however, are almost grotesque reflections of his loss. "Don't Leave Your
Wife Alone" treats marriage flippantly as it laughs at men who lead a
"double life":

> One they lead in cabaret,
> the other with their wife.

"Snookey Ookums" satirizes the penchant many newlyweds have
for baby talk. It portrays a newly married couple who drive their
neighbors crazy with such babble as,

> She's his jelly elly roll,
> He's her sugey ugar bowl.

However such nonsensical creations mixed into the chemistry of
grief, it was still nearly a year before Berlin agreed to take his brother-in-law's suggestion that he sail to England. Arriving in June of
1913, Irving Berlin found that his fame in Europe was equal to that
in America. British newspapers celebrated him extravagantly:

> Go where you will, you cannot escape from the mazes of
> music he has spun. In every London restaurant, park
> and theatre you hear his strains; Paris dances to it;
> Berlin sips golden beer to his melodies; Vienna has for-
> saken the Waltz, Madrid flung away her castanets, and
> Venice has forgotten her barcarolles. Ragtime has swept
> like a whirlwind over the earth and set civilization hum-
> ming. Mr. Berlin started it.

Despite all the laudatory press, Berlin's greatest satisfaction came
when he disembarked and the taxicab driver, not recognizing his
famous passenger, idly whistled "Alexander's Ragtime Band" as he
drove Berlin to his hotel.

Even more eagerly than the American press, British newspapers
seized upon Berlin as a musical demon, a genie who cranked out hit
songs even though he could not read music. They marveled at his
mechanical piano (even though it had been invented by an English
firm a hundred years before). They touted him as an American wizard of the machine age who had no need for traditional methods of

composition. He simply played his melodies to a trained musician who then transcribed them into sheet music. When he worked through the night without an amanuensis present, he employed a Dictaphone "until the cylinder choked with syncopation." "I hum the songs," Berlin explained, "hum them while I'm shaving, or in my bath or out walking," and the reporters marveled even more that "this boy—he looks nineteen—lathering his face to an unconscious tune one morning, four years ago, hit on the jerky, spasmodic bars of 'Alexander's Ragtime Band.'" Inviting a group of reporters to suggest a title (they tried to stump him with "That Humming Rag"), he composed a song on the spot. As they described his pacing, finger-snapping method of composition, he concocted a melody and lyric in twenty-nine minutes (he explained that was fourteen minutes longer than it usually took but that he wanted to write an especially good song for them). In their stories, Berlin came off like Paul Bunyan or John Henry, a human songwriting machine, relentlessly cranking out songs—and hits—from eight o'clock at night until five in the morning.

What really moved British audiences was the spectacle of Berlin himself performing his songs on stage at the London Hippodrome in the revue *Hullo, Ragtime*. Ragtime songs in England had been interpreted as wild and raucous dance numbers, but Berlin's rendition stressed the underlying melancholy beneath the music. Even the testiest critics found he sang

> his ragtime songs with such diffidence, skill and charm.
> In his mouth they become something very different from
> the blatant bellowings we are used to. All their quaint-
> ness, their softness, their queer patheticalness come out.
> They sound, indeed, quite new, and innocently, almost
> childishly pleasing, like a negro's smile.

Clearly, Berlin's personal grief underscored the "sadness" he always insisted lay at the heart of the most sprightly ragtime numbers. "That night in London," according to biographer Michael Freedland, "did more for Irving Berlin than anything he had ever before experienced as a songwriter." When he performed "The International Rag," a song he composed especially for the occasion,

> the audience reaction made him feel he had earned his
> billing as "The King of Ragtime." His "subjects" begged
> for more, shouting out requests one after another . . .
> "When I Lost You" had sold a million copies. Yet none of
> the money that came flooding in from that tune was
> compensation for what he had really lost. But in the

Hippodrome Theatre they were shouting for Irving
Berlin himself. In those cheers he was, for the first time
able to bury some of his grief.

When Berlin returned to America, he was given a smaller but in
its way equally significant reception by his peers. The Friars Club, in
October of 1913, which had invited Berlin to join its ranks in 1911,
now paid him the compliment of making him the subject of one of its
celebrated "roasts." In a tradition still carried on today, the subject
of a Friars' roast sits at the head table while his most notable colleagues subject him to gentle—and sometimes not so gentle—
ridicule. The prime roaster of the evening was George M. Cohan,
who had first nominated Berlin for membership in the show business fraternity. Like Stephen Foster, Cohan was Berlin's idol, and
his picture too hung in the young songwriter's office. Almost single-
handedly, George M. Cohan had tried to wrest the American musical
from the clutches of European operetta. Beginning in 1904, with
Little Johnny Jones, he wrote shows that employed ragtime rhythms,
colloquial speech, and contemporary American settings. Cohan's
roots were in the Irish-American tradition of vaudeville entertainers
like Harrigan and Hart, and his songs such as "Give My Regards to
Broadway" and "You're a Grand Old Flag" had a colloquial pugnacity that was a refreshing antidote to the Viennese schmaltz of Franz
Lehar and Victor Herbert.

For all Cohan's talent and flamboyance, however, the American
stage continued to be dominated by such lavish operettas as *The
Merry Widow* and *Naughty Marietta*, while the popular song industry
aimed its wares at vaudeville and musical revues. It may have been a
sign of Cohan's frustration over the diminishing hold Irish-
Americans had on Broadway that led him to refer to the guest of
honor as a "Jew boy." While ethnic slurs were much more common
in public then, Cohan's barb may reflect his resentment that Tin Pan
Alley was dominated by Jewish immigrants while the Broadway
stage continued to be the purview of European songwriters and their
American imitators. Cohan did praise "When I Lost You" as "the
prettiest song I ever heard in my life" and extended his young rival a
series of compliments:

> Irvy writes a great song. He writes a song with a good
> lyric, a lyric that rhymes, good music, music you don't
> have to dress up to listen to, but it is good music. He is a
> wonderful little fellow, wonderful in lots of ways. He has
> become famous and wealthy, without wearing a lot of
> jewelry and falling for funny clothes. He is uptown, but
> he is there with the old downtown hardshell.

At the conclusion of a Friars' roast, the victim is expected to rise and return the barbs of his colleagues, but Berlin's terror of speaking in public precluded such badinage. Instead, he composed a song in which he invoked the names of his fellow friars and expressed his appreciation to them, though he admitted "just why you honor me in vain I try to figure out" and "for days and days I worried what to say." Even with that self-armor, Berlin's shyness was clearly noticeable to the press, who reported that in performing "before the 'wisest' crowd in New York," he "was wobbly on his feet up to the moment he finished it."

Even as he basked in the encomiums of his peers, Berlin's sights were squarely fixed on the prospect of completing what his friendly rival George M. Cohan had begun: the Americanization of the Broadway musical. While acknowledging that Cohan was "his inspiration, the model, the idol" of his early career, Berlin added, "We all start as imitators of somebody," but "if you continue to imitate, you are not a songwriter. Once you express your own talent, it's a question of how good you are." The great Broadway producer Charles Dillingham had approached Berlin to write songs for his new musical comedy, *Watch Your Step*. Although Berlin had written songs that were "interpolated" into Broadway shows (single numbers added to the show's score after it had opened, usually to provide a star with fresh material), this was his first opportunity to write his own entire score. Berlin also recognized that Dillingham's invitation represented "the first time Tin Pan Alley got into the legitimate theater." What Berlin meant by that claim was that Broadway scores were usually composed by trained musicians, such as Victor Herbert, rather than the tunesmiths who cranked out individual songs for sheet-music sales. For a producer like Dillingham to turn to a pop songwriter—and an untrained one at that—and request an entire score was an unusual gesture, signaling Dillingham's determination to infuse modern American musical styles into the stuffy world of operetta.

Berlin would be working with librettist Harry B. Smith, a veteran who had written more than 300 "books" for Broadway musicals, many of which were simply updated versions of older plays. For *Watch Your Step*, Smith recycled an old French play, *Round the Clock*, about heirs to a fortune who have to compete for the $2 million legacy by adhering to the stipulation that they not fall in love. Given that story line, Berlin had to do something he had never had to do on Tin Pan Alley—integrate his songs into dramatic situations and tailor them to specific characters. Although far from the kind of thoroughgoing integration of song and story that Broadway would see in the 1940s, Berlin's original songs for *Watch Your Step* grew out of Smith's book in a surprisingly coherent fashion.

At first, Berlin confessed, he knew Smith "was a great versifier and I was a little insecure about my lyrics. So I said to him, 'If you want me to redo my lyrics, go ahead.' And he said, 'Irving don't ever let anyone touch your lyrics.'"

Berlin's ability to work songs into the libretto impressed the veteran Smith, as did the songwriter's skill with "inventing unexpected rhymes":

> Most bards would think it hopeless to attempt to find a rhyme for "Wednesday"; but Mr. Berlin found one. In one of the songs in this piece a matinee idol describes his persecution by women and alludes to the elderly worshippers who attend the afternoon performances:
>
> > The matinee I play
> > on Wednesday,
> > Is what I've nick-named
> > "My Old Hens' Day."

Along with the deft rhyme, Berlin's entire song went hand-in-hand with character and situation: the matinee idol, hired to seduce the innocent heroine, first complains that "They Always Follow Me Around," but when the heroine spurns his overtures, he is smitten by his first rejection.

Much of the integration between Berlin's songs and Smith's book went by the boards, however, when Dillingham chose to make Vernon and Irene Castle the stars of *Watch Your Step*. The Castles had done for the "dance craze" what "Alexander's Ragtime Band" had done for ragtime: they had toned down the sensual and frenetic animal dances into refined fun that all could enjoy. Starting out by introducing such American dances as the turkey trot and the grizzly bear in Parisian cabarets, the Castles had an informal, intimate style that was perfectly suited to the atmosphere of the cabaret. They began their act by strolling to the dance floor from one of the tables, as if they were merely two customers getting up to dance. Their sensational success in Paris brought invitations from New York, where they danced in Broadway shows, vaudeville, and revues. After their theatrical performances, they went to "roof-top," late-night cabarets, where they danced as part of the floor show. Soon they were in movies and opened their own cabarets—three of them—plus a studio where they provided dance instruction to the upper crust of society. Their ubiquity was satirized by a newspaper versifier:

> Castles in the playhouse, Castles on the roof,
> Castles in the movies, Ditto *op'ra bouffe*,

Irene and Vernon Castle, perhaps a publicity photo from the 1914 production of
Watch Your Step.

> Castles on the platform, Castles on the rug,
> Learn the Castle fox-trot, Do the Castle Hug,
> Castles in the cellar, Castles on the floor,
> "Castles," croaked the raven, "Castles evermore!"

As elegant and urbane as Fred Astaire and Ginger Rogers would be, the Castles drained the sensuality and tempestuousness out of the ragtime dances. Tutored by James Reese Europe, their black musical conductor, the Castles took black dances, refined them, and taught them to whites. With utter candor, Irene Castle explained the process:

> We get our new dances from the Barbary Coast. Of course, they reach New York in a very primitive condition, and have to be considerably toned down before they can be used in the drawing-room. There is one just arrived now—it is still very crude—and it is called "Shaking the Shimmy." It's a nigger dance, of course, and it appears to be a slow walk with a frequent twitching of the shoulders. The teachers may try and make something of it.

As a contemporary observed, the Castles "brought to the awkward and vulgar-looking dance forms of the current mode a combination of easy gayety and almost patrician fastidiousness. They sublimated the dance craze."

In uniting the Castles with Irving Berlin, Charles Dillingham had shrewdly cashed in on the very people who had brought ragtime and dancing into respectability. Placing them in the cast, however, presented problems with the script and songs, because while Vernon could sing, Irene Castle could not. Vernon therefore had to play opposite another leading lady but also wanted new songs like "I'm a Dancing Teacher Now," that would help plug the Castles' business enterprises. Irene, on the other hand, had to be given special numbers like "Show Us How to Do the Fox Trot," which were completely extraneous to the plot. Integration between song and story unraveled even more during the "doctoring" of the show. When the comedian W. C. Fields garnered more applause than the Castles from a tryout audience in Syracuse, Dillingham fired him rather than upstage his highly paid stars, and Smith had to write entirely new material for the new comic. Act One was to have ended with the floor of a ragtime dance school crashing down on a classical academy beneath it, but the set designer found it impossible to stage, and a new ending had to be created.

For some reason, perhaps that all-important requirement of fast-pacing, one of Berlin's best songs had to be cut even though it was intricately tied to the story. When the two young heirs dance, they realize they are falling in love and each tries to save the other's inheritance by insisting "I Hate You." Smith's script called for a duet that would be a "burlesque of the conventional love song in which the two declare their undying hate. 'I hate the ground you walk on just because you are you,' etc. The music pretty, the words comedy." Berlin took this suggestion and created a romantic "quarrel" song:

> "I hate the very ground you walk upon."
> "I hate your great big eyes of blue."
> "I hate the very phone you talk upon."
> "I don't give a rap for you."
> "I hope you never do."

Although the lyric is not especially witty, it looks forward to such brilliant duets as "Anything You Can Do" from *Annie Get Your Gun*. In 1940, he would recast "I Hate You" as "Outside of that I Love You" for *Louisiana Purchase*.

After more than the usual doctoring to pull a show into place, *Watch Your Step* opened on December 8, 1914, to critical and popular success. The lion's share of the credit went to Berlin's score, which wove an array of very different songs into a fluid skein of musical theater. In "Syncopated Walk" and "Settle Down in a One-Horse Town," he shifted between major and minor keys, sometimes in the space of a few bars. Other numbers were unlike anything he had ever written before. In "Ragtime Opera Medley," Berlin created a musical collage of several operas—*Faust, Carmen, La Bohème, Aida, Madame Butterfly, Pagliacci*—in a scene where the ghost of Verdi importunes the chorus at the Metropolitan, "Please don't rag my melody—let my *Rigoletto* be." The chorus, however, chants back. "We want you syncopated—even though we know you hate it."

Casting the opposition between modern and traditional musical styles in the form of a duet between Verdi and the chorus inspired Berlin to write "Play a Simple Melody," the first of his patented "counterpoint songs," where two different melodies and two different sets of lyrics are performed simultaneously. While it doesn't emerge from the dramatic context, the song creates its own little drama. One character leaves a theater singing one of the ragtime songs from the show he's just seen:

> Musical demon, set your honey a-dreamin',
> Won't you play me some rag?

> Just change that classical nag
> to some sweet beautiful drag.

Another character complains, "Oh, this new music gives me a pain. Why don't they sing some of the old stuff from Harrigan and Hart days? That was music!" Then a third character chimes in, "I know the kind you mean" and sings:

> Won't you play some simple melody?
> Like my mother sang to me.
> One with good old-fashioned harmony.

Then all characters sing in unison as the audience realizes that the melodies and lyrics of the two songs fit together perfectly. While the musical counterpoint is a far cry from that of Bach or Beethoven, it did require "filling in" the long notes of one melody with the quicker, rhythmic notes of the second melody. Lyrically, however, the song is as intricate as Gilbert and Sullivan, who sometimes crafted one romantic ballad for their leads to be sung against the snappy patter of the chorus. Berlin was cavalier about bringing off such a tour de force, saying "the musical part didn't give me any trouble" but "the difficulty was getting two lyrics so that they didn't bump into each other."

That musical and lyrical mastery was apparent to Broadway's harshest newspaper critics, some of whom merely mentioned that Vernon and Irene Castle were part of the show, on the opening night of *Watch Your Step*:

> Irving Berlin stands out like the Times building does in the Square. That youthful marvel of syncopated melody is proving things in "Watch Your Step," firstly that he is not alone a rag composer, and that he is one of the greatest lyric writers America has ever produced.

As music critic Ian Whitcomb observes:

> Berlin understood that syncopation is most effective when it is not used as a device or trick but when it springs naturally from conversation and, more especially, from the push and pull, parry and thrust, punch and duck, chatter battle of New York Swinglish-English.

Berlin always maintained that the opening night of *Watch Your Step* had been the greatest thrill of his life, because it was the first time he had heard his music performed by a full orchestra. When he imagined his earlier songs being performed by an orchestra, he thought only in terms of a small vaudeville orchestra termed a "piano and ten." For *Watch Your Step* his songs were orchestrated by a competent Broadway musician named Frank Sadler, who wrote out parts for instruments in a twenty-piece band. Those instruments, moreover, were as American as the music they played. Gone were the violins of the typical operetta orchestra; instead there were saxophones, brass, and banjos. Together, all of these elements made *Watch Your Step* a genuinely American musical production, one that challenged European imports even more powerfully than George M. Cohan's shows. The fact that the show premiered in the first Broadway season after the outbreak of World War I fueled its success, because now American audiences wanted to embrace native, rather than Germanic and Viennese, fare. "While the war was going on, operetta fell into disfavor with the majority of producing managers," noted librettist Harry B. Smith. "The Teutonic operetta crop failed."

Berlin spent the most memorable evening of his life in the audience with his mother and sisters. He had long before restored relations with his family, buying his mother her coveted rocking chair with some of his first earnings, then moving her out of the Lower East Side to her own apartment in the Bronx after his first big hit, "My Wife's Gone to the Country." Neither she nor her children, as one newspaper story put it in 1911, "has ever wanted for the good things of life since he began to dot notes on ruled paper." Although with her Yiddish she could follow little of the lyrics and stage patter of the show, Lena Baline certainly must have glowed when she saw her son, in response to cries of "Composer! Composer!" at the end of the performance, take to the stage, bow, and offer a few nervous words of thanks. After the performance, he dutifully escorted her and his sisters home, then retired to his apartment with his accompanist Cliff Hess and a few journalist friends to await what turned out to be smashing reviews.

While they waited, Berlin played over some of the songs from the show and showed his friends some of the china he had begun to collect. While reporters marveled that, after such a "successful first night," the "one most responsible for it could not be found after the performance at the most famous Broadway restaurant, the center of a large and admiring crowd," Irving Berlin, who had seen his share of glory in his climb up from the Bowery and Chinatown, was interested in something more lasting. Playing his score as he appreciated works of art may have strengthened his belief that he had produced, not ephemeral "hit" songs, but an artistic whole as intricately crafted as the work of ancient artisans.

It was with enormous pride that Berlin presented Charles Dillingham with a bound copy of the score, inscribed by the author, as if it were his first published book:

> To Charles Dillingham,
> First copy of my first score to the first manager who took
> a chance and made it possible.

Chapter 4

A PRETTY GIRL IS LIKE A MELODY

The reason our American composers have done nothing highly significant is because they won't write American music. They're as ashamed of it as if it were a country relative. So they write imitation European music which doesn't mean anything. Ignorant as I am, from their standpoints, I am doing something they all refuse to do: I'm writing American music.

With *Watch Your Step*, Irving Berlin moved from being a songwriter—who concentrated on individual songs that he hoped would become hits—to become a composer of musical scores for shows that strove for critical as well as commercial success. In short, he stepped up from Tin Pan Alley to Broadway. To underscore the distinction between those two worlds, he opened a separate office at 1571 Broadway, in the heart of the theatrical district, to handle his musical scores, while the Waterson, Berlin & Snyder office down at 38th and Broadway continued to publish his individual songs. The twenty-two songs he had worked on for *Watch Your Step* equaled half of his normal annual output of published songs, yet only one of these, "Play a Simple Melody," went on to sell significant numbers of sheet music and records. If he were to balance the elegance and sophistication of musical theater with the hard-nosed commercialism of the music publishing business, Berlin would have to achieve the seemingly impossible feat of writing songs that were tailored to shows but could also go on to become independent hits.

While a Broadway composer might not earn the royalties of a Tin Pan Alley songwriter, success in the musical theater brought other rewards, such as newspaper reports that George Bernard Shaw was interested in writing lyrics for a Berlin musical, and that Giacomo Puccini wanted to collaborate on an opera. Such accolades fueled Berlin's already boundless ambition, and he speculated to reporters that he would one day compose a "grand opera—not a musical comedy but a real opera on a tragic theme":

> You see, there's a real American opera coming along, and I want to write it. In syncopation, you understand. I'm going to prove that you can syncopate for people's hearts as well as for their toes. It's going to be a simple American story—men and women and love and adventure. And a good red-blooded fight. Whoever writes the book, I shall write my own lyrics, as I always do. And I don't want the critics to find my grammar crooked, my vocabulary of the twenty-word kind, and my sentences stilted and funny. When I begin to write seriously, I want no silly lyrics.

Such prospects did not seem impossible in 1914 when "classical" and "popular" culture were not as sharply divided as they are today, and opera had only recently become an exclusive entertainment for the elite. Berlin himself was a great lover of opera and frequently attended the Metropolitan's productions. He had shown, moreover, in the "Ragtime Opera Melody" from *Watch Your Step*, as well as other numbers, such as "Opera Burlesque" and "That Opera Rag," that he could parody such composers as Donizetti with dexterity. While Irving Berlin never realized his operatic ambitions, he did, by remaining within the confines of the thirty-two bar song format, manage to bring syncopation to the American ballad, even, as he would prove in the 1920s, to the waltz. Instead, Berlin's prediction would be fulfilled by a younger composer, George Gershwin, who would first try his hand at a one-act opera, *Blue Monday, Opera A la Afro-American*, in the Broadway revue, *George White's Scandals of 1922*. Then, in 1935, he would fully realize that ambition with *Porgy and Bess*. When not even Berlin himself could fulfill all of the works he envisioned, a younger generation of composers and lyricists were emerging who would make the next twenty-five years the richest era in American popular music.

In what little life he had outside of his career, Berlin turned more of his attention to collecting works of art, and to purchasing rare volumes of Shakespeare and other classic writers:

> I never had a chance for much schooling so I couldn't
> read the good books I wished to because I had to look up
> too many of the big words. I'm taking time now to look
> those words up. I'm trying to get at least a bowing
> acquaintance with the world's best literature.

Even as Berlin confessed to these cultural aspirations, his Lower
East Side defensiveness came out as he added, "I'm a little bit commercial in so doing. . . . I want to enlarge my vocabulary, with a definite purpose of bigger, better writing."

Berlin's turn toward the musical theater may also reflect his
recognition that music publishing was an increasingly perilous business. Tin Pan Alley was suffering from its own success, as Berlin
himself described how intricate and extensive the music publishing
network had become:

> The publisher sells his songs to the jobber or "the
> trade" for six and a half cents a copy. He pays a cent a
> copy royalty to the men who have written the song.
> That leaves him with a gross of five and a half cents a
> copy on the song. Out of this he must care for a tremen-
> dous overhead expense: the printing costs him a cent a
> copy; he has advertising he must keep up; he has
> branches and branches—staffs in half a dozen cities; he
> maintains a staff of eight or nine piano players in his
> home office, and staffs of two or three in branch offices;
> he keeps a force of "pluggers" or "song boosters"—who
> go over the cities singing his songs in motion-picture
> theaters and cafes—at work; he employs a force of "out-
> side men" whose duty it is to get his songs sung by the
> stage. . . . This cutthroat competition, which has recent-
> ly resulted in the failure of a number of publishing
> firms, operates in spite of the fact that it has become
> more and more difficult to make money out of the song-
> publishing business.

From the early days of Tin Pan Alley, when publishers could afford
to take risks on unknown songwriters with numbers like "Marie
from Sunny Italy," Berlin lamented that now "a publisher loses
money on a song unless he sells more than three hundred thousand
copies" and "must sell between five hundred thousand and six hundred thousand to make a fair profit." Songs for the musical theater
could be plugged through Tin Pan Alley's vast network, but touring
companies of a show could also carry its songs to theaters around

the country, so that a theater song made money through ticket sales as well as sheet-music and record sales.

At this time, however, an organization was born that would ultimately eclipse both Broadway and Tin Pan Alley as a source of revenue for songwriters, and save many from the pauper's death of Stephen Foster. In October 1913, Victor Herbert and eight other men met to discuss the organization at Luchow's restaurant on Union Square, ironically one of the many establishments that used Tin Pan Alley songs to entertain patrons—without paying compensation to the songwriters or publishers. The nine men agreed to lay plans for an organization modeled after the French group, SACÉM (Société des Auteurs, Compositeurs et Éditeurs de Musique), which, since 1871, had been collecting fees for public performance of songs by European composers, lyricists, and publishers. On February 13, 1914, they met again, with more than 100 other songwriters to form ASCAP, an acronym for "American Society of Composers, Authors (by which was meant "lyricists"), and Publishers." What ASCAP proposed to do was to sell licenses to restaurants and other establishments that would authorize them to perform the songs written by ASCAP members. ASCAP would then distribute the money it received for such licenses back to its members.

Initially, the owners of cabarets scoffed at ASCAP when the organization asked them to purchase licenses to perform songs that they had already been using for free. They even told the songwriters they should be grateful that cabarets were "plugging" their songs. ASCAP won a major victory the following year when Victor Herbert and his publisher, G. Schirmer Music, sued Shanley's restaurant for performing Herbert's song "Sweethearts" without authorization. Lawyers for Shanley's argued that it was a restaurant, not a theater, and that songs were performed only incidentally to the serving of food. In a decision that came from the United States Supreme Court, Justice Oliver Wendell Holmes ruled that the restaurant was performing the songs in order to attract customers. "If music did not pay," he wrote, "it would be given up." Even though tickets were not sold at the door of the restaurant, Holmes still regarded the unlicensed use of such songs as an infringement of copyright. With that ruling, any use of ASCAP songs, which soon would include the lucrative broadcast of music over a new invention called radio, earned profits for songwriters like Berlin that would supplement and ultimately outweigh the royalties that came from the sale of sheet music and records.

Although ASCAP could not pay its first dividends until 1921, spreading $24,000 in royalty fees among its members, by 1950 it was doling out between $15–16 million a year to songwriters who still only had to pay $10 a year in membership fees. Irving Berlin was not one of the founding fathers of ASCAP, but he soon became one of its most ardent supporters. He would sometimes stop a fellow songwriter on the street, ask to borrow $10, then shake his friend's hand and say, "Congratulations, you're now a member of ASCAP." Thanks to ASCAP and his ownership of his own songs, Irving Berlin could live in wealthy comfort long after his songwriting career was over.

In the years when ASCAP was establishing itself, a new development in American musical theater began to fill the vacuum left by the disenchantment the public felt toward Viennese operetta after the outbreak of World War I. Although Irving Berlin had established himself on Broadway, he was not in the forefront of the emergence of modern musical comedy, one of the few times in his career he turned out to be at the margins rather than the center of a major development in American popular music. If *Watch Your Step* fell at all short of what Berlin had hoped for it was in its lack of full integration between song and story. While he and Harry Smith had begun working with integration in mind, the addition of the Castles to the show, other cast and script changes, and the inevitable doctoring that cut and pasted the show together in rehearsals and out-of-town tryouts diminished the efforts of songwriter and librettist to have songs emerge logically from dialogue and action.

At that very same time, however, integration of story and song was being achieved by three other men—Jerome Kern, Guy Bolton, and P. G. (Pelham Grenville) Wodehouse—in an historic series of musicals at the tiny Princess Theatre, a small, intimate theater, where the emphasis was upon wit and sophistication rather than spectacular sets, costumes, and production numbers. While the Princess shows, such as *Oh, Boy!* and *Oh, Lady! Lady!* ran only from 1916 to 1918, they were crucial to the emergence of the modern American musical. The classically trained Kern could handle Tin Pan Alley formulas with elegant sophistication, Bolton's dialogue was clever and "smart," and Wodehouse's lyrics sparkled with the wit of Gilbert. It was his love of Gilbert and Sullivan, in fact, that initially made Wodehouse, an Englishman, wary of joining Kern and Bolton on a musical. Wodehouse knew that Gilbert's lyrics were always written first, and he feared that the American system of giving music precedence would make it impossible for him to ply his literate wit. Once he tried setting words to Kern's music, however, he found that, far from restricting him, taking his cue from the music actually enabled him to create effects he could not have achieved had he written words first. Citing one instance of how Kern's "twiddly little notes" inspired him to come up with a subtle rhyme in the phrase, "If every day you *bring* her diamonds and pearls on a *string*," Wodehouse said, "I couldn't have thought of that, if I had done the lyric first, in a million years. Why, dash it, it doesn't scan."

It was that regular, rhythmic "scansion" that marked Gilbert's lyrics as fundamentally poetic, thumping along in regular meters:

> When I *merely* from him *parted*,
>   We were *nearly* broken-*hearted*,
> When in *sequel* reu*nited*,
>   We were *equa*lly de*lighted*.

By letting music come first, Wodehouse wrote a more rhythmical-ly irregular—and therefore colloquial—line that sounded more like ordinary conversation than "poetry." He still could rhyme as cleverly as Gilbert but, where Gilbert's rhymes were blatant, Wodehouse's were so subtle one could barely detect them:

> What bad *luck! It's*
> coming down in *buckets*.

When Kern gave him a jazzy melody for "Cleopatterer," Wodehouse rhymed with slangy sophistication, as he praised the queen's "slim and svelte" figure that "gave those poor Egyptian ginks something else to watch besides the Sphinx." When Kern's music presented him with problems, such as an unexpected triplet (which Irving Berlin always said was the trickiest musical figure to set to words), Wodehouse used the three notes for a casual interjection that nicely deflated sentimen-tality: " I love him because he's—*I don't know*—because he's just my Bill." Ironically, it took the Englishman Wodehouse to show young theater lyricists that by following the music their words could sound less "poetic" and more colloquially "American."

It was the triumvirate of Bolton, Wodehouse, and Kern—rather than Irving Berlin—who laid the groundwork for a genuinely American musical comedy. While earlier attempts at homegrown musicals were little more coherent than revues, simply tossing in songs that had little relation to the book, the Princess shows created songs that emerged from dramatic situations, moved the plot for-ward, and defined character. Wodehouse also followed Gilbert in writing romantic songs that sidestepped sentimentality or even open-ly spoofed the clichés of romance. Gilbert would have his common-place lover lament his hopeless attraction to an aristocratic maiden with an outrageous pun: "I love a lass, alas, above my station." Similarly, Wodehouse had a jaded flapper confess that "at the age of five," she let herself be kissed at parties "by small boys excited by tea." Now that she has found true love, however, she declares to him:

> Had I known that you existed,
> I'd have scratched them and resisted.

Such spoofing of romance had always been the staple of light verse writers, but Gilbert carried it over into song. Wodehouse followed his example and showed how love could be treated with irony, understatement, and even sarcasm.

Young writers such as Ira Gershwin, Lorenz Hart, Cole Porter, and E. Y. "Yip" Harburg, who loved light verse and Gilbert and Sullivan, were completely entranced by Wodehouse's lyrics. They would go on to craft such witty declarations of love as "I've Got You Under My Skin," such tongue-in-cheek praise for a beloved as, "Your looks are laughable—unphotographable," and such literate laments as, "With love to lead the way I found more clouds of gray than any Russian play could guarantee." Teaming with composers like Richard Rodgers and George Gershwin, who were equally inspired by Jerome Kern's sophisticated transformation of Tin Pan Alley song formulas, these wunderkinder carried on the tradition of the Princess shows. By the mid-1920s they were creating elegant yet colloquial songs that were at once rooted in the plot and character of a Broadway musical yet achieved independent popularity on Tin Pan Alley.

Although Irving Berlin had been at the center of the development of American popular music up until this point, he did not follow the lead of the Princess shows, and for more than thirty years he would not be part of the development of the Broadway musical. Not until 1946 would he write a truly great integrated musical, *Annie Get Your Gun*, with songs such as "Doin' What Comes Natur'lly," "They Say It's Wonderful," and "Anything You Can Do" that were carefully integrated into the plot. Until that spectacular achievement, Berlin's route on Broadway took a very different course. His historical roots in the musical theater went back not to operetta but to the looser, more American forms such as the minstrel show, vaudeville, and the revue. *Watch Your Step* had been regarded by critics more as a "revue" than a musical comedy, and Berlin's next show, *Stop! Look! Listen!* had even less integration between song and story. Dillingham proposed it as a sequel to *Watch Your Step*, with Harry Smith again providing a book. He had wanted the Castles again, but their seemingly boundless success had been halted when Vernon Castle, sympathetic to his native England, had joined the Royal Air Force soon after the outbreak of World War I (he would later be killed in an airplane crash). Instead, Dillingham proposed building the show around the French sensation, Gaby Deslys. More noted for her lavish wardrobe than her singing abilities, Deslys, like Irene Castle, would not be able to step into an existing role in the script but would instead need special material written for her. Time, too, worked against Berlin's ability to wed his songs to Smith's story; where he had nearly half a year to work on songs for *Watch Your Step*, he would have less than three months to write the score for *Stop! Look! Listen!*

Many of Berlin's twenty-five songs for the show sounded as if they were retooled from the ragtime score of *Watch Your Step* (including "A Pair of Ordinary Coons," a throwback to the "coon" songs of the1890s, where two American blacks exult in their ability to "pass" as Hawaiians in Honolulu). One of the best songs was the kind of rhythmic syncopated number he had been writing for more than a decade. It was worked into the script on the flimsiest of grounds: a character insists upon taking several pianos on an ocean voyage, because, as he explains, "I Love a Piano":

> I love a piano, I love a piano.
> I love to hear somebody play
> upon a piano, a grand piano,
> it simply carries me away.

With his patented ability to "rag" words against music, Berlin crushed the three syllables of "pi-a-no" to fit two notes, so that it came out, slangily, as "I love a *pian-o*" (though in recordings of the song ever since, singers have missed the point, singing "on a pi-a-no" instead of "upon a pian-o").

In addition to his clever manipulations of words against music, one would almost think that—in Berlin's efforts to acquire the culture he had missed when he dropped out of school—he had been reading some of the new "Imagist" poetry that had begun to appear in the "little magazines" of the period, for he wove an artfully extended metaphor through the chorus that implicitly compares the piano to a woman. It is more likely, however, that he simply elevated the kind of risqué parodies he used to perform as a singing waiter to hint that the various parts of the instrument are transformed into erogenous zones by the performer's passion:

> I love to run my fingers o'er the keys—the ivories
> and with the pedal—I love to meddle. . . .

The subtle internal rhymes, such as *"o'er the keys—the iv-or-ies"* drive the lyric forward with the music to register the performer's exuberance. The metaphoric connection between piano and woman transforms the cliché "a fine way to treat a lady" into "I know a fine way to treat a Steinway." Berlin also reprises his characteristic balancing act between modern and traditional music by counterpointing the genteel "high-toned" piano/lady against the contemporary "baby" grand.

The climax of the song consists of an extended ejaculation of the word piano, lovingly spelled out letter by letter:

> Give me a P-I-A-N-O, oh, oh . . .

"I Love a Piano" was staged with six pianos on a set that resembled an enormous keyboard. What the song lacked in dramatic integration, it made up for in sheer spectacle.

Even as he continued to churn out ragtime songs, Berlin foresaw that the romantic ballad was making a comeback. The success of Kern's "They Didn't Believe Me" in 1914 signaled the return of the kind of simple, straightforward song such as Berlin himself had tried the year before with "When I Lost You." Other songwriters may have sensed the same development but Berlin's uncanny sensibilities enabled him to grasp the particular character the new ballad should have. His association with the Castles had given him a close perspective on how Irene was redefining the nature of the American woman. "Reversing the nineteenth century's view of women as frail and motherly," Lewis Erenberg explains, "Irene symbolized the active, free, and youthful women of the twentieth century." She spoke out against cumbersome corsets and gowns and wore fashions that accented her slim figure in free falling, even slit, skirts. Promoting dance and exercise, Irene urged women to shed pounds and maintain their appeal to men even when they were matrons. When she had to have her hair cut for surgery, she started a rage for bobbed hair that was called the "Castle clip." The image she projected was that of the modern, American "girl," rather than the traditional mature woman. Boyish in face and figure, she was the eternally appealing sprite—sexually attractive yet always innocently youthful.

Irene Castle frequently projected that new image of woman from the covers of magazines like *Vogue*, which, in turn, promulgated the image to its readers with articles about dieting, exercise, sports, and new fashions. It was Irving Berlin who crystallized this transformation of the American woman in a song, "The Girl on the Magazine Cover." It emerged from *Stop! Look! Listen!* as illogically as "I Love a Piano," with a character purchasing a magazine from a newsstand and being smitten by the clerk. Against a huge backdrop of *Vogue*, the girls on the cover literally came to life and stepped across the stage as the singer extolled the new ideal of American beauty:

> She's fairer than all the queens
> And loving her simply means
> That I'm kept busy buying magazines.

Berlin lavished a great deal of inventiveness on the song. While it had the now-standard thirty-two bar chorus, he did not rely upon one of the usual patterns such as AABA or ABAB, where the same eight-bar melodies are repeated as many as three times. Instead he created an ABCD pattern, where each of the four eight-bar sections introduces a new melodic phrase, making the song as constantly fascinating as the American girl it celebrates. The song and the spectacle rendered the image of the new American girl with such force that the hardened newspaper magnate William Randolph Hearst was so charmed by the girls on stage he returned for performance after performance. After working up the courage to approach one of these ethereal creatures, Marion Davies, he succeeded in making her his mistress, thus fulfilling the chorus-girl-as-Cinderella plot of Harry Smith's book.

While *Stop! Look! Listen!* started off well, Berlin soon got a lesson in how a Broadway star can make or break a show. Gaby Deslys's name attracted audiences, but her limitations as a singer necessitated restricting her to a single number, "Everything in America Is Ragtime," where she could play herself as the Parisian femme fatale caught up in the dance craze. Deslys did not take kindly to the cuts, however, and began turning in lackluster performances, dragging the show down with her, until Dillingham had no choice but to close *Stop! Look! Listen!* only weeks after it opened on Broadway. While Berlin's score went down with the show, "I Love a Piano" and "The Girl on the Magazine Cover" managed to establish themselves as independent songs. Thus his new music publishing company, Irving Berlin, Inc., helped salvage what for a purely theatrical songwriter would have been a total loss.

Turning his songwriting sights on the new American girl inevitably brought Irving Berlin into the orbit of the "great" Florenz Ziegfeld, who had been "Glorifying the American Girl" in annual editions of his *Follies* since 1907. Conceived as an American version of the Folies Bergère, the *Ziegfeld Follies* were notorious for the sumptuous sets and costumes by Joseph Urban, and the scantily— but elegantly—clad chorus girls, sometimes as many as fifty on stage at once. Ziegfeld was also noted for running up expenses, employing only the best names in show business, and throwing songs and acts in and out of his revue right up until opening night. The loose structure of a Ziegfeld production was heightened by the fact that the impresario never relied upon a single composer for all of the songs in a show. Berlin had written individual songs for Ziegfeld, such as the spoof "Woodman, Woodman, Spare That Tree," which black vaudevillian Bert Williams delivered in the 1911 edition of the *Follies*, but now Ziegfeld called upon the songwriter for his most ambitious project to date.

With his insatiable love of spectacle, Ziegfeld had purchased the enormous Century Theatre and planned to stage his most extravagant revue ever to celebrate *The Century Girl*—Ziegfeld's own interpretation of the newly emerging image of American womanhood—as the 1916 edition of his *Follies*. Combining forces with producer Charles Dillingham, Ziegfeld commissioned two equally big names to provide songs: Irving Berlin and Victor Herbert. Even though they represented two utterly different types of musical theater, Herbert and Berlin got along together personally. Berlin even asked the older, trained composer of operetta if he thought the "Ragtime King" should undertake the serious study of music. "Irving," Herbert advised, "You have nothing to worry about. You have a natural talent for putting words and music together—mind you, a little science wouldn't hurt." Spurred by Herbert's suggestion, Berlin said, "I tried to learn how to read and write music," only to find "I was not a student. Besides, in the time I spent taking lessons I could have written a few songs"; "I studied and practiced for two days and then gave it up."

Both men, however, found their songs eclipsed by Ziegfeld's dazzling celebration of the American girl:

> it was apparent as soon as the curtains parted that the show would succeed on the strength of its costumes and sets rather than its score, for this was the revue that introduced in its first scene the theatrical image for which Ziegfeld is best remembered: a celestial "staircase" devised to display the girls vertically as well as horizontally. Conceived by the Viennese designer Joseph Urban, the staircase extended from a trapdoor on the stage floor, through which emerged representations of women of all ages, who then began to ascend past pink and purple clouds.

In time, Berlin would devise a song that could match such opulence.

First, however, his meteoric career was put on hold by World War I. Although war had broken out in Europe in the summer of 1914, America had managed to stay out of the fray until the spring of 1917. Tin Pan Alley tried to straddle the fence between pacifists and isolationists on the one hand and proponents of making the world safe for democracy. Al Piantadosi, the piano player from Callahan's whose "My Mariucci Take a Steamboat" back in 1907 had first goaded young Izzy Baline into songwriting, gave voice to the former sentiment with "I Didn't Raise My Boy to Be a Soldier," but it was immediately answered by another song, "I Didn't Raise My Boy to be a Coward." Berlin's initial contribution had been "Stay Down Here Where You Belong," a 1914 number that had even the devil counseling against war, but when his friend George M. Cohan galvanized patriotic fervor with "Over There," Berlin followed suit with a song that helped the recruitment effort, "For Your Country and My Country." Although he did not go so far as to enlist himself, Berlin did make America his official country by becoming a naturalized United States citizen on February 6, 1918.

In taking that step, Berlin was again following a much larger historical pattern that revealed itself in the popular music of the time. As one song put it, "We're All Americans Now." What had once been a staple of Tin Pan Alley production—songs that poked fun at the ethnic stereotypes of recent immigrants—quickly disappeared under the pressure to put "America first." This pressure was exacerbated by the Bolshevik Revolution in Berlin's homeland, which toppled the czar and created what became known as the "Big Red Scare" in America. Suspicious of immigrants from eastern Europe, Congress passed a literacy test in 1917 and then the Immigration Act of 1921, which virtually cut off immigration from that part of Europe. In between those years, socialists and anarchists sympathetic to the Bolshevik cause set off bombs near the homes of Attorney General Mitchell Palmer in Washington and financier J. Pierpont Morgan in New York. On New Year's Day of 1920, the attorney general authorized raids in cities across the country that rounded up over 6,000 suspected communists, some of whom were deported to the new Soviet Union. The revived Ku Klux Klan, founded in 1915, railed against blacks, Jews, Catholics, and all other persons of "inferior" racial stock. Even Americans of German extraction, like H. L. Mencken, found themselves beleaguered by war zealotry; Irving Berlin must have wondered about the wisdom of his choice for a professional name, which he had made his legal one as well back in 1911.

While the immigrant songs that had once been Berlin's staple were out, war songs were in, from the grim, "Hello, Central, Give Me No Man's Land" to the comic farewell of a stuttering soldier to his girlfriend, "K-K-Katy." Berlin contributed his own comic perspective on the war with his characteristic knack of refracting the big historical picture through the lens of the particular individual. As a proud mother watches her son march off to war, she exclaims, "They Were All Out of Step But Jim." Berlin's own perspective on the war changed dramatically when, shortly before his thirtieth birthday, he was himself drafted into the army of his newly adopted country. As one newspaper headline declared, UNITED STATES TAKES BERLIN. By the time Irving Berlin became a soldier, the war was nearing its end, and that prospect made the routine of life at Camp Upton in Yaphank, Long Island, where Private Irving Berlin was stationed, all the more arduous. Marching, drilling, and doing "KP" (kitchen police) was intolerable for a man accustomed to working at all hours of the day and night, reveling in the bustle and glamour of Broadway, then being chauffeured back to his comfortable bachelor quarters where a cook served him a sumptuous meal before he slept late into the day.

"There were a lot of things about army life I didn't like," he recalled, "and the thing I didn't like most of all was reveille. I hated it. I hated it so much I used to lie awake nights thinking about how much I hated it." As with everything else he did, however, Berlin was determined to succeed. "I wanted to be a good soldier. Every morning when the bugle blew I'd jump right out of bed, just as if I liked getting up early. The other soldiers thought I was a little too eager about it, and they hated me. That's why I finally wrote a song about it." The song, of course, was "Oh! How I Hate to Get Up in the Morning," and it registered not only Berlin's but everybody's resistance to regimentation. Tying the insistent bugle call figure to the harsh slang expression, "You've got to get up, you've got to get up, you've got to get up," Berlin found another perfect match of words to music. Skillfully building his song to a climax, he repeats his opening musical phrase but instead of the helpless lament, "Oh! How I hate to get up in the morning. Oh! How I'd love to remain in bed," the lyric turns aggressive:

> Someday I'm going to murder the bugler,
> Some day they're going to find him dead.

In the final section of the ABAC chorus, Berlin introduces a new, more martial strain that accords with the even more graphic threat:

> I'll amputate his reveille,
> and step upon it heavily,
> and spend the rest of my life in bed.

As the song, which began so lamentably, comes to its rousing finale, the soldier glories in his fantasy of revenge.

"Oh! How I Hate to Get Up in the Morning" became enormously popular among soldiers as well as civilians. Soldiers found that soon

Irving Berlin in his World War I uniform for the 1918 production of *Yip! Yip! Yaphank.*

after they got to Europe, the rousing sentiments of "Over There" paled as homesickness for America set in. Much more to their liking were the insubordinate sentiments of "Oh! How I Hate to Get Up in the Morning," and they knew that only someone who had been a soldier himself was tormented by the question of why the bugler never overslept. In the second chorus of the song, Berlin delighted them with an answer and another murderous fantasy:

> And then I'll get that other pup—.
> The one that wakes the bugler up.

Another song beloved by soldiers of the American Expeditionary Forces (as the American army was grandly dubbed in Europe) was also, partly, by Irving Berlin. In 1913 he had written a song called "In My Harem," whose chorus began:

> In my harem, my harem,
> There's Rosie, Josie, Posie.

The doughboys set new words to the tune, which ran:

> In the army, the army,
> The democratic army,
> Your uncle clothes and feeds you
> Because your uncle needs you. . . .
> All the Jews and Wops,
> And the dirty, Irish cops,
> They're all in the army now.

Still another of Berlin's songs, "If I Had My Way, I'd Live Among the Gypsies," became a favorite among the doughboys. Written in 1917, Berlin never even published the song but he did play it at a Greenwich Village party one night before he was drafted. Another young songwriter at the party, Cole Porter, learned it by memory and then played it for the troops during his stint as an ambulance driver in Europe. It was especially beloved by Captain Eddie Rickenbacker's famed 94th "Hat-in-the-Ring" flying squadron, who may have found comfort in Berlin's reverie after the grueling air battles with Baron von Richtofen's "Flying Circus." The surviving flyers always sang it at their reunion, and, in 1943, when Hollywood planned a movie about Rickenbacker, Berlin learned his forgotten song from 1917 had long been an underground hit.

The success of "Oh! How I Hate to Get Up in the Morning" helped
Berlin, now Sergeant Berlin, mount a more ambitious project (and,
incidentally, to escape reveille forever). As his songwriter friend,
Harry Ruby, recalled, Berlin was so frustrated with army routine he
devised an "angle." Learning that the navy had staged a successful
fund-raising show at the Century Theater, Berlin pitched his scheme
to Major General J. Franklin Bell:

> Do you know how many people are in this Army who are
> from show business? The camp is full of them. Fine
> actors, vaudeville headliners, like Dan Healey, acrobats,
> singers—you never saw anything like it. Why don't we
> put on a show with these people? We could even play it
> on Broadway in one of the theatres—boost morale, help
> recruiting, everything!

Whether the general was moved by traditional rivalry with the
navy or whether he believed such a show could raise the money
needed for one of his own pet projects—a community house on the
campgrounds where relatives could visit soldiers—he gave Berlin
the go-ahead. It was at that point, according to Ruby, that Berlin
popped his question:

> "But here's the thing, General," he says, "I write at night.
> Sometimes I work all night when I get an idea. And I
> couldn't do that if I had to get up in the morning at five,
> you understand." "Why, you don't have to get up at five,"
> says the General. "You just forget about all that. *You write
> this show.*"

If it began as a ploy to escape reveille, Berlin's project catapulted
him into the role of producer as well as songwriter.

With the example of Ziegfeld before him, and the resources of the
United States Army behind him, Berlin commandeered the huge
Century Theatre, summoned 300 soldiers to be his cast and crew,
and started rehearsals for a revue he called *Yip! Yip! Yaphank*. He
devised songs and routines that satirized various aspects of army
life, but also, "recognizing how much theater was inherent in army
life, Berlin cannily included a series of military drills" that were "set
to his syncopated music." One of the highlights of the show was
Berlin's own mournful rendition of "Oh! How I Hate to Get Up in
the Morning," sung as he was dragged out of his tent, bleary-eyed
and yawning, by two burly fellow soldiers.

Knowing that the navy show at the Century Theatre had featured
sailors in drag, Berlin also used his production to spoof Ziegfeld's

lavish glorifications of the American girl. In one number, soldiers imitated such Ziegfeld starlets as Marilyn Miller and in another, a minstrel takeoff called "Darktown Wedding," the men wore black-face as well as dresses as they sang "Mandy" to the only real woman in the show: a stunningly beautiful black actress. Despite its comic setting, "Mandy" itself was a winsomely old-fashioned song, right down to its sixteen-bar chorus that was a throwback to nineteenth-century minstrelsy. The lyric, too, was simple and colloquial, rhyming "Mandy" with "there's a minister handy" and urging:

> here's the ring for your finger—
> Isn't it a humdinger?

Perhaps this dual exercise in satirizing the romantic ballad as well as returning to its roots provided Berlin with the perspective he would later use to create his consummate celebration of the American Girl in the *Ziegfeld Follies of 1919*.

Another number elicited Robert Benchley's remark that he "had never had such a thrill in the theater as that moment when the huge company receded from the vast Century stage and, left alone there with his scrubbing pail, Berlin's thin, shy, plaintive voice rose in this refrain":

> Poor little me, I'm a K.P.
> I scrub the mess hall upon my bended knee.
> Against my wishes, I wash the dishes,
> To make this wide world safe for democracy.

To bring his own revue to a close, Berlin contemplated using a patriotic song called "God Bless America." When he played it for Harry Ruby, then a staff pianist at Waterson, Berlin & Snyder who was brought in as his musical secretary for *Yip! Yip! Yaphank*, Ruby dutifully wrote down the melody but let Berlin know his reservations about the song:

> See, there were so many patriotic songs coming out everywhere at that time. It was 1918, and every song-writer was pouring them out. He'd already written several patriotic numbers for the show, and when he brought in "God Bless America," I took it down for him, and I said, "Geez, *another* one?" And I guess Irving took me seriously. He put it away.

Berlin would retrieve the "God Bless America" from his "trunk" twenty years later when America was poised on the brink of another world war.

For his finale, Berlin used a march, "We're On Our Way to France." Sung by the entire company in full battle gear as they marched off the stage on ramps and out the aisles of the theater, the song connected the world of the theater with the real "theater" of war. That connection became even more real on the last night of the show. The soldiers had received special orders that they were to board a troop carrier bound for France, and as they continued marching out of the theater and down the street the audience was awestruck with the realization that the cast was indeed living out the lyrics of the song.

Berlin himself remained at Camp Upton, returning to civilian life after the armistice was signed on November 11, 1918. Instead of diverting his career, the army experience had given Irving Berlin one of his greatest theatrical triumphs and one that placed him at the very center of national feeling. By extending his role to producer as well as composer, Berlin had added yet another dimension to his talents that strengthened his continuing resolve to become independent. He withdrew from the firm of Waterson, Berlin & Snyder but instead of joining another music publishing company, he established his own at 1607 Broadway under the title, Irving Berlin, Inc. This one firm would now handle all of his songs as well as publish songs by other composers and lyricists.

Within the world of musical theater, however, Berlin was still dependent upon Broadway producers. Approached by Ziegfeld, who had been duly impressed with the success of *Yip! Yip! Yaphank*, Berlin agreed to do the *Ziegfeld Follies of 1919*, but this time he made sure his songs were not upstaged by sets and costumes. His "Mandy" was recast as an opulent number for Ziegfeld's gorgeous star, Marilyn Miller, and Bert Williams sang the rhythmic dance song, "You Cannot Make Your Shimmy Shake on Tea." The latter was one of several numbers, including "Prohibition" and "A Syncopated Cocktail," that poked fun at the Volstead Act of 1920, which banned the sale and consumption of alcoholic beverages. (Berlin would have even more fun with Prohibition in another song, "I'll See You in C-U-B-A," where he naughtily spelled out the destination of thirsty Americans ninety miles from Miami.) Conceived with the same kind of high idealism that Woodrow Wilson had brought to both war and peace, Prohibition did have salutary effects on the nation's health, workforce, and home life, but it also spawned "bootleg" liquor, "speakeasies," and a network of criminal organizations that fought over the profits.

A big hit from the *Ziegfeld Follies of 1919* was Eddie Cantor's rendition of another of Berlin's slyly suggestive songs, "You'd Be Surprised." Taking an ordinary catch phrase, Berlin endowed it with sexual innuendo in a lyric that detailed the feats of a seemingly ordinary man who became quite extraordinary when with a woman:

> He's not so good in a crowd,
> but when you get him alone,
> You'd be surprised.

Cantor's notorious "banjo eyes" winked and rolled to underscore the surprising prowess of such an apparently diminutive lover. Also pleasantly surprising for Irving Berlin's new firm were the sales for Cantor's recording of the song. While recordings had been made since the earliest days of Tin Pan Alley, they were still regarded by music publishers as at best a sideline to sheet-music sales. As their technical quality improved and more homes purchased Victrolas, records began to rival sheet music as the mainstay of the music business. In the case of "You'd Be Surprised," Cantor's recording sold 800,000 copies—equaling its sheet-music sales.

Berlin's greatest artistic triumph in the *Ziegfeld Follies of 1919* was "A Pretty Girl Is Like a Melody," the elegant ballad he crafted as his new paean to the American ideal of femininity. Comparing its musical quality to that of a song like "Mandy," songwriter Alec Wilder concludes "it is extraordinary that such a development in style and sophistication should have taken place in a single year." Its sweeping melody that drives forward in subtly surprising contours is as beautiful as anything the classically trained Jerome Kern had written. The lyric is equally graceful—and forceful—elaborating a single extended simile in colloquial terms: a pretty girl is like an insistent melody that at first "haunts" your mind, then starts a ghostly "marathon" that gives your mind the "run-around," then finally produces a "strain"—at once musical and muscular—as her fleeting image reverses itself and imprisons her "pursuer." In the end, "you can't escape" because, paradoxically, "she's in your memory":

> She will leave you
> and then,
> Come back
> again

By breaking up this lyrical phrase against his chromatic melody, Berlin evokes not so much a flesh-and-blood reality but a tantalizing ideal of seductive beauty, the perfect evocation of Ziegfeld's floating, gossamer-clad visions.

Though usually modest, Berlin could not contain his realization that with this song he had truly mastered the ballad. One wonders if his forays into the classics had taken him to the poetry of Robert Burns. Surely, he would have known Burns's songs, such as "Auld Lang Syne" and "Comin' Thro' the Rye," and may have found his

simile between a pretty girl and a lovely melody in these lines from
"A Red, Red Rose":

> O My Luve's like a red, red rose
>   That's newly sprung in June.
> O My Luve's like the melodie
>   That's sweetly played in tune.

Whether or not Berlin took his simile from Burns, he certainly could
now regard the poet as a predecessor in the art of song.

While Burns, who had devised new words to old Scottish melodies, had been popular in America, his songs had nowhere near the
impact of those by Thomas Moore, who had followed a similar practice with old Irish airs. Musicologist Charles Hamm speculates that
Americans took to Moore's *Irish Melodies* because they had a "nostalgia" and "longing," musically and lyrically, not present in the
more robust and rustic songs of Burns. While the simile of a beautiful girl and a melody may have come from Burns, in Berlin's hands,
it takes on more of that haunting, melancholy character found in
Moore's exquisite songs, where the image of beauty flees "like fairy-
gifts fading away." Thomas Moore had, as we have seen, an enormous influence on Berlin's idol, Stephen Foster, and with "A Pretty
Girl Is Like a Melody," Berlin took his place among the pantheon of
these creators of timeless, classic ballads.

Ironically, this great song was added as an afterthought. After
Berlin had completed his score, Ziegfeld beseeched him for one
more song. Showing Berlin color plates of costumes he had ordered
for five of his lovelies, the impresario said, "Look at these costumes.
I have to have a number for them; my bookkeeper will kill me":

> So I went home. I looked at the costume plates. I
> thought of melodies to go with each girl and gown.
> "Traumerei," a Viennese waltz, etc. But I had to have a
> song to introduce the number and close it. Then I wrote
> lyrics and music to fit the action. It wasn't the hit of the
> show. "Tulip Time" was the hit then—"Pretty Girl" has
> become the hit.

Near the end of his songwriting career, Berlin could reflect comfortably on the durability of a song that has become a "standard."
"Today they play it when a pretty girl walks across a stage," he
observed, noting how it could also endure more questionable notori-
ety: "And stripteasers disrobe to it. That's show business."

Chapter 5

SAY IT WITH MUSIC

I suppose we all work best under pressure. I can't get to work until my partners tell me that sales are falling, that the rent is increasing, that salaries are going up— all because I'm not on the job. Then I sweat blood. Absolutely, I sweat blood between 3 and 6 many mornings and when the drops that fall off my forehead hit the paper, they're notes.

Irving Berlin's career as a businessman is almost as fascinating as his life as a songwriter. "Talent and business are wedded in him," quipped lyricist Howard Dietz, "like his words and music." From a lyricist who received only a few cents in royalties for a song, Berlin went on to establish his own music company and thus owned the copyrights for his songs. When he turned his business talents to Broadway, he saw that people who created songs and shows often did not reap the profits of their artistry. The experience of producing *Yip! Yip! Yaphank* and of working with Ziegfeld on the *Follies* gave him the confidence to undertake a lavish Broadway revue on his own. All that was needed for Irving Berlin the songwriter to become Irving Berlin the producer was a momentous opportunity and the wisdom to take advantage of it.

The moment came in 1920 in the person of Sam Harris. Like Berlin, Harris had come up through the Lower East Side, working his way up from laboring in a laundry to owning one, then branching out into boxing promotion and theatrical production. Harris had been George M. Cohan's partner ever since he helped Cohan produce his first successful American musical, *Little Johnny Jones*, in

1904. Even then, Harris still liked to wander down to the Bowery and Chinatown and frequently had a beer at "Nigger Mike's" Pelham Café while he listened to Izzy Baline and the other singing waiters. His long partnership with Cohan soured, however, when Cohan refused to accept the compromise that settled the bitter Actors' Equity strike of 1919, an obstinacy in which Cohan persisted even though he was virtually ostracized by the rest of his profession.

Harris realized that a producer had more control and flexibility if he owned his own theater. He recalled that Berlin once had given him a good tip at a Friars' gathering: "If you ever want to build a theater just for musical comedy," the songwriter had suggested, "why not call it the Music Box?" In the spring of 1920, Harris purchased a row of brownstone apartments in the heart of the theater district near Broadway and 45th Street. Hoping to engage Berlin as his new partner, he got on the phone and said, "I called you up to tell you that you can have your Music Box whenever you want it."

Building a theater was an enormously expensive and risky undertaking. The American economy was still recovering after its postwar slump, and no one could foresee the enormous boom years that lay ahead in the 1920s. The Music Box, moreover, would be a technological and aesthetic masterpiece, from its limestone facade, which featured a Renaissance loggia and columns, to its streamlined auditorium that had touches of the new style known as Art Deco, which emphasized machinelike design, textures, and colors. Berlin clearly brought the same kind of demanding artistry to building a theater that he did to crafting a song. As expenses mounted and details of its construction spread through the Broadway community, the Music Box looked like it would be Berlin's first folly. "The boys think they're building a monument," quipped one performer of Berlin and Harris, "but they're building a tombstone."

When their own funds were depleted, Irving Berlin turned to one of his oldest friends, Joe Schenck, the one-time clerk at Olliffe's Drugstore in Chinatown, who used to help his singing-waiter friend Izzy Baline with the rent when tips fell off. Just as Izzy had gone into Tin Pan Alley, Joe Schenck had abandoned his pharmaceutical studies and gotten in on the ground floor of another new American enterprise: the film industry. Still largely based in New York rather than Hollywood, silent films had started out as entertainment for lower-class, immigrant audiences, but now in the hands of directors like D. W. Griffith and stars like Mary Pickford and Charlie Chaplin, they were reaching a huge and broadly based audience.

A successful film producer, Schenck listened sympathetically to his old friend's plea, though at first he misconstrued it.

"I'm in trouble," Berlin stammered.

"Okay," Schenck shot back, "Who is she?"

"It's not a girl," Berlin explained, "It's a theater."

"Done," said Schenck, "Here's a check," though he felt he had to caution his old friend, "Irving, all I've put in this is some money; you've put your heart."

In return for putting up the needed funds, Schenck asked for a partnership in the enterprise, but his business acumen must have told him he had made a poor investment. Just building the theater would cost nearly a million dollars—an astronomical figure for the time—and mounting the first production would cost nearly $200,000, more than three times the expense for a normally lavish revue. Revues, moreover, were becoming increasingly commonplace on Broadway. The *Music Box Revue* would have to compete not only against Ziegfeld's annual *Follies* but against its many imitations, such as George White's *Scandals*, Edgar Selwyn's *Snapshots of 1921*, and other loose assemblages of songs, skits, and dances. New York audiences had already begun to weary of the formulaic glamour of these shows, so producers relied on profits from extensive tours in other cities; but the fledgling owners Berlin and Harris lacked the road companies to mount such tours. On top of that, other producers followed Ziegfeld's policy of using songs by a variety of composers, to ensure quality and variety, but Irving Berlin's independence would brook no interpolations. He himself would write all the songs for the *Music Box Revue of 1921*, and then for every annual revue at the theater after that. "The Music Box," as biographer Laurence Bergreen observes, "would be the first and only Broadway theater ever built to accommodate the songs and scores of a single composer." Joe Schenck had invested in a long-shot indeed!

As if all of these other expenses and risks weren't enough, Berlin commissioned Hassard Short as his director. While an acknowledged genius, Short was also known as "the wildest spendthrift director in town, a man with an abnormal passion for rising stage elevators, for Rube Goldberg mechanics." Short built the show around spectacular scenery, costumes, and special effects. In one number called "Dining Out," he displayed his gorgeous girls as huge pieces of food; in another, as gigantic pearls. Instead of the standard Ziegfeld staircase to display a bevy of chorines, the Music Box varied the effect by having an expensive moving staircase built under the stage so that it would arise from the floor and lift the girls to the ceiling of the auditorium. When Joe Schenck wandered into rehearsal to check on his investment, the notoriously unreliable staircase got stuck. Instead of panicking, Schenck slapped Berlin on the back and said reassuringly, "Never mind. It's no more than you or I would lose in a good stud game and never think of it again."

Fortunately, Berlin's songwriting skills were far more dependable. Drawing on his ragtime style, he wrote "Everybody Step,"

The Music Box Theatre on West 45th Street in 1922 (still there).

which invoked a "syncopated rhythm," a "jazzy fiddle," and a "clar-
ineter" (who "could not be better") in a sprightly invitation to dance
such as Berlin had been piping for years. Still, when he urged "be a
glutton when it comes to struttin' around," the call sounded as fresh
and lively as ever. The distinguished American composer, John
Alden Carpenter, included "Everybody Step" in his response to a
survey by *Etude* magazine asking him to name the "greatest masterpieces of musical art." Carpenter also included Bach's B-minor
Mass, Beethoven's Seventh Symphony, Wagner's *Die Meistersinger*,
Bizet's *Carmen*, Chopin's C#-minor polonaise, Debussy's *Pélleas et
Mélisande*, Moussorgsky's *Boris Godunov*, Stravinsky's *Petroushka*,
and Gilbert and Sullivan's *H.M.S. Pinafore*. He noted that his Chopin
and Berlin selections could just as easily been any of a " half dozen
masterpieces by the same composer."

When Berlin turned from ragtime to the ballad, he produced an
even better song than "A Pretty Girl Is Like a Melody." He had wanted to write a song that would serve to dedicate his new theatrical
house as well as capture the spirit of the revues he planned to mount
there. Taking a spare fifty-two note melody, Berlin enlivened it with
a bit of syncopation. He started off with a cellolike strain that deftly
matches long *a* and *u* vowels to lush whole notes:

> Say——it with mu——sic [rest]
> Beau——tiful mu——sic [rest].

The rest after the short second syllable of "music," however, abruptly cuts off the soaring progress of the melody, and, in the second section of the chorus, a rest made the shift from long to short words and notes even more abrupt:

> Some——how they'd rather be kissed
> [rest] To the strains of Chopin or Liszt.

The masterful manipulation of vowels and consonants, notes and rests, creates a ballad that combines both traditional melody and modern syncopation, not in counterpoint, as he had in "Play a Simple Melody," but molded together in one deceptively simple tune. Equally deft are the "memorable" rhymes he wove into the phrase " A melody mellow played on the cello" then continued into the next phrase with "helps Mister Cupid along."

By bringing syncopation into the ballad, Berlin paved the way for younger songwriters such as George Gershwin, who would begin such tenderly passionate songs as "The Man I Love" and "Embraceable You" on the upbeat. Berlin's allusions to Chopin and Liszt (who, after all, worked folk rhythms and melodies together in their most romantic compositions) was also part of his effort to incorporate jazz—and the Jazz Age—into his music. As he told a *Times* reporter in 1924:

> It was no more than being able to recognize what rhythm meant, and being with the times. It was the age of the automobile. The speed and snap of American jazz music is influenced by the automobile's popularity. Wagner, Beethoven, Mendelssohn, Liszt. All the masters of music knew the value of movement. . . . The automobile, however, is a new method of movement. All the old rhythm is gone and in its place is heard the hum of an engine, the whirr of wheels, the explosion of an exhaust. The leisurely songs that men hummed to the clatter of horse's hoofs do not fit into this new rhythm. The new age demands new music for new action.

If syncopating the traditional ballad was akin to merging romance with the automobile, then Berlin was putting into song what moralists were discovering with horror—that the automobile was doing far more than Freud to revolutionize America's dating and courtship practices.

Berlin realized that "Say It with Music" was one of the finest songs he had yet written, and he was eager to hear it performed. He violated a cardinal rule of show business by giving an advance copy of it to the jazz orchestra of the Sixty Club. They had promised to play it only once, but the song caught on so quickly Berlin had to squelch it lest it become popular before his show opened. When "Say It with Music" was officially premiered, Berlin was disappointed that it did not go over well with the audience of the *Music Box Revue*. Even though the song was performed beautifully, audience response was tepid. "We had a terrible time trying to get applause" for "Say It with Music," he told an interviewer. The problem was that Berlin did not want this superb song to be upstaged by scenery or costumes the way his songs had been when he wrote for the *Ziegfeld Follies*. Now that he was his own producer he could rein in the pyrotechnics of his director and insist upon a very simple staging for his masterpiece. But the audience, bedazzled by Short's staging of other numbers, was more interested in spectacle than song.

While "Say It with Music" was not the immediate hit Berlin had hoped for, the *Music Box Revue of 1921*, despite the doomsayers' predictions, delighted audiences and critics as much as his new theater. Even at the exorbitant ticket price of $4 a seat, it was sold out for months and eventually realized a profit of $400,000, providing ample returns on Berlin's, Sam Harris's, and Joe Schenck's investments. The *New York Times* critic, Alexander Woollcott, wrote floridly of both theater and show:

> Its bewildering contents confirmed the dark suspicion that Sam H. Harris and Irving Berlin have gone quite mad . . . they have builded them a playhouse in West Forty-fifth Street that is a thing of beauty in itself, and then crowded its stage with such a sumptuous and bespangled revue as cannot possibly earn them anything more substantial than the heart-warming satisfaction of having produced it all.

Although Woollcott may have been bedazzled by the spectacle of the theater and the revue, he made one observation that showed why he was regarded as one of the shrewdest and most demanding of theater critics. He astutely singled out "Say It with Music," but, instead of lavishing praise, Woollcott used understatement, calling it the "only one real song" in the show and predicting "by February you will have heard it so often that you will gladly shoot at sunrise any one who so much as hums it in your hearing."

Woollcott's standards and style were characteristic of a coterie of writers, entertainers, and socialites who regularly lunched at the Algonquin Hotel in New York's theater district. Woollcott served as the unofficial head of this sophisticated and acerbic group of wits—also known as "The Vicious Circle"— that included playwrights George S. Kaufman, Robert Sherwood, and Marc Connelly; humorists Robert Benchley and Ring Lardner; and the light verse poets F. P. A. (Franklin Pierce Adams) and Dorothy Parker. At their lunches, as in their writings, the Round Tablers place a premium on wit: the wisecrack, the fast comeback, the lethal retort. When Dorothy Parker was informed the notoriously stone-faced and stolid Calvin Coolidge had died, she quipped, "How can they tell?" When Kaufman patted Marc Connelly's bald pate and remarked, "Your head feels just like my wife's behind," Connelly placed his own hand on his head and exclaimed, without missing a beat, "You're right—it does."

Most of the Algonquinites wrote for newspapers, and their quips and parries were regularly reported in syndicated columns across the country. The big New York papers even carried regular columns of light verse, where writers like Parker could puncture romantic sentiments with a surgical aside:

> By the time you swear you're his,
> > Shivering and sighing,
> And he vows his passion is
> > Infinite, undying—
> Lady, make a note of this:
> > One of you is lying.

Such witty lines inspired young lyricists such as Lorenz Hart, Ira Gershwin, and E. Y. "Yip" Harburg to try to achieve similar effects in song lyrics. "We were living," Harburg recalled, "in a time of literate revelry in the New York daily press—F.P.A., Russel Crouse, Don Marquis, Alexander Woollcott, Dorothy Parker, Bob Benchley. We wanted to be part of it."

The songwriter who became most closely associated with the Round Table, however, was Irving Berlin, even though his personality and his songs seemed far removed from the cynical sophistication of the group. During the early 1920s, the Round Tablers became his closest companions, personally and professionally, and their urbane sensibility colored some of his songs, such as his 1922 "Crinoline Days," which celebrates traditional times but with a distinctly modern wrinkle:

Irving Berlin in the 1920s, perhaps in Palm Beach, Florida.

Back to the olden days
that were golden,
memory often strays,
before anyone could gaze
at Molly and May's
little ankle displays.

Similarly, in 1924, while vacationing in Florida with Dorothy Parker and other members of the "charmed circle," he displayed his own light verse rhyming in "Lazy," where he longed to roam in the *wild wood* as a *child would* and for "a great big *valise full* of books to read where it's *peaceful*." His lyric worksheets bristle with literary allusions to "Dickens" and "Omar Khayyam" (though Berlin paired them with homespun rhymes on "chickens" and "I am"). Musically, far from being lazily constructed, "Lazy" never repeats a phrase in its ABCD structure.

The Algonquin Round Table was a product of the continuing transformation of American culture from an isolated, rural, genteel society to one that, particularly after World War I, was cosmopolitan, urbane, and "smart." As his new circle of friends expanded, Irving Berlin came to know more and more fashionable people, such as the novelists Edna Ferber and F. Scott Fitzgerald, and theatrical figures who ranged from Noel Coward and Jascha Heifetz to Charlie Chaplin and Harpo Marx. The group's gatherings extended beyond the Algonquin to weekends at such fashionable estates as the Long Island mansion of Herbert Bayard Swope, the supposed inspiration for F. Scott Fitzgerald's *The Great Gatsby*.

The presence of Irving Berlin among these "sophisticates" indicates that the Round Table represented a safe and accepted haven for what, a few years before, had been a shocking revolt against traditional cultural and artistic values. That revolution pitted the cosmopolitan world of New York against the values of small-town America; when one member of the Round Table, Harold Ross, founded a magazine called *The New Yorker* in 1925, his masthead carried the slogan, "Not for the little old lady in Dubuque." This attitude was the culmination of a movement that had brought Midwesterners like Floyd Dell and Susan Glaspell to New York from small towns like Dubuque and Davenport. From Greenwich Village they looked back on their roots and scoffed at what H. L. Mencken labeled the "booboisie" of middle-class America and Sinclair Lewis caricatured in *Babbitt*. Along with flaunting Prohibition and every one of the traditional pieties they dismissed as "Puritan," these "flappers and philosophers"—as F. Scott Fitzgerald dubbed them— embraced every new and shocking cultural development New York could offer.

Berlin's own deepening sense of loneliness drew him closer to the fellowship of these urbane denizens of the Algonquin Round Table. In 1922, he moved from his Upper West Side apartment, where he had lived ever since his brief marriage, to a building in the theater district at 46th Street, close to his Music Box Theatre on 45th Street as well as to the Algonquin Hotel on 44th Street. Although it may seem strange that the shy, hard-working, and uncynical Berlin would be caught up in a set so bent on being sophisticated, irreverent, and "modern," he clearly found kinship in their talent, brilliance, and in what Edna Ferber termed their "terrible integrity." Mingling with this highly educated and literate company may have helped him focus his attempts to, as he put it "read the good books" and "get at least a bowing acquaintance with the world's best literature."

It was probably from poets like Dorothy Parker and George S. Kaufman that Berlin acquired not just a bowing acquaintance but an abiding interest in the poetry of Alexander Pope. While the eighteenth-century satirist might at first seem to be the remotest of poets from Irving Berlin, a little reflection will reveal the basis for their kinship. As the most supremely urban—and urbane—poet of London in one of its greatest eras and the center of his own circle of wits, Pope would have been a natural ancestor for all the poets of the Round Table. Irving Berlin, however, felt a special affinity for Pope's lifelong dedication to the "lean, compact heroic couplets"—the most constrictive of poetic forms. Pope's ability to compress his observations on politics, manners, and art within the confines of ten syllables parallels Berlin's devotion to the restrictions of the thirty-two bar chorus. Like the formula of the popular song, the couplet demanded ingenuity on the part of the poet in placing accent and pause, in avoiding banality of syntax and rhyme, and in achieving natural, even colloquial, expression within this most rigid of poetic forms:

> True Wit is Nature to advantage dressed;
> What oft was thought, but ne'er so well expressed.

While other songwriters, like George Gershwin, aspired to larger musical forms, Berlin, like Pope, was content to face, each day of his creative life, the rigors of the thirty-two bar formula. Observing that he thought Pope "would have made a brilliant lyric writer," Irving Berlin tried his hand at writing couplets:

> There goes Time with your last year's prize,
> Whittling it down to its proper size.

Like Pope, Berlin could render such a theme as mutability with deft wit and colloquial grace. Berlin would also have admired Pope as the most commercially successful of English poets, one who was alert to the shifting fashions of his time, to developments in the publishing business, and changes in copyright laws. Like Irving Berlin, "Pope became his own publisher, managed his rights with care, manipulated the booksellers, and planned his own career. . . . All he did was to write the most accomplished poems of his age, arrange for their publication at the most advantageous juncture, and harvest the returns carefully."

If the Algonquinites widened Berlin's literary horizons, he, in turn, drew them into his orbit of show business. In the spring of 1922, the group staged an amateur theatrical production, *No Sirree*, a send-up of a current hit revue called *Chauve Souris*. Berlin conducted the orchestra as Jascha Heifetz played the violin, Robert Sherwood sang songs by Dorothy Parker, and Robert Benchley did a comic monologue called "The Treasurer's Report." Recognizing the brilliance of Benchley's impersonation of a timid accountant suddenly stage struck as he delivers his report, Berlin hired him to do the bit in the *Music Box Revue of 1922*. Most of the comic sketches in the Music Box revues were not originally written for the show but, like Benchley's, recycled from vaudeville, burlesque, and other venues where they had already proven themselves.

Nor did the songs bear any relation to the comic sketches, though Berlin's songs for this second edition of his revue did reflect some of the irreverence of the Algonquin Round Table. His signature syncopated number, "Pack Up Your Sins (And Go to the Devil)," which rang down the curtain at the end of act one to thunderous applause, was a send-up of the moralists of the day who decried the exuberance of the Jazz Age. "They've got a couple of old reformers in heaven, making them go to bed at eleven," the song warned. Implying that such blue-noses were the aristocracy of the country, the song advised listeners to join the democratic and ethnically mixed mob:

> Pack up your sins and go to the devil in Hades,
> You'll meet the finest of gentlemen and the finest of ladies,
> They'd rather be down below than up above,
> Hades is full of thousands of
> Joneses and Browns, O'Hoolihans, Cohens, and Bradys.

Berlin's big ballad for the *Music Box Revue of 1922* was "Lady of the Evening," a "mature audience" version of "The Girl on the Magazine Cover" and "A Pretty Girl Is Like a Melody." Far from salacious, however, the song was only slightly suggestive, invoking angels, lullabies, and a metaphor lifted from no less hoary a poet than Henry Wadsworth Longfellow:

> You can make the cares and troubles that followed me
>   through the day
> Fold their tents just like Arabs and silently steal away.

Berlin introduces a minor seventh interval which, played against a major chord gives a "sprinkle of theatrical mystery" to the phrase. If Berlin's subject were indeed a lady of questionable morals, she was, like his fellow Round Tablers Tallulah Bankhead and Dorothy Parker, still very much a lady.

Once again, however, the success of the revue depended less on the quality of Berlin's songs and more on spectacular sets, costumes, and effects. In a "mirror" routine, dancers rehearsed before other dancers as their reflections; in another number, the singer wore a gold-sequined gown with a hooped skirt that, as she rose in the air, engulfed the entire stage; the show's finale featured endlessly streaming gold curtains. In his review, Woollcott sounded a prophetically sour note, not just with the *Music Box Revue of 1922* but with the whole tired concept of the genre. Making fun of Hassard Short's staging, he noted that performers, some attired in "gowns of sequins weighing about a ton each," could not simply walk on stage:

> No, they emerge from tree trunks and bird cages, spring up out of trapdoors and lightly swing down from high trapezes. When this is not possible they walk groggily down interminable staircases of black velvet.

Woollcott's criticism, which were echoed by other reviewers, could be construed as backhanded praise for Berlin's songs, which were upstaged by the revue productions. Still, he had clearly put his finger on a problem with the whole revue format.

Berlin may have sensed that the cure for the problem was not simply in new songs or new special effects but in new talent. Before beginning work on the 1923 edition of the *Music Box Revue*, he took a vacation in Paris, where he met a young American singer named Grace Moore, who was desperately trying to succeed in opera. Over a glass of wine, Berlin persuaded her to lend her magnificent voice to the *Music Box Revue of 1923*, and he wrote a contract for her on the tablecloth (for which the restaurant billed him along with food and drinks). Grace Moore clearly had the talent Berlin needed, but she was also high-strung, insecure, and inexperienced, all of which came across to the other members of the cast as the imperious posturing of a would-be prima donna. They greeted her transition from grand opera to Broadway revues with mockery, practical jokes, and back-stage bickering. Berlin now had to assume the role of producer at its most demanding, trying to heal the wounded feelings, jealousies, and back-stabbings of a disgruntled cast. As Robert Benchley, who was included again with an updated version of his "Treasurer's Report," noted, "Nothing could be more disconcerting than a rehearsal shortly before the opening of the Music Box":

A little man in a tight-fitting suit, with his hands in his pockets, walks on from the wings. He looks very white in the glare from the foots. You almost expect to have him thrown out, he seems so casual and like an observer. They don't throw him out, however, because he is Mr. Berlin. You are suddenly overcome with a feeling of tremendous futility. "Irving Berlin's Fourth Music Box Revue" it already says in the lights out in front of the theatre. And Irving Berlin is little. And the Fourth Music Box Revue is so big. And so far from articulation. Yet on opening night, not a week from the rehearsal, you won't feel any futility about it. If you are back-stage you will, if you can keep your head from being caved in, be impressed with nothing so much as the tremendous accomplishment of something out of what seemed to be nothing, or worse than nothing, chaos. For four months he has been working day and night, writing music, devising numbers, engaging principals and chorus, and having a terrible time with his digestion. And yet in all that time no one has heard him raise his voice. And in all that time no one has been hurt by him.

Berlin once again had managed to pull his show together, and while critics found it lacked the excitement and "lilt" of previous shows, it still had some wonderful moments. George S. Kaufman wrote a skit, "If Men Played Cards as Women Do," that was one of his classic bits of comic drama. Hassard Short outdid himself with a production number for a Berlin song called "An Orange Grove in California," that included orange scent that was released from valves under the seats of the audience. And Grace Moore proved to be the find Berlin believed she would be—on opening night, critics declared, "a new star was born."

Still, troubles with the cast only worsened after opening night and finally so upset Grace Moore she could not perform. Berlin again asserted himself as producer, forcing people to tender apologies and sending Grace Moore on a short vacation. As a songwriter, however, he believed he should also try to bolster his show with a song. Looking beyond his original score, Berlin decided to interpolate one of his own recent ballads. He had composed it at a birthday party Dorothy Parker and Neysa McMein had thrown for fellow Round Tabler Donald Ogden Stewart in November of 1923. As Stewart recalled, Berlin came to the party with several bottles of champagne:

> While we all sat around, celebrating and drinking the champagne, Irving went to the piano and kept on playing

> the first part of a song he had written. It was called,
> "What'll I Do?" But he hadn't been able to finish it. He
> played the part he had over and over, and we all liked
> it—but the best part of the evening was that after Irving
> had had enough of his champagne, he was finally able to
> finish the song that night.

The scene conjured up by Stewart shows how far Berlin had merged
into the Round Table and the heady atmosphere of the Jazz Age.
From a composer who normally worked alone throughout the night,
his creation of a song amid such elegant company suggests that he
had indeed found his new friends as intimate as family.

The song itself seems a far cry from the sophisticated set who first
heard it. A bone-simple melody and lyric, it nevertheless has some of
his most intricate manipulations of words with music. Rhythmically,
Berlin alternates between the three-beat measures of waltz time and
two-beat measures that give the melody the feel of a syncopated
waltz. Lyrically, he takes a common catchphrase of exasperation—
"What'll I Do?"—fitting the first three syllables to a triplet. Berlin
had long boasted that one of his secrets of success as a songwriter
was that he knew how to "vocalize" the triplet, and one way he did
so was to employ contractions, whose fluid syllables were perfectly
suited to the lilting rhythm of triplets. Contractions also give his
lyrics a colloquial character (as British listeners found when they
inquired about the meaning of the word "whattle"). The vernacular
"What'll" (instead of the more elevated "What Will I Do?") heightens
rather than dampens the singer's despair. In the next phrase, however, Berlin avoids the more common contraction "Who's" in order to
spell out the two words and create a rhyme: "when I am wond'ring
who *is* *kiss*ing you what'll I do?"

He crafted an even subtler off-rhyme in the final phrase:

> when I'm al*one* with *on*ly dreams of you.

The slight difference in sound between the *on* of "alone" and the *on*
of "only" is underscored by setting the two syllables to musical notes
that are only a faint half-interval apart.

In another phrase:

> what'll I do with just a photograph to tell my troubles to,

Berlin uses the same musical note to bring out the even subtler rhyme
between the way Americans pronounce *a* and *o* in "just *a* photograph"
then underscores the semantic difference between the two *tos* in "*to*
tell my troubles *to*" by putting them on widely different notes.

Such minute craftsmanship reveals how Berlin had mastered the art of fusing music and words, and while that mastery was probably not apparent to either the Algonquin circle who witnessed his creation of "What'll I Do?" amid clinking champagne glasses nor to audiences at the *Music Box Revue of 1923*, it would have been clear to Grace Moore, whose musical training enabled her to render its sophisticated simplicity with moving poignancy. Whether the addition of this single new song actually salvaged the show, cast squabbling calmed, and the *Music Box Revue of 1923* enjoyed a successful run, though none of the subsequent revues proved to be as profitable as the first.

With "What'll I Do?" Berlin not only advanced his mastery of the ballad but realized his earlier ambition to "syncopate for people's hearts as well as their toes":

> I would not want it said that I claim, by any means, to be the originator of modern ragtime, but I can truthfully say that I have accomplished a number of things which were thought impossible. I established the syncopated ballad and I have shown that the metre can be "chopped up" to fit the words.

He could manipulate the subtlest relations between words and music in a waltz as deftly as he had been "ragging" words against music in rhythmic songs since "Alexander's Ragtime Band." Moreover, just as those ragtime songs had an underlying current of sadness in them, these "sob ballads" as Berlin termed them, had a syncopated lilt beneath their poignant expressions of loneliness and loss. Although reporters tried to read into them a reflection of Berlin's personal life at the time, the songwriter insisted that the only song he had ever written directly from personal experience was "When I Lost You." In fact, he dismissed such speculation as "ridiculous":

> Just because a man writes sob ballads, he is not writing from his own experiences. It has always been assumed that whenever I've written a ballad I've been through some heartbreaking experience. But the real reason is that the public would rather buy tears than smiles—and right now they happen to want sob ballads.

Despite this businesslike approach to songwriting, one suspects Berlin doth protest too much. In July of 1922 he had lost his mother and then, just five months later, he learned of the death of a man who had been more of a father to him than anyone, "Nigger Mike" Salter. Berlin was the only one of Mike's old friends from the Pelham Café to show up for the funeral, and his comment to reporters echoes Hamlet's epitaph for his own dead father: "He was no angel, maybe," Berlin said, "But there are a lot of guys on the street today who would have been in jail if it hadn't been for Nigger Mike." Berlin was referring to Mike's penchant for getting criminals out of jail by having one of his aging prostitutes pose as the felon's distraught mother (a trick that sometimes backfired, as when Salter paired a Jewish prisoner with an Irish "mother" whose thick brogue gave away the ruse). Without ostentation, Berlin paid for his penniless friend's funeral expenses then paid off the $8,000 mortgage and turned the house over to Salter's widow and children. Ironically, "Nigger Mike" was buried in the same Brooklyn cemetery as Lena Baline had been only months before. As Laurence Bergreen speculates:

> They bore down heavily on Berlin, these two deaths, coming so close together, emphasizing a loneliness that no amount of acclaim could assuage. The applause at the Music Box, the thousands of copies of sheet music sold— that was all fine, splendid, in fact, until he came home to his penthouse, his books and art collection, and his toucans. And then he was alone. Single. Childless. A widower for ten years now.

Berlin's sense of isolation, emptiness, and loss was shared, beneath their banter and joviality, by most of the Algonquin Round Tablers. Dorothy Parker could write acerbically of suicide attempts in "Résumé"—

> Razors pain you;
> Rivers are damp;
> Acids stain you;
> And drugs cause cramp.
> Guns aren't lawful;
> Nooses give;
> Gas smells awful;
> You might as well live.

—perhaps because she had ventured them so often herself.

Whether or not Berlin's ballads grew out of his own loneliness, they certainly touched an audience in the early 1920s that was preoccupied with "the blues." The movement toward public expression of the private self that began with the cabarets and dance craze of 1910 had, a dozen years later, metamorphosed into a collective sense of solitude among the urban and urbane denizens of the Jazz Age. Many of these, particularly young women from small towns, had come to New York and other large cities to find jobs in offices, shops, and the still new and expanding "department stores." With a freedom unheard of a generation before, they lived on their own in apartments and pursued their own recreation unchaperoned. The new convenience of "canned" goods and laundromats made single life easier to sustain, but it created a new emptiness that T. S. Eliot captured in his poem of 1922, *The Waste Land*. In the sordid encounter of a young typist who invites a clerk to her flat for dinner, Eliot details how she serves "food in tins," engages in "caresses which still are unreproved, if undesired," then after capitulating in "indifference," accepts one "final patronising kiss" from her departing lover:

> When lovely woman stoops to folly and
> Paces about her room again, alone,
> She smoothes her hair with automatic hand,
> And puts a record on the gramophone.

The record Eliot's bored typist puts on her gramophone could easily have been "All By Myself," "What'll I Do?" or another of Berlin's "sob ballads." These songs spoke to their Jazz Age audience in their lonely moments, as his rhythmic songs did in their lively ones.

Such ballads, as Eliot notes, found their audience through the new medium of phonograph records. Records had been part of the music business since the turn of the century, but they had always been regarded by Tin Pan Alley as a sideline to the sales of sheet music. In 1910 the publishers succeeded in getting a copyright law passed that forced companies to pay publishers, lyricists, and composers a few pennies from each sale of a phonograph record or a piano roll. Still, to veterans of the music business like Irving Berlin, phonograph records represented a falling away from their mission to supply songs for the public to *perform*. Within the course of his lifetime, Berlin witnessed a shift in popular culture away from performance to consumption, in everything from songs to sports. Tin Pan Alley firms initially marketed sheet music to people who could play the piano in their own home. With the development of the player piano, however, one need not play at all, and Tin Pan Alley began to supplement sheet-music sales with piano player "rolls" that were cut by professional performers like George Gershwin and then purchased for home reproduction. With the increasing popularity of the player piano and the phonograph, which John Philip Sousa dubbed "canned music," people simply listened to songs. Indicative of this changing climate, "All By Myself" sold 161,650 piano rolls, 1,053,493 copies of sheet music, and 1,225,083 phonograph records.

At that very time, however, another technological innovation transformed the popular music business. On November 2, 1920, the first radio station, KDKA in Pittsburgh, broadcast the election returns that made Warren Gamaliel Harding the twenty-ninth president of the United States. Radio was slow to catch on as stations across the country tried broadcasting church services, concerts, even the boxing match between Dempsey and Carpentier. When they began playing popular songs, however, the entire country perked up its ears. "There is radio music in the air, every night, everywhere," newspapers announced, "Anybody can hear it at home on a receiving set, which any boy can put up in an hour." The president himself had a radio installed in the White House, and radio sales hit $60 million in 1922, doubled in 1923, nearly tripled in 1924, and finally reached half-a-billion dollars by 1925.

Had it not been for ASCAP, which insisted that radio stations, like cabarets, pay to play songs by its members, Irving Berlin and other Tin Pan Alley publishers would have opposed a medium that allowed people not only to listen to—rather than perform—their songs but to listen to them *free*. When Congress threatened to pass legislation allowing radio stations to play copyrighted music without paying royalties to ASCAP, Irving Berlin lobbied the Senate Patents Committee in Washington, along with other elder statesmen of popular song: Victor Herbert, Harry Von Tilzer, and even the venerable Charles K. Harris, whose "After the Ball" had galvanized the fledgling popular song industry back in 1893.

With their royalties protected, songwriters could embrace radio as the ultimate "plugger" of a new song. Radio, moreover, was the perfect vehicle for the new kind of "sob ballad" Irving Berlin had been writing. Intimate, introspective, reflective, the radio, like the phonograph, called for ballads aimed at the solitary listener, not for the group sing-a-long around the parlor piano. In 1924, "What'll I Do?" was sung over the radio by Frances Alda and "All Alone," was introduced by John McCormack, reaching millions of listeners without the extensive plugging network of Tin Pan Alley. As the Irish tenor's voice came over the new medium, it stimulated record sales rather than, as songwriters feared, obviated them by his "free" performance.

"All Alone," like "All By Myself" and "What'll I Do?," was a song tailor-made for the intimate new medium and its isolated listener. Berlin portrays the singer in a lonely room, waiting, obsessively, for a telephone's:

> ring
> a ting,
> a ling.

The song culminates on a pathetic sequence as Berlin first matches three musically parallel phrases with two lyrically parallel ones:

> Wond'ring where you are,
> And how you are.

But then, as Gerald Mast notes, the third lyrical phrase is a "syntactic surprise," which leaves the thought—and the listener—dangling:

> And if you are, . . .

The thought is only completed by a skillful return to that all-important title: "all alone too." The title itself is a commonplace phrase in
which Berlin discerned a singable and memorable faceting of sound:
"*All Alone.*" Such repetitive syllables, words, and phrases mirror the
self-enclosed lyrical "space" of both singer and listener of such radio
and phonograph ballads.

"All Alone" quickly became a hit, selling a quarter of a million
records in the first month. Berlin promptly interpolated it into the
Music Box Revue of 1924, as he had "What'll I Do?" into the previous
year's offering. Again, the song went to Grace Moore who sang it in
a duet, appropriately into a telephone, with her across-the-stage
lover. The theatrical performance, ironically, derived from rather
than inspired the radio and recording version of the song. As good
as Berlin's songs were for the *Music Box Revue of 1924*, the show
itself did poorly, as did Ziegfeld's own edition of his *Follies*. The
death knell for the big, lavish revue had finally tolled.

Meanwhile, on the same night the *Music Box Revue of 1924*
opened, two young brothers, George and Ira Gershwin, had the premiere of their first hit musical, *Lady, Be Good!* Cast in the mold of
the Princess Shows, *Lady, Be Good!* had a rhythmic thrust that was
new to Broadway. It was a "book" show with snappy gags, energetic
dance numbers, blackouts, and "crossovers" (brief musical scenes
played in front of the curtain while scenery was changed). Like the
Princess Shows, sets and costumes were scaled down from the spectacles of Ziegfeld's Joseph Urban and Berlin's Hassard Short;
instead, the sleek Art Deco designs of Norman Bel Geddes perfectly
matched the simplicity of the Gershwin brothers' songs. Beneath
that simplicity, however George Gershwin's score revealed his
assimilation of blues and jazz, and his brother Ira skillfully handled
the American vernacular so that, together, the Gershwin brothers
achieved the same deft interplay of words and music that Berlin had
mastered as his own composer and lyricist. The fact that *Lady, Be
Good!* starred another sibling team, the dancers Fred and Adele

Astaire, further indicates what a harbinger it was of things to come in American popular music.

Ironically, only a few years before, George Gershwin, then a lowly piano plugger on Tin Pan Alley, had approached Berlin for a job as his musical secretary. Berlin listened to the phenomenal youngster embellish his melodies, but, contrary to legend, did *not* offer Gershwin a job. Instead, Berlin gave him some advice: "Stick to your own songs, kid, you're too good to be arranging some other songwriter's music." Gershwin had done just that. He had also turned to Jerome Kern and the new tradition of musical comedy, wisely placing himself at the center of the most significant developments in American musical theater for the next ten years, while Berlin's work in the revue format seemed to be taking him farther and farther toward the margins.

The *Music Box Revue of 1924* was Berlin's last show of the decade at his own theater. While he would always consider his songs for these annual revues his best collective body of work, the revue format no longer drew audiences to the theater. The exhausting work of writing an entirely new score each year also took its toll on Berlin, especially because the most successful numbers, like "What'll I Do?" and "All Alone," turned out to be individual interpolations. Berlin's strength, it seemed, continued to lie with the individual song rather than the integrated score. The new technology of phonograph, radio, and in a few years the talking picture, however, provided him with wonderful showcases for those songs that compensated for his temporary withdrawal from the Broadway musical scene.

While Berlin the songwriter withdrew from Broadway, his theatrical business continued to be successful. With partner Sam Harris, he opened the doors of his lavish Music Box Theatre to other producers and shows. For the rest of the decade, the venture proved remarkably successful. By the mid-1920s it was clear that America had embarked upon an extraordinary period of prosperity. World War I had left European economies in shambles, but America was virtually unscathed. The country drew upon its enormous material resources, huge domestic market, and technological and managerial wizardry, typified by Thomas Edison and Henry Ford, to fuel an economic boom that carried everything from Broadway musicals to Florida real estate in its wake. Fostered by the Republican administrations of Harding and Coolidge (and epitomized by the motto, "the business of America is business"), business flourished and contributed to its own boom by persuading Americans to "exercise their credit" through the new phenomenon of installment buying.

The 1920s were also the decade that saw the development of advertising as an art aimed not at touting the product but of seducing the consumer. Ads stressed the symbolic values that came with the purchase of six-cylinder cars, cigarettes, rouge, and mouthwash. By 1927, business was spending more than a billion and a half dollars a year to "break down consumer resistance" and persuade Americans that everything from Lucky Strike to Listerine would make them more youthful, desirable, and successful. In the new emphasis upon advertising and salesmanship, American business was only adapting the techniques of plugging and mass marketing that Tin Pan Alley had espoused before the turn of the century.

That Irving Berlin's lavish theater with its top-drawer ticket prices should be a profitable, even a "charmed," house on Broadway seems only fitting, as does the fact that his musical evocations of the new American girl helped fuel the explosion in the fashion, cosmetics, and magazine industries. Even after the economic collapse at the end of the 1920s, a collapse brought on in part by the equivalent of "easy credit" buying on the stock market, Berlin's theater continued to thrive. In 1931, as the Depression worsened, the Music Box had one of the few successful shows, *Of Thee I Sing*, a political satire, cast squarely in the mold of Gilbert and Sullivan, with a book by George S. Kaufman and Morrie Ryskind and songs by the brothers Gershwin. The success of that satirical operetta, the first musical ever to receive the Pulitzer Prize, kept Berlin the businessman and his beloved theater solvent, but it also underscored how far he himself, as a songwriter, had drifted from the mainstream of American musical theater. "I am convinced," Berlin had told reporters in 1922, "that eventually the great American opera will be written" in jazz, and vowed, "I intend to do such a work" and "produce it myself at the Music Box." Berlin would have other triumphs in his own theater, notably the satirical revue, *As Thousands Cheer* in 1933. But it would be George Gershwin who would realize that operatic ambition in 1935 with *Porgy and Bess*.

Chapter 6

BLUE SKIES

When I say that jazz is the only great contribution of the twentieth century to the music annals of the world, I am speaking with the utmost seriousness. It is young, and being young, it has its faults. But none that can't be corrected. It will thrive because there is nothing artificial about it. Its tremendous popularity is due to the fact that it sounds a note to which millions of Americans are responsive.

One evening in May of 1924, Irving Berlin wandered down to Jimmy Kelly's. Throughout his life he had a habit of returning to his old haunts in Union Square, Chinatown, and the Bowery, a habit easily indulged in a city where no matter how far up—or down—the ladder of success you had climbed, you could reach your antipodes by walking a few blocks. On this particular night, Berlin may have been more than usually reflective about the course of his career. While he was undoubtedly the premier American songwriter, his hold upon that position was tenuous. It may have already been clear that he could not maintain it by writing scores for revues at the Music Box Theatre, and he was not ready to plunge into the newly emerging genre of the integrated musical comedy. Already, younger songwriters were vying for his mantle. On February 24, 1924, Paul Whiteman presented a concert at Aeolian Hall that purported to fuse jazz with the classics. Much of that program, however, including a "Semi-Symphonic Arrangement" of Irving Berlin's songs, proved drearily monotonous; only when young George Gershwin strode to the piano, nodded to Whiteman, then plunged into *Rhapsody in Blue*, did it become clear that jazz had found a new spokesman.

If Berlin could not clearly foresee his future in American song, a look backward at his past seemed to suggest that his stunning career had reached a plateau. His friend Alexander Woollcott was writing a biography of the songwriter—an enormous tribute, yet one that suggested a sense of closure. Woollcott traced Berlin's rise from the immigrant Lower East Side to the heights of American success, romanticizing his subject as an untutored genius who drew upon his melancholy heritage as a Russian Jew. Woollcott predicted that his music would endure only after a trained composer had transmuted it, as Liszt and Chopin had taken anonymous folk melodies and lifted them into the realm of classic art. While Woollcott acknowledged that it was unusual to write the biography of a man in his mid-thirties, his book implied that Berlin had come as far, creatively, as someone like him possibly could.

What may have made Irving Berlin especially reflective on this particular night, however, was that he had not come to Jimmy Kelly's alone. With him was a lovely and sophisticated young lady named Ellin Mackay. Earlier that evening, they had met at a fashionable dinner party. She had charmed him by saying, "Oh, Mr. Berlin, I do so like your song, 'What Shall I Do?'" And, he, after correcting her about the title of his latest hit, graciously acknowledged the propriety of her distinction between *shall* and *will*: "Where grammar is concerned," he joked, "I can always use a little help." After dinner, he invited her to accompany him to Jimmy Kelly's, which had become, in the parlance of the Prohibition era, a "speakeasy." Kelly had also moved from his old Union Square location to Sullivan Street in Greenwich Village, the heart of artistic experiment, social protest, and Bohemian lifestyles in the Jazz Age.

The transformation of Jimmy Kelly's was indicative of the vast changes in American social mores that had taken place since Berlin had worked there as a singing waiter. The coming of the cabaret around 1910 had threatened to break down the barriers between the social classes, to place young girls from the highest echelons of society next to men from the lower and even immigrant classes. Dancing, dining, and the intimate floor show invited the expression and exploration of private experience, once confined to the homes of a closely knit society, into the open, public domain. The redefinition of the American girl that had started out with Irene Castle as the healthy, active, fox-trotting playmate of 1914 had, ten years later, transmogrified into the Jazz Age flapper, kicking up her stockingless legs in the Charleston.

The encounter between Irving Berlin and Ellin Mackay was the most dramatic upshot of these changes in American society. Barely twenty-one, the lithe, blonde Ellin came from the highest reaches of society. Her father, Clarence Mackay, on the strength of his father's fortune, spawned by the fabled Nevada Comstock silver mines and invested in the telegraph system, was one of the wealthiest and most prominent men in New York. Ellin had grown up at his estate on Long Island, gone to the finest private schools, and in 1922 made her debut into society at a ball at the Ritz-Carlton. In the fall of 1924, she would dance with the Prince of Wales, who was destined to become King Edward VIII of England until he, in an even more scandalous crossing of class barriers, gave up the throne to marry a divorced commoner.

Ellin, however, had literary aspirations and found herself drawn to Greenwich Village and to her mother's cousin, Alice Duer Miller, a member of the Algonquin Round Table. The Round Table itself exemplified social mixing among people like Woollcott and Franklin Pierce Adams, who came from solid gentility, George S. Kaufman and Dorothy Parker, who stemmed from wealthy Jewish families, and Jews like Berlin and Herbert Swope, who had struggled up from poverty. For a flower of New York society like Ellin Mackay to mingle with such a mongrel group, however literate, testified to the breakdown of class distinctions. Ellin knew it and capitalized upon it. In 1925, she would write an essay, "Why We Go to Cabarets: A Post-Debutante Explains," for *The New Yorker*, the new magazine founded by Round Tabler Herbert Ross to set a standard of wit, insouciance, and urbanity.

Ellin's essay gleefully satirized the dreaded influence of cabarets on American society:

> Our Elders criticize many things about us, but usually they attribute sins too gaudy to be true. The trouble is that our Elders are a trifle gullible; they have swallowed too much of F. Scott Fitzgerald. . . . They believe all the backstage gossip that is written about us. . . . Cabaret has its place in the elderly mind beside Bohemia and bolshevik, and other vague words that have a sinister significance and no precise definition. . . . We have privacy in a cabaret. . . . What does it matter if an unsavory Irish politician is carrying on a dull and noisy flirtation with the little blonde at the table behind us? We don't have to listen; we are with people we find amusing.

In just such a cabaret Ellin Mackay had fulfilled the worst of those fears by finding companionship with an immigrant Jewish songwriter. In Ellin, Berlin found the high spirit of his first wife, Dorothy, together with the literate sophistication of his current friends from the Algonquin Round Table.

When he learned that his daughter was involved with Berlin, Clarence Mackay was incensed. The fact that his family was Catholic made him vigilant in guarding his social standing. While Mackay could be friendly with wealthy Jews who moved in his own social circle, such as Otto Kahn and Bernard Berenson, it was unthinkable that his daughter would be courted by an immigrant Jew from Tin Pan Alley. His vigilance was heightened by the fact that his own wife, Katherine Duer Mackay, had earlier become entangled in an affair with a prominent society surgeon, Doctor Joseph Blake. When Clarence Mackay refused, on Catholic tenets, to grant her a divorce, Katherine traveled to Paris, where Doctor Blake headed an American Red Cross hospital during World War I. There she married her lover and left Mackay to Harbor Hill, his magnificent Long Island estate, and to his bitterness.

That bitterness flared anew over his daughter's association with Irving Berlin. Although he himself had taken a mistress, Anna Case, she was from the upper echelon of the musical world, a concert singer who had been a star at the Metropolitan Opera, where Mackay was a member of the board of directors. When he learned that Ellin and Berlin were seen together at parties, he hired private detectives to investigate the songwriter and keep him away from Harbor Hill. When he could turn up nothing damaging, he whisked his daughter off to Europe in the hope that other suitors would expunge the memory of Berlin.

What Mackay did not realize was that removing his daughter from New York would only intensify Berlin's feelings, which do not seem to have been as committed to the relationship, until that point, as Ellin's were. Later, she admitted that in those early days she had been the pursuer. However, in her absence, Berlin seems to have felt his mid-life emptiness all the more keenly. A newer, youthful era was emerging as epitomized by the success of the Gershwins' *Lady, Be Good!*, while Berlin, along with the revues to which he had committed himself and his theater, seemed to be ebbing into the past. In his first marriage he had hoped to find an escape from the demons that drove him to maintain the success he had achieved with "Alexander's Ragtime Band." As he contemplated this new commitment, it may have seemed a bulwark against the vicissitudes of time and fortune.

By the end of 1924, songs such as "What'll I Do?" and "All Alone" had become enormously popular, and newspapermen would later ascribe them to Berlin's longings for his departed Ellin. While "What'll I Do?" had been written before they met, "All Alone," according to their oldest daughter, was "clearly written for my mother during their courtship (however often the composer might try, self-consciously, to deny this)." In December of 1924, he took out

a song he had been working on, on and off, for two years. He had
given it the minimalist title, "Remember," and took great pride in
"the little musical phrase that is coupled with the word 'remember'
in the song." The word begins the chorus on a syncopated upbeat, so
that the waltz rhythm is slightly out of kilter, reflecting the singer's
consternation. The second syllable of "remember" then climbs up
three notes, an unusual rising interval that leaves the question—and
the chord—unresolved. When the word is repeated at the end of the
A-sections, it stretches over a full octave, intensifying the singer's
despair. Then, at the beginning of the release, "remember" traverses
four intervals beyond the octave, yet still follows that haunting pattern of the rising third. Only when "remember" recurs at the very
end of the song is the chord resolved, though the effect is more one
of resignation than resolution:

> You promised that you'd
> forget me not
> But you forgot
> to remember.

It was when this final "turnaround" phrase came to him as a "tag
line" that Berlin felt his two years of work had reached an end. That
line "made the song," illustrating his conviction that "it's the lyric
that makes a song a hit, although the tune, of course, is what makes
it last."

If "Remember" was inspired by Ellin Mackay's absence, the song
also registers Berlin's gnawing sense of insecurity as he entered
such a critical period in his professional as well as his personal life.
"With 'Remember,'" he said, "I tried to express a feeling or an emotion that had been embodied in me," and he was "a bit sensitive and
enthusiastic concerning it." Berlin recalled:

> On Christmas morning I called Max Winslow and Saul
> Bornstein, my publishing associates, to my studio room
> in the Music Box Theatre to hear the new song I had
> composed. I sang it, certain I had a hit. When I
> finished . . . Bornstein said that it was not so good.
> Winslow said it was terrible. I told them I thought the
> song was good and would be a hit. They tried to per-
> suade me from publishing it and suggested I throw it
> into the wastebasket and forget about it. . . . During the
> spring and summer I remembered "Remember" and
> worried about it. I thought I had lost my skill, my talent.
> I was afraid to write anything for fear Winslow would

> say it was terrible. I was developing an inferiority com-
> plex, which is the greatest hindrance a writer can
> have. . . . I worried so much that I was becoming a bun-
> dle of nerves. . . . That Christmas Day was the worst one
> I had ever spent in my life. Every time I felt worried or
> troubled I remembered that day and felt worse.

Berlin worried about how long his talent would endure, and part of his drive reflects his fear that one day he would find he could not come up with another successful song. Earlier he had speculated that while his ability to concoct tunes was safe, he feared that lyrics would one day be his downfall. Now, in the creation of a single song, he seemed to be at a dead end. If the song reflected the absence of young Ellin Mackay, Berlin's loss was doubly poignant.

"After much worrying and thinking," Berlin decided to "publish the song against the advice of Winslow and Bornstein and let the public judge." Its success buoyed Berlin's confidence, and, though Ellin had returned from Europe only to be sent off to the West for the summer of 1925, his professional life seemed to revive when an opportunity presented itself to work on a genuine "book show." His collaborator would be George S. Kaufman, yet another of his Round Table friends and already recognized as one of the finest playwrights of his era, the comic counterpart to Eugene O'Neill. Kaufman approached playwriting with as businesslike an attitude as Irving Berlin approached songwriting. Although he once quipped, "Satire is what closes on Saturday night," Kaufman had a brilliant sense of the excesses and foibles of the Jazz Age.

The show he envisioned would send up one of decade's biggest fads, the Florida real-estate boom which reached its peak in 1925. In that year in Miami alone there were 2,000 real estate offices and more than 25,000 agents (or, as they preferred to be called in typical 1920s grandiosity, "realtors"). The city, which had grown from 30,000 residents in 1920 to 75,000, had to pass an ordinance forbidding the sale of property—even the showing of maps—in the street to try to stem congestion. Kaufman's satire targeted the wildest get-rich-quick-schemes that the most megalomaniacal American could want. The success of Coral Gables spawned other developments, some sunny and some shady, and people around the country wrote out their checks for unseen lots. Stories of fabulous profits abounded. Lots that cost $800 in 1920 were selling for $150,000 in 1924. People began to buy land solely with the notion of reselling it at such enormous profits, but by early 1926 the bubble began to burst. By that summer, people who had put all their money into "binders" on lots found they could not sell them and could not make the payments. Then in September a hurricane hit Florida and "piled the waters of Biscayne Bay into the lovely Venetian developments, deposited a five-masted schooner high in the street at Coral Gables, tossed big steam yachts upon the avenues of Miami, picked up trees, lumber, pipes, tiles, debris, and even small automobiles and sent them crashing into the houses."

The zaniness of the Florida boom made Kaufman's script a perfect vehicle for the Marx Brothers. Harpo Marx, also a member of the Algonquin group, solicited Berlin's help in persuading producer Sam Harris to use him and his brothers in the show. Berlin prevailed upon Harris who, with some trepidation, agreed to use the unpredictable foursome in *The Cocoanuts*. The Marx Brothers ensured the success of the show, but at the expense of Berlin's songs and Kaufman's script. Groucho, Harpo, Chico, and Zeppo threw in their own routines, ad-libbed lines, and treated songs as "throwaway" comic material. "I never knew that musical comedy was so difficult to produce," Irving Berlin said, "until we began working with the Marx Brothers on *The Cocoanuts*":

> When we started to rehearse we had our plan well-formulated. But 'ere long suggestions began to come in from the Marx Brothers, from Kaufman, from Harris—in fact, from everybody—and before we knew what had happened the general scheme of things had been turned topsy turvy. My well laid score was opened up and I wrote new songs, new lyrics and eventually we had an entirely different production than had been planned.

When the show ran long in rehearsals and out-of-town tryouts, Kaufman had to cut his script and Irving had to drop songs. But when the show opened in December 1925, the Marx brothers convulsed audiences with their comic shtick. Groucho at one point tries to bamboozle Chico into buying real estate at an auction. "I know an auction," Chico pipes up, "I come from Italy on the Atlantic auction." When Groucho shows him a map of a development with levees, Chico says he knows a family of "Levys," but when Groucho points out a "viaduct," Chico is stymied. "Why a duck?" he demands and the two are off on another verbal rollercoaster. How could mere songs follow an act like that?

The only Berlin song that might have become a hit from *The Cocoanuts* had been cut from the score early in the "doctoring" process. It had supposedly started out as a syncopated waltz for a young woman named Mona, who was the girlfriend of Berlin's musical secretary at the time, Arthur Johnston. One day, so the story goes, she asked Berlin and Johnston to write a song about her. Berlin hummed a melody, Johnston jotted it down, then Berlin

The Marx Brothers (*clockwise:* Groucho, Harpo, Chico, and Zeppo) in *The Cocoanuts*.

added a lyric that began, "I'll be loving you, Mona." The story is probably apocryphal, reminiscent of the legend that George Gershwin had a private song that he used to impress whatever young lady he happened to be interested in at the time; the lyric was designed to allow the insertion of any girl's name to convince her that she had inspired Gershwin's spontaneous flight of creative fancy. The punch-line to the Berlin story is that, while working on

the score for *The Cocoanuts*, he took out "Mona" and changed her
two-syllable name to "Always." Whatever the song's genesis, its construction is a subtle variation of the standard thirty-two bar AABA
chorus. The first three sections start off with the same syncopated
waltz phrase but then each section goes a different melodic way to
create an unusual ABCD pattern. Berlin not only shifts melody but
even shifts keys. Each of these innovative variations, however,
returns to the title word, "Always" but always on a different pair of
notes. Only in the fourth and final section did Irving Berlin return
to the same two notes on "Always" that had concluded the initial
phrase of the chorus.

Such melodic invention Berlin dismissed as easy—"but not the
lyric," Berlin affirmed. "Off and on, I spent a year on it. If I'd hur-
ried, the melody would have been the same, but the words wouldn't
have been so plain and simple. That's what I aim at—always." Once
again, it was the "tag-line" of the lyric that bedeviled him. "I just
couldn't get the last three lines, so I ad-libbed—'Not for just an hour,
not for just a day, not for just a year—but always.' And there it was—
exactly what I wanted to say." Where the earlier sections had two or
even three rhymes (including the subtle *"Days may* not be fair
al*ways*), this last had none. Such simple artistry was lost on
Kaufman, who admittedly knew nothing about music. His cynical
wit, however, turned on the sentimental lyric. "'Always' was a long
time for romance," quipped Kaufman when Berlin demonstrated the
song for him. As someone who thought romantic love one of the silli-
est of cultural artifices, Kaufman suggested "the opening line might
be a little more in accord with reality—something like 'I'll be loving
you Thursday.'" Given Berlin's recent doubts about his creative powers, Kaufman's quip seemed probably twice as cutting, but he soon
had a better use for his waltz than as grist for the Marx Brothers
comic mill.

In September 1925, Ellin Mackay returned from the West; after
almost a year, her ardor for Berlin had not abated, and the two
resumed their courtship. As they did, they were caught up in a new
phenomenon, then called "ballyhoo," now, less poetically, "publicity"
or "media blitz." "Ballyhoo" was the result of the consolidation of
newspapers into national chains, such as the Scripps-Howard and
Hearst systems. Instead of newspapers developing local coverage
and features, the syndicate office in New York now provided their
chains "editorials, health talks, comic strips, sob-sister columns,
household hints, sports gossip, and Sunday features prepared for a
national audience and guaranteed to tickle the mass mind." This
consolidation helped solidify New York as the cultural center of
America and had people across the country delighting in Dorothy
Parker or Robert Benchley's latest quip at the Round Table.

Helped by the increase of national magazines with their large circulation and advertising revenues, as well as by radio broadcasting,
the newspaper chains began to play upon the national mind with a
series of riveting stories that for a time dominated the headlines. The
Scopes "Monkey Trial" in Dayton, Tennessee; Charles Lindbergh's
flight across the Atlantic; the athletic feats of Babe Ruth, Red
Grange, or Bobby Jones—these events were "hurled at one in huge
headlines, [the reader] waded through page after page of syndicated
discussion of it, heard about it on the radio, was reminded of it
again and again in the outpourings of publicity-seeking orators and
preachers, saw pictures of it in the Sunday papers and the movies,
and (unless one was a perverse individualist) enjoyed the sensation
of vibrating to the same chord which thrilled a vast populace."

The courtship of Ellin Mackay and Irving Berlin was fodder for
this new mass-media machine. Even before Ellin returned from
Europe, newspapers rumored they were engaged, and Broadway
shows featured skits of the lovelorn songwriter pining for his missing high-society beauty. The biggest ballyhoo, however, came on
January 4, 1926, when Ellin eloped and married Irving Berlin at
City Hall in a civil ceremony. The couple was dogged by reporters to
Berlin's apartment, from there to Penn Station, then to Atlantic City,
where they spent a tense few days, then back to New York, until they
sailed to Europe. During that week, they were besieged by reporters,
sometimes fifty at a time, who asked about their relations with
Clarence Mackay. *Variety* reported that Clarence Mackay had vowed
their marriage would only happen "over my dead body," and *The
New York Mirror* even invented an angry exchange between the telegraph magnate and his songwriter son-in-law.

The most poignant aspect of the marriage was one that did not
get to the newspapers. While Clarence Mackay's statement to the
press was simply that his daughter had married without his "knowledge or approval," he quietly took more forceful steps, cutting Ellin
out of his will (although he could not touch her substantial trust).
Irving Berlin's response was to take his ballad "Always" and dedicate it to his bride as a wedding present, signing over its copyright
so that the royalties would go to her. It was the sentiment, rather
than the royalties, that Berlin tendered in his lyric that envisioned
"caring each day more than the day before." "'Always' was a love
song I wrote because I had fallen in love," he said simply. What
Kaufman and other sophisticates dismissed as sentimentality, however, was Berlin's heartfelt musical and lyrical expression of his
marriage vow, and his life with Ellin would quickly displace his
intimacy with the Algonquin Round Table.

The Berlins spent nearly a year abroad, but the ballyhoo rekindled
when they returned. Reporters hounded them with rumors that

Mr. and Mrs. Irving Berlin in Atlantic City in 1927, still annoyed at the ballyhoo over their marriage.

Berlin planed to convert to Catholicism and that the whole marriage had been a publicity stunt to promote his songs. Berlin grew more testy under the pressure and Ellin more withdrawn, responses heightened by the fact Ellin was expecting a baby. When Mary Ellin Berlin was born on November 25, 1926, the frenzy of reporters reached its climax. As the couple left the hospital, reporters crowded around snapping flashbulbs and shouting questions. The Berlins were one of the first couples to be subjected to ballyhoo, but they soon learned that its saving grace was brevity—it could concentrate on only one headline story at a time. When other events grabbed the public's attention—the death of Valentino, the Dempsey-Tunney fight—the spotlight mercifully turned from Mr. and Mrs. Irving Berlin. Their other children were born without ballyhoo—Linda Louise on February 21, 1932 and Elizabeth Irving on June 16, 1936. A son, Irving Berlin, Jr., was born on December 1, 1928, only to die a few weeks later, on Christmas Day.

After nearly a year's absence from songwriting, Berlin returned to his craft. One evening late in December of 1926 he got a panicked phone call from the singer Belle Baker. Baker had introduced several of Berlin's songs in vaudeville over the years, but now she found herself in unfamiliar territory. She was starring in *Betsy*, a new musical by the young songwriting team of Richard Rodgers and Lorenz Hart. Even more than George and Ira Gershwin, Rodgers and Hart symbolized the emergence of the sophisticated song and the integrated Broadway musical. Steeped in Gilbert and Sullivan and the Princess Shows, Rodgers and Hart were at first dismissed by Broadway producers as "too collegiate." In 1925, however, a satiric revue called the *Garrick Gaieties* featured their songs, and one, "Manhattan," became a hit. Audiences loved Hart's clever rhymes from the opening, "We'll have Manh*attan*, the Bronx, and *Staten* Island too" to the closing, "The city's clamor can never *spoil* the charms of a boy and *goil*." A year later, a second *Garrick Gaieties* featured the even more pyrotechnic, "Mountain Greenery" where "God paints the sc*enery*" and "beans could get no *keener re*-ception in a *beanery*." Suddenly *Variety* magazine was hailing a "lyrical renaissance," overlooking Irving Berlin's twenty years of skillfully fusing words and music. Until Rodgers and Hart, *Variety* lamented, the "general run of musical comedies were stupidly worded" but "in the last two or three seasons, things have taken a change." *Variety* then quoted extensively from Hart's lyrics, openly comparing him to Gilbert, and also praised Ira Gershwin, Howard Dietz, and other new lyricists—but there was no mention of Irving Berlin.

As far as Belle Baker was concerned, however, the two wunderkinder had not given her one good song in *Betsy*. Following the Princess tradition, Rodgers and Hart had tried to integrate songs into the characters and dramatic context of the story. Their score bristled with rhymes like "Iskowitz . . . thiskowitz . . . joykowitz . . . hoi-polloikowitz . . . goykowitz," with a vocabulary seldom found in Tin Pan Alley songs—"het'rogenous," "panegyric," "afflatus," and "supernal." Belle Baker understandably felt out of her element, and even though Rodgers and Hart had written a rueful ballad for her called "This Funny World," Baker cried, "Irving, I'm opening in a show tomorrow night, and there isn't a 'Belle Baker' song in the score, and I'm so miserable. What can I do?"

"Belle, I'll be very honest with you," Berlin replied cautiously, knowing how much he resented interpolated songs by other composers in his own shows. "All I have is a song in my trunk. I've often thought it would be great for you, but I never got around to finishing it." Baker pleaded for him to bring the song over to her. "Even something half-finished by you is better than what I've got now, which is nothing," she said. Perhaps Berlin was flattered to hear his work praised in such terms over Broadway's latest "whiz kids," perhaps he wanted to do a friend a favor. In any case he took the song to Baker's apartment and, with her help and that of her husband,

Maury Abrahams, with whom Berlin had collaborated early in his career, he went to work on "Blue Skies," one of his most masterfully crafted songs and one he wrote to celebrate the birth of his first daughter.

His efforts reflect how subtly he could manipulate words and notes within the confines of the standard thirty-bar chorus. When he arrived at Baker's that evening, all he had was the first eight-bar segment of the chorus completed, but it was an auspicious beginning. The first two notes scaled the range of the five black keys. and Berlin matched that arching interval with a title phrase that progressed from a long open vowel in "Bl*ue*" to a long closed vowel in "Sk*ies*." Then, with a dash of syncopation, he wove those open and closed vowels through the first eight bars:

> Bl*ue* sk*ies* sm*i*ling at m*e*, nothing but bl*ue* sk*ies* do *I* s*ee*.

For the second eight-bar section of the chorus, he repeated that same melody but varied the lyric with a parallel image of "blue birds singing a song."

It was when Berlin got to the third section of this AABA song, the eight-bar "bridge" or "release," that the chemistry of genius and hard work coalesced. Because it had to introduce a new eight-bar melody and a lyric that acted as a fulcrum to lead back to the final eight-bar A-section, the bridge was usually the hardest part of a song to complete. For Berlin, the bridge to "Blue Skies" proved excruciatingly difficult, taking him, according to Max Wilk, the entire night. He may have recalled some phrases from the verse to "Always," such as "the whole day through I'd feel so blue," "time will fly," and "now that my blue days have past." If so, these remembered shards reworked themselves into his bridge and final eight-bar A-section. Finally, at six in the morning he had it.

> Never saw the sun shining so bright.
> Never saw things going so right,
> Noticing the days hurrying by,
> When you're in love, my!
> How they fly.

One of his most brilliant bridges, this eight-bar strain brings out the latent sadness of the song, sounded in the minor key beginning of each of the A-sections and hidden in the underside of the meaning of "blue." Here, those grayer meanings emerge with the preponderance of negative terms—"nothing," "nothing," "never," "never"— even the neutral "noticing" seems negative with its initial syllable.

The emphasis on participles—"shining," "going," "noticing"—draws "nothing" into its orbit and hints that the singer's present happiness may only be fleeting, as does the melancholy chromatic note on the word "shining." The note of mutability, at the song's emotional pivot, turns the joyous "blue" of "blue skies" and "blue birds" into the "blue" of the blues as the bridge turns into the final A-section:

> Blue days—all of them gone—nothing but blue skies from
> now on.

Unlike "blue skies" and "blue birds," these last "blue days" are the departed days of sadness, but the preceding recognition that "when you're in love" the days go "hurrying by" also hints that despondent times can return. While the song ends on a note of affirmation, the lingering rhyme on "gone" underscores that melancholy awareness.

"Blue Skies" was indeed an extraordinary song, the work of a craftsman, who unlike the young Rodgers and Hart, disguised his intricate artistry under a veneer of utter simplicity. The seasoned star Belle Baker knew what a gem Berlin had crafted for her and immediately went to the producer of *Betsy*, Florenz Ziegfeld, who could also discern a great song when he heard it. While Ziegfeld continued to mount his annual *Follies*, he was a shrewd enough showman to see that integrated musical comedy was becoming the order of the day. He also saw that *Betsy*, despite the talents of Rodgers and Hart, had its problems. Though he knew an interpolation would infuriate the young songwriters, he agreed to let Belle Baker sing "Blue Skies" on opening night, December 28, 1926. The audience, too, knew a good song and applauded until Baker had to sing encore after encore. Overwhelmed by the response, Baker blanked on the last encore, and Berlin himself, in a throwback to his singing stooge days at Tony Pastor's, rose from the audience to help her out with the lyric. The only unhappy members of the audience were Rodgers and Hart. Outraged by the surprise interpolation, they felt the failure of their score all the more acutely against the reception for Berlin's "Blue Skies," a song that, as Rodgers himself admitted later, was simply better than any song they were capable of creating at that point in their career.

While Berlin had his moment of triumph with "Blue Skies," however, the future of American musical theater lay with songwriters like Rodgers and Hart. In the next year, 1927, Broadway saw its greatest array of shows yet. Rodgers and Hart took Mark Twain's *A Connecticut Yankee in King Arthur's Court* and turned it into a witty musical with such clever songs as "Thou Swell" and such moving ones as "My Heart Stood Still." George and Ira Gershwin had anoth-

Irving Berlin at the piano surrounded by Eddie Cantor, Florenz Ziegfeld, dance director Sammy Lee, and the chorus girls from the *Ziegfeld Follies of 1927.*

er hit musical with Fred and Adele Astaire in *Funny Face*, then
broke new ground with a political satire by George S. Kaufman
called *Strike Up the Band*.

The greatest triumph, however, was Jerome Kern and Oscar
Hammerstein's *Show Boat*, which transformed European operetta
into an American setting. In Edna Ferber's novel, Hammerstein
found a story of racial conflict that approximated the class conflict
that usually complicated romance between a prince and a commoner in European operetta. Adapting the novel into his own musical
script, he deftly wove songs into Ferber's story and characters. From
the opening curtain, where blacks work along the Mississippi "while
the white folks play," the story introduces the carefree gambler
Gaylord Ravenal who sings of drifting along as fancifully as the
river, while the black Joe voices a contrasting sentiment of stoic resignation in "Ol' Man River." In the same sequence he counterpoints
"Make Believe," which Gaylord and the youthful Magnolia sing
when they fall in love at first sight, with the fatalistic "Can't Help
Lovin' Dat Man" that the seasoned Julie intones. That song, in turn,
actually advances the plot, for it is described as a "colored" song and
is the first hint that Julie herself is part black.

Such intricate weaving between song and story marked a major advance in American musical theater, an experiment made possible by the prosperity of the era and one that would be halted by the Depression, only to resume again in the 1940s with Rodgers and Hammerstein's *Oklahoma!* Surprisingly, *Show Boat* was also produced by Florenz Ziegfeld, another sign that the impresario knew when the public was ready for such serious themes as racism and tragedy on the American musical stage.

Amid all of this innovation and experiment, however, Ziegfeld still produced his 1927 *Follies*, and it was for this fading enterprise that he commissioned Irving Berlin to do the songs (the first time he relied upon a single composer for the entire score of his revue). Neither songs nor show were successful, despite the presence of Eddie Cantor as the star and a young singer from Chicago, Ruth Etting, who did an electrifying shimmy to "Shaking the Blues Away." Irving Berlin, as a result, was relegated even further to the margins of American musical theater in its most bounteous season of plenty. Nonetheless, in this same year, Berlin would find "Blue Skies" at the very center of a different but equally significant development in popular music that would help sustain him for the rest of his career.

Chapter 7

THE SONG IS ENDED

You do it piece by piece by piece. You go into a projec-
tion room, and you'll see what they call the rushes of
the day. It becomes a bit monotonous and boring. And
then, when you see the first rough cut, then you out-
and-out wish you hadn't done this. A lot of the things
that you liked wind up on the cutting room floor.

In 1889, when Irving Berlin was barely a year old, Thomas Alva
Edison invented the Kinetoscope, a machine that could show
motion pictures. When he connected it to the phonograph, which he
had invented a decade earlier, sound and film were wed. At the
Paris Exhibition of 1900, his Kinetophone displayed Sarah Bernhardt and other luminaries on a hand-cranked projector while their
voices were reproduced—talking and singing—by wax cylinder
recordings. It would not be until the late-1920s, however, that "talking pictures" were a commercial reality. The two fundamental problems were amplification of sound and synchronization between
sound and image:

> The big horns over which the recordings were played
> were insufficiently audible, and there was the intractabil-
> ity of coordinating the film projector with the phono-
> graph, both machines with peculiar concepts of speed
> and consistency. Anything less than perfect synchroniza-
> tion, even a hair's-breadth separation between picture
> and sound, could be magnified many times in just a few
> seconds. And was.

While sound and film waited to be wed, they carried on a more distant relationship.

Music had always been present in film theaters, from a single
piano or organ in small-town nickelodeons to the full orchestras of
New York's movie palaces. In his early days as a street busker, as
we saw, Irving Berlin had sung for the "song slide" intermissions
between reel changes of silent films. Among his many innovations,
director D. W. Griffith commissioned the first musical score to be
composed specifically for a film, his 1915 production of *The Birth of
a Nation*, thus adding an entirely new member to the team of film-
makers, the "film scorer," whose craft, until the age of computers,
required sitting before a screen with a stopwatch and composing
discrete musical segments to fit every scene in a film. By the 1920s,
movie "theme" songs, usually based on the title of the film, were
included on the score that was played in movie houses to accompany
the films, helping make both song and the otherwise–silent film a
success. In 1926, when Dolores Del Rio warbled the title song for
Ramona on a coast-to-coast radio broadcast before the movie's premiere, it galvanized both record and ticket sales.

In the mid-1920s, Bell Telephone Laboratories improved Edison's
system by connecting a projector and phonograph with a belt that
kept sound and image in synchronization. At the same time, Lee
DeForest developed Phonofilm, a process that actually put a sound
track on the film itself. At first, the studios were not interested in
either device, but one, Warner Brothers, saw possibilities in the Bell
system, which they purchased and dubbed "Vitaphone." Warner
Brothers had long been a poor cousin to big studios like MGM and
Paramount. Its biggest star was Rin-Tin-Tin, and it was notorious for
the parsimony of its owner/brothers, Sam, Jack, and Harry. The
brothers were also known for shrewdness, however, and they had
been among the first to realize the impact of radio. Knowing audiences would tune in for "free" music, they bought KFWB Los
Angeles in 1925 and plugged their films on the air.

The Warner brothers did not, however, envision film musicals,
songs sung from the screen, or even talking pictures. As one of the
brothers, according to legend, put it, "Nobody wants to pay money
to hear actors talk." What they wanted from their new Vitaphone
process was a sound track recording that would accompany their
films and allow even small-town movie houses to regale their audiences with full orchestral background music. About the farthest
beyond that the Warner brothers could imagine was the filming of
vaudeville acts in sound "shorts" to be shown between reels in movie
houses. It would take a great song by Irving Berlin—and a great performance of it by Al Jolson—to consummate the marriage of song
and film.

To launch its new Vitaphone device, Warner Brothers commissioned the New York Philharmonic to record the score for its new silent film, *Don Juan*, starring John Barrymore. As a prelude to the film, Warners put together a program of operatic and concert numbers to demonstrate the Vitaphone process in all its glory (as well as its limitations, most notably that the presence of the microphone in the studio meant that the camera had to be put in a soundproof box to conceal its whir, rendering motion pictures virtually immobile). At the premiere on Broadway on August 6, 1926, it was this sound prelude that stole the show from *Don Juan*. In particular, as film historian Richard Barrios points out, it was opera star Giovanni Martinelli's rendition of an aria from *Pagliacci* that demonstrated the power of song emanating dramatically from the screen:

> The laugh-clown-laugh aria was ideal material for his ringing tenor, his exceptional breath control enabling him to take the piece at a slow tempo in extremely long phrases, extracting the maximum amount of pathos through good musicianship and communicating it directly to the audience. The flat one shot/one camera format could not deter his stunning impact, and this single, three-and-a-half minute performance was crucial to the successful entry of sound film.

As Al Jolson might have told the assembled audience, however, "You ain't seen nothing yet."

Nineteen-twenties ballyhoo focused on the new phenomenon as the "greatest sensation of the decade—next to radio." These responses prompted theaters to install sound equipment and inspired Warner Brothers to go a little further with their new process. In addition to making more Vitaphone "shorts," featuring vaudeville stars, they decided to include a few songs within their next major silent movie. However, this decision brought them up against a problem that would plague all films with songs in them. Put in its simplest terms, how do you "include" a song in a film? By its very nature, film is a realistic medium. What could realistically account for characters suddenly switching from talking to singing—and back again? In opera, the least realistic of theatrical genres, audiences must accept, among its many other conventions, that everything—even the most mundane conversation—is sung. In operetta and musical comedy, there is the more easily accepted convention that at certain dramatic points conversation turns to song, and the customary applause afterwards eases the transition back to spoken dialogue. But in a film, what could possibly justify having a character suddenly burst into song and then—without even the cushion of applause—just as abruptly resume talking?

The solution Warner Brothers and other studios struck upon—
and maintained throughout the history of film musicals—was to
make movies about singers. That way, actors sang because they were
playing the role of singers; songs were done as "performances,"
rehearsals, or simply because singers "naturally" burst into song—
even in the rain. From Broadway hoofers hammering out numbers
for opening night in *Broadway Melody* or *42nd Street* to Mickey
Rooney and Judy Garland inspired to "put on a show" with the
neighborhood kids, the Hollywood musical, from its very inception,
was tied to the idea of song as performance.

The Jazz Singer—the story of a cantor's son who breaks his
father's heart by using his talent in show business rather than the
synagogue—was thus a logical choice for including songs within a
silent film. It had been a successful play on Broadway, and its star,
George Jessel, had performed in a Vitaphone short. When contract
negotiations broke down with Jessel (who wanted to tour with the
stage version of *The Jazz Singer*), Warners turned to Al Jolson, another Vitaphone star, who was a far more engaging performer than
Jessel. While *The Jazz Singer* was a silent film, Jolson would sing six
songs on the Vitaphone sound track, each synchronized to his image
on screen. The six songs were all staples in the Jolson repertory—
such as "Yes Sir, That's My Baby"—and one, "When I Lost You," was
to be a Berlin song.

Incorporating established hits into films was an outgrowth of the
decision to present songs as performances. When actors played the
part of singers, what they sang, "naturally," would be popular songs
of the day. These songs, moreover, need have no relation whatsoever
to the characters or story of the film. Although such "ease" in pre-
senting songs would soon present major artistic problems for musical films, initially Hollywood producers saw it as a commercial
windfall, because a song that had already proved itself popular could
help boost the movie where it was performed.

As plans developed for *The Jazz Singer*, it was decided that a more
recent Berlin hit, "Blue Skies," would be used in the scene where
Jolson, having run away from home as a boy to pursue his career in
show business, returns, flushed with his Broadway success, to see
his mother. The scene, like so much of the story, evoked Berlin's
own rise to success as the son of a cantor, and Jolson's promise to
move his mother out of her tenement and into a fancy new apartment in the Bronx was actually fulfilled by Berlin for his own mother. The choice of "Blue Skies" was also dramatically apt; while
Jolson sings it to his mother as a "performance," to demonstrate the
kind of song he sings on Broadway, the lyric clearly expresses the
bittersweet happiness of their reunion.

Al Jolson sings "Blue Skies" to his screen mother, Eugenie Besserer, as his irate
father, played by Warner Oland, stops the music in the 1927 film *The Jazz Singer*.

Jolson's rendition of "Blue Skies" is now part of the annals of film
history: this single performance vividly revealed what tremendous
power a song could have when it emanated from the screen. The fact
that it emerged from a silent film made that power even more dramatically clear. As the title cards have Jolson telling his mother—
played by Eugenie Besserer—he will show her how he sings his
songs on the stage, the saccharine background music stops and, as
Jolson steps to the piano, we hear real sound. Suddenly, it becomes
clear that a song in film is utterly different from a song on stage.
Jolson's performance, for all its vaudeville bravado, is not aimed at a
theater audience but at a single person, his mother, and with close-
up camera work, the song between two people has an intimacy no
stage performance could rival.

What was even more extraordinary was what happened after he
sang "Blue Skies." According to Hollywood legend, Jolson started
ad-libbing dialogue about how he was going to buy his mother a
pink dress to impress "the Goldbergs and all the other bergs," take

her to Coney Island, and, raising Freudian shivers, kiss her in the Tunnel of Love. There is evidence that some dialogue had been planned for the song sequences in *The Jazz Singer* and that these would be left to Jolson to improvise, given his stage fright when called upon to "act" rather than sing. However, the terrified expression on Eugenie Besserer's face as Jolson rambles on, and her own lack of any dialogue, make the moment seem utterly spontaneous. In either case, she was the first screen personage cast in the unenviable position of having to react to someone singing—and talking—a song to her. When Jolson then reprises "Blue Skies" in a jazzier version, the historic demonstration that song and dialogue could be seamlessly meshed was completed. After the song, Jolson's screen father, the old cantor played by Warner Oland (later of *Charlie Chan* fame), bursts into the room and, as the title card flashes his screamed "Stop!," *The Jazz Singer* reverts to a silent film. But after hearing Al Jolson sing his way through a great Berlin song on screen, audiences would never again settle for silent films.

Apart from the "Blue Skies" number and a few of the other songs, however, *The Jazz Singer* was a creaky tearjerker. Jolson was a singer, not an actor, and his voice and mannerisms, while superb for the stage, seemed overblown in the realistic and intimate medium of film. The presence of songs in film, always dangerously intrusive, seemed even more so in a silent film, particularly one with a melodramatic and sentimental story. It would be years before song found its true voice in the witty, casual films of Fred Astaire and Ginger Rogers, most notably in their 1935 hit *Top Hat*, featuring Irving Berlin's first great film score. Until then, "talkies"—and Irving Berlin—would have to suffer years of growing pains. Some of these pains were technological ones that, as Gerald Mast explains, centered on the problem of obtaining a "satisfactory simultaneous direct recording of image and sound on the set":

> Early microphones were large and insensitive (so speakers sat or stood very close to the bush or canister where it had been buried). There were no sound mixers to permit the use of two recording microphones (so actors huddled together to speak into the same bush or canister). There was no boom (so actors could not simultaneously walk and talk). And the noisy camera had to be encased in a soundproof booth with a single glass window to view the set (restricting both camera movement and character movement). Oddly imbalanced and meaningless compositions, based on the maximum number of persons who would eventually enter the frame, were very common in early sound films. . . . Musicals were even

more cramped by these restrictions than other films. To record a musical number, the entire orchestra trekked to the sound stage, where performers sang directly into the recording microphone, during filming, backed by the musicians in their off-frame "pit."

In addition to surmounting these technical difficulties, musicals would have to develop new artistic conventions that transcended the premise that songs must be presented as performances by characters playing the part of singers. What that meant was that songs did not grow out of the story, as they do in opera, operetta, and, after the 1920s, musical comedy, where characters sing to express what they feel at a particular moment. Such dramatic occasions lend "particularity" to a song's music and lyrics, and explain why songs for musical theater are generally superior to those written for Tin Pan Alley.

Yet it was precisely such simple fare that studio heads wanted, and to get it they literally bought out Tin Pan Alley itself. When the Warner Brothers saw that the royalties for songs for Jolson's next film, *Sonny Boy*, which truly was "a "talkie," went to the songwriters and the music publishers, they simply bought out one of Tin Pan Alley's biggest publishers, Witmark's, and acquired the rights to all their catalogue of songs as well as the services of their composers, lyricists, and arrangers. MGM did the same with the Robbins Company, and other studios devoured other music publishers. By 1929, almost all popular songs were emanating from Hollywood rather than Tin Pan Alley. In an article entitled, "Westward the Course of Tin Pan Alley," a new magazine, *Photoplay*, "detailed the exodus":

> By the middle of 1929 songwriters had replaced the sound men as the most conspicuous new presence at the studios. Few of the best or busiest tunesmiths were able to resist the call and the money, and the result was an immense quantity of songs emanating from Hollywood in the first two years of talkies.

Irving Berlin alone held out against the ravenous studios, and Irving Berlin Music remained the last of the independent Tin Pan Alley music publishers. Recognizing the westward course of the popular music industry, however, Berlin did open a Hollywood office for his firm in the late 1920s.

On the one hand, Hollywood's appetite for songs was a blessing for songwriters like Irving Berlin, who had mastered the formulas of Tin Pan Alley. Supplying simple songs for performance numbers in movie musicals was easier than trying to keep up with experiments in musical theater, such as *Show Boat*, that increasingly called for "integration" between song and story. Hollywood, however, frequently stifled songwriters' creativity. Instead of trying to develop a wholly new kind of song, one specifically tailored to the medium of film, studios wanted songwriters to turn out, almost by the yard, formulaic love songs that would satisfy the public's fascination with "all-talking, all-singing, all-dancing" spectaculars. "In their crassest manifestations," according to Richard Barrios, "the studios became ditty factories where style and substance were tertiary considerations." This crassness was most blatant when Hollywood studios made film versions of Broadway shows, such as *No! No! Nanette!* for which they did not own the musical rights. In this case, they jettisoned the very songs that had made the show a stage success. Instead, they would hire their newly acquired composers and lyricists to write new scores so that the studios captured the royalties. Irving Berlin was nearly implicated in what would have been the greatest such travesty: a film version of *Show Boat* without "Ol' Man River," "Can't Help Lovin' Dat Man," and other songs from Kern and Hammerstein's score! Universal Studios had the film rights to Edna Ferber's novel and, rather than have to bargain with Ziegfeld over using the score to the stage musical, announced that Irving Berlin would write a theme song and possibly a special score for *Show Boat*. Fortunately, the Kern and Hammerstein songs soon became so popular that a film version of *Show Boat* without them was unimaginable—even to the studio heads.

Irving Berlin was one of the first songwriters who made the transition from Broadway to Hollywood. The last Broadway show he even considered writing in the 1920s was a musical called *Paris* that was proffered to him by his former brother-in-law, Ray Goetz. Goetz wanted Berlin to write the score for a vehicle for his wife, the French star Irene Bordoni, but Berlin recommended another songwriter for the cosmopolitan enterprise—Cole Porter. "You can find him in Venice," he told Goetz. Although Porter, born in 1891, was nearly Berlin's age, he had tried unsuccessfully to break into songwriting for many years. Born into a wealthy Midwestern family, educated at Yale and Harvard, Porter had written songs that had long been dismissed as too sophisticated for Broadway. The lyrical renaissance sparked by Rodgers and Hart and the Gershwins, however, paved the way for Porter, and in 1928, he finally found a success with *Paris*. The big hit from that show was "Let's Do It," a jazzy, risqué version of a Gilbert and Sullivan catalog song that listed all the creatures that did "it," from shocking "electric eels" to goldfish "in the privacy of bowls." Despite their difference in background and song style, Irving Berlin and Cole Porter became admiring friends, the only major songwriters of their day who wrote both their own words and music. When Porter scored another triumph with *Fifty Million Frenchmen*, Irving Berlin paid for a newspaper ad that extolled the show as "the best musical comedy I have seen in years" and added "It is worth the price of admission to hear Cole Porter's lyrics." With that tribute to the new generation of literate sophistication on Broadway, Irving Berlin turned his talent for brilliant simplicity to Hollywood.

Berlin's old friend from Bowery days, Joseph Schenck, was now a major force in Hollywood at United Artists, the studio started by some of Hollywood's greatest silent film stars. That association, however, was a mixed blessing. Because Schenck was wary of the new wave of talkies, Berlin's film projects were, for a songwriter who had always been at the forefront of his craft, mired in the past. When Samuel Goldwyn wanted to feature one of his new stars in a 1928 film called *The Awakening*, he called upon Irving Berlin to supply words and music. Berlin came up with a formulaic girl's-name number, "Marie," a throwback to his very first song, "Marie from Sunny Italy." *The Awakening* proved unsuccessful as a film—despite the direction of Victor Fleming, who would go on to direct *Gone With the Wind*—and "Marie" went unnoticed until Tommy Dorsey, a decade later, revived it and turned it into one of the classics of the swing era. The first film for which Berlin wrote a theme song, *Coquette*, marked the talking picture debut of the great silent screen star, Mary Pickford. At its New York premiere on April 5, 1929, the amplifier fuses blew during the opening credits and, the dialogue—and Berlin's song—were barely audible. Although Pickford went on to win an Academy Award for her performance, *Coquette* was not a success nor was Berlin's theme song, despite the presence of Pickford's face on the sheet music cover.

What made writing songs for Hollywood films especially frustrating, not only for Berlin but for the Gershwins, Cole Porter, and other theater songwriters, was their relative lack of involvement in the production. On Broadway, songwriters were in on a show from the beginning, working closely with dramatists, directors, choreographers, performers, and even technicians. In Hollywood, however, songwriters were often just told to write songs, sometimes without even seeing a script. Berlin had little involvement with these early films where his songs were used, and in fact spent most of his time in New York rather than Hollywood. That lack of involvement was particularly unfortunate in the first film for which Berlin actually supplied a full song score, the filmed version of *The Cocoanuts*. Once again, the Marx Brothers dominated the show—and Berlin's songs— when the very absurdity of the comedians' antics might have helped ease the transition from realism into song. In later Marx Brothers films, having Groucho burst into song seems no more illogical than

Chico's puns or Harpo's pantomimes, but in *The Cocoanuts* songs stood out oddly from the rest of the film. Berlin had written three new songs for the film, but the most-featured number, "When My Dreams Come True," cast in the ultra-simplified style Hollywood demanded, seemed particularly out of place. Its old-fashioned melody and lyric sounded quaint against the up-to-date dadaism of the Marx Brothers, and critics pointed out how far it fell from Berlin's own normally high standards of songwriting.

Equally out of place, though in a different way, were songs Berlin wrote for *Hallelujah*, one of the first black musical films. It might seem strange that major studios would make feature films about blacks, given the prejudices of the time. To be sure, the 1920s had seen the "Harlem Renaissance," when white Americans began to take note of black writers, painters, and, most of all, jazz artists like Louis Armstrong, Bessie Smith, and Duke Ellington. That renaissance even at the time, however, was dismissed by some blacks as a brief period "When the Negro Was in Vogue," and certainly could not in itself prompt Hollywood studios to make musical films aimed at white audiences, using black casts. With the advent of sound, however, a door opened, if ever so slightly, for black musicals. Ironically, it was because of the prejudicial view that blacks were more spontaneous and rhythmic than whites that made it seem more realistic to have black characters suddenly burst into song and dance without the excuse that they were playing the roles of professional singers who rendered songs as performances. While a normal white American could not suddenly switch from talking to singing, blacks, or so studios reasoned, might naturally do so.

The first black musical film was *Hearts in Dixie*, which relied exclusively upon the spirituals that had become so popular during the Harlem Renaissance. The spirituals were sung, for the most part, by an off-camera choir, as a background to dialogue and action, and nowhere in the film did any of the principal characters break into song. Irving Berlin, however, was the first songwriter called upon to supply original songs for a black musical film, *Hallelujah*. Its director, King Vidor, a Texan who had deeply admired black culture as a child, approached Joe Schenck with the idea of making a musical film about black rural life. MGM resisted the proposal, saying such a film would lose money because many theaters—not only in the South—would refuse to show it. But when Vidor offered to waive his director's fee, Schenck gave his go ahead, but placated MGM by having his old friend Irving Berlin supply some of the songs for *Hallelujah*.

Berlin's contributions were a mixed blessing for *Hallelujah*. He was called upon to write numbers that sounded like folk songs and would fit into a score that included spirituals, work chants, and even

Nina Mae McKinney performs Irving Berlin's "Swanee Shuffle" as co-star Daniel L. Haynes looks on in wonder in King Vidor's all-black musical *Hallelujah* (1929).

Stephen Foster songs . A song like "Swanee Shuffle" could sound perfectly authentic as a performance song in a rural black night club, though some of the deft rhyming sounded less than "folksy." "Waiting at the End of the Road," however, was just too polished a song to fit into the score. With its artful AABA structure that slickly modulates from release back to the main melody, it seems the hero should be serenading a Cotton Club audience rather than singing as he delivers a wagon load of cotton to market. The sophistication of the song is even more glaringly apparent later in the film when it is reprised as a revival meeting song that calls sinners to Jesus who, in an altered lyric, is now "Waiting at the End of the Road."

These experiences in early musical films made Berlin, with his rigorous perfectionism, determined to involve himself more fully with the overall creation of a film, rather than take the piecework assignments that other songwriters accepted. Given his enormous stature—and the fact that he owned his own songs—he could insist that studios purchase not only his songs but his ideas for the story in which they were to be used. Berlin actually wrote extensive treatments (plot summaries without dialogue, showing where his songs were to be worked into the story). As an artist, this helped him ensure that his songs would fit into the texture of the film; and the businessman in him knew that studios would have to pay him more if he made them buy both script and songs.

Berlin developed the story idea for *Mammy*, a 1930 film that portrayed Al Jolson as part of a touring minstrel show. For several years he had been working on a stage musical about a minstrel troupe. Perhaps inspired by the success of *Show Boat, Mr. Bones* was to be a vehicle for Al Jolson, but with the shift of musical activity from Broadway to Hollywood Berlin transformed his project into a film. Film musicals about performing troupes, such as MGM's 1929 *Broadway Melody*, provided all the excuse needed for having characters break into song as they created, rehearsed, and, always at the end of the film, put on their show. But this kind of musical, dubbed the "backstager," had already begun to wear thin. *Mammy*, despite its title and Jolson's presence, was "one of the more creative backstagers," which, from its opening scene of a minstrel parade during a rainstorm, gave a "convincing and energetic simulation of the one-night stands and transience that constituted minstrel life." Berlin provided Jolson with a signature song, "Let Me Sing and I'm Happy," which captured his blackface stage persona as a minstrel who sings of "cotton fields" and "Mammy's arms" not out of his own experience but as an expression of his country's history. In a very different song, "Across the Breakfast Table," Berlin drew upon the screen's power to render a song more intimately and informally than stage performance ever could, a power first registered in the "Blue Skies" scene of *The Jazz Singer*. In *Mammy*, Jolson quietly and dramatically sings to his beloved of the simple joys of domestic bliss, "Across the breakfast table, looking at you." The song comes across not as a performance but an expression of the character's feelings at a particular moment in the story. Despite these innovations, critics and audiences wrote the film off as a creaky remake of Jolson's previous backstagers, and *Mammy* was the first of Jolson's films to lose money. That loss was particularly telling because Warner Brothers had poured an enormous amount of money into the film; Jolson's salary alone was bigger than the budget of most films.

For his next film, Berlin involved himself fully in the production, again writing not only the songs but the script for *Say It With Music*. It would be filmed in New York, so Berlin could be in close contact with the filming. Indeed, Berlin was so heavily involved in the day-to-day making of the film that he assumed something like the role of producer, as he had for his *Music Box Revues*, even to soothing relations between the brash nightclub star, Harry Richman, and his teenaged costar, Joan Bennett. Still, Berlin had far less control than he had in stage productions, and the film was beset with problems that delayed production for more than a year. Berlin's original script for a musical that would trace the evolution of American popular song was replaced with a tired backstager about a singer whose success goes to his head as he spurns his true love and turns to drink, finally going blind from bad bootleg liquor. Plans to film in New York were scrapped, and the picture was done in Hollywood. Still, Berlin had enough stake in its quality that he moved his family to a house on the West Coast so that he could be on the set each day.

Despite his efforts, the film, whose title changed from *Tin Pan Alley* to *The Song of Broadway* to *Broadway Vagabond* and, finally, *Puttin' on the Ritz*, exemplified everything that was wrong with early backstage musicals. It opens, as did *Broadway Melody*, in a Tin Pan Alley publishing office where Harry Richman and other singers and pianists are plugging songs for vaudeville performers looking for new material. The first song played and reprised is not even by Irving Berlin, but a recent hit of the previous year, "I'll Get By," inserted simply because of its current popularity. Richman the song plugger then meets Bennett the neophyte composer and finds, miraculously, that words he has written to another song will fit her inspired melody. Their song, "With You," is Berlin's but one of his lesser creations, fittingly characterized by Richman, when he first hears Bennett's melody, with the crack, "They stopped writing songs like this twenty years ago." Even after he "jazzes it up," however, the song cloys as it is endlessly reprised through the film, with its "With you . . . Without you . . ." formulaic lyric.

Other faults of early musicals are present as well. Harry Richman was captivating on stage but, like Jolson, too brash and histrionic for the more intimate medium of film. Conversely, Joan Bennett, while lovely and understated on screen, lacks the power to put over a song and dance. *Puttin' on the Ritz* also follows *Broadway Melody* and all its other imitators in including a special fantasy sequence shot in primitive technicolor. A filmed remake of the "Alice in Wonderland" number from Berlin's fourth *Music Box Revue*, it consists of little more than Joan Bennett becoming a Broadway star merely by walking among dancers costumed as characters from the Lewis Carroll classic.

Even the big production number for "Puttin' on the Ritz" has Richman and dozens of dancers (one very noticeably out of step) cavorting across the stage, gesticulating wildly, but coming off as very stagey and even static. In yet another imitation of *Broadway Melody*, the backdrop for the number is the Manhattan skyline and, at the conclusion, the skyscrapers turn out to be inhabited by dancers who clumsily sway to the music. Finally, all of the technical limitations of early sound film are glaringly apparent. Because the camera was immobilized (its noisy operation muffled by encasing it in a booth), the dancers must move back-and-forth before the lens in boring waves. On the other hand, because the microphone was also immobile, Richman must stay planted at dead center stage to sing the song, ironically separating song and dance in a number that calls for their joyous integration.

And yet, despite all of its flaws, the title song, one of Irving Berlin's greatest, reaffirmed the extraordinary possibilities of song in film with an intricate interplay between words and music. "Puttin' on the Ritz" carries the principle of ragging words against music to the furthest possible extreme, so distorting verbal accents against musical ones that the lyric comes out as Gertrude Steinese or a jazzy idiom that might be dubbed "Berlintz":

> *Spang*led *gowns* up*on* a bevy
> *of* high *browns* from *down* the *le*vee,
> *all* mis*fits*—*put*tin' on the *ritz*.

What the lyric describes—Harlem blacks parading in elegant finery (a black version, musically and lyrically, of "Easter Parade")—it also mimics in its own clever misfits of rhythmic and verbal accents.

Equally discordant is the mix of diction, as Berlin sets slang and elegant terms side by side—as in "swell beaux" and "rubbing elbows"—or weaves them throughout the lyric:

> Come with me and we'll attend their jubilee
> and see them spend their last two bits
> puttin' on the ritz.

To his credit, Richman, wooden in his melodramatic scenes, rises to this occasion and radiates the verve that made him a top night-club performer.

While mildly successful, *Puttin' on the Ritz*, like *Mammy*, did not justify the enormous expense it took to mount. Moreover, it exacerbated the public's growing antipathy to the limiting conventions of film musicals, primarily the premise that songs must be presented as performances. In March of 1930, *Billboard* ran an editorial, under the title "Backstage Stories Bane to Exhibitors," that lamented the fact that "ever since talking pictures found voice enough to sing and to record a rat-tat-tat of tap dancers on a hard-wood floor these backstage stories have been done and re-done ad nauseam." Small-town theater owners were particularly fed up with musicals because they were required to book blocks of films from distributors and sometimes wound up showing a different film each night, with the possibility of two or three being backstager musicals. By July *Variety*

Harry Richman and chorus girls perform Irving Berlin's title song in the 1929 film *Puttin' on the Ritz*.

was reporting that customers at theater ticket counters were asking "Is it a musical?" If so, they were walking away. By late August, *Billboard* ran a headline "MUSICAL FILMS ARE TABOO." In less than three scant years, the vistas opened by Jolson singing "Blue Skies" were closing.

Adding to the disenchantment with musicals, particularly those that presented songs as giddy effusions of joy, was that the Roaring Twenties had come crashing down with the stock market in October of 1929. A decade that had lived on ballyhoo now had its biggest story, which *Variety* emblazoned in the headline, "WALL ST. LAYS AN EGG." Berlin learned of the Crash while he was working on *Puttin' on the Ritz* in Hollywood, and he, like others, lost millions of dollars due to the unregulated buying on margin, which allowed investors to buy more stock on the basis of the supposed increase in the value of their current stocks.

Fortunately, Berlin still had something worth far more than stocks and bonds: his own song copyrights. Those, together with Ellin's substantial trust fund, enabled the Berlins to survive, while Clarence Mackay, by contrast, "had the hideous distinction of incurring the largest loss suffered by an individual in the Crash." Ellin and her father had already begun to move toward reconciliation, albeit through a series of tragic family events: the death of her son, Irving Berlin, Jr., then, a year and a half later, the death of her mother. When Clarence Mackay married his mistress, opera singer Anna Case, in 1931, Mr. and Mrs. Irving Berlin were in attendance.

While Berlin survived the Crash financially, he entered a period of personal despair that paralleled his country's plunge into the Great Depression. For several years, his confidence in his creative powers had been waning. The Crash had shaken America's distinctive optimism and self-reliance like no event since the Civil War, and Irving Berlin, always attuned to the spirit of his times, registered that same crisis on a personal level. "I developed the damnedest feeling of inferiority," Berlin later recalled. "There were times between 1930 and 1932," he said, when "I got so I called in anybody to listen to my songs—stock room boys, secretaries. One blink of the eye and I was stuck."

Even though Berlin had written some of his greatest songs in these years, such as "Puttin' on the Ritz," as well as some of his most buoyant, such as "Let Me Sing and I'm Happy," his depression deepened. Other songs he wrote, such as "The Song Is Ended" and "How About Me?," seemed to reflect his fears, as if, before his muse deserted him, she would inspire him with songs of her imminent departure. In 1929, he wrote a similar song "Where Is the Song of Songs for Me?" for the film *Lady of the Pavements*, which was directed by the great D. W. Griffith. It was a silent film, but a musical soundtrack was added that featured Irving Berlin's song at three different points. Griffith was by this time himself the prototype of the genius whose creative powers had languished. Even before the advent of talkies, his great days were behind him, and when *Lady of the Pavements* proved a dismal failure, Griffith quickly moved toward retirement. Berlin must have wondered if it were time for him to do the same.

The nadir of his despair came with a film entitled *Reaching for the Moon*. To read the scripts for this film, then to watch it as it exists today in the butchered form in which it was issued, is painful. *Reaching for the Moon*, as originally conceived—and filmed—could have been an exquisite musical comedy—lively, witty, and sophisticated—a forerunner of the films of Fred Astaire and Ginger Rogers. Even watching what remains of it with the Astaire-Rogers films in mind, one sees many of the same elements. To begin with, we have a pair of urbane, witty, and quarrelsome society lovers in Bebe Daniels, who would go on to star in *42nd Street*, and Douglas Fairbanks, Jr. While Fairbanks was no dancer, he brings his acrobatics from swashbuckling silents to the film and, leaping, bounding, swinging across the sets, he is almost as much an effervescent physical presence in the film as Astaire (though his muscular movements

Douglas Fairbanks and Bebe Daniels in the 1931 film *Reaching for the Moon*.

are more suggestive of Gene Kelly). In Berlin's original script, entitled, *Love in a Cottage*, Fairbanks was called upon to sing several
duets with Daniels, and one can easily imagine Fairbanks talking his
way through a song with gusto and aplomb. Even some of the
Astaire-Rogers supporting team are present, such as Edward Everett
Horton, as are the elegant costumes, the luxury-liner setting, and the
droll banter ("Are you a misogynist, sir?" "No, a Presbyterian.").

The final irony to this aborted masterpiece is that Berlin had created his story against the background of the stock market crash, a bold attempt to confront his own—and the country's—crisis in a musical comedy. Berlin's story envisioned Douglas Fairbanks, Jr. as an irrepressible stock broker who giddily buys and sells stocks before the Crash until he is smitten by love for Bebe Daniels, who, in a nod toward 1920s ballyhoo, portrays an aviatrix modeled on Amelia Earhart. This typically frothy musical plot takes a new direction, however, when Fairbanks, who has invested all he has in the market, learns of the Crash. The stoic grace with which he accepts his loss, his cavalier optimism that he and the country will recover, and the newly discovered tenderness he feels for Daniels all find expression in song.

The real innovation of Berlin's original score is that he conceived the songs not as the usual performance numbers (neither Fairbanks nor Daniels plays the role of a singer) but as integral songs that arise out of a dramatic situation and render the particular character's emotions at that moment. There had been a few such experimental numbers in other early musical films, but Berlin planned nearly a dozen songs to be woven throughout the story: ensemble numbers where brokers extolled the upward swing of the market then lamented its downward plunge; love songs such as "Lucky Break," which crystallized Fairbanks' discovery of love; "If You Believe," which counseled faith after the Crash; and "The Little Things in Life," where Daniels and Fairbanks tried to accustom themselves to simple domestic charms after the loss of wealth (though while she takes comfort in "A little can, a little jar," he can't relinquish the thought of "A little tin of caviar"). Only one song, "Doin' the Low Down," was to be presented as a performance number at a dance aboard the ocean liner, largely to provide newcomer Bing Crosby, who had no other role in the film, a chance to sing.

After filming was completed, however, the studio panicked over the public's increasing aversion to musicals. The costs for filming had mounted to nearly a million dollars and in a last-ditch effort to salvage profits, the studio gutted all but the "Doin' the Low Down" number so that *Reaching for the Moon* could be marketed as a non-musical film. Other studios were doing the same thing. Warner Brothers, after buying the rights to Cole Porter's hit Broadway show, *Fifty Million Frenchmen,* cut all of the songs out to market it as a purely dramatic film. All that was left was a few bars of the hit of the show, "You Do Something to Me," playing in the background. But in the case of *Reaching for the Moon,* the cuts backfired, creating unexplained lapses in plot and awkward moments when a character, about to break into song, is suddenly cut off and a new scene ensues. The overall fluidity of the film is lost without the musical numbers, and the total length is less than seventy minutes instead of the standard ninety. The original film, with musical numbers intact, has never been found.

This butchery, of course, did not save the film but doomed it even more surely to oblivion. *Reaching for the Moon* came to epitomize the demise of the film musical, when it could have been its renaissance. Had the film been made as he intended, the history of the film musical might have been radically altered and Berlin's own deepening personal depression alleviated. Instead, it exacerbated his own crisis and remained a lifelong source of frustration. Those who knew him say that, even at the end of his long life, four words would never fail to dismay him: *Reaching for the Moon.*

Chapter 8

HOW DEEP IS
THE OCEAN?

I was scared. I had had all the money I wanted for the rest of my life. Then all of a sudden I didn't. I had taken it easy and gone soft and wasn't too certain I could get going again. . . . I found I'd have to go back to work, and I wasn't sure I could make the grade. I used to write a song and take it for granted that it was all right. Now I found I was very critical of myself and would ask opinions of all sorts of people before putting a number out.

Just as Berlin's personal depression mirrored that of the country, so his painstaking climb back paralleled America's step-by-step recovery in the 1930s. The very magnitude of the Depression was slow to dawn on a people who wanted to believe President Herbert Hoover's assurance that "Prosperity is just around the corner." As more businesses closed, and more people found themselves out of work, even out of a home, the most insidious effect of the economic collapse spread—that pervasive loss of hope, of trust, of will that the newly inaugurated president, Franklin D. Roosevelt, tried to address in 1933 when he said "The only thing we have to fear is fear itself." To overcome that fear Roosevelt proposed not a single panacea but a battery of new economic initiatives. Berlin's recovery, too, would take place on a variety of fronts.

One took him back to the ballad. Berlin's preeminence in this form was freely acknowledged by other songwriters; Cole Porter, in his list

of supreme compliments in "You're the Top," his witty catalog song
of 1934, ranks "a Berlin ballad" with such other masterpieces as "a
Waldorf salad," "an O'Neill Drama," and "Whistler's Mama." Yet it
was precisely here, in what had always been his greatest strength,
that Berlin feared his greatest loss. Among his papers are worksheets
from these years featuring such weak efforts as "Butterfingers" ("You
let my heart slip through your fingers and break . . . I'm not the same
since my heart started to ache"). No longer did he feel he was the
master of saying "I love you" in the thirty-two bar format of popular
song. He had written two such ballads, both solemn songs musically
that had undertones of loss in their lyrics. They were superb songs
but, like the country, Berlin had lost his confidence. He no longer
had the resolve to promote them, as he had with "Remember," over
the negative reactions of his most trusted associates.

Fortunately, one of those associates, Max Winslow, who had been
an early champion of "Alexander's Ragtime Band," took one of these
songs to radio crooner Rudy Vallee in the summer of 1932. Radio
was an ironic salvation for Berlin, who had been suspicious of the
new medium that offered "free music" to the public since its inception in the early 1920s; by the 1930s, he was openly critical of the
threat radio posed to his business—and his art:

> We have become a world of listeners, rather than
> singers. Our songs don't live anymore. They fail to
> become part of us. Radio has mechanized them all. In
> the old days Al Jolson sang the same song for years until
> it meant something—when records were played until
> they cracked. Today, Paul Whiteman plays a song hit
> once or twice or a Hollywood hero sings them once in
> the films and radio runs them ragged for a couple of
> weeks—then they're dead.

Winslow knew, however, that radio was the kind of tonic Berlin
now needed for his latest song. "Irving's all washed up, or at least he
feels like it," he told Vallee, "He thinks he's written out as a songwriter. But here's a song of his I'd like you to look at and please,
sing it for him." Vallee, who was going through his own personal
crisis in a divorce, resonated to the lyric; he commented, "There was
I singing that song about my girl seeing someone else and going
away—it was all true and happening to me." For all of Irving
Berlin's antipathy to radio as the bane of sheet-music and record
sales, it was Vallee's rendition of "Say It Isn't So" that gave Berlin
his first genuine hit in two years.

In the construction of this song, Berlin went back to the basics in
his craft as a songwriter. He began with an ordinary catchphrase,

an American vernacular expression of desperation, evoked most poignantly in the previous decade during the infamous Black Sox scandal, when a boy supposedly pleaded to "Shoeless" Joe Jackson, "Say it ain't so, Joe." Within that phrase, Berlin discerned a progression of long, open vowels, "Say It Isn't So," that were tailor-made for a radio crooner's lingering tones. Berlin set each syllable on the same note, G, then repeated the phrase by dropping down dramatically a half-interval to G-flat. When he repeated the phrase again, however, at the end of the first eight-bar section, he dropped down even more dramatically—almost a full octave between "Say" and "it"—giving the plea an even more desperate insistence. Each section varies the same musical and lyrical phrases as it repeats them, culminating in the final, colloquial, "Say that ev'rything is still O-Kay," where that most American of expressions, "Okay," reverses the order of the long vowels in "Say It Isn't So." By the end of the song, the singer cannot even repeat the feared rumor, alluding to it through conversational circumlocution, "and what they're saying—say it isn't so."

Irving Berlin took a second step toward the recovery of his creative powers with "How Deep Is the Ocean?" The composition of this classic song, however, seems to have been especially excruciating. As he sometimes did with the construction of a new song, Berlin rummaged about in some of his older ones. Just as he had found the "blue skies" phrase in "Always," now he came across the questions, "How deep is the ocean? How high is the sky?" in "To My Mammy," which he had written for Jolson in the film, *Mammy*. "I keep taking lines and other bits out of bad songs," he later confided, "And I'll tell you something else—all songwriters do." (Berlin could have added that poets do the same, particularly his beloved Alexander Pope, who frequently mined his old couplets for new ones.)

After eliminating a first-draft melodramatic protestation ("So much I love you, dear, to measure it all/the heavens must fall, the sea must be dry"), he seems to have conceived the song as a series of questions, perhaps drawing upon the Yiddish penchant of answering a question with another question. ("How much do I love you?—How deep is the ocean?"). But it took several days for him to strike the precise tone—not desperate yet not flippant—for those questions. In manuscripts dated over early August 1932, we can see Berlin tossing out the chatty, "How far is it, honey?" as well as the overly formal "How far would I journey?" for the perfect balance between colloquial ease and solemn pledge:

> How far would I travel
> To be where you are?

How far is the journey,
From here to a star?

By avoiding rhymes on "travel" and "journey," Berlin gives the lyrical line a longer, open development, yet he still seeds his internal rhymes with "far," "are," and "star." Reaching back to one of his oldest tricks, "vocalizing" the triplet, Berlin deftly placed triplets on such phrases as "far-would-I" and "be-where-you" that are completed with "travel" and "are," giving the questions a lilting quality that echoes nursery rhyme riddles.

Berlin heightened that simplicity by eliminating the verse from the song. His various attempts to write a verse led him either toward a tone that was too casual ("How can I tell you of the things I've planned?/ How can I really make you understand?") or too melodramatic ("Measure the ocean and the sky above,/Then you will know the greatness of my love"). By eliminating the verse altogether, Berlin gave the song an abruptness that underscored its intensity. Here again he anticipated a trend in writing verseless songs that would soon be followed by such hits as "Stormy Weather," by Ted Koehler and Harold Arlen in 1933. By placing all of his emphasis upon the chorus, Berlin concentrated all his powers of matching words and music. Just as the lyric moves from hesitancy to affirmation, the music progresses from a brooding minor key to conclude with a joyous resolution in the major. Of "Say It Isn't So" and "How Deep Is the Ocean?" Berlin said, "Those two songs came at a critical time, and they broke the ice." Clearly, the answer to any question about the depth of Irving Berlin's creative resources was another question: "How Deep Is the Ocean?"

Even before the success of these two songs, Berlin had begun making his comeback on another front—the Broadway stage. Berlin's comeback was aided by changes the Depression wrought on Broadway. Where there had been some fifty musicals on Broadway in 1929, there were fewer than half that by 1931 and only twelve in 1932. The most successful of these had a new, satirical cast to them that was in strong contrast to the frothiness of 1920s shows. The most telling instance of that change was George and Ira Gershwin's *Strike Up the Band*, which had flopped in 1927 but was successfully revived in 1930 with audiences much more willing to accept its premise that wars were precipitated by the profiteering of large corporations. Even more successful was the Gershwins' satirical operetta, *Of Thee I Sing*, which made fun of the presidency and much else in American politics in a fashion never before seen in the American musical theater. So innovative was this particular show, which ran at Berlin's own Music Box Theatre, that it won the Pulitzer Prize, the first ever awarded to a musical.

The success of such operettas may have prompted Irving Berlin to try his hand at political satire. He turned to his old Algonquin Round Table friend, George S. Kaufman, who had worked on both *Strike Up the Band* and *Of Thee I Sing*. Kaufman brought with him a young playwright named Moss Hart, with whom he had just collaborated on a hit comedy, *Once in a Lifetime*. Like Berlin, Hart had grown up in abject poverty but had always imagined the theater as his escape from drab reality. As a teenager, he relished reading about Berlin, George S. Kaufman, and other members of the Round Table in the *New York World*. In F. P. A.'s "Conning Tower" he found:

> not only the world of the theatre, but the world of wit and laughter as well, making them both seem even more desirable. . . . I would breathlessly go through the week with him on a round of opening nights, opening-night parties afterward, lunches at the Algonquin Round Table, poker parties at the Swopes', and all kinds of high jinks at Neysa McMein's studio, where all these giants seemed constantly to forgather as if by magic and spin out the nights in a spate of insults and ribaldry. Famous initials and names spattered the diary like a translucent Milky Way: GSK and Beatrice—A.W. and Harpo—Alice Duer Miller and Smeed—Benchley and Dottie—Bob Sherwood and Marc—I. Berlin and J. Kern.

After getting nowhere with serious drama, Hart decided to lower his aspirations and try his hand at a comedy that satirized Hollywood's sudden transition to the talkies. Sam Harris, Berlin's partner in the Music Box, telegrammed the young author to see if he would be interested in making a musical of *Once in a Lifetime* with Irving Berlin doing the songs. With the memory of a flop musical, *Jonica*, still fresh in his mind, Hart had the gritty integrity to pass up this chance of a lifetime. "I do not write musical comedies," he insisted, "I'm a playwright. I write plays—*only* plays." Harris responded with another offer—if young Hart would agree to collaborate with George S. Kaufman, Harris would produce *Once in a Lifetime* as a straight comedy. At the risk of having his own work subsumed by one of his idols, Hart agreed. After excruciating revisions—and near abandonment of the whole enterprise—*Once in a Lifetime* was a success, and Kaufman stepped forward at the opening-night curtain call to say, "I would like this audience to know that eighty per cent of this play is Moss Hart."

Whether it was because of that resounding success or Kaufman's prompting, Hart overcame his sense of himself as a pure playwright and once again entered the dreaded world of musical comedy. With

Hart as his playwright, and Kaufman directing, Berlin set to work on *Face the Music*. For Berlin, too, the enterprise meant breaking into new and less familiar territory. He told Hart he did not want to write another revue. Instead, he wanted to try a book show, and when Hart outlined an idea, Berlin suggested they work together for a few weeks. Those weeks turned into months, as Hart learned that "writing a show with Irving Berlin is tantamount to entering a monastery. . . . you not only write a show with Irving Berlin, you live it, breathe it, eat it and were it not for the fact that he allows you no sleep at all, I should say sleep it." The intense effort paid off; when *Face the Music* opened in February of 1932, Irving Berlin had his first hit on Broadway in years.

Inspired by actual investigations into New York City government, Hart concocted a story about corrupt policemen who try to launder some of their graft by backing a Broadway show they are sure will flop. Once it adds a healthy dose of fleshy titillation, however, *The Rhinestone Girl* is an unexpected hit. Berlin's thirteen songs fit neatly into the story and several became independent hits as well. "Let's Have Another Cup O' Coffee" was written for a scene where former socialites are reduced to eating in an automat. Berlin's lyric takes the clichés of Tin Pan Alley and equates them with the equally groundless political and economic reassurances of the Hoover administration, particularly its pledge, laughable by 1932, that "prosperity is just around the corner":

> Just around the corner,
> There's a rainbow in the sky,
> So let's have another cup o' coffee
> and let's have another piece o' pie.

Berlin's lyric runs through the litany of Pollyanna weather songs—"let a smile be your umbrella," "the clouds will soon roll by," and "just an April shower"—then crowns his list with the kind of topical allusions that were typical of 1930s catalog songs:

> Even John D. Rockefeller is looking for the silver lining.
> Mister Herbert Hoover says that now's the time to buy.

"Let's Have Another Cup O' Coffee" quickly became identified with the Depression, a less bitter anthem than Yip Harburg and Jay Gorney's "Brother, Can You Spare a Dime?"

A very different song, "Soft Lights and Sweet Music," captured another aspect of the 1930s, its fascination with class, charm, and sophistication, soon to be crystallized in the films of Fred Astaire and Ginger Rogers. Against the very backdrop of breadlines and bank closings, the public was intrigued by the world of luxury, and Berlin, just as much as Cole Porter, responded to that interest with sumptuously elegant songs. Porter's *The Gay Divorce* featured "Night and Day" (indeed, was sometimes referred to as "The 'Night and Day' Show"), and *Face the Music* had the equally lovely "Soft Lights and Sweet Music," which, like Porter's song, made deft use of plaintive chromatic chords and long musical and lyrical phrases:

> Chopin and pale moonlight
> Reveal all your charms,
> So give me velvet lights and sweet music,
> And you in my arms.

Here Berlin places "Chopin" on a chromatic E-flat, then makes the melody flow back to the key of F major, while the lyric smoothes the way with softly—and sweetly—alliterating *v*, *m*, and *l* consonants.

Face the Music also had the kind of number that took a satirical wink at contemporary mores, "I Don't Wanna Be Married, I Just Wanna Be Friends," where an independent woman tells her lover, "You're compromising me but that's exactly how it ought to be":

> Don't speak of wedding chimes
> Because we mustn't be behind the times,
> Besides a wedding isn't necessary at all . . .
> I never would change my name
> Even after the baby came.

The song's shocking "modernity" reflected the realities of the Depression when couples simply could not afford to get married, but its sentiments were still a far cry from a song Irving Berlin wrote back in 1914, when a woman confronts a beau who has not proposed marriage with the colloquial admonition, "If You Don't Want My Peaches, You'd Better Stop Shaking My Tree." Another witty *Face the Music* number, "I Say It's Spinach—And the Hell with It," took the caption from a popular newspaper cartoon and transformed it into a stoical retort to hard times.

The success of *Face the Music* prompted Irving Berlin to conceive of a show that would combine the new emphasis on satire with his long-standing love of the revue format. The 1930s saw the disappearance of the lavish revues of Ziegfeld and other producers, many of whom had been devastated by the Crash. In their place came the "little" revue, where the emphasis was upon satire and sophistication rather than elaborate costumes and scenery. Skits and songs were woven together around some topical theme, and a new group of songwriters—Harold Arlen, Yip Harburg, Howard Dietz, and Arthur Schwartz—were blending jazz and wit in songs like "I Guess I'll Have to Change My Plan," "It's Only a Paper Moon," and "Dancing in the Dark." Once again, Irving Berlin proved his remarkable versatility by not only adapting to this new kind of satirical revue but creating one of its greatest manifestations in *As Thousands Cheer*.

First, however, he had to persuade Moss Hart to be his collaborator. Hart, who disliked writing musical book shows, thought the loose format of the revue even further below his stature as a "playwright. Together, however, the two men struck upon an idea that challenged each of them creatively. As Moss Hart recalled:

> We both agreed that we had no desire to do a conventional sort of revue with the usual blackout sketches, songs, and dances. So we hit upon the idea of writing a topical show right off the front pages of the newspapers. That was the beginning of the thing.

Hart, however, was pressed for money and wanted to try his fortunes in Hollywood, but what he quickly came to call "that city of dreadful night" put him off as it had Berlin a few years earlier:

> After I had been in—I shudder to mention the name!— Hollywood for some time I received word from Mr. Berlin that he'd like to come out and talk over the entire thing with me. He came—venit!—and in ten short days we had practically laid out the entire plan of action. It was remarkable the amount of work we were able to accomplish in so short a time

Berlin was so impressed by the young playwright's talent, he lent him money to do *As Thousands Cheer*, then borrowed funds himself to stage it at the Music Box Theatre.

Knowing how sweet a taste of luxury is to someone who grew up in poverty, Berlin also took Hart on a trip to Bermuda where they could work on the script together. Hart recalled:

> And so, Mr. Berlin and I took ship to Bermuda last April, after I had shaken the last dust of Hollywood from my brogans. There, in the most idyllic land that one can possibly imagine and one designed by an all-embracing Nature for the convenience and inspiration of writers, we completed the first act and laid out the second.

The songs and sketches fit into the various sections of a newspaper: society page, comics, advice to the lovelorn, the fashion column, and so forth. Brilliant in its simplicity, this structure ran the risk of predictability unless each song and skit surpassed what preceded it.

The tropical isle of Bermuda gave them a remote perspective on modern society—from evangelist Aimee Semple McPherson to John D. Rockefeller. "There are some persons," Berlin explained, "who need no distortion to caricature, and the same is true of much of the world's news. . . . It is satire in itself and has only to be photographically reproduced to be the most gorgeous kind of irony." Together, the veteran songwriter and young playwright concocted sketches that satirized everyone from Herbert Hoover to Noel Coward. Director Hassard Short curbed his legendary penchant for expensive sets and instead designed dramatic—and economical—lighting effects, including a way of flashing newspaper headlines across the proscenium arch of the stage before each number. Strikingly realistic masks enabled Clifton Webb to impersonate such figures as Gandhi and Douglas Fairbanks, Jr., and Marilyn Miller, in her last stage appearance, to send up Joan Crawford and Barbara Hutton. For these performers, Berlin created one of his finest and most wide-ranging scores. There were mournful ballads, such as "Lonely Heart," and rhythmic ones like "How's Chances?" and patter songs like "The Funnies," which invoked such popular comic strips as "The Katzenjammer Kids," "Bringing Up Father," and "Skippy."

The real star of the show, however, was Ethel Waters, once known in Harlem night clubs as "Sweet Mama Stringbean." She broke into mainstream popularity in 1925 with "Dinah," a song by Harry Akst and Joe Young, two Tin Pan Alley songsmiths. When they demonstrated their number to Waters, they sang it in a typically 1920s ricky-tick style. "Is that the way you want me to sing it?" Waters asked skeptically. The songwriters had the good sense to urge her to sing it her way. When Waters gave it a torchy blues delivery, "Dinah" became a major hit, and she soon became the first black woman to star on Broadway and in Hollywood. She had a spectacular voice and could dance and act in both comic and straight dramatic roles.

As he did for all the great singers he wrote for, Berlin tailored his songs to his performer. "Berlin obviously listened very carefully to this lady sing and found notes and phrases and words to her liking." "Harlem on My Mind" was a slow blues number that had Waters paying tribute to Josephine Baker, the black singer who had left America for Paris, convinced that a black woman would not be accepted on Broadway. With so many Americans living as expatriates in Paris, newspapers frequently carried regular columns that reported on the doings of the likes of Stein, Hemingway, and Baker.

In "Harlem on My Mind," Berlin imagined the cosmopolitan Baker homesick for life in America, first in a chatty verse:

> Em'ralds in my bracelets,
> And diamonds in my rings,
> A Riviera chateau, and a lot of other things,
> And—I'm blue—so blue am I.

At the phrase "I'm blue" the music drops down in a series of notes that composer Alec Wilder describes as "perfect" for Ethel Waters' "voice and style."

When he shifts to the chorus, Berlin gives Waters a powerful blues melody that she rendered with her deep, resonant delivery:

> I've got Harlem on my mind,
> I've a longing to be low-down,
> And my "parlez vous,"
> Will not ring true,
> With Harlem on my mind.

Given Waters's penchant for imitating male singers like Louis Armstrong, Berlin inserted a lyrical allusion to Cab Calloway's classic growl:

> I go to supper with a French Marquis,
> Each evening after the show,
> My lips begin to whisper "Mon Cheri,"
> But my heart keeps singing "Hi-de-ho."

"Harlem on My Mind" combined the extremes of 1930s urbane sophistication and earthy blues into a number that was at once satirical and poignant—the chic lament of an American black woman who can only find creative fulfillment by leaving her homeland.

Drawing upon Waters' wide range of talents, Berlin crafted a dynamic rhythmic number, "Heat Wave," which she sang torridly as the "Weather Report" section of the newspaper. Rolling her rs for a Caribbean flavor, Waters attributes the heat wave to a dancing lady from the tropics:

> A heat wave blew right into town last week,
> She came from the Island of Martinique.
> The can-can she dances will make you fry.

Berlin's lyric matches slang expressions to Waters' voice that could sustain closed *e* vowels the way other singers projected *a*s and *o*s:

> Gee! Her anatomy
> made the mercury
> jump to ninety-three.

Waters could also drop her voice dramatically to underscore the sensuous dancer she celebrates:

> She started the heat wave
> By letting her seat wave.

Waters also had impeccable control of rhythm, so Berlin could give her syncopated phrases where music and words tugged against each other as they did in "Puttin' on the Ritz":

> The way that she moves that
> Thermometer proves that
> She certainly can
> CAN-CAN.

He also expanded the standard verse-chorus pattern of popular song by inserting a patter section full of rhythmic tricks that enlivened a litany of weather clichés, from getting a tan "in the shade" to "a chicken laid an egg on the street—and it fried."

When they were working on *As Thousands Cheer* in Bermuda, Berlin proudly demonstrated "Heat Wave" for Moss Hart. Hart's initial impression was that the song "sounded terrible," and he asked Berlin to play it again. "It sounded even more terrible," Hart thought. But then it occurred to him that the problem might lie with Berlin's piano-playing and singing. "Play 'Always,'" Hart diplomatically urged his collaborator, curious to see how Berlin rendered one of his greatest songs. The results were equally appalling, so much so that Hart found "Always" almost "unrecognizable." "I thought so," he muttered to himself but breathed more easily, his confidence in "Heat Wave"—and his collaborator—completely restored.

More remarkable still was another song Berlin wrote for Ethel Waters, "Supper Time," a song, musically and lyrically, more innovative than anything the Broadway stage had yet seen. Lights flashed the newspaper headline UNKNOWN NEGRO LYNCHED BY FRENZIED MOB over the stage, then Ethel Waters stepped out to sing the anguished lament of the victim's wife, who must now attend to the

Ethel Waters and dancers performing "Heat Wave" in *As Thousands Cheer* (1933).

prosaic task of feeding her children and telling them their father is dead. Berlin had once again struck upon the individual perspective on a historical occasion, and the lyric focuses poignantly on the predicament of the mother and wife as she forces herself to start her daily routine. Eliminating a verse, Berlin plunges directly into the chorus to make the woman's outpouring more immediate. The title phrase is set to notes that sound much like a streetcall, anticipating Gershwin's similar music for "Summertime" in *Porgy and Bess:*

> Supper time, I should set the table,
> 'Cause it's supper time,
> Somehow I'm not able,
> 'Cause that man o' mine,
> Ain't comin' home no more.

Blue notes (E-flat and B-flat) on "table" and "able" provide chromatic hints at the grief that seethes under her immediate concerns, and when that phrase "Ain't comin' home no more" is repeated at the end of the second A-section, Berlin shifts to a dark minor key with a poignant two-note lilt on "more."

The song then overflows the standard thirty-two bar format as Berlin expands the release from eight to sixteen bars, giving this series of questions a growing, yet still helpless, intensity:

How'll I keep explainin' when they ask me where he's gone,
How'll I keep from cryin' when I bring their supper on?

Here, the contraction "How'll" actually comes out as the very "howl" the woman longs to utter, and the next phrase builds toward that outcry with an abrupt key change:

How can I remind them to pray at their humble board,
How can I be thankful when they start to thank the Lord, Lord!

The chromatic melody line arches, drops, then suddenly soars up and above the octave, as Berlin deftly underscores the lyrical repetition of "Lord," first as noun then as harsh exclamation, with a corresponding shift from D to D-sharp. With the return of the title phrase on the highest notes of the song, Berlin plunges back down the octave in his final A-section with the woman's resignation in the face of the fact "that man o' mine ain't comin' home no more." In an extra pair of measures, Berlin repeats the phrase but, instead of the traditional resolution to the tonic, he leaves the end hanging, unresolved, like the singer's inconsolable grief.

Remarkably, Berlin avoids the twin pitfalls of sentimentality and preachiness. Lynching is never even mentioned in the song, which could conceivably be a lament for a man who simply deserted his wife and children. By focusing upon the woman's concentration on fixing dinner, Berlin creates a lyrical marvel of understatement. Here again, he was writing *for* Waters, and her delivery of the song drew upon her own quiet outrage (as Billie Holiday did in her rendition of "Strange Fruit") at the wave of lynchings that spread across the South—and beyond—during the bitter years of the Depression. Waters recalled:

I was telling my comfortable, well-fed, well-dressed listeners about my people. . . . When I was through and that big, heavy curtain came down, I was called back again and again. I had stopped the show with a type of song never heard before in a revue, and a number that until then had been a question mark.

"Supper Time" went far beyond the satiric formulas of 1930s revues, and had not Irving Berlin mounted the show at his own Music Box Theatre, it is unlikely the song would have survived another producer's cuts. Berlin exercised his power as producer in other ways as well. In her memoir of her father, Mary Ellin Barrett tells the story of how, in the Philadelphia tryout, the white stars of *As Thousands Cheer* "refused to take a bow with Ethel Waters, she being black, they white. He would respect their feelings, of course, my father had said, only in that case there need be no bows at all." The next night "they took their bows with Miss Waters."

Despite these extraordinarily innovative songs, the biggest hit from *As Thousands Cheer* was an old song. Berlin had written a melody back in 1917 with a lyric that went:

> Smile and show your dimple,
> You'll find it's very simple.
> You can think of something comical,
> In a very little while.
> Chase away the wrinkle,
> Sprinkle just a twinkle.
> Light your face up,
> Just brace up and smile.

Even for 1917 this was not a stellar piece of craftsmanship, with its forced rhyme (comic*al/while*) and the heavy-handed internal rhyme (*wrinkle/sprinkle/twinkle*). Nonetheless, the firm of Waterson, Berlin & Snyder made the song the focus of an extensive and innovative plugging campaign. Realizing that new songs needed to reach people from beyond theaters and cabarets, they experimented with the techniques of the advertising industry, then in its infancy. Choosing Philadelphia as their marketing target, they took out big advertisements in newspapers extolling the song, put up huge posters in department store windows, had newsboys deliver circulars, and sent sandwich-board men around town to tout the song. Still, "Smile and Show Your Dimple" sold only a paltry 2,500 copies of sheet music.

Now, in 1933, Berlin needed a number to close the first act of *As Thousands Cheer*. "We wanted a big Fifth Avenue number," Berlin said, "I wanted an old-fashioned type song, but I couldn't come up with anything. The most difficult thing to do is to consciously create an old-fashioned tune." So Berlin took the seventeen-year old song out of mothballs. Keeping the catchy opening phrase, he changed the rest of the melody and recast it in the now standard AABA pattern. Then he gave it a completely new lyric for the fashion column number that closed the first act. Fortuitously, he linked fashion to a holiday setting, imagining the informal stroll along New York's Fifth Avenue in spring finery as an "Easter Parade." The number was staged as a throwback in time with the cast costumed in brown to simulate the sepia tones of a newspaper rotogravure section. As the cast paraded across the stage, they suddenly stopped, as if frozen in a snapshot, while Clifton Webb and Marilyn Miller sang Berlin's new version of his old song:

> In your Easter bonnet, with all the frills upon it,
> you'll be the grandest lady in the Easter parade.

"Easter Parade" is one of Berlin's most deceptively simple songs. From the very first word and note of the chorus—the seemingly unimportant word "In" placed, oddly, on a sustained note—Berlin gave a demonstration of how a master songwriter knew how to break one of the most fundamental rules of his craft, which dictated that long notes must be fitted with long vowels. Another of those rules was to avoid what are called "feminine" rhymes, two-syllable rhymes where the last syllable is unaccented (*bon*net/up*on* it). The only time a songwriter wanted feminine rhymes was when he wanted to create a comic effect. Berlin had studiously followed the rules in "Always," never rhyming his two-syllable title. When another songwriter, probably Buddy De Sylva, wrote a parody of "Always," he relied on such feminine rhymes for his humor:

> I'll be loving you always,
> Both in very big and small ways.
> With a love that's grand
> As Paul Whiteman's band
> And 'twill weigh as much as Paul weighs,
> Always.
> In saloons and dark hallways,
> You are what I'll grab always.
> See how I dispense
> Rhymes that are immense,
> But do they make sense?
> Not always.

Berlin took this volatile form of rhyming and used it, sparingly, to create not a comic song but one of nostalgic warmth.

After rhyming "In your Easter bon*net*" with "with all the frills up*on it*," he deftly avoids rhyme altogether for several bars. Instead, he knits words and music together with vowels instead of rhymes (you'll *be* the grandest *lady* in *the Easter para*de).

With its long notes and rests, the release suspends the lilting melodic and rhythmic patterns of the A-sections, as if the song itself were striking a pose for the approaching photographers:

> On the Avenue (rest, rest),
> (rest) Fifth Avenue (rest, rest)
> (rest) the photographers will snap us.

Then the melody, like the flash of a camera, pushes up to its highest note and the lilting patterns return in a magnificent, sweeping burst:

> And you'll find that you're
> in the rotogravure.

At this point a lesser songwriter would have tried to create another clever feminine rhyme, such as "trap us," but Berlin snapped his lyrical as well as melodic pattern, and found a one-syllable rhyme between a colloquial contraction and a four-syllable word. That word, "rotogravure," some people suggested, was so tied to the production number in *As Thousands Cheer* that it would prevent "Easter Parade" from becoming an independent hit.

The song made the production number one of the most memorable moments in musical theater history. Its nostalgia evoked an era of prosperity and gaiety before the Depression. Marilyn Miller, it had been said, was washed up as an actress, as outmoded as the *Ziegfeld Follies* where she had starred. Ziegfeld himself had recently died, penniless, and though Miller herself would also soon die suddenly at 38 years of age, her rendition of "Easter Parade" was a final moment of theatrical glory.

The extraordinary match of words and music is amazing in light of the fact that Berlin revised an old melody and added a new lyric. As he himself observed, however:

> A song is like a marriage. It takes a perfect blending of
> the two mates, the music and the words, to make a per-
> fect match. In the case of "Easter Parade" it took a
> divorce and a second marriage to bring about the happi-
> est of unions.

Even more than a "standard," "Easter Parade" has become a timeless song, one that would seem to be a folk song if it were not so urbane. "I can never guess a song," Berlin reflected, citing "Easter Parade" as his prime example. "I just thought it was something to

The company of *As Thousands Cheer* recreate Fifth Avenue in the 1880s for "Easter Parade."

take care of the rotogravure idea for that particular production. Moss Hart said it would be a hit and it has turned out to be a natural."

Just as novel as Berlin's technique in "Easter Parade" was his conception of the song as an urban and secular holiday celebration. Much has been made of the fact that the lyric ignores all of the religious connotations of Easter, but it also evades the even more ancient pastoral celebrations of the coming of spring. Instead, Berlin transforms this natural holiday of fecundity into an urban ritual of donning new clothes as a sign of rebirth. The only allusion to greenery is the line "I'll be all in clover," whose American, urban, commercial meaning refers to the green of wealth—not nature. While the lyric is up-to-date, musically the song evokes such old melodies as "Put On Your Old Gray Bonnet" and "Pack Up Your Troubles in Your Old Kit Bag."

As Thousands Cheer concluded as innovatively as it began, though it took some last-minute heroics on Berlin's part to add that finishing touch. The closing number was to have been "Come Along and Skate with Me," sung by the cast on roller-skates at a high-society cocktail party. Just before opening in Philadelphia, however, the director,

Hassard Short, discovered that the theater there did not have the linoleum floor needed for smooth skating. Without linoleum, he explained to Berlin, the cast could not roller-skate.

"But we open on Saturday night," Berlin lamented, "They can't sing a skating song if they're not on skates. What are we going to do?"

"That, my dear sir," Hassard replied, "is up to you."

Berlin walked out of the theater and conferred with Moss Hart in the alley. Hart, who had been reminding himself how precariously a musical had to be put together ever since rehearsals began, mustered a suggestion that Berlin go back to a song he had originally planned to use for the show. Berlin worked on the song in one of his by-now classic all-night stands, and then rewrote the opening number of the show to set up the new finale. As the curtain went up, the chorus announced a piece of "news": there will be no reprises in this "newspaper" show. Then, true to their word, the final number was not the standard reprise but an entirely new song, "Not for All the Rice in China." As delivered by Clifton Webb, who could be both debonair and deftly daft, the absurdly hyperbolic list was a send-up of the era's endless catalog songs that listed all the commodities a lover would not exchange for his beloved: "all the rice in China"; "all the grapes in France"; "kilts in Scotland"; "onions in Bermuda"; and "beans in Boston." The roller-skating number went into Berlin's trunk, to be resurrected in 1940 for *Louisiana Purchase* as "(Come Along and) Dance with Me (At the Mardi Gras)."

The combination of old and new, satiric bite and warm nostalgia, understated tragedy in "Supper Time" and riotous sensuality in "Heat Wave," together with Hart's sketches, made *As Thousands Cheer* the longest-running show of 1933, a triumph for the songwriter who for several years had been haunted by the fear that his talent had deserted him.

The only casualty of the show was Moss Hart, who, once rehearsals began, found his antipathy to musicals revived. "Doctoring" a play was one thing but performing surgery on a musical involved recasting songs, dances, and orchestrations. Interviewed shortly after opening night, Hart's "first and last words were an emphatic 'Never again!'"

> Still a bit shaken by the experience, he roundly denounced the sin of revue composition—into which he had fallen—as a delusive craft designed to ensnare the unwitting into eternal bondage in purgatory; and he swore to lead henceforth a noble and upright life, following virtuous pathways and never touching pen to paper again—that is, to write musical shows.

The success of *As Thousands Cheer* wore down Hart's resistance long enough to lay plans, with Berlin, for a sequel called *More Cheers*, but the two men reconsidered their idea in the light of the failure of a similar project. The Gershwins had mounted a sequel to their hit, *Of Thee I Sing*; called *Let 'Em Eat Cake*, it was, musically and lyrically, richer and more experimental than the original, but audiences were put off by the bitter satire of the book, which depicted a fascist takeover of America. *Let 'Em Eat Cake* failed miserably, giving credence to the old show-biz adage, "Never do a sequel." That failure, coupled with the sudden death of star Marilyn Miller, prompted Hart and Berlin to scrap plans for *More Cheers*.

Berlin shelved the musical but not before he had written several songs for it. Following the experimental character of his work in *As Thousands Cheer*, some of these songs were innovative, even daring in the way they pushed the boundaries of the thirty-two bar format. They would be money in the bank for his next big project.

Hart was relieved to return to pure playwriting but, thankfully, his aversion to musicals crumbled many times. He went on to write *Jubilee* with Cole Porter, *Lady in the Dark* with Kurt Weill and Ira Gershwin, and the filmscript for *A Star Is Born* with Harold Arlen and Ira Gershwin. He directed Irving Berlin's *Miss Liberty* in 1949, as well as Lerner and Loewe's *My Fair Lady* in 1956, Never again, however, did he write with the man who had helped him find his first success in musical theater.

For the moment, the driven songwriter could relax, bask in the success of his hit show, and take stock, along with the American public, of his extraordinary achievements. In May 1934, as Berlin turned forty-six, he was pictured on the cover of *Time* magazine, and the story portrayed him as an American institution, a man whose songs had encapsulated the history of America for more than a generation. Coinciding with the *Time* story, NBC presented a five-part radio series that traced Berlin's songwriting career from his 1910 hit "My Wife's Gone to the Country" to "Easter Parade." The series prompted Berlin to reassess radio as the nemesis of songwriters and music publishers. "Radio's most valuable asset is in the old songs," he declared, "Catalogues of yesterday's tunes are the backbone of radio today." As Laurence Bergreen observes:

> Despite Irving's misgivings, it was apparent to listeners that a remarkable number of Berlin's old songs held up well, even after two decades. They now revealed a timeless quality that outlasted fashion. . . . Though he wrote for the moment, he lavished extraordinary care on his creations; a large part of his genius consisted of his willingness to

take infinite pains in fashioning them. They were built to
last. Suddenly people were talking about Irving Berlin
again, and not just on Broadway. His songs had seeped
into the national consciousness: after twenty-five years,
they seemed to have been there forever. The retrospective established Berlin as the great musical consolidator,
whose melodies had become part of the ineffable glue of
society. They were something Americans had in common, like the weather, the Depression, the bittersweet
memories of a romance or vanished youth.

If radio had concentrated on these old songs, it could create a repertory of classical songs to be reinterpreted and revived over generations. However, if it only sought out new songs to air, Berlin wondered "how in the world radio can keep on going? Where will it get
the material?" What he did not venture to speculate, but perhaps
realized, is that radio would corrode the quality of American songwriting with its appetite for new hits. The craftsmanship that went
into songs of the 1920s, 1930s, and even into the early 1940s, simply
could not be sustained in a market that demanded new songs with
ever increasing frequency. Shows like "Your Hit Parade" set a frenetic pace for songwriting that soon would sacrifice quality for
quantity. In 1934, however, that threat was still years away, and
radio was America's most powerful medium. Fittingly, it served to
highlight Berlin's achievement—and his triumph over his worst personal crisis—in grand fashion.

Chapter 9

CHEEK TO CHEEK

I'd rather have Fred Astaire introduce one of my songs than any other singer I know—not because he has a great voice, but because his delivery and diction are so good that he can put over a song like nobody else.

Just as Irving Berlin had successfully engineered a comeback, so had the Hollywood musical. While other studios curtailed musical productions in the early 1930s, Paramount had forged ahead with an innovative series of comic operettas. Directed by Europeans such as Ernst Lubitsch and Rouben Mamoulian, films like *Monte Carlo* (1930) and *Love Me Tonight* (1932) radiated wit, sophistication, and a knowing naughtiness. As in stage operetta, songs were not confined to the performance mode but emerged out of character and situation. Because the films were set in Europe, it seemed less odd that someone like Maurice Chevalier would suddenly burst into song. In *Love Me Tonight*, in fact, Rodgers and Hart used rhymed dialogue to ease the transition from talking to singing, and songs such as "Isn't It Romantic?" actually defined characters and advanced the story.

While Paramount fused film with European operetta, Warner Brothers, which had initiated the backstager, revived that genre in 1933 with *42nd Street*. Although the formula was the same, *42nd Street* was no tired backstage story with static performance numbers reprised ad nauseam. It combined the jazzy rhythms of Harry Warren with the vernacular grit of Al Dubin's lyrics to evoke "hot-shot, ace-high, lowdown, dirty, crazy, New York show biz." While the songs in *42nd Street* are all done as performances, they resonate with the story and characters in subtle ways. "You're Getting to Be a

Habit With Me," for example, is sung in rehearsal as exhausted chorus girls are given a brief respite from the fiercely driving—and driven—director, played by Warner Baxter. Lyrics like "Ev'ry kiss, ev'ry
hug seems to act just like a drug" underscore Baxter's own frenzied
addiction to the excruciating work of putting on a show.

The success of *42nd Street* launched Warner Brothers on a series
of *Gold Diggers* films that confronted the hard-nosed realities of the
Depression in the story line even as they escaped them in fantastical
musical numbers. Those numbers were made even more spectacular
by the choreography of Busby Berkeley, who made the camera move
as it had never done before: pushing it along in waves or through
inverted V's of legs; shooting dancers from above so that they
formed kaleidoscopic patterns; pulling back from a confined space
to create the illusion of enormous vistas that had no relation to real
space; and reducing human bodies to abstract geometric patterns. At
last, sound movies truly moved—and moved audiences to wonder.

What was needed was a fusion of these two developments—the
operetta-based European musicals of Paramount and the jazzy backstagers at Warner Brothers—some new kind of musical that would
present ordinary Americans breaking into song and dance as an
integral expression of their character and dramatic situation. New
technological developments stood ready to make this possible: the
Moviola allowed for editing of both sound and picture elements;
movable cameras and microphones could follow performers, even
outdoors; and most important, songs could be prerecorded and then
lip-synched by singers to their own playbacks, making singing seem
as effortlessly natural as talking. These possibilities were realized
most fully by one of the smallest Hollywood studios, RKO (Radio-
Keith-Orpheum), which had declared bankruptcy in 1933 and was
ready to take risks larger studios could not afford.

One performer RKO was willing to gamble on was Fred Astaire.
Since his childhood in vaudeville, he had been teamed with his sister
Adele, and they had scored successes in the 1920s with Gershwin
musicals such as *Lady, Be Good!* (1924) and *Funny Face* (1927).
When Adele quit show business to marry an English nobleman, Fred
found himself looking for solo work in a Depression-pinched
Broadway. His first—and last—Broadway show without Adele was
The Gay Divorce (1932), whose doddering book needed Cole Porter's
extraordinary "Night and Day" to keep the show afloat. Astaire had
come to Hollywood to try his luck, but his facial features, particularly what RKO executive David Selznick described as "enormous ears
and bad chin line," did not show up well on camera. The now-
famous result of his first screen test—"Can't act. Can't sing. Balding.
Can dance a little"—did not deter RKO, which put Fred Astaire
under contract.

Building an entire film around an untried screen star was risky even for hard-pressed RKO, so they first lent Astaire to MGM where he played himself for a few dancing scenes in a Joan Crawford vehicle called *Dancing Lady*. While not stellar, the performance prompted RKO to include him in *Flying Down to Rio*, a 1933 Latin American extravaganza (with Europe and Asia steeped in political turmoil and the Roosevelt administration promoting its good-neighbor policy in the Western Hemisphere, South America became the setting of many 1930s films that wanted to let audiences forget the grim realities of the day). Astaire did not star but played the musical equivalent of comic sidekick to Gene Raymond as he romanced Dolores Del Rio against such spectacles as chorus girls dancing on (and nearly falling off) the wings of airplanes that fly in formations over Rio de Janeiro. He might have gone virtually unnoticed except for a dance number called "The Carioca," where, teamed with the wise-cracking Ginger Rogers, he managed to balance her sensual vitality with a casually comic style that would become their hallmark.

Rogers was an established figure in Warners musicals such as *42nd Street* and *Gold Diggers of 1933*, where she played a tough-talking showgirl whose tartiness nicely contrasted with the saccharine innocence of star Ruby Keeler. In coming to RKO, Rogers hoped that she could leave musicals behind her for straight dramatic roles, but when she saw "The Carioca," with its torrid forehead-to-forehead step, she had to admit it was more electrifying than any other dance number that had been seen on the screen.

Excited by the possibilities he saw in "The Carioca" after filming was completed, Pandro S. Berman, a young producer at RKO, followed Astaire to London, where the dancer was joining the stage company of *The Gay Divorce*. Initially, Berman planned to propose a follow-up film, to be called *Radio City Revels*, where Astaire and Rogers would star (radio musicals also became very popular in the 1930s, because they enabled listeners to see their favorite stars, such as Rudy Vallee and Kate Smith, on film). Once he saw Astaire in *The Gay Divorce*, however, Berman bought the screen rights. He knew the script was too racy for Hollywood, which, under increasing scrutiny by the Legion of Decency, had reluctantly established the Production Code Administration, which strictly policed visual and verbal naughtiness. The story would need rewriting, Cole Porter's sophisticated songs, except for "Night and Day," would have to go (Berman asked Porter to write new songs but the songwriter refused, so he turned to Hollywood songwriting teams like Mack Gordon and Harry Revel as well as Con Conrad and Herb Magidson), and the title had to be changed to *The Gay Divorcée*. While divorce can't be gay, a divorcée could, since it was a time-tested truth that a widow could be merry.

Astaire eagerly listened to Berman's pitch for the film but balked at the thought of teaming with Ginger Rogers, who he thought was too earthy to play the refined female leading role. He may also have been concerned that Rogers might overshadow him as his sister Adele always had. "I did not go into [pictures] with the thought of becoming part of a team," he insisted, "and if that's what RKO has in mind for me, we'd better end the contract right now." Berman offered Astaire the unusual (for a performer) prospect of ten percent of the film's profits as well as the kind of artistic control over musical numbers that Warner Brothers granted to Busby Berkeley. A rigorous perfectionist from his years in vaudeville and on Broadway, Astaire was appalled at the slipshod nature of dance numbers in musicals, and insisted Berman commit six full weeks of rehearsal time to the musical numbers alone. He was determined that his films be top-notch. When he saw *Flying Down to Rio* in a theater, he said "I was amazed that the reaction could be so good because I knew I hadn't yet scratched the surface with any real dancing on screen." Like Berlin, Astaire's long experience on the stage made him skeptical about Hollywood glitz and hype. "Unless I can do something outstandingly important," he insisted, "I don't think I want to be bothered with movies."

The Gay Divorcée was a film that looked two ways: back to the dreary past of backstage musicals but also forward to the great Astaire-Rogers films to come. There are endlessly reprised performance numbers like "The Continental" (seventeen minutes long; still, it was the first song to win an Academy Award). More forward looking was "Night and Day," which is presented not as a performance but as the emanation of Astaire's enthrallment with Rogers. The transition from dialogue to song is awkward, with Astaire pleading, "Don't go, I have so much to say to you," then sliding into Porter's verse with "like the beat, beat, beat of the tom-tom when the jungle shadows fall. . . ." Once Astaire is into the song, however, the magic unfolds, and his delivery is effortlessly debonair, almost like musical talking. After a bit of uncertainty as to how to react when someone sings to you, Rogers finds her solution. Instead of swooning over his serenade, she alternately looks away, looks disapproving, even looks to leave, then, when he's not looking, her face reveals how pleased she is with him.

As with the stage production, the success of "Night and Day" made a hit of *The Gay Divorcée*. Oddly, Astaire seriously considered dropping the song from the film for fear that it had become too familiar already; if this had happened, the picture may not have enjoyed the success it achieved. With that success, RKO was poised to mount more musicals built around Fred Astaire and Ginger Rogers. *Roberta*, another film remake of a Broadway show, definite-

ly established the couple as a team. It was at that point that Irving
Berlin returned to Hollywood. Wiser to Hollywood ways after his
first experiences with film musicals, Berlin was also, thanks to several hit songs and the smash production of *As Thousands Cheer*, back
to his old confident self. Just as he had once plunged into his first
musical for the Castles and gambled on writing annual revues for his
own Music Box Theatre, Irving Berlin now was willing to gamble on
little RKO, Fred Astaire, and Ginger Rogers. Like Astaire, he asked
for and got a profit-sharing stake in the film and a tremendous
amount of artistic control that enabled him to sit in on every script
conference. Where other performers and songwriters had to suffer
the whims of producers and directors, Fred Astaire and Irving
Berlin had daily input on the set and behind the scenes that brought
their extensive experience in musical theater to bear on the next
great Astaire-Rodgers musical, *Top Hat* (a title Astaire suggested).

With one eye on Paramount's sophisticated European operettas
and the other on Warner Brothers' jazzy, spectacular backstagers,
the RKO team of Berman, Berlin, Astaire, choreographer Hermes
Pan, and director Mark Sandrich set about creating the definitive—
and definitively American—film musical. With a bow to Warner
backstagers, they made Fred a performer and, with another nod to
Paramount, they set *Top Hat* in Europe. From there on, however,
everything about *Top Hat* was RKO. From the opening scene where
Fred Astaire disrupts the funereal quiet of a gentleman's club in
London with his finger and toe tapping, *Top Hat* is militantly
American and full of sound—not the "silence" proclaimed by the
Thackeray Club.

Top Hat started with a script—in Hungarian—from a play called
Scandal in Budapest, where a country girl flees from an arranged
marriage to Budapest. There she shrewdly resolves to slap the face of
a prominent politician in the lobby of a fashionable hotel, knowing
the incident will create a scandal that will suggest she is his mistress
and free her from her dreaded marriage. When Astaire read an early
adaptation, however, he was appalled: "In the first place—as this
book is supposed to be written *for me* with the intention of giving me
the chance to do the things that are most suited to me—I cannot see
that my part embraces any of the necessary elements except to *dance,
dance, dance.*" He then complained about his character as "a sort of
objectionable young man without charm or sympathy or humor," the
fact that he had "practically no comedy of any consequence," and
that love interest consisted of his "forever pawing the girl or she is
rushing into my arms." One stipulation he laid down was that he
would not give Rogers the obligatory Hollywood on-screen kiss.

Given Astaire's contractual control, the story went through many
revisions and "treatments," each of which was reviewed by Irving

Berlin, until virtually only Ginger's slap of Fred's face (twice) remains. The nature of their relationship is closer to the witty sparring of couples in the so-called "screwball" comedies of the 1930s, such as Cary Grant and Katharine Hepburn in *Bringing Up Baby*. Still, the original European sophistication surrounds the story of Americans abroad in London and Venice. Their misunderstandings, disguises, and sexual peccadilloes become more entangled and embroiled, until, as in the films of Lubitsch and Mamoulian at Paramount (as well as Shakespearean and Restoration comedies), the witty posturing of sophisticates gives way to honest revelations of simple affection.

Although Irving Berlin brought with him a trunk of great songs from *More Cheers*, the shelved sequel to *As Thousands Cheer*, he quickly found that *Top Hat* would not be a simple backstager where any good song could be performed, but an integrated story, like his aborted *Reaching for the Moon*, where songs had to be tailored to character and situation. He "holed up in his hotel for the next six weeks, composing music by night, in his pajamas and slippers, and writing lyrics by day." Although he came up with twelve new numbers tailored to the script, only five were used in the film, and some of these were songs he had brought from Broadway, for which the script was rewritten. Berlin was used to such ratios from his early days as a songwriter, when he would write "four to five songs a week, and, by elimination, but one out of ten reaches the public."

The first of the new songs, "No Strings," was the first number in the film, and it was presented, integrally, as a spontaneous effusion of Astaire's joy in bachelorhood. Striking a dramatic pose that begins to set up the transition from dialogue to song, he declares, with subtly long vowels that move him closer to singing, "In me *you* see a *youth* who is completely on the loose." The next line is pure talk:

No yens, no yearnings.

But it parallels the opening line of the song, which Astaire delivers as dialogue:

No strings and no connections.

And only with the next line, "No ties to my affections," do we get rhyme and singing.

With that deft transition, Astaire established the principle that he was one American performer who could burst into song as readily as any of Paramount's European stars.

Berlin's lyric drives home Astaire's casual elegance with a series of American vernacular expressions:

> Bring on—the big attraction
> My decks—are cleared for action.
> I'm fancy free—
> and free for anything fancy.

Dramatically, the song emerges from a lecture on the joys of marriage he receives from Edward Everett Horton, who, along with Eric Blore, Helen Broderick, and Erik Rhodes, would become staples in the Astaire-Rogers films. All exquisite character actors, they emphasized, by their contrasting looks, age, and manner, the romantic rightness of Astaire and Rogers for each other.

The first dance number for Fred and Ginger was actually one of the songs from *More Cheers* Berlin had brought with him from New York, but it was beautifully retailored to its new dramatic context. Initially the script called for a daffy number, "In the Birdhouse at the Zoo," where Astaire, impersonating a horse-cab driver, chariots Ginger to Regent's Park, where she goes horseback riding. In the original scene, he intercepts her and invites her to the London Zoo, where he was to sing, in the birdhouse:

> If I can, you can—so can the toucan do what two can do.
> You'll not be heard but we'll get the bird in the birdhouse
>   at the zoo

Then the script was changed so that a sudden rain shower drives Ginger and Fred to a bandshell for shelter where they perform "Isn't This a Lovely Day (to Be Caught in the Rain)?" Sitting on a bench under the canopy, he edges closer to her protectively when the thunder roars. The sound of thunder subtly prompts music to arise and the fact that they are on a stage—a bandshell—helps excuse the transition from dialogue to song. The transition is underscored visually by the camera's focus on the lyres of the musical stands. Astaire, cued by Ginger's frightened observation that only the sound of the thunder bothers her, exquisitely talks his way from dialogue into the chatty verse of the song. With the camera taking in more shots of the musical lyres and the stage, the singing and dancing unfold to create an integral number that expresses the feelings of these characters in a dramatic situation as well as a performance enacted on a bandstand, the perfect blend of—and advance over—the experiments in film musicals by Paramount and Warners.

The scene also carried the RKO hallmark for dance numbers, which, at Astaire's insistence, were done in long takes instead of being broken up into kaleidoscopic shots like Busby Berkeley's. Mark Sandrich made his three cameras move with his dancers, each

Fred Astaire and Ginger Rogers perform Irving Berlin's "Isn't This a Lovely Day?" in the 1935 film *Top Hat*.

of which framed Astaire and Rogers head to foot. Such camerawork, according to Gerald Mast, "emphasizes the wonder of movement in space" but in a completely different way from Berkeley's pyrotechnics. Berkeley made his camera move, often while his dancers stood still, but in RKO films, Astaire and Rogers always move in real—not camera-created—space. In later Astaire-Rogers films, Sandrich, an engineer, had a special "Astaire dolly" constructed so a camera could track, glide, and turn with them perfectly. "Either the camera will dance," Astaire insisted, "or I will."

The inspiration for the next number, "Top Hat, White Tie, and Tails," came to Astaire one night when, like Berlin, he could not get to sleep. After tossing and turning, he jumped out of bed at five in the morning, grabbed his umbrella, "blasted away" with it, then "crawled sheepishly back into bed." Even though it is done as a straight performance number by Astaire in his role as a world-famous dancer, the film imaginatively integrates the song into the story. As he and Horton chat in the dressing room before Astaire goes on stage, Horton receives a telegram with news that Ginger's character—for whom Astaire has been searching—has arrived in Italy. Astaire grabs the telegram, tells Horton to charter a plane so they can fly to meet her the next day, then rushes on stage, waving the telegram.

As in "Puttin' on the Ritz," "Top Hat, White Tie, and Tails" uses misplaced accents to "rag" words that express Astaire's giddy happiness:

> *I* just got an *invitation through* the *mails*:
> "Your *presence* re*quested*, this *evening*, it's *formal*."
> A top hat, a white tie, and tails.

As he moves from verse to chorus, Berlin lengthens his rhythm—and his syllables—to bring out his long vowels, and Astaire's dancing follows, shifting from rhythmic cane and toe-tapping to long, elegant strides:

> *I'*m—puttin' on m*y* top hat,
> *Ty*in' up m*y white tie*.
> Brushin' off *my* tails.

Then, in the release, when Berlin again rags his phrases into abrupt rhythmic bursts, Astaire resumes his frenetic tapping with cane and feet:

> I'm steppin' *out*, my *dear*,
> To breathe an *at*-mos-*phere*
> that simply *reeks* with *class*.

The clash of high and low diction in these phrases is repeated when Berlin juxtaposes the arch "I trust that you'll excuse" with the vernacular "my dust when I step on the gas." He makes formal language dance against colloquial shards and musical jarring, reflecting Astaire's own glee as he looks forward to "Puttin' down my top hat" and "Mussin' up my white tie."

The visual and aural spectacle of this number shows the advancement in film technology since the days of *Puttin' on the*

Ritz. Astaire sings to his own prerecorded playback, including his taps that ring out like machine-gun bursts. A mobile camera captures a genuinely moving performance in which Astaire dances with a chorus line of men attired, as he, in tails, then he "shoots" them all down with his cane at the end. Berlin clearly sensed the revolutionary implications of such technology for songwriting. When writing for a performer who would sing a song on stage, a songwriter had to supply long notes and open vowels so the singer, be it Ethel Merman or Fred Astaire, could project a song to the back of the balcony. With microphones and prerecording, however, those old rules for singability went out the soundstage window. In Hollywood, Berlin could concentrate on Astaire's ability to enunciate syllables and follow the trickiest rhythms. Using shorter vowels and clipped consonants, Fred Astaire's singing could now sound more like Astaire talking.

Short consonants and stresses, moreover, are more natural in the English language. The earliest poetry in our language was created not with rhyme and meter but alliteration and accent. From old Anglo-Saxon verse ("Bitter breast cares have I abided"), through Shakespeare ("I had rather hear a brazen candlestick turned or a dry wheel grate on the axletree") down to modern advertising ("When Better Cars Are Built, Buick Will Build Them"), the deepest music of English lies in its rough consonants and harsh accents. Berlin, the Gershwins, and other songwriters realized this in writing for Astaire and Rogers, producing such previously unsingable lines as "The way you wear your hat," "A fine romance, my dear, this is," and Berlin's marvelously clipped phrases from "Top Hat, White Tie and Tails":

> I'm dudein' up my shirt front,
> Puttin' in the shirt studs,
> Polishin' my nails.

Songwriters who wrote primarily for the stage, such as Rodgers and Hammerstein, would never enjoy such freedom. Hammerstein fretted, for example, over ending a song, for dramatic reasons, with the unsingable line, "all the rest is talk."

Irving Berlin violated that principle of singability again with "Cheek to Cheek." When Astaire saw the song, his instinctive reaction was to sing it "as though he were talking" and Berlin responded "Oh, that's great, I love it." In *Top Hat*, "Cheek to Cheek" is presented as another hybrid between an integral and a performance song. Astaire and Rogers get up from a night club table to dance, but

Rogers mistakenly thinks he is married to her friend, played by Helen Broderick. Broderick, in turn, is playing matchmaker and signals Rogers to move closer to Fred as they dance, to be, in effect, "cheek to cheek." Rogers does, with the kind of cavalier disregard of bourgeois morality Ernst Lubitsch's Paramount musicals flaunted. "Well, if she doesn't care, I don't," she declares, to which Astaire blissfully agrees, "Neither do I." Then, almost before we notice it, he moves from talking into singing "Cheek to Cheek." The graceful transition is even more amazing because Berlin wrote the song without a verse, the more conversational portion of a song that songwriters usually relied upon to ease out of dialogue.

Even without a verse, "Cheek to Cheek" gave Astaire an abrupt but still perfect transition from chatting with Ginger to saying: "Heaven, I'm in heaven and my heart beats so that I can hardly speak." Another songwriter would have started with the same two pick-up notes Berlin used when he repeated the initial phrase ("I'm in heaven, I'm in heaven, . . ."). The elimination of those notes, together with the not so singable short and long closed e's and aspirating h's give the song a breathless immediacy. Berlin concludes this daring opening phrase by placing the word "speak" two intervals above the octave, stretching Astaire's vocal range to the limits so he can barely sing the word "speak," close cousin to Hammerstein's unsingable "talk" (making his singing, of course, still more like speaking).

Berlin's innovations in "Cheek to Cheek" have only begun, however. He compensates for the lack of a verse by writing a chorus more than twice the length of the normal thirty-two bars. Over the course of seventy-two bars, Berlin writes two A-sections of sixteen bars each, then an eight-bar B section that repeats the same melodic phrase ("Oh! I love to climb a mountain," and so on) no fewer than six times. When Astaire sings this section of the song to Rogers, he actually stops dancing and comically lectures to her about his fondness for these traditional male activities.

Just as the song threatens to become monotonous, however, Berlin is off on an entirely new C-section that dramatically shifts to a deep minor key as the lyric turns from sprightly to passionate with "Dance with me—I want my arms about you." At this point, Astaire gathers Rogers in his arms and sweeps her off the crowded dance floor into a garden patio where they dance alone after Astaire—and Irving Berlin—have returned this long and complex song back to its beginning with the words "will carry me thru to—heaven. I'm in heaven." Their dance floor has a sunburst pattern on it and classical urns that recall the lyres on their other private stage of the park bandshell, linking "Isn't This a Lovely Day?" and "Cheek to Cheek" together visually, as well as thematically. The casual daytime song, danced by Astaire and Rogers in riding clothes, is recalled in the sumptuous formal dance in evening attire, precisely at the point when Astaire and Rogers leave the other dancers and swirl outdoors again to dance in the sun as they had danced in the rain, a silent, symbolic allusion to "Night and Day."

The set for "Cheek to Cheek" is one of the loveliest Art Deco creations of designer Van Nest Polgase. Eastman Kodak had recently developed film that could capture white. Previously, in the 1920s, white caused such glare that sets had to be painted pink or pastel green. RKO's art department developed what it called "The Big White Set," with stunning contrasts between black and white, perfect for the sleek, streamlined lines of Art Deco as well as for Fred Astaire in his formal black tails and gleaming white shirt front.

Even though such a classic—and classy—number seems so perfectly suited to this moment in the film, Berlin had written "Cheek to Cheek" in New York before he came west to work on *Top Hat*. Moreover, as he had done with "Smile and Show Your Dimple" in writing "Easter Parade," he had taken a musical phrase out of another song, "Moon Over Napoli," to use in "Cheek to Cheek." "Moon Over Napoli" had been intended for *More Cheers*, but Berlin was intrigued by a rising, step-wise sequence of notes for the lyric phrase, "When a dark-eyed maid invited me to 'See—Naples and Die.'" Subtly changing some of the intervals, he reworked the first eleven notes of the phrase to what became the music for "And my heart beats so that I can hardly speak" in "Cheek to Cheek." With that transplanted cutting, Berlin created a new melody and lyric for "Cheek to Cheek," forging that intricate blend of words and music in a single intense day of labor, which, given his work habits, probably meant more night than day. Equally incongruous is the behind-the-scenes squabbling that underlay Astaire and Rogers' elegant enchantment with each other in "Cheek to Cheek." Rogers showed up at dress rehearsal for the number in a gown covered with ostrich feathers, and as they danced, "feathers started to fly," Astaire recalled, "as if a chicken had been attacked by a coyote." Astaire sneezed so much he could not complete the number, and when the efforts of the costume designer failed to fix the gown, feathers flew in another sense as Astaire tore into Rogers, insisting she change to another dress. As Ginger burst into tears, Lela Rogers, the classic stage mother, swooped down to defend her daughter—and the dress she herself had chosen for the number. Astaire stormed off the set, and rehearsal stopped until tempers cooled and the costume designer went back to work on the dress.

Later, Astaire and Hermes Pan concocted a parody of "Cheek to Cheek":

Fred Astaire and Ginger Rogers (in her famous feathered gown) dance to Irving Berlin's "Cheek to Cheek" on RKO's "Big White Set" for *Top Hat*.

> Feathers—I hate feathers—
> And I hate them so that I can hardly speak.
> And I never find the happiness I seek
> With those chicken feathers dancing cheek to cheek.

Perhaps all of these sparks gave an edge to "Cheek to Cheek" that makes it a rival, albeit less erotically overt, for the elegant passion of "Night and Day."

With the finale of *Top Hat*, Berlin and the RKO team tried to solve the problem faced by every musical: how to end the film with a musical number that would not seem like the ending of virtually every other musical film. Audiences had come to expect such a conventional ending—particularly from Warner Brothers, where Busby Berkeley had streamlined a formula that always concluded with a Big Number like "42nd Street"—but audiences also demanded their formulas with a degree of variation. RKO decided, daringly, to conclude *Top Hat* with a spoof of such numbers that would be so overblown, so elaborate, that it would refreshingly send up all musical finales.

Ever since the story—itself an overtly contrived sequence of coincidences and mistaken identities—had taken the characters from London to Venice, the Italian sets had given the film a surreal quality with buildings that looked like flimsy cardboard and canals that seemed an inch deep. While these backdrops may reflect the studio's financial straits, they were perfect for a finale that would parody the artificiality of musical film conventions, particularly those of Busby Berkeley, with dancers twisting among huge scarves to form intricate patterns in black and white. The number Berlin wrote for the absurd frolic, "The Piccolino," took him back to his own lavish production numbers from a decade before. "I hadn't done a tune like that since the Music Box Revues in the 1920s," he recalled. It was not an easy task, however, to satirize one's own extravaganzas. "I worked harder on 'Piccolino' than I did on the whole show," Berlin recalled, an effort matched by the entire company, which devoted a staggering 125 hours of rehearsal time to the number.

It begins conventionally enough, alluding to the film's setting:

> By the Adriatic waters,
> Venetian sons and daughters
> are strumming
> A new tune upon their guitars.

That wrenching off-rhyme (*waters/daughters/guitars*) not only sounds wrong, the accents are off, and Berlin's music highlights the skewing by placing "waters" and "daughters" on descending notes, while "guitars" rises up musically even as its verbal accent falls.

The lyric undercuts itself even more sharply in the next lines:

> It was written by a Latin,
> A gondolier who sat in
> his home out in Brooklyn
> and gazed at the stars.

The true rhyme on *stars/guitars* only highlights the jarring "Brooklyn" which makes the whole romantic foundation of the song totter like the flimsy Venetian set.

The chorus takes Berlin even further back than his Music Box days to "Marie from Sunny Italy" and his many immigrant songs, but now he pushes his rhymes over the top:

> Dance—with your Bambino . . .
> Drink—your glass of Vino,
> And when you've had your plate of Scalopino,
> Make them play the Piccolino.

This self-parody came hard, but Berlin later said of "The Piccolino," "I love it, the way you love a child that you've had trouble with." To further emphasize the silliness of the number, it is first sung not by Astaire but by Rogers, who seems more suitable to the silliness given previous comic roles in musical films (such as her inspired pig-Latin version of "We're in the Money" in *Gold Diggers of 1933*).

Although it is now recognized as one of the greatest of film musicals, *Top Hat* did not go over well with its first audience. When the film was previewed in Santa Barbara, people walked out and complained that the ending was too long. No one was more despondent than Berlin, who may have feared that he would relive the horrors of *Reaching for the Moon*. By cutting just a few minutes of running time, *Top Hat* fared much better at a second preview, then opened at Radio City Music Hall and broke that theater's attendance record, bringing in $350,000 in ticket sales its first three weeks. The film went on to earn more than $3 million, repaying Berlin and Astaire for their shrewd gamble on the film's profitability (it had cost only $620,000 to make). The film was nominated for many Oscars and, though it did not win (*Mutiny on the Bounty* won Best Picture, and Berlin's "Cheek to Cheek" lost out on Best Song to Al Dubin and Harry Warren's "Lullaby of Broadway"), Astaire and Rogers became top box-office attractions surpassed only by Clark Gable and Shirley Temple. By September 1935, three of Berlin's songs—"Cheek to Cheek," "Top Hat," and "Isn't This a Lovely Day?"—held the first, second, and fourth spot, respectively, on *Your Hit Parade*.

In Hollywood, Irving Berlin, now approaching fifty, was regarded with the same respect he had earned on Broadway with *As Thousands Cheer*. In typical filmdom style, he was regaled with a dinner that included moguls from Darryl F. Zanuck to Samuel Goldwyn, and that featured a full-scale replica of "'Nigger Mike's'

Irving Berlin, Fred Astaire, and Ginger Rogers on the set of *Top Hat*, perhaps rehearsing "The Piccolino."

Pelham Café" As he "was led through the swinging doors into the sawdust floors of Mike's," *Variety* reported:

> the little fellow whom they called Izzy in these lean days of his career turned on the tear duct and little beads of emotion crept down his cheeks as he gulped in amazement at the duplication of scenes that were so dear to him.

Accompanied by his old rival from Chinatown days, Al Piantadosi, Berlin sang a medley of his hits, from "Alexander's Ragtime Band" to his latest "Cheek to Cheek." This lionizing of Berlin solidified his repute among studio heads and started several of them thinking about making a movie based on his extraordinary life story. This speculation, coupled with the falling off in quality of the next RKO film featuring Astaire and Rogers, eventually altered Berlin's course in Hollywood.

Instead of following the successful formula of *Top Hat*, the next Astaire-Rogers picture, *Follow the Fleet*, reverted to the model of *Flying Down to Rio*. Fred and Ginger portrayed the comic couple opposite the serious romantic leads played by Randolph Scott and

Harriet Hilliard (later of *Ozzie and Harriet* fame). While Fred and Ginger played professional singers and dancers, the story was less of a backstager than a ship-to-shore romance with Astaire and Scott as sailors who woo Rogers and Hilliard in between being called back to their ship for war-game maneuvers.

Berlin was successful in getting Pan Berman to include seven of his songs in the film, but all were done as straight performance numbers. Of these, the most engaging are "I'm Putting All My Eggs in One Basket," which begins with Fred Astaire playing the piano (*really* playing, showing the musicianship he had developed since his childhood days of playing the drums). With a cigarette dangling from his mouth, he plunks the song out in honky-tonk style, then Ginger joins him in a song and dance as they "rehearse" the number for a benefit show.

In the show, itself, Astaire and Rogers perform "Let's Face the Music and Dance" as another production number, but it is preceded by a pantomime that gives the song a dramatic—indeed a melodramatic—context. Within the set of a European casino, Astaire suavely accepts the loss of all his money at the roulette wheel, then strolls out to the balcony just in time to prevent Rogers, who has also lost heavily, from committing suicide. With such a somber preface, "Let's Face the Music and Dance" went beyond the confines of most film songs to reflect some of the real grimness of the Depression and the prewar jitters raised by the advances of Hitler and Mussolini. Although its carpe diem theme is as old as literature itself, "Let's Face the Music" counsels seizing the day for pleasure in the teeth of a very contemporary despair. It is also, like "Cheek to Cheek," another very innovative song, with sections running to as many as eighteen measures rather than the standard eight bars and subtle shifts of key at dramatic points.

While a good film, *Follow the Fleet* was nowhere as creative as *Top Hat* in integrating songs into the story, and this decline in quality may have made Berlin more receptive to an invitation from Darryl F. Zanuck to do his next musical with Twentieth Century–Fox. Zanuck, who had produced gangster movies at Warners in the early 1930s, joined forces with Berlin's old friend Joe Schenck and together the two had taken over Fox in 1935. Because Zanuck, a Catholic from Nebraska, was an anomaly in Hollywood (though Fred Astaire himself was born in Omaha of Austrian parents), Fox became known as the "non-Jewish studio" and soon evolved its own distinctive brand of musicals. Its first forays, like Berlin's *On the Avenue*, were highly derivative, however. Borrowing Dick Powell from Warner Brothers' Busby Berkeley spectaculars and a story line from RKO's Astaire-Rogers films, *On the Avenue* was another backstager. Originally entitled *Out Front*, it took a phrase from Berlin's "Easter Parade" for its

new title and clearly depended on the songwriter's work to carry the
film. In a scribbled note on an early script, Zanuck, who always prid-
ed himself on his involvement with story development in his films,
scrawled a comment: that the film "depends on numbers":

> This is a clever frame for good numbers, comedy and
> cast—it does not have the original novelty of *Thanks a
> Million* or the underlying drama of *Burlesque* or the star
> attraction of *Top Hat*, therefore it must depend on clever
> comedy, songs, and interesting people.

From the very first scene, songs are done as a stage performance
with no relation to the story; much of the film, in fact, takes place in
the theater where Dick Powell and Alice Faye perform in a typical
satirical revue of the 1930s.

The brightest spots in this tired formula are Dick Powell's rendi-
tions of "I've Got My Love to Keep Me Warm" and "You're
Laughing at Me." Powell was more of a singer than a dancer, and
Berlin took advantage of his greater vocal range. Attired in Astaire's
classic top hat and tails, Powell's lusty tenor belts out "I've Got My
Love to Keep Me Warm" (yet prerecording still enabled Berlin to
end his title line with the clipped "warm" rather than the long open
vowels he would have had to use for a stage performance). The
lyric's colloquially elegant phrases perfectly match conversational
stress with musical accent:

> I *can't* remember a *worse* December,
> Just *watch* those *i*cicles *form*!
> What do I *care* if *i*cicles *form*?
> *I've* got my *love* to *keep* me *warm*.

"I've Got My Love to Keep Me Warm" with its unusually long sixteen-bar A-sections (but cleverly standard eight-bar release), clearly
derived from Berlin's work on *Top Hat*. "When I had to write for
Fred Astaire, I learned something," Berlin said. "Instead of having
him dance a chorus and then repeating it, it gave me the idea of
writing an overlong song like 'Cheek to Cheek' and that keyed me
into 'Let's Face the Music and Dance.' You see, once I found certain
harmonies in rhythms, I completely exhausted them." He continued
to attribute his harmonic discoveries to his musical limitations. "The
fact that I compose only in F-sharp gave me certain harmonies that
other writers missed, because they knew more about music."

Harmonically, his romantic ballad, "You're Laughing at Me," was
an especially intricate song, "as far out and as unanticipatable,"

notes songwriter Alec Wilder, "as anything in popular music." Berlin changes keys, drops in intervals that are difficult to sing, and covers as wide a range as he had ever done before in a song: five notes beyond the octave. Powell had the voice to handle the song, but an attempt to "integrate" it into the story line resulted in stopping the number half-way through while the zany Ritz brothers took over the stage from a flummoxed Powell besieged by the laughter of the audience. Even though it was given short shrift in the film, "You're Laughing at Me," like "I've Got My Love to Keep Me Warm," still became a hit.

For all its drawbacks, *On the Avenue* helped establish a musical style for Twentieth Century–Fox. The key to that stylistic evolution was Alice Faye, who played the singer who loses Powell to an elegant, wealthy socialite. Faye's big number in the film was "Slumming on Park Avenue." The song clearly derived from "Puttin' on the Ritz," but recast the notion of slumming by having the poor folks invade the domain of the swells, and the lyric had some social bite to it:

> Let's go smelling—where they're dwelling,
> Sniffing ev'rything the way they do.

Faye proved she could sing, dance, and even do comedy as she strutted through the number, urging "let's go slumming—nose-thumbing" and counterpointing the arch pronunciation of "cl*awh*sses" with the Brooklynese of "*peah*sses." Even though she could look—and talk—like a platinum bombshell, she had a Madonnalike sweetness and vulnerability that fit in perfectly with Zanuck's "Catholic" studio.

Faye was given the lead in Berlin's next film, *Alexander's Ragtime Band*, which, according to Gerald Mast, set the pattern for later Twentieth Century–Fox musicals:

> Twentieth Century–Fox spun variations on a single theme before, during, and after the war: the relation of extraordinary musical performance to normal American life. The one studio that competed with MGM in the quantity and quality of musical production, Fox built its musicals on female performers attended by nonsinging men. In movie after movie, Alice Faye, Betty Grable, Marilyn Monroe, Carmen Miranda, Sonja Henie, and Ethel Merman carried the musical performance while Tyrone Power, Don Ameche, John Payne, and MacDonald Carey smiled encouragement from the pit, the piano bench, or the front row.

Just as *Top Hat* had defined Astaire-Rogers films for RKO, *Alexander's Ragtime Band* gave Irving Berlin the distinction of helping another studio establish its distinctive musical style.

Berlin found this type of film even more suited to his songs than the Astaire-Rogers classics. Where *Top Hat* had used only five songs, *Alexander's Ragtime Band* incorporated more than twenty. A few of these were new ones Berlin composed for the film, but most were older songs, some famous ones, like the title song, others, like "The International Rag," that had been popular once but had long since faded. Hollywood films, even more than radio, Berlin found, could revive old songs and help them become standards. Berlin would continue making such "retrospective" films that incorporated his older songs for many years for Fox, MGM, and other studios. The fact that these films presented songs as performances rather than integrally related to plot and characters also appealed to Berlin, who—despite all of his success with the integrated songs of *Top Hat*—was always more at home with the looser format of the revue.

Alexander's Ragtime Band started out as a thinly veiled biography of Berlin himself. Zanuck commissioned Berlin to work on a script, which the songwriter turned into a history of modern American popular music, using twenty-two of his own songs to illustrate America's liberation from European models and the creation of a musical idiom that finally culminates in a Carnegie Hall performance. Zanuck, again with his devotion to script development, insisted upon revisions that would make it a "character story" rather than a "situation story" about the history of American song. "Maybe our trouble is that we are trying to tell a phase of American musical evolution," Zanuck said in one of his memos on the script, "instead of a story about two boys and a girl." Still, Zanuck balanced that love story with the evolution of American popular song:

> Give Alexander credit for every innovation that has been given to bands in the last couple of decades. He is the first one who uses someone to get up and sing in a megaphone, the first one to introduce specialties. But Alexander can't be a prophet—his innovations are casual inspirations—must be shown and let audience draw its own conclusions. We want to introduce as many varieties of entertainment as we can put over songs in sock-o fashion. Each time lapse should introduce something new.

With any other songwriter, Zanuck's demand would have seemed absurd, but all Irving Berlin had to do to trace every important development in twentieth-century American song—the dance craze,

Jack Haley as the drummer, Tyrone Power as the violinist bandleader, and Don Ameche as the pianist play the title song from the 1938 film *Alexander's Ragtime Band.*

World War I patriotism, sob ballads of the 1920s, 1930s radio croon-er fare—was to reach into his catalog and pull out not one but a handful of classics.

The filmed version traces Berlin's professional—but not his per-sonal—life as it follows the career of bandleader Tyrone Power (who never sings), pianist-songwriter Don Ameche (who sings passably), and Alice Faye and Ethel Merman (who both sing wonderfully). Songs are woven throughout the film, from "Alexander's Ragtime Band" and "Everybody's Doin' It," through "Oh! How I Hate to Get Up in the Morning," "A Pretty Girl Is Like a Melody," "Blue Skies," "Heat Wave," and "Easter Parade." At some points, song follows song to trace plot and character developments as well as historical changes, with no dialogue whatsoever. Instead of integrating his songs into a story, *Alexander's Ragtime Band* wove a story of American music and American history around a progression of Irving Berlin's songs—a feat that would not have been possible with any other songwriter of his generation. Berlin wrote some new songs for the film, such as "Walking Stick," which Merman delivers in a rhythmic tribute to Astaire, and "Now It Can Be Told," which Faye renders in typically opulent 1930s "sweet music" style.

In the words of film historian, Gerald Mast:

> What keeps the twenty-seven-year chronicle together is
> not the attempt to tie some story to the string of songs
> but to make the songs and musical styles into the chroni-
> cle itself. *Alexander's Ragtime Band* is the first film musi-
> cal to realize that the history of American popular music
> is the history of America. Irving Berlin is a historian; to
> hear his songs is to read that history. . . . Over twenty-
> seven years, the actors don't age. Nor do the songs.
> Ageless, ever fresh and young, the songs are America—a
> union of past and present, dance dive and concert hall.
> No previous Hollywood musical demonstrated a closer
> bond between social history and cultural artifact.

The first film ever to carry a songwriter's name above the title and
ahead of any other name in the credits, *Alexander's Ragtime Band*
was a tremendous tribute to Irving Berlin's great body of work.

The extensive script changes Zanuck mandated for *Alexander's
Ragtime Band* delayed its completion and the start of work on
Berlin's second film for Fox, *Second Fiddle*. An undistinguished vehicle for Sonja Henie, playing a skating teacher from Minnesota who
achieves stardom in Hollywood, *Second Fiddle* did produce a hit in
"I Poured My Heart Into a Song." Between the two Fox films, Berlin
returned to RKO to do one more score for Astaire and Rogers. In his
absence RKO had turned out more films for their charmed and
charming pair with other songwriters such as Dorothy Fields and
Jerome Kern (*Swing Time*) and George and Ira Gershwin (*Shall We
Dance?*). Cast in the mold of *Top Hat*, these films define the quintes-
sential Astaire-Rogers style and produced such great songs as "Let's
Call the Whole Thing Off," "A Fine Romance," and "The Way You
Look Tonight." Those songs, moreover, are intricately woven into
the dramatic texture of the film and in some cases were not even
dance numbers. (George Gershwin was upset when his and Ira's
"They Can't Take That Away From Me" was not given the full-scale
dance treatment, but Astaire's poignant, understated delivery to a
tearful Rogers was far more effective than any dance.)

RKO had managed to keep the Astaire-Rogers formula alive by
carefully balancing repetition with variation: returning to the same
sophisticated stories, stock characters, and integrated songs, yet
refreshing these with such new wrinkles as having Fred and Ginger
dance on roller-skates. Even so, the formula was beginning to wear
thin. Astaire himself recalled that he and Rogers "wondered how
long it would be safe to carry on this cycle of team pictures. We
didn't want to run it into the ground." He remembered one ominous
review of *Swing Time* in 1936:

THE SINGING AND DANCING LIMIT

Ginger and Fred are at it again in "Swing Time," singing and dancing like anything. One begins to wonder how many more of that type of film the public is prepared to enjoy. I know of at least one member of it who has reached the limit.

Astaire had a five-picture contract with RKO with a "Ginger clause" that allowed him to work independently of her in two of those films. He exercised his option for *A Damsel in Distress* in 1937. It is an excellent musical except for the painfully obvious fact that his beautiful costar, Joan Fontaine, could neither sing nor dance and thus suffered the inevitable comparisons with Rogers. *A Damsel in Distress* was also the first Astaire film to lose money, so he agreed to work again with Rogers. Banking on the appeal of the magical pair, RKO put *Carefree* into production at the end of 1938 and brought Irving Berlin back to write songs for them. Although the film is good, it strains for novel effects to refresh the Astaire-Rogers formula. Rogers plays a singer, but Astaire is cast as a psychoanalyst who tries to cure her of continually breaking her engagement to Ralph Bellamy only to find himself falling in love with her. In one number, Rogers dreams of Astaire singing and dancing with her. A complex production was planned to include several lifts that would be filmed in slow motion. Originally, the dream sequence was to be shot in Technicolor, a device that had been used in several films, and seemed an especially dramatic way of highlighting the transition from the "reality" of black-and-white to the colorful world of dream, then back again. This contrast would also underscore the movement from talking to singing and dancing, easing the transition that was at the heart of all film musicals. Berlin therefore wrote a song, "I Used to Be Color Blind" especially for the scene. Another gem of simplicity, the original lyric had the phrase, "I never could see the green in the grass, the gold in the moon, the blue in the skies." But after looking at it, Berlin realized that it was "redundant and negative," so he revised it to what he felt was more "direct and positive":

> I used to be color blind,
> But I met you and now I find
> There's green in the grass,
> There's gold in the moon,
> There's blue in the skies.

In such subtle intricacies of artistry lay the seeming naturalness of his blend of words and music.

After the color tests were screened the results were disappointing and the idea was shelved. Shot entirely in black-and-white, the dance is charming in its slow movement over various platforms but Berlin's lyric seems oddly out of place with its stress on "the red of your lips, the blue of your eye" and other color imagery. As a "dream-dance" that reveals character and advances plot, "I Used to Be Color Blind" anticipates Agnes de Mille's revolutionary dream-dance for Laurey in *Oklahoma!* The number was also a landmark in Astaire-Rogers films, culminating in their first on-screen kiss. Astaire had long resisted the Hollywood cliché of the kiss, but he finally relented, though there is still a refreshing twist: as film historian John Mueller points out, "it is *Rogers* who consummates the kiss (after all, it's her dream)."

Two of Berlin's other songs for the film, "The Night Is Filled with Music" and "Let's Make the Most of Our Dreams," were filmed but cut from the final print, while "Since They Turned Loch Lomond into Swing" and "The Yam" were overwhelmed by their production numbers: one a bizarre golf dance by Astaire and the other the stock finale of silliness. Only "Change Partners" stood out from the film. An all-purpose song designed for any Astaire-Rogers vehicle, "Change Partners" was given a dramatic framework as Astaire tries to lure Rogers out of Bellamy's embrace—and out of a posthypnotic trance. Once again, Berlin blends words and music together in perfectly matched cadences:

> *Must* you dance,
> *ev'ry* dance
> *With* the same
> *for*tunate *man*?

Weaving triplets and chromatic notes through perfectly colloquial phrases, Berlin captures Astaire's tone of elegant seductiveness:

> Ask him to sit this one out
> and while you're alone
> I'll tell the waiter to tell him
> he's wanted on the telephone.

Then, as the release shifts back to the final A-section with an expression of passionate exasperation—"You've been locked—in his arms—ever since—heaven knows when"—Astaire fully clasps Rogers in his own arms, emphasizing the pivotal point in the lyric. Such an interplay of words, music, and dance testifies to the way Berlin and Astaire wed their artistry together.

Carefree was successful with critics but wound up losing money, yet another sign that the Astaire-Rogers partnership was coming to an end, although over the course of their teamwork they had brought in more than $38 million for RKO. Their parting signaled the end of an era of sparkling elegance and casual urbanity that had flourished since the end of World War I. It had been nurtured by the wit of the Algonquin Round Table, honed in the pages of *The New Yorker*, and sung in the songs of Cole Porter, Rodgers and Hart, and the Gershwins. The 1929 Crash had not destroyed that debonair style; instead, it deepened and matured it, giving it a greater range that paralleled the lengthening of song titles themselves, from Berlin's minimalist titles of the 1920s like "Always" and "Remember" to the expansiveness of "How Deep Is the Ocean?" and "Top Hat, White Tie and Tails." It was manifest in the streamlined, gleaming style of Art Deco films like *The Thin Man* with William Powell and Myrna Loy, and the elegant and witty "screwball comedies." It was a style that identified with New York, with its attendant penthouse cocktail parties, black tie and evening dress and all the "hip hooray and ballyhoo" of Broadway.

Even before the parting of Astaire and Rogers, George Gershwin had died suddenly from a brain tumor in 1937 at the age of only 38. The genius who had captured the "Fascinating Rhythm" of New York in his music was mourned by shocked friends and colleagues; Irving Berlin contributed an elegy to the young man who had once come to him for a job. In it he acknowledged how different he and George Gershwin were. Gershwin was a trained musician and composer, a brilliant pianist who had pushed beyond popular song into classical compositions—rhapsodies, concerti, tone poems—and had just completed one of America's few great operas in *Porgy and Bess*. Berlin recognized Gershwin's range, but warmly welcomed him into the one realm where Berlin had been and would be content to remain throughout his musical career: "A chorus of thirty-two bars."

While other purveyors of the musical style of elegant wit remained, time was taking its toll on them as well. Lorenz Hart's alcoholism grew worse and, as Rodgers searched in vain for him for days during crucial rehearsal periods for their musicals, his thoughts turned to finding another collaborator. Cole Porter, who epitomized the style of the 1930s, suffered a terrible accident while horseback riding one morning in 1938 that slowed his songwriting career and left him crippled the rest of his life (though Porter boasted that—while he lay under the horse, his legs crushed—he composed one of his most flippant catalog songs, "At Long Last Love").

Irving Berlin could write music and lyrics in the style of casual elegance but he always kept a certain distance from it. This better positioned him to revert to more heartfelt and simpler sentiments when the times called for them. He once quipped, in fact, that "nothing is so corny as last year's sophistication." As the clouds of another world war loomed over the closing years of the decade, the American sensibility turned to more sombre and prosaic fare than the graceful charm of Astaire and Rogers, dancing in evening clothes on an Art Deco set to a witty catalog song by Cole Porter. An era and a songwriting style were passing, and Irving Berlin would once again prove to be at the forefront of the transition.

Chapter 10

GOD BLESS AMERICA

I'd like to write a great peace song, but it is hard to do, because you have trouble dramatizing peace. . . . Yet music is so important. It changes thinking, it influences everybody, whether they know it or not.

When Irving Berlin turned fifty in 1938, American spirit was at its lowest ebb. The Depression had been dragging on for nearly a decade and another economic slump, dubbed a recession, made recovery seem even more remote. Franklin Delano Roosevelt's various initiatives had not rejuvenated the economy, and even nature seemed to turn against the country with a terrible drought that made the Great Plains a gigantic "Dust Bowl" and drove poor farmers and sharecroppers from the land. Meanwhile, around the world, the threat of war mounted. Then, Japan attacked China, Mussolini invaded Ethiopia, and Hitler entered the Rhineland. Together the two European dictators supported Franco in the Spanish Civil War, then, in 1938, Hitler forced an *Anschluss* with Austria. The League of Nations, established after World War I to prevent such aggression, stood helplessly by.

Radio brought these frightening developments into the homes of the American people. In September 1938, most of them tuned their dials to H. V. Kaltenborn, who broadcast the latest news from what he called, in his clipped, crisp voice, "Yirrup." For eighteen tense days, Kaltenborn kept vigil over a new crisis: Germany's claims to Czechoslovakia's Sudetenland. From his CBS studio in New York, Kaltenborn reported the latest developments then napped on an army cot till more news poured in. In eighty-five extemporaneous broadcasts, he traced the course of negotiations in Munich on September 30, when Hitler cowed British Prime Minister Neville

Chamberlain into ratifying Germany's seizure of the Sudetenland.
The next day newspapers carried photographs of Chamberlain,
holding his furled black umbrella in one hand and waving what
would turn out to be a worthless "Anglo-German Pact of Friendship" with the other. The headlines announced his ringing assurance to the cheering crowds that greeted him back in England that
he had brought "peace for our time."

Irving Berlin was in London on business during those fateful
days, and, like everyone, he wanted desperately to believe
Chamberlain's pledge. He also wanted to capture that widespread
sentiment, as he alone could do, by writing a "peace song." "I
worked for a while on a song called 'Thanks, America' but I didn't
like it," he told reporters. "I tried again with a song called 'Let's
Talk About Liberty,' but I didn't get very far with that. I found it
was too much like making a speech to music." After he returned to
America, he went to his "trunk" of unused songs and found a song
from 1918 called "God Bless America." Its title had been inspired
by Berlin's mother who, despite their poverty as Berlin was growing up, would frequently murmur, "God Bless America." "And not
casually," Berlin recalled, "but with emotion which was almost
exaltation." He had intended to use it as the finale for *Yip! Yip!
Yaphank* but cut it because it seemed too solemn for the upbeat
revue. Besides, Berlin noted, "We weren't 'God-blessing America' at
the time—we were going to beat the Hun":

> When I saw the show in rehearsals, I realized that the
> song was just a bit too much. After all, it was a soldiers'
> show, the boys were in uniform—it was like gilding the
> lily. I put the piece away and didn't think of it again until
> that moment in the Autumn of 1938.

Taking another look at "God Bless America," Berlin found its sentiments much more appropriate to the new, troubled times. The very
title dated the song, since by the 1930s people had begun to refer to
the country as the "United States," a shift in nomenclature that
reflected "the era of the Depression and growing worldwide
Fascism, when the limits of American power became painfully visi-
ble." By bringing the old term "America" back into his song, Berlin
evoked in his listeners' minds an era when "America" was strong,
unified, and indivisible.

Still, he needed to make some changes to bring the song up to
date for 1938:

> I had to make one or two changes in the lyrics, and they
> in turn led me to a slight change and, I think, improve-

ment in the melody. One line in particular; the original line ran: "Stand beside her and guide her to the right with a light from above." In 1918 the phrase "to the right" had no political significance, as it has now. So for obvious reasons I changed the phrase to "Through the night with a light from above," and I think that's better.

Because he wanted a "peace" song rather than a "war" song, Berlin also changed the original line, "Make her victorious on land and foam," to a lyric that required him to lengthen the melody. What resulted was the most majestic section of the song:

> From the mountains
> to the prairies
> To the oceans
> white with foam

Where another songwriter would have followed "To the oceans" with another parallel phrase (such as "to the stars!"), Berlin's lyric takes a surprising swerve with "white with foam." Into that phrase went his mastery of vowels, the long *o* of "foam" echoing "oceans" and "white" resonating with the long *i*s of "land that *I* love, stand bes*i*de her and gu*i*de her, thru the n*i*ght with a l*i*ght from above."

The music reinforces this climactic moment by building a melody, as it has throughout the song, in wavelike, repeated intervals; here the sequence of repeated phrases rises to progressively higher notes, then the next phrase begins on the highest note of the song, appropriately enough on the word "God," which returns, like yet another huge musical wave, to the opening theme of the chorus as the melody, with "home sweet home," returns to its own home key on the last note.

Once he had refurbished his old trunk song, Berlin offered it to Kate Smith, the strapping radio singer who had the voice and dignity he felt "God Bless America" required. While Berlin still viewed radio as a threat to the quality and commercial success of popular songwriting, he recognized the medium's power to reach people, particularly in such critical times. When Kate Smith sang "God Bless America" on her Armistice Day broadcast of November 11, 1938, the song struck a chord in the American people. Proud, strong, yet humble, even prayerful, the song crystallized the feelings of Americans as the Depression continued and war clouds gathered.

Berlin had once again written a song that transcended the ephemeral boundaries of "popular song," and he tried to explain its sudden and enduring success:

> The reason "God Bless America" caught on is that it hap-
> pens to have a universal appeal. Any song that had that
> is bound to be a success; and let me tell you right here
> that while song plugging may help a good song, it never
> put over a poor one. . . . The mob is always right. It
> seems to be able to sense instinctively what is good, and
> I believe that there are darned few good songs which
> have not been whistled or sung by the crowd.

Like "Alexander's Ragtime Band," "God Bless America" was a simple but superbly crafted work that captured both its own historical
moment as well as an enduring, universal sentiment.

So eagerly did Americans embrace "God Bless America" that soon
there were calls for it to replace "The Star-Spangled Banner" as the
national anthem. While replacing the national anthem might seem
unthinkable to many Americans today, in 1938 its stature was not
quite so venerable. "The Star-Spangled Banner" had only been named
the national anthem in 1931, near the end of Herbert Hoover's administration, over strong calls for "America" and "Columbia, the Gem of
the Ocean," which George Washington had commissioned as the
nation's official song. "The Star-Spangled Banner" had not even been
composed as a song. Francis Scott Key had written a poem about the
British bombardment of Baltimore's Fort McHenry in the War of
1812, employing a galloping anapestic meter:

> Oh say, can you *see* by the *dawn's* early *light*
> What so *proud*ly we *hailed* at the *twi*light's last *gleam*ing

This was a popular poetic meter in the nineteenth century (Clement
Clarke Moore, for example, used it for "A Visit from St. Nicholas"—
"'Twas the *night* before *Christ*mas and *all* through the *house* . . .).
Like all poets, however, Key varied his meter, so that when people
tried to sing it to the tune of an old British drinking song, "To
Anacreon in Heaven," the irregular poetic meter did not fit the exact
musical rhythm. To make words and music match, therefore, certain
syllables had to be elongated, from the initial "O-oh say" to the cumbersome ending: "ba-ah-ner-er ye-et wa-ave." Along with these mismatches of lyrics and music, the melody itself was so wide-ranging
that few people could sing it—an oddly elitist national anthem for a
democratic country. Several people, including Eleanor Roosevelt,
had been calling for a simplification of "The Star-Spangled Banner,"
so that, as she put it, "it could be sung by those of us who have little
or no voice." Others had been protesting its martial tone and
imagery, and one New York school official proclaimed the anthem
"too militaristic to be sung by high school students."

By contrast, "God Bless America" was a masterfully simple song that anyone could sing and was especially designed for a large group to carry words and melody easily. Kate Smith sang it before a huge crowd at the 1939 New York World's Fair, and it was featured at both the Republican and Democratic conventions in 1940. The *New York Times* reported that "people like to wear buttons and wave pennants labeled 'God Bless America.'" When the song was played at Brooklyn's Ebbets Field on Memorial Day of 1940 "the crowd rose and uncovered as if for the national anthem." "Americans who find 'The Star-Spangled Banner' hard on their voices," the *Times* proclaimed, "have found a patriotic song they can sing."

Not all Americans embraced Irving Berlin's song, however. "America-first" patriots rallied round "The Star-Spangled Banner" and began shouting down efforts to sing "God Bless America" at public gatherings. Prominent clergymen attacked the song from the pulpit as "patriotic pretense" and a "specious substitute for religion and patriotism." Headlines like "G-A-W-D Bless A-M-E-R-I-K-E-R!" decried the song as the slick, commercial product of Tin Pan Alley, and an editorial writer haughtily observed, "One does not 'croon' 'The Star-Spangled Banner!'" Behind this backlash was the smoldering anger of the WASP establishment over what Irving Berlin and other immigrants had been doing to American popular culture since 1910. The editorial writer referred to Berlin as "nee-Izzy Balinsky, ex-Singing Waiter" and denounced "God Bless America" for failing to express "the real American attitude." Instead, he sneered, "It smacks of the 'How glad I am' of the refugee horde." The head of the New Jersey Ku Klux Klan was more to the point in calling for a boycott of "God Bless America" simply "because its author Irving Berlin is Jewish." Someone even concocted a parody lyric that indicted all the Jews who purportedly controlled America's popular entertainments: "God lives in Hollywood—he just planed in." After having the Almighty consorting with "the Zanucks" (who, while not Jewish, was nevertheless Catholic) "and the Mannix," it culminated in "God lives in Hollywood—and prays—to—Mayer."

"God Bless America" found a defender in the poet Carl Sandburg, who was also a prominent scholar of American folksong. Describing a political rally in Chicago, Sandburg delivered the following encomium for Berlin's song:

> The high spot of the evening for me was when a frail gal from Hollywood, l'il Judy Garland, stepped up to a mike and let her warm tremulous contralto go on the first line of "God Bless America." Before she had reached the second line, at least half of the audience on the main floor

> rose from their seats and joined in the singing. Not from anywhere came a hoot or a protest—not a sign of one person in a murmuring demurrer to Irving Berlin's song. Then the magnetic little Judy, beating time with the sway of her arrow-like figure, carried the song through to a massive choral effect.

Sandburg then turned his ire on the "racists" who had booed the song at other rallies and proclaimed "God Bless America" "one of our national songs worth community singing no matter what the race of the author of the song." While Carl Sandburg defended the song on political grounds, the great conductor Leopold Stokowski, stood up for its artistry against charges of Tin Pan Alley "slickness." "It is what you might say very singable," observed the maestro, "that is, it can be carried along handsomely by a great number of people and it has dignity, simplicity, and a wonderful sincerity."

Berlin himself opposed any suggestion that his song replace "The Star-Spangled Banner" and soon after his company published "God Bless America," he signed over all of its royalties, which soon reached a quarter of a million dollars, to the Boy Scouts and Girl Scouts of America. While he wanted no profits from his song, Berlin did control its use to make sure it was rendered with the proper dignity. Through ASCAP, he was able to limit radio performances of the song as well as ban Harry Richman from using it in a chorus-girl routine at the Chez Paree Chicago. Kate Smith, Berlin felt, had given the song its definitive performance, and he wanted no "swing" versions of "God Bless America."

Radio stations saw Berlin's control as another battle in their ongoing war with the songwriters of ASCAP. A station director wrote Berlin an open letter, carried in newspapers across the country, demanding that he turn over his song completely to the American public. Praising "God Bless America" for "the genuine emotion of its lyrics, the moving simplicity of its melody," the director predicted, with a back-handed compliment, that the song would earn Berlin "an acclaim and an immortality" that will endure long after the "tawdry sentimentality" of his "Tin Pan Alley effusions." Then, using an argument frequently directed at creative artists—but never, say, at inventors—he implied Berlin could not take personal credit for so inspired an achievement:

> You, Mr. Berlin, have no more right to a personal interest in "God Bless America" than the descendants of Abraham Lincoln have a right to a restricting copyright on the Gettysburg Address. That great document passed into the public domain as the words fell from his lips.

Berlin should be content with nothing more than "the glory of having achieved greatness" and present his song "to the United States Government so that it may be played and sung everywhere at any time."

Berlin struck back at the medium he had regarded warily for twenty years. After a lifetime of plugging his songs, he pointed out, "God Bless America" was "the first song I ever wrote which required no push to get it started." As for the station manager, Berlin shot back that his editorial "would I think be in much better taste if advanced by an executive of a radio station which had not been a party to defrauding composers and authors of their royalties for a period of years."

Berlin and ASCAP won the battle over "God Bless America," but they would ultimately lose their war with radio. The medium's incessant airing of a song boosted short-term gains but quickly exhausted its popularity. Radio then demanded songwriters turn out songs more and more quickly—albeit shoddily—to fill its voracious appetite for new "hits." While ASCAP could not limit radio's use of its songs, the organization could at least demand an increase in what seemed to songwriters the ridiculously low fees stations paid for ASCAP material, given the profits those songs earned for the stations and their advertisers. In 1940, ASCAP demanded that radio stations pay double the $4.5 million dollar fee to renew their five-year license to play the music of ASCAP members. Radio stations, which had always taken the position that songwriters should be grateful for the "free" plugging radio gave their songs, refused to pay the increase. For months, the two sides bickered and radio listeners had to be content with a fare of non-ASCAP songs. Because virtually ever major living songwriter was a member of ASCAP, radio first turned to dead songwriters. Stephen Foster's "Jeannie With the Light Brown Hair" was aired so frequently that an ASCAP songwriter penned a parody called "Jeannie's Light Brown Hair is Turning Gray."

Radio soon found other living songwriters who were not members of ASCAP, and as the war dragged on, a new organization emerged that would eventually change the character of American music. Broadcast Music Incorporated (BMI) was a rival of ASCAP that had been quietly signing up songwriters in the south and midwest. BMI was not interested in sheet music or songs for musical theater and films; instead, it concentrated on record sales and radio. The songwriters BMI sought out were a far cry, as historian Tony Palmer observes, geographically and stylistically, from those of Tin Pan Alley, Broadway, or Hollywood:

> Those who benefited immediately were the hillbillies, who by now had their own well-established network of

local country radio shows, and the black musicians, who
for years had been recorded for little or no financial
reward. The ASCAP monopoly was broken and the
absolute domination of Tin Pan Alley came to an end.

BMI provided radio stations with songs that had a distinctly different twang from the urbane New York polish of ASCAP writers. A
country-western song, "You Are My Sunshine," became a hit in
1941, and was soon followed by "Deep in the Heart of Texas" and
"Pistol Packin' Mama."

Although ASCAP and radio finally reached an agreement later
that year, as Charles Hamm explains, "BMI had at least a foot in the
door of the popular music industry":

> As mid-century passed, New York had been the center of
> the publication and composition of popular song for
> some sixty years. An urban song style had grown up in
> the city, a style combining elements of the previous gen-
> erations of American song with fresh harmonic and
> melodic ideas from nineteenth-century European classi-
> cal music—and this mixture spiced with rhythmic and
> instrumental idiosyncrasies of the music of black
> Americans. The resulting product was the vehicle for
> some of the finest and most successful songs in the histo-
> ry of the genre. But the mood of America was changing,
> the Tin Pan Alley style had lost its freshness and cutting
> edge, and it was only a matter of time before another
> corner would be turned and American song would once
> again incorporate new elements from the rich and com-
> plex musical heritage of the country.

The change would be so profound that not even Irving Berlin would
be able to adapt.

Berlin was one of the first songwriters to sense that there was a
shift away from the New York sophistication of the 1930s. With
"God Bless America," he deliberately revived what he called, from
his early days on Tin Pan Alley, a "home" song. With the advent of
World War II, he and other songwriters turned away from the
world of skyscrapers and cocktail shakers to America's regions, to
rural life, to hearth and home. As early as 1938, Berlin, with his
remarkably attentive ear to shifts in the national sensibility,
planned a Broadway show, *Holiday Revue*, that would be based
upon American holidays, just as *As Thousands Cheer* had been built
around the sections of a newspaper. Broadway, however, had completely turned away from the revue format to the more integrated

book show, and soon would reflect the larger shift in national taste with Rodgers and Hammerstein's 1943 musical, *Oklahoma!* Berlin had better luck selling his holiday revue to Hollywood, where it became *Holiday Inn*.

Like later film musicals of the 1940s, such as *Meet Me in St. Louis* and *The Harvey Girls*, *Holiday Inn* emphasized American rural life over New York glitz and glamour. As Laurence Bergreen notes:

> In the face of the threat of war, holidays acquired a new significance; they affirmed the values of heart, home, and country. A traditionalist, Berlin sensed that people would cling to holidays at a time when the nation's well-being was imperiled. Conceived as escapism, *Holiday Inn* took on a new function; like "God Bless America," it served as a vehicle for endorsing the American way of life at a time when all hell was breaking loose in Europe. *Holiday Inn* was still entertainment; no thought of politics intruded on its timeless appeal. But the threat of war, and what war would mean for the nation, informed every aspect of the movie.

As a dramatic showcase for his holiday numbers, Berlin imagined an entertainer who left the bustle of show business behind him to refurbish an old country inn that would be only open on holidays. In 1938, Berlin had bought a country house in the Catskills as a Christmas present to his wife. As Mary Ellin Barrett describes her first glimpse of "Our very own 'country house'":

> No pillars, no broad terrace and tall French windows, just an old, low-slung dwelling with peeling white paint and a dingy roof. "It needs a little work," my father said as we looked about the icy inside. "A lot of work. . . . "Are you excited?" my father asked, and before I could answer, he said, "*I* am."

Bing Crosby's pastoral longings in *Holiday Inn* clearly reflected Berlin's own. With the added twist that the entertainer would put on shows for the benefit of other entertainers, for whom holidays always meant work, and absence from their families, Berlin had his dramatic vehicle for including songs. While most of these songs were done as performance numbers, their staging and the way they resonated to the film's story and characters made *Holiday Inn* one of the most innovative of the 1940s musicals.

Berlin sold his idea to Paramount, whose trademark was the musical built around the star performer—in the 1930s, it had been

Irving and Ellin Berlin, "Portrait of a Happy Marriage," 1942.

Maurice Chevalier, Mae West, the Marx Brothers, and Marlene Dietrich (in later years Paramount would wrap musicals around Dean Martin and Jerry Lewis as well as Elvis Presley). In 1940, however, Paramount's musical centerpiece was Bing Crosby. Crosby, who had begun as a radio crooner, had a casual, informal style that was perfect for film songs, yet he could handle the most intricate movements of melody and rhythm. Crosby played the entertainer who longs for the simple life in the country, while his big-city rival—

in show business and in love—would be Fred Astaire. Since his split with Ginger Rogers, Astaire had been struggling to redefine himself in the new decade of homespun musicals. In *Holiday Inn* he plays the dark underside of his 1930s persona of elegance and charm. Representing the world of the big city and show business in their crasser commercial incarnations, Astaire tries to bring Crosby back out of the woods. In one number he even dances drunk and has to be carried from the floor!

The film was directed by Mark Sandrich, who staged the musical numbers with the pictorial and dramatic flair he had developed in *Top Hat* and other RKO films. Berlin wrote more than a dozen songs for the film, which, together with older songs like "Easter Parade," give *Holiday Inn* the song-packed feel of *Alexander's Ragtime Band*. The film opens in a Broadway nightclub with Astaire and Crosby doing a charming "challenge" song to woo their costar, Virginia Dale. Crosby warbles "I'll Capture Your Heart Singing" and Astaire retorts, with his feet as well as his voice, "I'll Capture Your Heart Dancing." In the backstage romance, Dale leaves Crosby and his dream of a country retreat for the promise of stardom with Astaire. The song and dramatic situation set up a contrast to the rest of the score of holiday songs, which are staged in the rural world of Holiday Inn. Each of these receives the kind of lavish treatment that made Berlin prefer the revue format over integrated songs for his film scores. Most of the performances, nevertheless, are tied to the story in a complementary, if not an integral, way. "Let's Start the New Year Right," for example, not only inaugurates the first show at the inn, it establishes the romance between Crosby and his new discovery, Marjorie Reynolds. He and Reynolds move from entertaining the audience to cooking domestically for the guests in the kitchen.

One of those songs, however, raised an issue of what today would be termed "political correctness." For the Lincoln's Birthday number, Berlin wrote "Abraham," a minor-key gospel song which focused on Lincoln's emancipation of the slaves. The song fits dramatically into the film when Crosby, in an effort to hide his beautiful new discovery from Astaire and other Broadway types, has her black up for the number. While blackface had been commonplace in earlier films, by the 1940s organizations like the NAACP made their objections to the demeaning practice heard. Although the film could not be redone after it was released, Irving Berlin was sympathetic to the racial issue and took the unusual step of revising his lyric in the sheet music for "Abraham" to change the objectionable word "darkey" to "Negro." "No song," he said, "is important enough to offend a whole race." The change made the newspapers and Berlin's gesture was a small but significant step toward more sensitivity to racial representation in the media.

The other songs that unfold through *Holiday Inn* trace the most ancient of ritual patterns as the holidays mark not only national and religious occasions but the cycle of the seasons. The romance between Crosby and Reynolds takes root with the Valentine number, "Be Careful, It's My Heart," a lovely ballad with long notes tailor-made for Crosby's delivery, which many people thought would be the popular hit of the film. The romance blossoms in "Easter Parade," one of the few numbers that emanates directly out of a dramatic moment. Despite the big-city references of its lyric, that occasion is not an urbane stroll up Fifth Avenue but a congregation's exodus from a country church after Easter morning services. At the end of the song, the rural peace is broken when Fred Astaire ominously returns. By midsummer, when he tapdances around exploding fire-crackers for the Fourth of July number, "Say It with Firecrackers," Astaire emerges as the villain who has insinuated himself into Crosby's Edenic romance. After he has lured Reynolds to Hollywood, winter sets in and Crosby is unable to eat his lonely Thanksgiving dinner as he sings "Plenty to Be Thankful For" with rueful irony.

The story of *Holiday Inn* is framed dramatically by one of Berlin's greatest songs, "White Christmas." Berlin had written this song back in the Christmas of 1937. Filming on *Alexander's Ragtime Band* had finally begun, but that meant Berlin had to stay in Hollywood, while his family spent the holidays without him back in New York. Lonely and gloomy, he decided to work on a Christmas song for his holiday revue. Starting with a verse about the palm trees and balmy weather of Beverly Hills in December, he envisioned "White Christmas" sung as a mournful carol by a group of sophisticates gathered around a Hollywood swimming pool. With cocktails and cigarette holders in hand, they would reminisce about the white Christmases of their youth. In contrast to the days, weeks, even years it took him to complete other songs, Irving Berlin wrote "White Christmas," start to finish, in one of his classic all-night marathons. As he himself described it, the song came to him in one of those rare cases of inspiration:

> We working composers all too often, in the interests of expediency, sharpen our pencils, get out that square sheet of paper and become too slick. Those forced efforts are "square" songs. But sometimes a song is a natural. We may start it to order for a specific scene or show, but our subconscious beings go to work and the song is just there. This is what I call a "round" song.

The result of that unusual night's work was a song that subtly departs from the most fundamental tenets of songwriting. Berlin's innovations were effective, in part, because "White Christmas" was recorded in a Hollywood sound studio, so he could take greater liberties with short vowels and crisp consonants than he could in a song that had to be sung from the stage. The innovations themselves, however, came from a lifetime of manipulating words against music.

From its haunting opening to its last syllable and note, "White Christmas" seems utterly simple, yet beneath that simplicity the song never ceases to surprise. Another songwriter would have made the first line emphasize such important words as "dreaming" and "Christmas," verbs and nouns, with long, emphatic notes, so that they might have come out something like this:

I'm *dream*ing of a white *Christ*-mas

But Berlin deftly emphasizes the seemingly unimportant "I'm" with a whole note, then races over the other syllables to another whole note on "white," emphasizing the long *I* in each word:

I'm dreaming of a *white* Christmas

Although written in the most basic key of C, the melody wanders chromatically. While it generally stays within the octave, it climbs above it at the beginning, "just like the *ones* I used to know," then again in the phrase "with ev'ry *Christ*mas card I write." Despite these upward strains, the melody's progress is steadily and almost despondently downward. After one last upward climb to "bright," it drops one note below middle C on "may all your Christ-*mases be* white" to give the ending a wandering, unresolved quality. The lyric too hesitates, particularly on the unsingable, almost unpronounceable, word "Christmases" that only a singer with Crosby's talent could enunciate with apparent ease.

The rhymes drift as elusively as the melody. The initial "know" does not find its simple, solid rhyme until we traverse the clipped, double rhymes of:

> where the treetops glisten
> and children listen
> to hear . . .
> sleigh bells in the snow.

Even these short lines make us linger, as "listen" is not followed by the normal noun telling us *what* they listen to, but instead by "to hear" that makes us, too, pause in anticipation. The song ends on the tonic note of middle C, but that musical return to the home key is offset by the aimless, drifting off of the lyric on the word "white," which for the first time in the song is not followed by Christmas but hangs alone to resonate with all of its ambiguous connotations.

This tension between distant wandering, musically and lyrically, and the rootedness of rhyme and melody reflects the singer, who is so remote from the very memories he recalls so vividly. Like "Easter Parade," "White Christmas" sidesteps all religious associations, but where "Easter Parade" converted the religious holiday into a communal urban festival, "White Christmas" evokes the associations of home, family, and landscape that are as endemic to Christmas as the religious celebration, but makes them all the more poignant by having them voiced by a singer who cannot share but only recall them. If Berlin's melancholy Russian heritage ever came to bear on the perfect subject, it was in this secular carol of nostalgic loneliness.

As a song, "White Christmas" is the counterpart to Robert Frost's great modern poem, "Stopping by Woods on a Snowy Evening," which uses the simplest of rhymes and the barest of imagery to evoke a beautiful but melancholy scene. Both Berlin and Frost expressed amazement at the dark "meanings" people read into their simple creations. Another poet, Carl Sandburg, found in Berlin's song the undertones of a world at war:

> Away down under, this latest hit of Irving Berlin catches us where we love peace. The Nazi theory and doctrine that man in his blood is naturally warlike, so much so that he should call war a blessing, we don't like it . . . the hopes and prayers are that we will see the beginnings of a hundred years of white Christmases—with no bloodspots of needless agony and death on the snow. . . . Where there is will and vision men and women may hope. They may even dream of a century of white peace where treetops glisten and children listen to hear those sleigh bells in the snow.

Little wonder that "White Christmas" was embraced by American soldiers stationed in the South Pacific during World War II. "It became a peace song in wartime," Berlin reflected, "nothing I'd ever intended. It was nostalgic for a lot of boys who weren't home for Christmas. It just shows that inspiration can produce anything."

When he handed the song to Bing Crosby, the singer looked at it, took his pipe out of his mouth, and, with characteristic nonchalance, quipped, "You don't have to worry about this one, Irving." But, equally characteristically, worry Berlin did. Those working on *Holiday Inn* recalled his infatuation with his latest creation:

It was as if he were going to have a baby when he was working on that song. I never saw a man so wrapped up in himself. It was all a tremendously traumatic experience for him.

Musical director Walter Scharf recounted how Berlin could not keep off the set. On the day "White Christmas" was to be filmed, Scharf told him that it would be a long time before they would be ready, and Berlin agreed to leave until it was time for Crosby to sing:

It was then that I noticed that one or two of the flats—you know, the screens we use to dampen the sound—were out of place. I went behind to investigate and there was Irving, bent low down. "I'm sorry," he apologized, "I just had to stick around."

Berlin was not disappointed with the way "White Christmas" was integrated into *Holiday Inn*. Early in the film, Crosby and Marjorie Reynolds sit in the deserted inn he is trying to refurbish, and she notices a song he has written on the piano and asks him to sing it for her. Such an introduction of a song had long been commonplace in musical films, but in *Holiday Inn* it defines "White Christmas" as a commercial song yet one that "integrally" evokes the rural world Crosby loves more than wealth and success. When he reprises it to her at the end of the film on a busy Hollywood set, the song's quiet power reunites the lovers and transcends the crass commercialism that surrounds them.

The song was powerful enough to sustain one of the most innovative camera shots in film musicals. As Reynolds prepares to sing the song on a Hollywood sound studio, her director points out it is an exact replica of Crosby's country inn where she first heard the song. For her motivation, the director tells her "Your Hollywood success was empty, you've lost the one man you love—the usual hoke." Reynolds, of course, really is unhappy about losing Crosby and when suddenly he appears to sing "White Christmas" to her, the camera pulls back from the reunited lovers to reveal that the scene is actually shot on the *Holiday Inn* set itself, with cameras and crew in clear view this time. Instead of being a replica of the real thing, there is no real thing—only as John Meuller points out, "the set that has been used throughout the film, and there is something intriguingly disorienting in the way the film calmly shatters its own artful illusion by showing its beautiful central set to be merely that—a set."

Although "White Christmas" became the best-selling song Irving Berlin—or anyone—ever wrote, Berlin had written most of his score for *Holiday Inn* with the realization that by tying each song to a holi-

Bing Crosby sings "White Christmas" to Marjorie Reynolds in the 1942 film *Holiday Inn*.

day, it was unlikely any would achieve independent popularity. Not only did "White Christmas" overturn that expectation, the all-purpose "Happy Holiday" has also become an evergreen (which most people mistakenly sing as "Happy Holiday*s*"). In fact, the latter song has become even more popular with the increasing emphasis upon the various holidays that are celebrated by different American religions and cultures near the end of the calendar year.

Berlin seemed equally unconcerned about royalties as he turned out an array of songs specifically aimed at the war effort, knowing full well that none would outlast its era. During World War I, the songwriters of Tin Pan Alley wrote prowar (as well as antiwar) songs without prompting, because popular songs were primarily topical by nature, many suggested by headlines in the newspapers. In the 1920s, however, as popular songs began to emanate from Broadway musicals and Hollywood movies rather than the cubicles of Tin Pan Alley publishers, these songs tended to be about romance, to suit the stories of the shows. Between 1920 and 1940, according to one estimate, 85 percent of popular songs were love songs, a much greater proportion than songs of earlier or later periods.

For World War II, consequently, it was the government itself which took the initiative and sought out songwriters to write songs in support of specific agencies and causes. When songwriters used to saying "I love you" with a trenchant twist took up the cause of America, they brought their Broadway wit to bear on patriotism. In response to Secretary of the Treasury Henry Morgenthau's request for a song for the war bond drive, for example, Ira Gershwin came up with "Let's Show 'Em How This Country Goes to Town," rhyming "V for Vict'ry" with "nothing contradict'ry." Irving Berlin, whose career harked back to the early days of Tin Pan Alley well before World War I, came up with a more direct approach:

> Any bonds, today?
> Bonds for freedom that's what I'm selling.
> Any bonds, today?

Later in the war, as the tide began to turn in America's favor, Berlin added new lyrics to its catchy bugle-call melody and provided "Any Bombs Today?" for the "Buy Bombers with Defense Stamps" drive. Still another set of lyrics adapted it for the Australian Armed Forces!

In the early years of the war when morale was low, Berlin became a songwriting juggernaut, turning out "When That Man Is Dead and Gone," which pointedly alluded to a Satanic figure "with a small mustache." He then wrote "Arms for the Love of America" for the Ordnance and Ammunition Department. When the Red Cross asked him for a song, he put in a forty-eight hour stint and came up with "Angels of Mercy" and donated all proceeds from the song to the charity. After listening to reports of the London blitz, he penned "A Little Old Church in England." In recognition of Franklin Delano Roosevelt's favorite charity, he wrote "The President's Birthday Ball" for the March of Dimes. If ever a song was written in the composer's full knowledge it could never become a hit, Irving Berlin wrote a joyous ode to a joyless duty: "I Paid My Income Tax Today" for the Internal Revenue Service. At the end of the war, he turned comic with an exultant number for the women in the armed forces, "Oh, to Be Home Again":

> There's no romance when you dance
> Cheek to cheek and pants to pants
> Oh for an old-fashioned dress.

As if writing all these songs were not enough, Berlin undertook an enormous patriotic project that would engage him for the remainder of the war. Calling upon General George Marshall in Washington, he proposed a sequel to his World War I *Yip! Yip! Yaphank:* a new all-soldier show called *This Is the Army*. It would play on Broadway with all proceeds going to the Army Emergency Relief. This project not only channeled Berlin's patriotism, it provided him with the chance to write another revue. General Marshall gave the songwriter the go-ahead, and Berlin was, once again, songwriter, performer, and producer in charge of a cast and crew of 300 soldiers. The company rehearsed at Camp Upton, where Berlin had been a soldier a generation before. The songwriter turned out a score in three weeks, working in a barracks on the base alongside his scenery and costume designers. The proximity to a new generation of American soldiers gave Berlin a basis of comparison with his World War I show:

> The boys are different from those who served in 1918. They had different upbringing and the ideals which were held up to them were different. They have seen many of those ideals shattered. They are more serious and grim. They know what they are up against.

As he worked longer with the troops, he extended his comparison of World War II to World War I:

> Parades are out, cracks, happy songs, all the stock standard forms of patriotism are out of this war. Because this war is too terrible and everybody knows how long and how hard a fight it's going to be for us. This Army makes the other Army, at least while the other Army was on our soil here, look like college boys larking for a big football game. Nowadays, the fellows go off quietly and we watch them go quietly.

The army—and America—had undergone profound changes since then, but Berlin was instrumental in an additional transformation. At his insistence, Laurence Bergreen points out, the company included black soldiers:

> In his show business milieu, of course, Blacks had long been stars, popular with both black and white audiences. By integrating the revue, Berlin was simply importing familiar conventions into the Army. However, he was not blind to appearances; he knew his gesture would be progressive, at the least, and probably controversial. But he believed in the armed forces as the great leveler in American society. In his youth he had seen the Great War reduce barriers separating Jewish, German, Irish, and Italian ethnic groups in the United States. Yet Blacks had been excluded from this quiet revolution; even in *Yip! Yip! Yaphank*, the black numbers had been

performed by whites in blackface in the manner of a minstrel show. His insistence on including Blacks in *This Is the Army* suggested he believed the Second World War might do for them what the Great War had done for other minorities. . . . black and white members of the *This Is the Army* unit lived as well as worked together. "We had guys who were crackers when they came into the outfit," said Alan Manson, one of the white actors who took to the novel arrangement with enthusiasm. "But after two or three weeks of living together you couldn't say a word against a black man in our company. It really was an enormous experience. Berlin is a fairly conservative guy, but this meant a lot to him."

Perhaps Berlin's insistence upon an integrated company had been sparked by the controversy over the blackface routine for the song "Abraham" in *Holiday Inn*. Whatever inspired his decision, the result was that the *This Is the Army* company was the only integrated armed service unit in World War II.

This Is the Army opened on Broadway July 4, 1942. Audiences that expected an amateur fund-raiser were thrilled by a first-rate production presented by seasoned theatrical pros. Many of Berlin's songs, from the comic march "The Army's Made a Man Out of Me" to the winsomely syncopated ballad, "I Left My Heart at the Stage Door Canteen," became popular hits, though their topicality has prevented them from becoming standards. Only the title song, with its rousing imperatives that seem to emanate from a drill sergeant, has endured as a military anthem:

> This is the Army, Mister Jones
> No private rooms or telephones.
> You had your breakfast in bed before
> But you won't have it there anymore.

The song captured Berlin's first-hand sense of how different the army of World War II was from that of World War I—more grim, more professional. Still, he could find flashes of soldierly humor:

> This is the army, Mister Brown,
> You and your baby went to town.
> She had you worried
> But this is war
> And she won't worry you anymore.

Singer Kate Smith pays $10,000 for opening night tickets to *This Is the Army* as Irving Berlin and soldiers look on.

The highlight of *This Is the Army*, as it had been in *Yip! Yip! Yaphank*, was Irving Berlin himself singing "Oh! How I Hate to Get Up in the Morning," in his old World War I uniform. For his new show, Berlin added some verses to his classic that bridged the gap between the two wars:

> When I was in the army five and twenty years ago,
> I wrote a song and sang it in another soldier show. . . .
> The army's very different now, they've changed it quite a bit,
> The soldier boys are fashion plates in uniforms that fit.
> The sergeants wear pajamas, they're as gentle as a dame,
> It's all so very different but the bugler's just the same.

This Is the Army was so successful it played through September 1942. Partly through the enthusiasm of Eleanor Roosevelt, who saw the show three times, it went on a national tour. Starting in Washington, with the president himself in the audience, it traveled to cities across the country, where, as one cast member recalled, its integrated company ran into racial problems:

> We always insisted that the black guys stay with us. And
> if a place wouldn't take us, all three hundred of us would
> go where the black guys could go. We wouldn't play in a
> segregated theater—and that's that. We were invited to a
> party on occasion, and a couple of times, they didn't
> include the black guys. We said, "We're sorry, we're not
> coming. Forget it."

The tour concluded in San Francisco in February 1943; by then the
show had earned $2 million for the Army Emergency Relief Fund.

This Is the Army was not through, however. Warner Brothers
turned it into a movie and, again at Berlin's insistence, agreed to
give all earnings from the film to the relief fund. Hollywood added
some film stars to the company, including a young actor named
Ronald Reagan. Berlin had to tone down his risqué lyrics to songs
such as "Ladies of the Chorus," sung by soldiers in drag, as well as
turn the violent "Dressed Up to Kill" to the more innocuous
"Dressed Up to Win." When it came time to film "Oh! How I Hate to
Get Up in the Morning," Berlin fretted about his first performance
before the camera and became so nervous he forgot his own lyrics
on the first take. After he finally squeaked and quavered through the
song, a grip on the set, unaware who the performer was, supposedly
muttered, "If the fellow who wrote that song could hear this guy sing
it, he'd roll over in his grave."

Even after filming was completed, *This Is the Army* refused to die.
First, the show was taken to London, where Berlin added some new
skits and a song, "My British Buddy." Inspired by an air-raid black-
out, the song helped relieve some of the mounting tensions between
British soldiers and the "Yanks" who were crowding into their country. After touring other cities in the United Kingdom, *This Is the Army*
returned to London where Eisenhower was so taken with the performance he urged General Marshall to send it to soldiers around the
world as a morale booster. The company—including Berlin himself—
went to North Africa then to Italy, still in the midst of heavy fighting.
After Allied troops took Rome, *This Is the Army* rolled in, and started
putting on two shows a day at the Royal Opera House. Berlin also
toured military hospitals and sang Italian songs he'd learned growing
up on the Lower East Side. He even did shows for local civilians and
donated the proceeds to Italian charities:

> I shall never forget a performance in Rome where I
> don't believe one-tenth of the audience could understand
> a word of the show. If anyone does not think that music
> is the universal language I wish he could have attended
> that performance at the Royal Opera House. I spoke

Irving Berlin performing in *This Is the Army* aboard the U.S.S. *Arkansas* in the Pacific in 1944.

through an interpreter at the end of the show. I told how as a kid who had been born in Russia my folks went to America and settled in an Italian neighborhood. We youngsters knew no distinction of race or creed and I used to sing Jewish songs for them and they sang Italian songs for me. By the time I was through talking the audience and I were singing songs we both knew in chorus. One that I never forgot was "Oi-Marie." It was heartwarming to see those fascists stand up and sing this simple Neapolitan folk song as though it were their national anthem.

Berlin returned to America for a brief respite in 1944, but the company went on with the show through Egypt and Iran and into the South Pacific.

The songwriter rejoined them in New Guinea at the end of the year and proceeded on a dangerous tour of the South Pacific in a rickety old freighter. Conditions were even more makeshift than they had been in Europe, but there were moments of unexpected delight as when Berlin overheard natives chanting the melody to "White

Christmas." Not only did Berlin endure the hardships along with his company, he kept adding new songs to the score—"Heaven Watch the Philippines," "I Get Along with the Aussies"—and continued to battle racial prejudice as the army tried to segregate the company in the outposts where it toured. After island-hopping with his men, Berlin took another trip back to America but rejoined his company for the final run of the show in Hawaii in October 1945. *This Is the Army* had been playing for more than three years, literally around the world, to two-and-a-half million people. At fifty-seven years of age, Irving Berlin had performed an astonishing service to his country, for which President Harry Truman, in the wake of the death of Franklin Delano Roosevelt and the dropping of the atomic bomb, conferred upon him the Medal of Merit. The medal was pinned on the songwriter by General Marshall. "He has set," the citation read with remarkable understatement, "a high standard of devotion to his country." For Berlin, the ceremony was "the biggest emotional experience of my life. Nothing," he said, "ever matched this."

Chapter 11

ANYTHING YOU CAN DO

The Hollywood yardstick for success is business. At the end of the year, perhaps longer, they'll tell you how much gross business your picture did and then you'll know whether it was a success or not. With a Broadway show you get the bad news or the good right away. You don't have to wait. And you get to hear people singing your songs right away, too, which is very pleasant.

By the early 1940s, the Theatre Guild, the prestigious organization that had been founded in 1918 "to present classic and contemporary dramatic works on Broadway," was on the verge of bankruptcy. Codirector Theresa Helburn envisioned the Guild's salvation in a musical. Musicals had long been regarded with a mixture of admiration and condescension by people in the "serious" theater. On the one hand, musicals had become practically synonymous with Broadway and could be counted upon to attract far larger audiences than straight dramatic plays. Yet the very audience they attracted, known as the "tired businessman," seemed to relegate musicals to the most superficial level of theatrical art. What Helburn had in mind, however, was not another "Bring on the Girls" show but "a new type of play with music, not musical comedy, not operetta in the old sense, but a form in which the dramatic action, music, and possibly ballet could be welded together into a compounded whole, each helping to tell the story in its own way."

Only a few previous musicals had approached such integration of song, story, and dance. Kern and Hammerstein's 1927 production of *Show Boat* had started the movement toward integration, followed by the Gershwins' political operettas, *Strike Up the Band*, *Of Thee I Sing*, and *Let 'Em Eat Cake*. The Depression slowed the development of the serious musical, but it was the Theatre Guild that backed the 1934 production of *Porgy and Bess* when George Gershwin's insistence upon a black cast turned other producers away. By the early 1940s, several shows—Ira Gershwin and Kurt Weill's *Lady in the Dark*, Rodgers and Hart's *Pal Joey*—anchored songs closely to characters and dramatic situations. Irving Berlin had anticipated this trend in his 1940 musical *Louisiana Purchase*, which spoofed Southern politics and featured both witty catalog songs, such as "What Chance Have I with Love?" ("If an apple could ruin Adam, they could knock me off with a grape"), and sumptuous ballads like "It's a Lovely Day Tomorrow." Still, for all of their "integration" of songs with story, these musicals smacked of the sophistication, satire, and urbanity of the 1930s. Helburn's idea was to make a musical out of Lynn Riggs's play, *Green Grow the Lilacs*, a folksy, homespun tale of the Oklahoma Territory at the turn of the century. The play had been a Theatre Guild production in 1931, and she was convinced that it could be transformed into a successful musical.

Helburn first approached Richard Rodgers and Lorenz Hart with the project. The composer and lyricist seemed the logical choice, because they had gotten their first big break by writing songs for the *Garrick Gaieties*, a 1925 revue designed as a fundraiser for the Theatre Guild. They had created many successful shows since then, but Hart's self-destructive drinking had finally strained the partnership to its breaking point. When Hart dismissed the project as hopelessly corny, Rodgers turned to Oscar Hammerstein. Hammerstein's career had languished since *Show Boat*, and he had never been able to interest his long-time collaborator, Jerome Kern, in following that historical musical with another fully integrated show. He himself had proposed the Riggs play as a musical but Kern at that time was bent on success in Hollywood. Hammerstein, who found little interest among Hollywood producers in his dramatic and poetic lyrics, then retreated to his Pennsylvania farm to work on a labor of love—a black version of Bizet's great opera, to be called *Carmen Jones*.

When approached by Rodgers with the Theatre Guild project, Hammerstein at first demurred and even offered to work—without credit—on lyrics with Hart. Only when Rodgers insisted that his partnership with Hart was over did Hammerstein agree. Completely different from the acerbic, urbane, and clever Hart, Hammerstein was a master of the kind of lyric that, like a soliloquy, revealed character and grew out of dramatic situation. Among all the great lyricists of his generation, moreover, he was the most adept at adapting a novel, play, or collection of stories into a musical. Other lyricists, such as Hart and Ira Gershwin, relied upon playwrights to supply them with a book for a musical, and they would work with the play-wright and composer to locate the best points in the script for a songs. Hammerstein, as he had done with Edna Ferber's sprawling novel, *Show Boat*, could take an existing literary work and recast it to provide the richest openings for songs. Although it is now common for a single person to be credited with "book and lyrics" of a Broadway show, Oscar Hammerstein was the first major American lyricist to assume both roles and thus could achieve much closer integration between song and story. That integration was further strengthened by bringing in Rouben Mamoulian, who had directed *Porgy and Bess*, and choreographer Agnes de Mille, fresh from her work on Aaron Copland's Americana ballet *Rodeo*.

The intimate linkage between songs and story forged by this creative team surpassed even that of *Show Boat*. Coupled with its regional character, that integration made *Away We Go*, as the show was originally called, a daring departure from the usual run of Broadway musicals. Even a theatrical pro like Mike Todd, when he saw the New Haven tryout quipped, "No gags, no girls, no chance." Yet after some final doctoring, and a title change, suggested by Helburn, *Oklahoma!* was an extraordinary success on Broadway when it opened in March of 1943, running for more than 2,000 performances over five years.

Almost as groundbreaking as the musical itself, as theater historians Amy Henderson and Dwight Bowers point out, was a set of 78-rpm recordings of the score by members of the cast:

> These were not, contrary to legend, the first American recordings of a theater score made by its original New York cast [Marc Blitzstein's 1938 *The Cradle Will Rock* had been similarly recorded]. However, no previous effort had captured quite so vividly on disc the sheer exhilaration of the Broadway musical experience from overture to finale, from the out-and-out hits to the less familiar character songs. More than anything, these recordings solidly confirmed that the music and lyrics for *Oklahoma!* are essential ingredients in the narrative structure of the show and not just a series of traditionally catchy, easily isolated popular songs.

Cast albums made it possible for any song from a Broadway musical, even one most intimately tied to the story, to become a popular hit. In earlier musicals, it was usually only the romantic ballads that were published independently as sheet music and turned into recordings. With the cast album, however, such integrated songs from *Oklahoma!* as "The Surrey with the Fringe on Top," "I Cain't Say No," and even the title song of the show became popular. Creating a fully integrated show, therefore, no longer meant that the composer and lyricist had to abandon hope that their songs could achieve independent popularity. As the tradition of the integrated musical grew, cast albums turned the most unlikely numbers—such as "The Rain in Spain" from *My Fair Lady* and "Trouble" from *The Music Man*—into major popular hits. The lesson was not lost on Irving Berlin, who always maintained that a good show was one that produced a lot of hit songs.

While Berlin toured the battle zones with *This Is the Army*, the Broadway musical struck off in the direction of *Oklahoma!* This development was a great boon to certain lyricists, such as Yip Harburg and Dorothy Fields, who, like Hammerstein, had always thought more in terms of the show rather than the individual song. Dorothy Fields, daughter of the great vaudevillian Lew Fields, had started out writing lyrics for such hits as "On the Sunny Side of the Street" and "I Can't Give You Anything But Love." Gradually, she had moved toward integration by writing books for Cole Porter musicals with her brother Herbert Fields. She came to see herself as a "book-writer" even "when I'm working on songs":

> I'm not out to write popular song hits, though I've writ-ten songs that have *become* popular; I'm writing a song to fit a spot in the show. To fit a character, to express something about him or her . . . to move that story line forward. You can't fool that audience out there. They'll always tell you whether a song is right or not.

Given her sense of how song and story went together, Dorothy Fields was the logical person to receive the inspiration for one of the greatest of all musicals:

> During the war, my late husband did volunteer work down at Penn Station for Traveler's Aid, from midnight to seven a.m. And one of the ladies told him one night about a kid who'd just come in, a young soldier. Very drunk, he'd been to Coney Island and had kewpie dolls and lamps and every piece of junk you could possibly win. How come? Across his chest he had a row of sharp-shooter's medals.
>
> And as if out of the sky, from Heaven, comes this idea . . . Annie Oakley—the *sharpshooter!* With Ethel Merman to play her!

Imagining herself as writing both book and lyrics for such a production, Fields took her idea to Oscar Hammerstein because she knew "he and Dick Rogers were producing shows as well as writing them":

> I said, "Ockie, what do you think of Ethel Merman as Annie Oakley? He said, "We'll do it." That's all! And then he said, "Talk to Dick after the meeting." I talked to Dick, and Dick said the same thing—"We'll do it."
>
> Then they both said, "But can you get up to see Ethel?" She'd just gone into the hospital to have a child, by Cesarean, and she was feeling awful. I had a hell of a time getting into the hospital, but I did, and I went over to her bed and I leaned down and said, "Merm. What would you think of yourself as Annie Oakley?"
>
> She looked up from her hospital bed, and blinked, and said, "I'll do it." It was as simple as that.

When Rodgers and Hammerstein persuaded Jerome Kern to return from Hollywood to write songs with Dorothy, the collaborative team seemed complete.

Working with her brother, Dorothy found that "writing the book was a dream. It's the one show out of all the shows I've done that went so beautifully." Then, just as her inspiration seemed blessed by the gods, tragedy struck. The day after Kern arrived in New York, he suddenly collapsed from a stroke on the sidewalk of Park Avenue. "Jerry came to New York," Fields recalled, "And then he dropped dead—on a street. Unknown. That was the worst week of my life. The worst week of everybody's life. Horrible." Like many show business people, Kern carried no wallet with him, so the ambulance took him to City Hospital and placed him in the charity ward. Ironically, it was in this same ward that Stephen Foster had died, penniless, more than eighty years before. With another twist of historical irony, what helped save Jerome Kern and many other songwriters from Foster's fate was the organization ASCAP. Kern was carrying his ASCAP card and, through his member number, the hospital was able to identify their renowned patient. Although family and friends rushed to his side, Kern never recovered consciousness.

After such backstage drama, Fields now had to live up to that tiredest of cliches, "the show must go on":

> After the funeral, we were all sitting at a restaurant, and we started discussing whom we could get who could possibly replace someone as gifted as Kern. And Dick finally

said, "Well, I know somebody, but it means that Dorothy can't do the lyrics."

Fields never described her reaction at hearing that blunt prospect, but she put the good of the show above her own ego. Such altruism was characteristic of Broadway in this period; where the talented stars of Hollywood were sometimes self-centered, New York theater people had a tradition of sacrificing their own glory for the sake of the production. "I have enough to do with the book," Fields said, "I don't care. Who is it?" "Irving," Rodgers replied.

"We all thought that was fabulous," Fields said, but when she called Irving Berlin, he was hesitant. "Well, I don't know whether I'd want to do a show that isn't 'Irving Berlin's whatsoever.'" Showing her own Annie Oakley grit, Fields barked back, "Irving, sorry, but this is our idea, our play, and it can't be 'Irving Berlin's Annie Oakley.'" Berlin said he would think about the project for a few days, then sat down with Richard Rodgers to talk about writing songs for a "situation show," Berlin's down-to-earth term for the "integrated musical." Rodgers urged the veteran to embrace the new genre, where "he wouldn't have to find ideas in the sky. They'd be there on paper, they'd be in the book." Rogers recalled, "I begged him to go home with the book and fool around over the weekend and see how things worked, whether he got any ideas, whether it felt comfortable for him"

Irving Berlin, nearing sixty, was struggling not only with a new genre of Broadway show but with a different kind of music, "hillbilly music," as he dubbed the new regionalism that was competing with Tin Pan Alley's mainstream New York style. As Laurence Bergreen speculates:

> He knew nothing about hillbilly music, but he reached
> the conclusion that it had no place in *Annie Get Your
> Gun*; ultimately, it was a musical about show business,
> not hillbillies, and show tunes did have a place.

He may also have seen himself in the character of Annie Oakley— a poor, uneducated, feisty, and enormously talented performer. Berlin certainly demonstrated his talent and determination in the first few days he worked on songs for *Annie Get Your Gun*. Years later, Dorothy Fields was still astounded, that he asked to look at the script for act one, the outline for act two, and "in the twelve days he agreed to do the show, he wrote *five* songs."

Berlin's remarkable score for *Annie Get Your Gun* bridged the gulf between the new kind of integrated song Broadway called for and Irving Berlin's notion of a good, old-fashioned Tin Pan Alley hit. The nineteen songs he wrote—all new, not one a hangover or trunk song—establish character and grow out of the story yet manage to transcend the show as self-contained popular numbers. One of the first songs that he completed follows Hammerstein's advice that Berlin could achieve folksiness by dropping final letters from words. "Doin' What Comes Natur'lly" was what was known, in the new integrated musical, as an "I am" song, in which a character defines himself to the audience. Berlin went beyond that simple formula and had Annie define—and defend—her entire "hillbilly" culture:

> Folks are dumb
> Where I come from,
> They ain't had any learnin',
> Still they're happy as can be,
> Doin' what comes natur'lly.

"Doin' What Comes Natur'lly" is a classic patter or "catalog" song that goes back, via Cole Porter, to Gilbert and Sullivan, and Berlin knew he could rely on Merman's projection and enunciation to articulate the consonants in such tricky lyrics as:

> You don't have to go to a private school
> not to turn up your bustle to a stubborn mule.

Berlin's own humble upbringing as well may have gone into this spunky retort to a social elite he had been satirizing in such songs as "Slumming on Park Avenue."

The next song, one that Berlin rattled off in the first frenzied weekend of work on the show, was critical in the development of Annie's character, as well as Ethel Merman's career. The script called for the brash, tomboyish Annie to fall in love at first sight with handsome Ray Middleton in the role of sharpshooter Frank Butler. Director Josh Logan wrestled with the problem of Ethel Merman's stage persona, which, from her debut in the Gershwins' 1930 production of *Girl Crazy*, had always been the brassy, big-city dame, wise to all guys:

> I felt the only way I could show such an abrupt change was to have her collapse inwardly and outwardly as if she were a puppet whose strings had been cut quickly. I told Ethel to keep her eyes fixed on Ray but to let everything else in her body and mind go.
>
> She tried it. Her mouth dropped open, her shoulders sank, her legs opened wide at the knees, her diaphragm

caved in. It was an unforgettable effect. Later we dubbed
it the "goon look."

The catalog song Berlin devised for this moment, "You Can't Get a
Man with a Gun," maintains Annie's pugnacity but also reveals a
new vulnerability in her as she longs for the traditional feminine role
she outwardly scorns. As Ethel Merman succinctly put it, "Irving
made me a lady":

> The gals with umbrellers
> Are always out with fellers
> In the rain or the blazing sun.
> But a man never trifles
> With gals who carry rifles,
> Oh, you can't get a man with a gun.

Even as she bemoans her plight, Annie's pathos turns to outrage
over the fact that "You can't shoot a male in the tail like a quail." In
Annie, Berlin found the perfect vehicle to give voice to earthy
American slang:

> If I went to battle with someone's herd of cattle,
> You'd have steak when the job was done.
> But if I shot the herder,
> They'd holler bloody murder.

With her impeccable delivery and soaring voice, Ethel Merman
enshrined every syllable, particularly the inspired "hillbilly" touch of
dragging "gun" over two notes, a rising interval that makes the unro-
mantic monosyllable sound like a mournful wail.

For "Doin' What Comes Natur'lly" and "You Can't Get a Man
with a Gun" Irving Berlin used larger musical forms of fifty and
sixty measures to handle more fully integrated songs, but for the
show's big ballad, he returned to his old thirty-two bar AABA chorus. With "They Say It's Wonderful," he gave his heroine a hesitant
foray into the unfamiliar territory of romance. The vernacular
catch phrase, "so they say," provides Annie with a defensive retreat
from the exuberance of "They say that falling in love is wonderful,
it's wonderful." Merman heightened the tension by booming out
the word "wonderful" with an open-mouthed wonder of its own,
then quickly adding the qualifying "so they say" with almost legal
detachment.

> I can't recall who said it,
> I know I never read it.

Only the Annie who had mocked "book larnin'" in "Doin' What Comes Natur'lly" would confess with such comic innocence that she certainly would not have *read* about the grandeur of love.

Fittingly, the emotional crux of her first love song hinges upon the simplest of terms:

> I only know they tell me that love is *grand*—
> *and*—
> the thing that's known as romance is wonderful, wonderful,
> in ev'ry way—
> so they say.

The emotional charge Merman gave that "and" balanced, for a dramatic moment, Annie's romantic eagerness and wariness.

Annie's romantic opposite is Frank Butler, the crack sharpshooter—until Annie Oakley joins the troupe—of Buffalo Bill's traveling Wild West Show. In his "I Am" song, a country-fiddle melody like Annie's "Doin' What Comes Natur'lly," Butler paints himself as "A Bad, Bad Man," a womanizer who leaves broken hearts (and shotgun-toting fathers) behind in every town. That exaggerated self-portrait is matched by an equally hyperbolic song, "The Girl That I Marry," where Butler, a confirmed bachelor, reveals how he can stave off marriage by insisting upon an impossible ideal:

> The girl that I marry will have to be
> As soft and as pink as a nursery.
> The girl I call my own
> Will wear satins and laces and smell of cologne.

Although "The Girl That I Marry" was comically ironic in *Annie Get Your Gun*, the folksy waltz became independently popular as a straight paean to conventional matrimony. Followed almost immediately by "You Can't Get a Man With a Gun," it establishes the characters of the two principals and sets up the central conflict of the plot.

As Richard Rodgers had predicted, Berlin found that writing for a book musical was inspiring and, given the wonderful characters of Annie Oakley and Frank Butler, the songs complemented one another. After introducing himself with "I'm a Bad, Bad Man," Frank

Butler, by the end of Act I, finds that he what he wants is not "a doll I can carry" but his rival in sharpshooting. As he excuses his fall for Annie with "My Defenses Are Down," he secretly envisions marriage as "Being miserable is going to be fun." With equal dexterity, Berlin weaves the verbs *get* and *got* through Annie's songs, from her own dazed rationalization for falling in love, "I Got Lost in His Arms," through her exultant, "I Got the Sun in the Morning," to a reprise of her frustrated "You Can't Get a Man with a Gun."

Berlin's wonderfully comic and touching songs traced the course of romance between these two characters, but as rehearsals approached it became clear to director Josh Logan that the two lovers needed a song in Act II that would complement their first act duet, "They Say It's Wonderful." He whispered his concern to Hammerstein at a staff meeting but Hammerstein hushed him with "Listen, Josh, don't bother Irving with that now. Don't bring it up. It'll worry him, and he won't be able to finish his work, so you keep quiet about it—we'll bring it up when the time is right." Hammerstein's hush may have been a stage whisper, for Berlin overheard. "Another song?" he called out:

> Just a minute, please, everybody quiet. A discussion has just come up about a new song. They think there's got to be one for Annie and Frank. Let's have a conference right now. If I'm going to write a song, I have to know what *kind* of song.

In earlier times Berlin would have simply approached a new song as a new *song*, but he now thought in terms of the characters and situations of an integrated musical and relied upon all of his collaborators, from librettists to choreographers. After a long discussion about where the song should go, it was agreed Frank and Annie, even though they were not on speaking terms at that point, had to sing a duet just before their climactic marksmanship contest (which Annie, upon the advice of Chief Sitting Bull, deliberately loses to win Frank's love). Suddenly, Berlin had his inspiration: "The only thing I can possibly think is that if it's before a shooting contest, it has to be some sort of a challenge song. Okay, challenge song. Right?"

At that point the conference broke up and Logan took a cab back to his apartment some dozen blocks away. As he entered, the telephone rang and he ran to answer it. Irving Berlin was on the line, eager to demonstrate a "challenge" song he had just written:

> "Hello, Josh—this is Irving. What do you think of this?"
> And then he sang the whole damned first chorus of

"Anything You Can Do." Most amazing thing I ever experienced in my whole life! It couldn't have been more than, at most, fifteen minutes from the time he'd first heard about it to the time he had me on the phone. He'd written the song—the entire first chorus. It was done like that.

In rising to a challenge of his own, Berlin had crafted an extraordinary song that proved he could do anything his rival songwriters on Broadway could do. On the one hand, "Anything You Can Do" is a witty catalog duet like Cole Porter's "You're the Top," but it also is rooted in character and dramatic situation as are the songs of Oscar Hammerstein. In the tradition of the western tall tale, Annie and Frank trade brags and insults. When he boasts, "I can shoot a partridge with a single cartridge," she goes him one further with "I can get a sparrow with a bow and arrow." To his "I can drink my liquor faster than a flicker," she retorts, "I can do it quicker and get even sicker." To vary the litany of boasts, Berlin throws in a challenge that stumps both characters, "'Can you bake a pie?' 'No.' 'Neither can I.'" Not only are they western braggarts, they are show business rivals, and when Frank says "I can knit a sweater," Annie answers, with a bit of cheesecake, "I can fill it better." The crux of the song turns on singing itself rather than marksmanship (the stage persona of Merman upstaging the character of Annie Oakley). While Annie loses to Frank in her efforts to sing softer and sweeter (as Ethel Merman inevitably would), she triumphs by holding a note longer than he or anyone can—another Mermanism. In fifteen minutes of inspired work, Berlin had written a song that was perfectly suited to his characters, the dramatic moment, and his star.

Another show-stopper in this remarkable musical was a song that has become the anthem of the American theater, "There's No Business Like Show Business." It was one of the first songs Berlin wrote for the show and may have crystallized his realization that *Annie Get Your Gun* was "a musical about show business." In the script by Dorothy and Herbert Fields, Annie Oakley is part of Buffalo Bill's Wild West Show, as she was in real life. The wild west show, moreover, was a major part of New York show business in the late nineteenth century. It was a New York writer of western novels who invited Buffalo Bill Cody to come East and star in a play about cowboys, which was so successful Cody stayed on Broadway and mounted his own wild west show. Replete with Indians and sharpshooters, Cody's enterprise was a long-standing hit that for a while even featured "Wild Bill Hickock," until the gunman's penchant for firing blanks at his fellow cast members forced Cody to send his

William O'Neal, Murty Moy, Ethel Merman, and Ray Middleton sing "There's No Business Like Show Business" in the 1946 production of *Annie Get Your Gun*.

sidekick back to South Dakota where he was killed in a Deadwood saloon. Eventually, Cody's show was superseded by a more realistic form of western entertainment called the rodeo, and Cody died penniless, like so many theater impresarios before him, though not before having influenced America's romantic image of the west, from dime novels to Hollywood movies.

The wild west show belonged to Broadway as much as the circus or vaudeville. Berlin, who had grown up amid that era of true "variety," evoked it in the old-fashioned, verse-chorus structure of "There's No Business Like Show Business":

> The cowboys, the tumblers, the wrestlers, the clowns,
> The roustabouts who move the show at dawn . . .
> The sawdust and the horses and the smell.
> The towel you've taken from the last hotel.

"There's No Business Like Show Business" was an integrated number for *Annie Get Your Gun* but it could also ring down the curtain on any show about the theater:

> There's *no* bus'ness
> like *show* bus'ness
> like *no* bus'ness
> I *know*.

Here the internal rhyme falls on a thumping downbeat, and, as Gerald Mast points out, *"know"* is "heard as a repetition of 'no' but seen imaginatively as a rhyme with *show*."

Berlin breathes new life into the oldest backstage clichés by pushing them over the top:

> You get word before the show has started,
> That your fav'rite uncle died at dawn,
> Top of that your Pa and Ma have parted,
> You're broken-hearted—but you go on.

In Berlin's lyric manuscripts for "There's No Business Like Show Business" he caricatured less glamorous stereotypes: "the stage director everlasting who does his casting upon a couch" and the "leading man who gives you doses of halitosis."

Berlin also toyed with the argot of the theater district, the area, according to Walter Winchell, that had produced such colorful slang as "click," "hit," "fan," "flop," "baloney," "cinch," "turkey," "squawk," and "gyp." Irving Berlin, who had heard some of these terms when they were freshly minted, wove them throughout his paean to what insiders called "the business":

> Even with a turkey that you know will fold,
> You may be stranded out in the cold . . .
> There's no people like show people,
> They don't run out of dough.
> Angels come from ev'rywhere with lots of jack.
> And when you lose it there's no attack.
> Where could you get money that you don't give back?

Within the lyric itself, Berlin manages to capture, by deft phrasing, the very suspense he celebrates:

> Yesterday they told you would not go far,
> That night you open—and there you are,
> Next day on your dressing room they've hung a star!

"There's No Business Like Show Business" is steeped in Berlin's lifetime involvement in the theater, from his earliest days of busking in the Bowery, to his long residence on the heights of his profession.

Still, when he played "There's No Business Like Show Business" for Rodgers and Hammerstein, the Fields, and Logan, all his years in the theater did not sustain his confidence in the song against what he assumed was their lack of enthusiasm. In truth, the group was so stunned by the quality of the song that they did not respond with the usual cheering. "Irving was very proud of it," Logan recalled," but when he sings right into your face, he's *reading* you, studying you every second for your reactions." "Only by fixing his eyes on the listener could he sense if the song worked. If one blinked too often or one's eyes glazed for a second, Irving was apt to put the song away."

For Berlin, their dumbfounded awe seemed a tepid response. He had always "pitched" his songs to anyone who would listen, and if they did not show enthusiasm, he would shelve or rework the song. During his creative crisis of the early 1930s he had lost all faith in his songwriting abilities, but even though his confidence had long been restored, he still depended on audience reaction—even an audience of one—to judge the quality of his work. The first person for whom he had played "There's No Business Like Show Business" was a secretary in his office and she had dismissed it, so when he thought his collaborators evinced a similar lack of enthusiasm, he quietly put the song aside.

Later, when he played through the existing score for them, Logan said, "Irving, what's the matter? You left out the finale!"

"Oh, well," Berlin explained, "I didn't like the way you all reacted this morning. It didn't register."

Logan recalled:

> It wasn't petulance. He meant it. I was astounded. I asked him what he'd done with the lead sheet, and he shrugged and said he'd put it away in his files somewhere, and I said, "Irving! Get it out of those files." . . . He argued with me, but I kept on insisting, until finally he gave in and went out to his secretary and asked her to dig it out of the files, and do you believe this—*they couldn't find it*? They searched and they hunted, arguing back and forth, all the while, rummaging through his whole office. Eventually, thank heaven, they came up with his original lead sheet. There wasn't even a copy. Can you imagine—for a good ten or fifteen minutes there, "Show Business," that show-stopper, that standard, an absolute classic of popular music, was missing!

Once found—under a telephone book—Irving Berlin became the composer of his profession's—as well as his country's—unofficial anthem.

Annie Get Your Gun opened in New York on May 16, 1946, a few days after Berlin's fifty-eighth birthday. It went on to a smashing run of 1,147 performances, earned critical raves, and produced more hit songs than any Broadway show before or since—virtually every song became an independent success through the original cast album.

Berlin followed his success on the "new" Broadway with an equally significant achievement in Hollywood. Except for the filmed version of *This Is the Army*, the only film score Berlin had written since *Holiday Inn* was for *Blue Skies* in 1946. The film featured Paramount's big star, Bing Crosby, again teamed with Fred Astaire but in an even lesser role than he had in *Holiday Inn*. Crosby crooned a string of Berlin classics—"All By Myself," "Always," "White Christmas," as well as the title song— and also introduced a hauntingly beautiful new ballad, "You Keep Coming Back Like a Song," reprised throughout the film, as well as the charming "(Running Around in Circles) Getting Nowhere." The story was not strong enough to hold the songs together, but *Blue Skies* is notable for what many consider Fred Astaire's greatest dance number in "Puttin' on the Ritz." Taking his most complex rhythmic song, Berlin rewrote the original lyric, which portrayed Harlem blacks strutting along Lenox Avenue, to portray instead the "well-to-do" parading "up and down Park Avenue." The new lyric reflected Berlin's continuing sensitivity to racial sensibilities, but it still ragged lyrical against musical accents in a playful idiom that might be dubbed "Berlintz":

> *Come* let's *mix* where *Rock*-e-*fell*-ers
> *walk* with *sticks* or "*um*-ber-*el*-las"
> *in* their *mitts—put*tin' on the *ritz*.

Astaire's dance to this masterpiece redeemed it from the stiff and smarmy rendition by Harry Richman fifteen years earlier. Working alone with only a cane, Astaire mimes slow motion in counterpoint to Berlin's staccato melody, then strikes a brittle pose, relaxes and snaps back into the song's rhythms. Throughout the routine, he slams, kicks, and makes the cane seem to dance by itself (at one point, a trick spring sends the cane leaping into Astaire's hand). The overall effect, as dance critic John Mueller observes, is "intense, controlled, with a hint of something like hostility . . . the number is unrelievedly and cumulatively assertive, and has a rather unsettling drive."

Part of the dark, menacing character of the dance may reflect the fact that Astaire intended it to be his final performance on film. As the decade progressed, his career fell further from the glory days at RKO, and the advent of more athletic dancers like Gene Kelly threatened to render his suave elegance passé. Determined to go out on a dazzlingly high note, Astaire put in "five weeks of back-breaking physical work" on "Puttin' on the Ritz," filming the complex number eight separate times to create seven images of himself as his own chorus. After the final take, Astaire reportedly took off his toupee, threw it on the floor, and shouted, "Never, never. Never will I have to wear this blasted rug again!"

While his best friend might be retiring from the changing musical scene, Irving Berlin was once again adapting to the change in Hollywood musicals as he had on Broadway. In the 1940s, producer Arthur Freed and his creative team at MGM had advanced the film musical as dramatically as Rodgers and Hammerstein had its stage counterpart. Freed had started out in Tin Pan Alley as a lyricist and was one of the first wave of songwriters to migrate to the west coast after the birth of the talkies. There, working with composer Herb Nacio Brown, he ground out the simple lyrical fare, such as "Singin' in the Rain" and "My Lucky Star," that early film musicals demanded. Freed, however, set his sights beyond songwriting and, by the end of the 1930s, had established himself as the head of what would come to be called the "Freed unit" at MGM, a branch of the studio that specialized in top-quality musicals. Beginning with *The Wizard of Oz* in 1939, Freed and his collaborators created a series of brilliant film musicals—*Meet Me in St. Louis*, *Summer Stock*, *The Harvey Girls*—that continued the tradition of Astaire-Rogers films at RKO. Like the stage shows of Rodgers and Hammerstein, MGM's musicals carefully worked songs into the story and characters, used choreography, sets, and all other aspects of the production to enhance the script, and employed such superb talents as Judy Garland, Gene Kelly, and director Vincente Minnelli. The films also evoked America's rural and small-town past for a postwar audience.

Berlin had his first dealings with Freed while negotiating the motion picture rights to *Annie Get Your Gun*. Freed was impressed with Berlin's tough business sense during their negotiations. Eventually, the songwriter, along with Dorothy and Herbert Fields, sold the rights to MGM for $650,000—an astronomical figure for a script and score. "It took longer to write one of Irving's contracts than it did the script," Freed recalled, "but after it was done, he forgot about the contract and gave you anything you wanted."

At the same time Berlin was negotiating with Freed and MGM, he was dickering over another film project with his old friend Joe Schenck. Schenck had just been released from prison after serving

Fred Astaire, in what was to have been his final performance, dances with seven images of himself in Irving Berlin's "Puttin' on the Ritz" from the 1946 film *Blue Skies*.

four months for income tax evasion, and, though he returned to Twentieth Century–Fox, he no longer held the same power there that once he had. Perhaps in an effort to ease his friend's transition back into the film business, Berlin proposed another film, like *Alexander's Ragtime Band*, which would be built around a collection of his old hit songs, with a few new numbers tossed in. With the new process of Technicolor in mind, Berlin suggested "Easter Parade," which had been so colorfully staged in *As Thousands Cheer*, as the logical title song.

Schenck agreed, but in his new subordinate position he had to clear the arrangement with Fox executives, who balked at Berlin's demand for a share of the film's profits. While RKO may have cut Berlin such a deal in its struggling days during the Depression, a major studio like Fox would not abide such an unusual arrangement for a mere songwriter, even one as prestigious as Irving Berlin. When Schenck telegrammed his old friend the news, Berlin wired back, "Dear Joe—You and I shook hands on a deal for *Easter Parade*, so let's forget about it." Berlin was then approached by MGM, whose imperious head, Louis B. Mayer, offered the songwriter the staggering sum of $500,000 to write the score for *Easter Parade*. Berlin held fast to his demand for a percentage of the film's profits and wired back the great mogul, "Dear Louis—why should I ask for one thing from Twentieth and do another for you?"

Amazingly, Louis Mayer gave in, granting Berlin his percentage as well as his half-million fee, and placing Arthur Freed in charge of producing *Easter Parade* as he had for *Annie Get Your Gun*. In order to have *Easter Parade* ready for release in time for Easter of 1948, work began on the picture first. Now that he was part owner of the film, Berlin took part in every aspect of production. Because the film was to be set in 1912, he felt qualified to advise the young, first-time screenwriters, the married couple Frances Goodrich and Albert Hackett, who were especially amenable to his advice. "Sometimes," Goodrich recalled, Berlin "would come in with an idea and a song to illustrate it."

Under Berlin's tutelage, the script emerged as an historically accurate but also grittily realistic evocation of the show business world of the early century. Berlin "was eager for their script to avoid the saccharine tone that had plagued *Blue Skies*," which, despite the presence of Bing Crosby and Fred Astaire, had not fared well with audiences or critics. MGM musicals had delved into such darker territory before, most notably in *Meet Me in St. Louis* and *Summer Stock*, but Berlin's realism went too far for director Charles Walters, "who privately complained to Freed that the script was, if anything, too authentic and harsh":

> It was important for all concerned to recognize that they were not setting out to make the next *42nd Street*; *Easter Parade* was to be light, escapist fare, whose darkest emotion was nostalgia.

Freed agreed and brought in Sidney Sheldon, at that time a young writer for Broadway as well as the movies, to soften the story line and characters. Still, Berlin's influence can be felt in the period character of the script and its hard-nosed look at show business realities.

One of those realities struck *Easter Parade* itself early in production. The film was to star Judy Garland and Gene Kelly, who had been paired in several MGM musicals and clearly had replaced Ginger Rogers and Fred Astaire as the singing and dancing couple of the 1940s. More folksy and childlike, Kelly and Garland exuded energy, heartfeltness, and small-town America. Kelly seldom danced with Garland in the kind of romantic clasp Astaire had held Rogers; instead, they danced as chums, frequently alongside others, including children. Kelly matched Astaire's urbane grace with boyish athleticism. However, his athleticism cost him the part in the film, because, while playing touch-football with his family, he broke his ankle. In the world of show-biz cliché, the accident would have resulted in the chance of a lifetime for an unknown star; in real-life Hollywood, Arthur Freed brought an old-timer out of retirement.

The prospect of Fred Astaire starring opposite Judy Garland struck Sidney Sheldon as preposterous. "You can't put Judy Garland opposite a grandfather," he told Freed, "The audience will be rooting for them *not* to get together." "Write the script," was Freed's reply. The script not only worked for *Easter Parade* but set a pattern for Fred Astaire that enabled him to make a spectacular comeback playing opposite younger stars—Garland, Cyd Charisse, even Leslie Caron—well into the 1950s. Even more than the script, the songs and dances had to negotiate these May-December relationships, and Irving Berlin set the standard with his songs for *Easter Parade*. Replacing Gene Kelly with his old friend Fred Astaire brought out the best in Berlin, as a challenge always did:

> If Kelly had played it, the picture could have been heavier. In fact, we planned it as a heavier story. Kelly can do that sort of thing. With Astaire it was all lighter. . . . There's not only his dancing, but he has class, style, anything you want to call it. It's corn maybe, but in a different way. It's—what do you want to call it?—it's Country Gentleman corn.

Astaire's presence reconciled Berlin to the lightening of the script, and his old songs fit even more comfortably into the story of the veteran Fred Astaire tutoring neophyte Garland in the art of song-and-dance. As they run through such classic Berlin hits as "I Love a Piano" and "When the Midnight Choo-Choo Leaves for Alabam'," the master-apprentice relationship between the two stars paves the way to their romance. Their relationship culminates in the title song, which Garland, now the seasoned professional herself, sings *to* Astaire, as she places his classic top hat upon her tutor who beams as she serenades him.

Berlin was even more than his usually inventive self with the seven new songs he wrote for *Easter Parade*, such as "Steppin' Out with My Baby," a debonair rhythm number for Astaire, cast in the syncopated, minor mode of "Puttin' on the Ritz" and "Top Hat, White Tie, and Tails," as well as haunting, vernacular ballads like "Better Luck Next Time." "It Only Happens When I Dance with You" is not only integral to the story line but to the Hollywood history behind the film. *Easter Parade* begins when Astaire is dropped by Ann Miller, his long-time lover and dance partner, a clear allusion to the dissolution of his partnership with Ginger Rogers. The song asserts that the Astaire-Rogers magic will never be recaptured; when he and Miller perform a sensuous, graceful dance reminiscent of the Astaire-Rogers classics, it truly does seem that Astaire can never dance as romantically with another.

The break-up with Miller prompts Astaire to make a drunken bet that he can teach any woman to dance like his estranged partner. The woman he chooses to demonstrate his Svengali powers, is, of course, Garland, but she proves utterly recalcitrant material until Astaire realizes that her genius lies in comedy rather than elegance. Once he comes to that realization, it is Astaire who must change, revealing a new dimension of his screen personality (though one that had long been a staple in his farcical vaudeville routines with his sister Adele). The Berlin number that crystallized their new comic partnership was originally to be "Let's Take An Old-Fashioned Walk," but Freed asked for a different kind of song. "Let's have a 'tramps' number," Berlin suggested and in an hour wrote "A Couple of Swells." Casting it in the musical style of the turn-of-the-century, with a verse longer than the chorus, Berlin developed a simple, "walking" melody that advances upward like the determined pair. "A Couple of Swells" did more than any other number to exorcise the ghost of "Astaire-Rogers."

In a parody of his elegant top hat, white tie, and tail costumes, Astaire and Garland play hoboes in tattered evening clothes, their top hats crushed, their teeth blacked out. As such, Astaire and Garland parody rather than compete with the image of Astaire and Rogers, and the lyric underscores that relationship by freeing Garland from the responsibility of having to perform a romantic ballroom dance with Astaire. Instead, in their rough-and-ready penury, Astaire and Garland complain that, because there is no way to ride or sail "up the avenue," they will "walk" (rather than "dance") up the avenue "till we're there." Their comic walking turns out to be as satisfying as the audience's memories of Astaire and Rogers dancing and, within the film, triumphs over the image of Astaire reenacting those 1930s dances with Ann Miller.

Easter Parade is an extraordinary musical film, the counterpart of Berlin's achievement with *Annie Get Your Gun* on the Broadway stage. The movie rekindled Fred Astaire's career and may have altered the course of MGM musicals under Arthur Freed. Before *Easter Parade*, Freed's unit had built musicals around original stories and scores. While most of these could be superb, some—such as *The Pirate*, even with Garland, Kelly, and a Cole Porter score— were less than stellar. When Irving Berlin proposed *Easter Parade* as a film for MGM, he presented it in the same mold as *Alexander's Ragtime Band:* an anthology of old and new songs placed in a story designed to showcase them. He may well have given Freed the idea to build other movies around collections of older songs. Shortly

Fred Astaire and Judy Garland do their "tramps" number, "A Couple of Swells" from the 1948 film *Easter Parade*.

after *Easter Parade*, Freed's unit at MGM embarked on a series of musical revivals—*An American in Paris* in 1951, which wove a new story around songs by the Gershwins, *Singin' in the Rain* in 1952, which recycled Freed's own songs with Herb Nacio Brown, and *The Band Wagon* in 1953, which again starred Fred Astaire in a story that resonated with old songs by Howard Dietz and Arthur

Irving Berlin, Judy Garland, and Fred Astaire on the set of *Easter Parade*.

Schwartz, to which they added "That's Entertainment," a paean to
the movies that took its place beside Berlin's "There's No Business
Like Show Business" as an anthem for the stage. Like Berlin's
blend of old and new songs in his score for *Easter Parade*, these
MGM films combined tradition and innovation in their development
of the American film musical.

Chapter 12

COUNT YOUR BLESSINGS

I've always thought of myself as a songwriter. What else would I want to be? I'm a songwriter, like dozens and dozens of others, and so long as I'm able, whether the songs are good or bad, I'll continue to write them, because song-writing is not alone a business or a hobby with me. It's everything.

In 1947, as Irving Berlin neared sixty years of age, he invited a reporter to accompany him on a nostalgic journey back to his old haunts on the Lower East Side As they got out of the car in the Bowery, Berlin's memories came flooding back. "There was a saloon right there," he exclaimed before a bank building, "I used to go in there and pass the hat. Blind George was the piano player—I'll never forget him." Their next stop was a saloon once owned by a boxer named Steve Brodie—"Brodie who jumped off the Brooklyn Bridge," Berlin explained, "There was always a picture around of him doing his stunt." Berlin recalled:

> These places were bars with back rooms. People who were around here, when I was on the loose, have gone— the bums and the riffraff stayed and died off. Others like myself were only waiting to get the hell out of here. Right across there was Diamond Lottie's place—she had

a diamond in her tooth—and this place was the Saranac, run by Biggie Donovan, a bar with a back room. I sang in there, too. Beer was 5 cents a glass. Wilson whiskey cost 10 cents. Whiskey was called a stack of reds and gin a stack of whites.

He also recalled a "terrible joint" at No. 9 Bowery, "inhabited by the drunkenest sailors and the oldest hags. But I went there and passed the hat."

It was in those grimy origins that Berlin's remarkable talent was nourished, where, as he put it more simply, "I got to know songs and got to know words." Much of his ensuing success came from this early schooling in what people wanted to hear and how to put over a song. His ability to give the public the songs they craved had lasted for nearly half a century, longer than that of any other songwriter. He had survived many changes in the style of popular music and was one of the few songwriters to have equal success on Broadway and Hollywood. Yet even as *Annie Get Your Gun* continued to run on stage and *Easter Parade* completed filming, time was beginning to leave Irving Berlin behind. Inevitable turns of events, coupled with some unfortunate luck, made his last twenty years of songwriting the least satisfying phase of his career. There would still be hit songs and hit shows, but there would be more failures and disappointments. Then, for another twenty years, there would be nothing—no published songs, no shows, no films, virtually no public appearances, even when he was honored with spectacular tributes.

He had always feared the loss of his talent, but in these years that loss seemed inevitable. "Who is going to tell me that I'm washed up as a songwriter?" he wondered. "That day is sure to come, and I'm always afraid my friends won't have the courage to tell me. I don't want to make my exit in the midst of a bunch of mediocre songs. I want my last one to have just as much merit as the first."

The first indication that Berlin was losing step with the times was the 1949 musical, *Miss Liberty*. The success of *Annie Get Your Gun* made him eager to begin another Broadway musical, and when his old friend from the Algonquin Round Table, playwright Robert E. Sherwood, presented an idea for a show, Berlin seized upon it. Sherwood had been aboard a troop ship in 1944 as it left New York harbor for England, and he was amazed that the 15,000 GIs cheered like schoolboys as the ship passed the Statue of Liberty. "It had all the qualities of a good musical," Berlin thought, undoubtedly bringing his own immigrant heritage to mind, "And I told him this was our opportunity to do a show together."

In the age of the new integrated musical, however, the most successful shows emerged when a single person wrote both the book and the lyrics. Oscar Hammerstein, in particular, would adapt an existing play, *Liliom* (*Carousel*); a novel, *Anna and the King of Siam* (*The King and I*); or a collection of short stories, *Tales of the South Pacific* (*South Pacific*), into a libretto. Such an adapation began with a proven story, then streamlined it into a musical where the most dramatic scenes would flower into song. This procedure ensured the fullest integration between song and character and story, as Alan Jay Lerner would prove again with *My Fair Lady* (from George Bernard Shaw's play *Pygmalion*), and *Camelot* (from T. H. White's novel, *The Once and Future King*).

It was possible, of course, to produce a great musical, such as *Annie Get Your Gun*, by dividing the labors of story and songs, but it required intricate and extensive collaboration. Dorothy and Herbert Fields had worked on many books for musicals and Dorothy herself was a superb lyricist; both were willing, as was Berlin, to revise and fine tune their work throughout rehearsals and out-of-town tryouts. Sherwood, by contrast, was a distinguished playwright—"too distinguished," Berlin later said, "for this kind of show"—with little experience in musicals. He was accustomed to having his plays produced as he had written them and was inimical to the constant doctoring required to pull a musical into shape.

When Sherwood researched the history of the statue, which France had presented as a gift to the United States on the centenary of its Revolution, he learned that there were no funds to provide a base or to erect the monument. Sherwood found his dramatic conflict in two rival newspaper publishers, Joseph Pulitzer and James Gordon Bennett, who made a campaign for funds to complete the statue into a circulation war. Sherwood then tried to inject love interest into the show with a plot that revolved around a search for the model for the statue, who, in his script, was a glamorous Parisian girl of the streets. Berlin, who also threw himself into research on the statue, came across the more prosaic truth when he investigated the life story of its sculptor, Frédéric Bartholdi. "Look, Bob," he told Sherwood, "His mother posed for it." "I knew that," Sherwood replied, pulling out his poetic license, "But there must have been younger models who posed, say, for hands."

As Sherwood veered from history into fantasy, Berlin went his own way with the songs for *Miss Liberty*. Insead of trying to integrate each song into the characters and story, as he had done in *Annie Get Your Gun*, he composed most of his songs before Sherwood had even completed the script. "In *Annie Get Your Gun*," he told reporters, "I had to defer to the book. These songs will be hits all by themselves." In particular, he thought "Give Me Your Tired," his musical setting of Emma Lazarus's poem on the base of the statue, would be as stirring as "God Bless America." The song that held the greatest promise,

Irving Berlin, Moss Hart, and Robert E. Sherwood at work on *Miss Liberty* in 1949.

"Mr. Monotony," was not even written for *Miss Liberty* but was a left-over from *Easter Parade*. When Rodgers and Hammerstein watched a tryout performance, they recognized the lack of integration between "Mr. Monotony" and the rest of *Miss Liberty*. "You must have the courage to cut out the one show-stopper," they advised Berlin, "Because it is bad for the character of the girl singing it." Berlin took their advice, but the lack of integration overall was crippling. Although *Miss Liberty* ran for 308 performances, it was lambasted by the critics. Brooks Atkinson in the *New York Times* called it "a disappointing musical comedy . . . done to a worn formula . . . put together without sparkle or originality." His most stinging criticism, however, was that, despite the fact that Berlin and Sherwood had found the perfect subject for their talents in the story of the Statue of Liberty:

> they have not written it. Bogged down in the clichés of old-fashioned musical comedy, they have not even written about the grand lady who holds the torch over our harbor. In view of their special gifts as writers, they have missed the opportunity of their Broadway careers.

Even by Berlin's oldest test of a musical's success, long before the days of "integration," *Miss Liberty* was a flop. Not one of the songs he had written for the show, not the charming "Little Fish in a Big Pond" nor the moving "Just One Way to Say I Love You," ever became a hit. Only "Let's Take an Old-Fashioned Walk," recycled from *Easter Parade*, was an independent success. To make matters even worse, the failure of *Miss Liberty* contrasted sharply with the triumph of other brilliantly integrated musicals of the day, including Rodgers and Hammerstein's *South Pacific* and Cole Porter's *Kiss Me, Kate*.

Berlin experienced similar setbacks in Hollywood. Film studios had always produced their own versions of successful Broadway musicals, but they often took great freedom with the original story, characters, and songs. It was not unusual for a studio to keep only a song or two from the original score of a musical like Rodgers and Hart's *Babes in Arms* or the Gershwins' *Strike Up the Band*, adding new songs by its house composers (which meant the studio could collect royalties on songs from the film). After *Oklahoma!*, however, studios approached a Broadway show more reverently and tried to adhere more faithfully to the original stage production. In part, this reverence was dictated by the popularity of original cast recordings of shows; audiences went to a film version of a musical expecting to hear all the songs that were on the records. Because those songs were integrated into the story, the studios had little choice but to stick to the original. About the only way they could put a Hollywood imprimatur on a musical was to substitute film stars for the original Broadway leads, such as Mitzi Gaynor for Mary Martin in *South Pacific*. If the film star could not sing—such as Rossano Brazzi, who assumed Ezio Pinza's role in *South Pacific*—the studio simply dubbed his voice with that of a professional singer—a tawdry use of the device of prerecording that had made the musicals of Astaire and Rogers seem so effortless in their singing and dancing. When Fred Astaire lip-synched to his own playback recording, he did it with the facial expression and carriage of a consummately professional singer and dancer. When an actor who has never sung professionally tries to lip-synch to a recording made by a singer with a full voice, the discrepancy is ludicrously apparent.

Although these Broadway remakes usually did well at the box office and frequently won Academy Awards, they had a devastating effect on the original film musical. Faithful adherence to the stage production, which was after all created with stage rather than film conventions in mind, resulted in lavish but stiff musical films (*South Pacific* is a perfect example). By the mid-1950s, competition with television and a Supreme Court "antimonopoly" ruling that divested studios of their nationwide chain of theaters made it difficult to maintain the array of songwriters, choreographers, and other talent needed to create original musicals. When Hollywood did mount a musical, it was either a filmed version of an established Broadway hit or a low-budget vehicle aimed at the newly flush teenage consumers of the 1950s.

Given the superb work Arthur Freed and MGM had done on his original screen musical, *Easter Parade*, however, Irving Berlin expected great things from the film version of his Broadway smash, *Annie Get Your Gun*. While he accepted the fact that his beloved Ethel Merman could not star in the film, her role was to go to her closest counterpart in Hollywood, Judy Garland. (Among Broadway songwriters, Merman was known as "La Merman," and in Hollywood the composers and lyricists called Judy "La Garland.") Working with screenwriter Sidney Sheldon again, Arthur Freed stayed close to the book for *Annie Get Your Gun* but "opened it up—broadening its physical layout, taking advantage of the potential of the camera." To meet the objections of the Breen Office, which censored motion pictures, several lyrics had to be changed, such as Annie's wonderful lines in "Doin' What Comes Natur'lly":

> My tiny baby brother,
> Who's never read a book,
> Knows one sex from the other,
> All he had to do was look . . .

Also cut were these lines from "You Can't Get a Man with a Gun:"

> A man's love is mighty,
> He'll even buy a nightie
> For a gal who he thinks is fun.
> But they don't buy pajamas
> For pistol-packin' mamas.

Fortunately, the censor missed the joke that opens the song, when Annie innocently explains her marksmanship by revealing that her imminent birth prompted a shotgun wedding: "Oh, my mother was frightened by a shotgun they say, that's why I'm such a wonderful shot."

As filming neared, however, problems began to center on Judy Garland. One problem became apparent when she prerecorded her songs for *Annie Get Your Gun*—her first experience with the integrated Broadway musical:

> Judy was unsure about what to do with the part. It was the first time in her career that she was not doing a "Judy Garland picture." Here she had to portray a character independent of her own personality. Perhaps during the recording sessions Judy was only vaguely aware of this, just aware enough to make her insecure.

"In the monitor booth," recalled a member of Freed's staff, we "smiled each other into a more or less artificial enthusiasm. 'That was very nice, wasn't it?' we said. 'Nice' was a term we had never used for Judy before." Far worse than these artistic problems, Judy Garland was suffering from the effects of years of taking drugs: to sleep, calm down, perk up. Some days she called in sick, showed up late, or collapsed during filming.

Finally, Freed had to find a replacement for her, and he turned to Betty Hutton, a dynamic but far less luminous star. Hutton, who idolized Ethel Merman, did a superb job once the director managed to rein in her zaniness and channel it into the character of Annie Oakley. While Hutton may well have done a better job than Garland with the role, the film version of *Annie Get Your Gun*, without Garland, was not the great success Berlin had hoped it would be. By 1950, at the age of sixty-two, he said, "I've never been in a tougher spot than I am right now. . . . Talent is only the starting point in this business. You've got to keep working at it. And some day I'll reach for it, and it won't be there."

The next time—for one last time—it was there. For his next project, Berlin turned back to Broadway, Ethel Merman, and the days when a musical took its story off the front page of the newspaper. Howard Lindsay and Russel Crouse, who had collaborated on the book for Cole Porter's *Anything Goes* back in 1934, had always wanted to write another show for its star, Ethel Merman. It wasn't until 1949, however, while Lindsay was vacationing at a resort in Colorado where Merman was also staying that he wrote to his collaborator about an idea he had for the perfect vehicle for her. "I have been studying her," Lindsay wrote as he watched Merman sitting by the pool in a yellow swimsuit and bandana, she seems so *American*—raucously, good-naturedly, almost vulgarly American. I got to wondering how we could spot her in a foreign setting. And then I thought of Perle Mesta. How about making her Madame Ambassadress? She would be very funny as an American Ambassador. Give her a very proper First Secretary, strong on protocol and manners,—the kind that would try to stop her from crossing her legs, etc. He isn't the love story. I don't know where that is. She could get the government into trouble and then get it out by using sound American instinct and common sense. There is room for comment. And she could turn out to be a hell of a good Ambassador in the end and spread the democratic idea. The title could be "Call Me Madame" or is that terrible?

When Crouse presented the idea to Merman, she loved it—title and all. The problem was she didn't know who Perle Mesta was. Lindsay explained that Mesta had long been the most prominent hostess in Washington, D.C., and, reportedly in return for munificent campain contributions, President Harry Truman had just appointed her to the position of Ambassador to Luxembourg.

Lindsay went on to point out that such a blatant bit of favoritism could be the basis of some good old-fashioned musical satire, and Merman would be perfect for the brassy lead role. Ethel, however, had another problem with the idea—she didn't want to sing. Ever since her first Broadway show, the Gershwins' *Girl Crazy*, Merman had shown she could be a wonderful comic actress (as her mother gleefully bragged to friends, "Ethel can *talk* too"). "I want a good, solid dramatic role," she insisted—not another musical. When Lindsay refused to outline the plot to her unless she agreed to sing, she caved in: "All right—a few songs if they could be worked in." Lindsay asked her about possible composers and Merman shot back, "Why not Irving?" They both agreed that, after the failure of *Miss Liberty*, Berlin "was in a spot now to do his damnedest."

When the collaborators approached him, Irving Berlin seized the chance to write a score of top-notch songs. Unbeknownst to Lindsay and Crouse, however, he went through his own agonies with the score:

When Howard and Buck asked me if I would write the score for a Merman show, I said yes. They worked on it by themslves a long time, then they sent me the script while I was in Nausau. I wrote six songs very quickly, then I just went blank for two months. I got terribly worried. I couldn't sleep. . . . I like to work under pressure,

against a deadline, in New York. But these boys—
Lindsay and Crouse—wrote this show like a straight play
and then sent it to me, and I had to find a way of getting
songs into a play that was strong enough to stand by
itself without music, instead of a libretto full of song
cues. Besides that, they never seemed to worry about me
or my work. They just sent me the text. Then as they
revised it and changed scenes, they would send me the
new ones. They just didn't worry about my part in it at
all. They just said: "Oh, send it off to Berlin. He'll take
care of the music."

Perhaps it was his collaborators' faith in his talent that restored
Berlin's own, for after a two-month drought, "suddenly, everything
was all right again, and I wrote two or three songs in one week."

Although not a fully integrated "musical drama" in the mold of
Rodgers and Hammerstein, *Call Me Madam* had songs that resonat-
ed with its story and characters. Berlin gave Merman a brassy "I
Am" song, "The Hostess with the Mostes' on the Ball," as well as an
aggressively passionate love song, "The Best Thing for You (and the
Best Thing for You Would Be Me)," that suited her role as a persua-
sive diplomat. Berlin himself coached the Hungarian actor Paul
Lukas in how to put over his song, "Marrying for Love," despite the
limitations of his untrained voice. For the young romantic lead,
Russell Nype, who helped set a 1950s style with his crew cut and
horn-rimmed glasses, Berlin came up with a charming song, "It's a
Lovely Day Today," a revamping of his classic "Isn't This a Lovely
Day?" from the film *Top Hat* and "It's a Lovely Day Tomorrow" from
Louisiana Purchase.

Once tryouts began, however, it was clear that some major doctoring was needed for what Berlin termed a "big hole" in the second
act. Berlin first tried to fill it with "Mr. Monotony," which he had cut
from both *Easter Parade* and *Miss Liberty*. Over the objections of
Lindsay and Crouse and the doubts of director George Abbott, he
insisted on inserting it into the show. But when New Haven audience response was lukewarm, Ethel Merman weighed in, saying
"I've gone along, I've cooperated, I've sung the song and it doesn't
fit. It's out." Berlin then wrote a new, more integral song, "Free," for
Merman to give an ambassadorial lecture on the American way of
life, but that song also failed to fill the hole. Through all of this doctoring, the most worried member of the production was young
Russell Nype, whose first-act number, "It's a Lovely Day Today,"
was the biggest hit of the show. He had enough Broadway experience to know that stars as big as Ethel Merman sometimes had newcomers fired if they stole too much glory from the top of the bill.

When Berlin finally came up with "Something to Dance About" for Merman to sing in the second act, it helped but did not cure the problem. Merman, the woman who had initially demanded a dramatic role where she didn't have to sing, said to Berlin, "I want a number with the kid."

George Abbott suggested Berlin write one of his classic counterpoint songs for Merman and Nype. The songwriter's first such number, the 1914 "Play a Simple Melody," was enjoying new popularity on a recording by Bing Crosby and his son Gary. Berlin had written six tricky counterpoint songs through his career, but the most recent had been twenty-six years earlier. Rising, as ever, to the challenge, he took to his hotel room for an all-night session and emerged with the finest of all his counterpoint songs, "You're Just in Love." When it was finished, he called Russell Nype up to his room and, still in his pajamas, demonstrated the number, singing Merman's lyric himself and coaching Nype on his part. Once he was sure the song worked, Berlin told the youngster, "Don't tell Ethel you heard this before her."

What made the song so effective was Berlin's juxtaposition of age and youth. Perhaps suggested by Bing Crosby's version of "Play a Simple Melody" with his own son, "You're Just in Love" does not treat the conflict between generations but the guidance the old can offer the young, as the worldly wise Merman counsels the bespectacled Nype about the ways of love. Nype's lyric, set to a sweet melody, voices the oldest clichés of romance with the innocent wonder of youth:

> I hear singing and there's no one there,
> I smell blossoms and the trees are bare
> All day long I seem to walk on air,
> I wonder why, I wonder why.

At that point Merman chimes in on the upbeat with punchy wisdom set to a syncopated melody:

> —You don't need analyzing,
> —It is not so surprising
> —That you feel very strange but nice.
> —Your heart goes pitter patter.
> —I know just what's the matter,
> —Because I've been there once or twice.
> —Put your head on my shoulder.
> —You need someone who's older,

—A rubdown with a velvet glove.
—There is nothing you can take
—To relieve that pleasant ache.
—You're not sick—you're just in love.

It was a new kind of love duet, for an older woman mothering a younger man. Berlin created imagery—"a rubdown with a velvet glove"—that was sensuous without being sexual, and he alluded to the vogue of psychoanalysis, which friends like Moss Hart relied upon, only to debunk it with old-fashioned vernacular advice: "You're not sick—you're just in love."

When he demonstrated the song to Ethel Merman and Nype, who had heeded Berlin's advice to keep silent, La Merman said simply, "We'll never get offstage." The seasoned trouper was a good prognosticator; at the first tryout performance in Boston, the audience applauded for seven encores of "You're Just in Love." Integrated musicals did not receive ovations for individual songs; audiences were now expected to be sophisticated enough to respect the overall fabric of drama and song and not to create show-stoppers by cheering for individual numbers to be sung one more time. For Irving Berlin, who had grown up with vaudeville, the smashing success of "You're Just in Love," which topped *Your Hit Parade* for weeks, must have touched the seasoned veteran, as well as the perennial youth, inside him.

Call Me Madam opened in New York on October 12, 1950—Columbus Day—and, boasting the biggest advance ticket sale in Broadway history, ran for eighteen months to critical raves. In Ethel Merman, once again, Berlin had found the perfect vessel for his words and music:

> Give her a song and she'll make it sound good. Give her a good song and she'll make it sound great. And you'd better write her a good lyric, because when she sings the words, the guy in the last row of the balcony can hear every syllable. . . . She's a lyric writer's dream; nobody in show business can project the lyric of a song like Ethel. She times a lyric as carefully and brilliantly as a comedian timing a gag. . . . I love to write songs for Ethel. I guess it's a little like a dress designer getting an extra kick when he dreams up a gown for a beautiful woman with a perfect figure.

The *"American"* quality about Merman that had so struck Howard Lindsay at the Colorado resort pool was perfectly in tune with the

Ethel Merman and Russell Nype sing Berlin's counterpoint duet "You're Just in Love" from the 1950 production of *Call Me Madam.*

songs of Irving Berlin. The combination of singer and songwriter captured the exuberant, prosperous spirit of the early 1950s, when America, after the Depression and World War II, was finally emerging from decades of scarcity and anxiety. Songs like "Can You Use Any Money Today?," where Merman plays Perle Mesta offering American "dollar diplmacy," gently satirized both the nation's sense of limitless wealth and its giddy recognition of itself as the dominant world power:

Two million, Four million, Six million, Eight million, Ten,
Take what you want when it's gone you can come back again.

It was an age of dynamic expansiveness, and Ethel Merman singing
Irving Berlin epitomized it.

Perhaps the most surprising hit from the show was "They Like
Ike," which alluded to the movement to draft General Dwight D.
Eisenhower for president, despite his lack of political experience
("Ike is good on a mike"). Although Eisenhower continued to insist
that he would not run, Berlin had clearly supplied him with a campaign song. This was not his first attempt at a political campaign
song. In 1924, he had written "We'll All Go Voting for Al" to boost Al
Smith's bid for the presidency, but Smith had long been associated
with the classic song, "The Sidewalks of New York." For a Madison
Square Garden rally in support of Eisenhower's candidacy, Berlin
revised his lyric from *Call Me Madam* and then, in front of 15,000
supporters, sang "I Like Ike." While the song has not endured,
Berlin's title phrase became the most successful campaign slogan of
all time. The distinguished linguist, Roman Jakobson, has subjected
the phrase "I Like Ike" to intense scrutiny, finding its magic lies in
the way the "I" who voices the phrase is subtly included in the verbal
embrace of the "i" in "like" and then even more grandly in the "I" of
"Ike." Berlin probably would have shrugged his shoulders at such a
tribute to what he would have considered merely a trick of a songwriter's trade.

When he became president, Eisenhower, in turn, helped plug
Irving Berlin's last true hit song in 1954. Berlin had written it after a
particularly bad bout of insomnia (a problem that would grow
increasingly worse as he aged). He complained to his doctor that he
had even tried counting sheep. "Did you ever try counting your
blessings instead?" the doctor replied, unwittingly giving him his
title phrase. A young singer, Eddie Fisher, performed "Count Your
Blessings" at the American Jewish Tercentenary banquet to commemorate the first immigration of Jews to America. For Irving
Berlin, who had also been an immigrant, it was a fitting hymn that
expressed a gentle word of caution to America's current prosperity.
Eisenhower, who attended the event to give a televised speech after
the dinner, found himself "very much touched" by "Count Your
Blessings," and once the television cameras came on, he asked
Eddie Fisher to sing the song again so that all Americans could hear
it. For one last time, the aging troubadour had captured the national
spirit in a song.

The year 1954 saw the last films with scores by Irving Berlin.
White Christmas gave Berlin the chance to work on an idea he had
had since the end of World War II about a general who is forgotten

Irving Berlin, President Eisenhower, and Ellin Berlin at the White House in 1955, where the songwriter receives a Congressional Gold Medal for his work.

during peacetime. Originally conceived as a stage musical, Berlin adapted it for a film that was originally to star Bing Crosby and Fred Astaire, in an obvious recasting of *Holiday Inn*. However, things quickly became chaotic. "For some reason," Berlin recalled, "Bing suddenly didn't want to do it. Astaire didn't like the story, this one and that one said no." Berlin talked Crosby into reconsidering and Donald O'Connor replaced Astaire, but then O'Connor became seriously ill. "We were frantic," Berlin said. "It seemed a doomed film." Then somebody recalled "a lad on the lot who bristles with talent. Fellow named Danny Kaye." Kaye lived up to billing, but the upheaval left songs like "The Best Things Happen When You're Dancing," somewhat out of place with a singing, rather than dancing, cast. In all, Berlin wrote nine new songs for the film, including "Sisters," a witty duet for Rosemary Clooney and Vera Ellen, but it was "Count Your Blessings" and the established songs that charmed audiences. Compared to *Holiday Inn*, with its darker, satirical look at the entertainment business, *White Christmas* is heavy on sentiment and nostalgia, right down to a bald, retired general who looks much like Ike. The lavish, glossy rendition of the title song, with all four leads sparkling in Santa outfits, overwhelms the simplicity of the music and lyrics, which were presented with such casual understatement in *Holiday Inn*.

Like *White Christmas*, *There's No Business Like Show Business* reflected the opulence and bigness of the 1950s as much as the decade's car fins and bosomy starlets. Both features were even filmed, respectively, in VistaVision and CinemaScope, those technological breakthroughs that forced directors to film performers in broad, horizontal shots that would fill the wide screen. Understandably, such movies turned out to be as static and stilted as the first wave of talkies back in the 1920s. Still, there were wonderful numbers in *There's No Business Like Show Business*, such as Marilyn Monroe singing "Heat Wave." Ethel Merman, who starred in the film with Dan Dailey, was originally slated to do the number, but when Berlin saw a photograph of Monroe at Joe Schenck's house, he beseeched his old friend to get her to do the song in the picture. Filmed at Twentieth Century–Fox, still very much the "Catholic" studio under Zanuck's control, *There's No Business Like Show Business* had to stress family values.

Just as Zanuck had insisted on cutting much of the satire from *Call Me Madam* when Fox did the film version in 1953, he now focused *There's No Business Like Show Business* on the sentimental story of a show business family. For Zanuck the story of a film was uppermost, even in a musical, and numbers had to take a back seat. Prerock stylist Johnnie Ray might be in the film to wail his heart out, but he also had to play a role in the narrative by entering the priesthood at the end of the film.

Even as he worked on *There's No Business Like Show Business*, rumors began to circulate that Irving Berlin was again suffering from depression and that he had had to spend a week in a rest home. When columnist Louella Parsons asked him if he had recuperated, Berlin denied the rumor of any illness with a laugh, affirming, "I've just eaten the biggest lunch" and "I've never been better." The truth was he had begun to slide into another period of depression much more severe than his creative crisis of thirty years before. "I got really sick," he admitted later, "I worried about everything, when, really, I had nothing to worry about." Perhaps the onset of his breakdown can be glimpsed in an incident during his work on *White Christmas*. He had completed the songs for the picture and asked Bing Crosby to come to his house to hear them. When Crosby arrived, however, Berlin was overcome with insecurity in the singer's presence. The painful episode resembled young Irving Berlin's humiliating terror in 1910 when he had the chance to audition his songs for the great Broadway magnate, J. J. Shubert, only to find himself dumbstruck. When Crosby realized the songwriter could not demonstrate his songs, he graciously asked, "Do you like them, Irving?" When Berlin nodded, Crosby said, "Then they're good enough for me."

After 1955, Berlin wrote less and less and worried more and more about it. One song he did produce was ironically titled, "Anybody Can Write." Plans for a new musical with George S. Kaufman and S. N. Behrman, two of Americas best playwrights, fizzled. It was to have been about the Mizner brothers, two real-life characters from the Jazz Age, and could have made for a wonderful period musical. Berlin had been a friend of Wilson Mizner, playwright, "versifier," and wit, who was credited with coining the phrase, "Never give a sucker an even break." Meanwhile, a property that Irving Berlin had turned down when the estate of George Bernard Shaw offered *Pygmalion* to him as the basis of a musical, became the spectacularly successful *My Fair Lady* in 1956. He tried taking up painting as a hobby but expressed his frustration in a song called "(You Can't Lose the Blues with) Colors." In 1957, when Hollywood asked him to write a theme song for a Marlon Brando movie based on James Michener's novel about postwar Japan, Berlin simply dug into his trunk for "Sayonara, Sayonara," which he had written four years earlier when he and Josh Logan planned to turn *Sayonara* into a stage musical, plans that also never materialized. The following year, when he turned seventy, there was not one new song copyrighted by Irving Berlin—something that had not happened in over fifty years. He still wrote songs for his family, always, along with his songwriting career, the most cherished thing in his life. When Ellin, who had continued to write throughout their marriage, published a bigraphy of her grandmother, Berlin honored the book with a title song, "Silver Platter." For his grandchildren, he wrote "Irving Berlin Barrett" and "Song for Elizabeth Esther Barrett." For the public, however, all he could manage in 1959 was one song, "Israel," in honor of the new Jewish homeland. Even then, he admitted, he felt "as if he were heading for a breakdown":

> There was everything a man could want. Money? It no longer meant anything. It came in, it went out. It would always come in, I decided to quit, to retire. I took up painting. Painting? That's a laugh. Daubs. They were awful. They had no meaning. I wrote no music, I made no songs, I idled. For five years, first, health troubles. Nerves, ague pains, twitches. Then depression. I got to a point I didn't want to leave my room when daylight came.

Eventually, he had to be hospitalized, and it was publicly announced that Irving Berlin had at last retired.

Although Berlin's despair seems to have been wholly personal, it coincided with a vast change in the world of popular music, a change that, for once, Irving Berlin could not adjust to. The change

Irving Berlin, age 69, at the piano in his office in 1957.

was signaled by a popular song of 1954, "Rock Around the Clock," which became the basis for a movie that ushered in the newest form of American music since ragtime. The new music had its roots in the black and country music that had been seeping into the mainstream through BMI since ASCAP's struggle with radio in the early 1940s. As Irving Berlin had foreseen many years before, radio was shortening the shelf life of a popular song with its incessant airing of "hits," and the quality of songwriting had suffered from this medium's insatiable appetite for songs. That appetite grew even more voracious when television commanded the attention of the major broadcasting networks, who stopped producing national radio programs and left local stations to find their own material. Most turned to disc jockeys, who would endlessly spin hit records to attract listeners. The Top Ten of the old Hit Parade expanded into the Top Forty, and songs had to be turned out by the yard for an ever more youthful audience. "We don't like rock 'n roll," one of the new "A&R" (artist and repertory) men at the big recording studios piously lamented, "But we discovered that's what the teenagers want, and that's what we're going to give them":

> No A & R man in his right mind is going to turn down a song he thinks is a hit. We need hits to keep our jobs. If a songwriter like Irving Berlin were to write a new song tomorrow, the chances are that any A & R man in the business would jump to record it, but I'm not going to keep recording Berlin's old hits, just because they're Berlin's. What some of the old-timers don't realize is that Tin Pan Alley isn't the heart of the music world anymore. Hits today can spring up from any part of the country and on any one of some 700 record labels.

Although they insisted "we don't dictate the public taste, we go along with it," the "payola" scandal revealed that these same A&R men were bribing disc jockeys to play their wares. They righteously—but rightly—countercharged that Tin Pan Alley publishers had long bribed big stars like Al Jolson to plug their songs by putting their names on sheet music and cutting them in for a share of the royalties. Still, as Edgar Leslie, one of Berlin's old collaborators, put it:

> What are they trying to tell us, that all this talent that produced this wonderful music has disappeared overnight? At 70, I'm willing to concede the parade may have passed me by, but it's going at least 100 miles an hour when it passes writers like Irving Berlin.

The state of music was changing, but there was clearly something more involved than a shift of musical styles.

Before he succumbed to depression, Berlin had been more generous than other songwriters of his era toward the new music. While cautioning that "One 'Sh-Boom' or 'Oop-Shoop' doesn't make a hit writer," he noted that the reputation of songwriters like Vincent

Youmans subsisted on only a few hits. Giving "Rock and Roll Waltz," his highest praise, he said, "I wish I had thought of it," and in later years he would praise the Beatles' "Michelle" and other songs such as "Little Green Apples" (though he observed, "A professional song-writer would never have rhymed 'little green apples' with 'it don't snow in Minneapolis'—he would have said 'We don't pray in church-es and chapels'"). Nor did he scorn "hillbilly and cornball songs," like "Tennessee Waltz," even though it was a BMI rather than an ASCAP song. A young singer, Kathy Linden, made a hit out of his old song, "You'd Be Surprised," though Berlin winced at the way she gulped phrases in the new rock style. He drew the line, however, when Elvis Presley recorded "White Christmas," and even tried, unsuccessfully, to prevent its airing on radio.

What Berlin also recognized in the Presley phenomenon was that it was now a performer's "interpretation" that made a song, though he indicated that much the same had been true of performers like Jolson. What was different in the rock era was that songwriting had become less important than song performance, and that change took hold during Berlin's years of depression. Several of Presley's early hits were written by the team of Leiber and Stoller, who freely acknowledged that they were in the business of writing "disposable" songs. For a songwriter like Irving Berlin—or Cole Porter or the Gershwins—who wrote songs in the hope they would become stan-dards, such a notion of a disposable song was anathema. But where, he must have wondered, would standards continue to be heard? Commercial radio was not interested in playing older songs, no mat-ter how good they were, and classical stations narrowly viewed clas-sical music as European concert works.

By the 1960s, the role of the pure songwriter diminished even more as performers increasingly wrote their own songs. "The ama-teurs," some of the more disgruntled older songwriters termed them. What had once been the very specialized crafts of the lyricist, com-poser, and performer now were all combined in one person, with an understandable decrease in song quality. In Berlin's generation, only he and Cole Porter had mastered the art of combining music and words; and Berlin alone had been a successful performer, though he had largely abandoned the profession of singer once he had estab-lished himself as a songwriter. Performers in the age of rock who wrote the words and music to their own songs would have had to possess Irving Berlin's unique and prodigious talent to match the quality of the songs of his era.

While the rock revolution was the major cause for the change in popular music, Broadway also turned away from the world of popu-lar song in these years. Younger songwriters like Stephen Sondheim and Sheldon Harnick advanced the integrated musical into more innovative directions, but with that advance came the loss of popular songs emerging from the musical theater. The shows, not the songs, were now uppermost on Broadway, and, by the 1960s, it was not unusual for a successful musical to produce not even one hit song. Where Cole Porter, Berlin, and the Gershwins measured a show's success by how many of its songs became hits, a songwriter like Stephen Sondheim would never consider himself a writer of popular songs.

The separation between Broadway musicals and popular song was particularly noticeable in the realm of dance music. It was Berlin who married the dance craze with the Broadway musical when he wrote *Watch Your Step* for Vernon and Irene Castle in 1914. For the next forty years, as Gerald Mast observes, "songs that were once sung or danced on theater stages and movie screens were the songs to which Americans danced offstage and off screen as well." The songs Irving Berlin, Rodgers and Hart, Cole Porter, and the Gershwins wrote for Broadway and Hollywood musicals were danceable as waltzes, fox trots, or other popular couple dances. Beginning with Rodgers and Hammerstein's musicals, Mast argues, show tunes became increasingly less danceable:

> The divorce of American theater music from its dance music made it more serious and more grand, even as it made it less American and less popular—particularly with the young. The Broadway musical grew steadily older through the 1950s and 1960s, and its audiences grew older with it—in taste and in fact. Broadway shows abandoned their old friends, pop singles and sheet music, for the new LP record, born in 1948. Like operas and symphonies, Broadway shows were recorded as Columbia Masterworks and RCA Red Seals, and the Broadway hills were alive with a sound of music as Masterworky as the recordings.

For Irving Berlin, who had written so many of his songs not only for dancing but *about* dancing, from "Everybody's Doin' It Now" to "Something to Dance About," the new Broadway offered little room.

Paradoxically, despite all these changes in his professional world, Irving Berlin pulled himself out of his depression by returning to songwriting:

> One day, after five years of it, I looked at myself and said, "What you need is to go back to work. What made you think you ever could quit?" It was wonderful. I threw out the medicines, paid off the doctors and sat

down and did what for almost 60 years I have done
best—I started writing music again. My spirits soared,
my aches and pains disappeared. And that's the truth I
want every man with any kind of talent to look at me and
heed—don't quit, don't turn your back on the mystery of
talent, don't abandon what was given to you, don't scorn
your gifts. Use them until your last day on earth and live
a full, rich and rewarding life.

It sounded as if it didn't matter what project he undertook; if so, that
may have helped him weather the debacle that was to come.

Berlin went to Howard Lindsay and Russel Crouse, the playwrights who had concocted his last great stage hit, *Call Me Madam*,
and told them he wanted to do another show. His idea was to do the
show about a retired general, *Stars on My Shoulder*, but they told
him they had a new idea for a musical about what happens to a president after he leaves office. Given the youthfulness of President
Kennedy, the idea was intriguing, and it promised to capture the
vitality and charm of the Kennedy White House. "I told them I liked
the idea very much," Berlin explained to reporters with all of his old
exuberant modesty, "and that I'd go home and see if I could still
write a song." What he did was create the biggest score—twenty-two
songs—he had ever composed for a musical. "It would have been
easy to have gone into the trunk for the songs," he confided, "but I
wanted to see if I could still reach up and find it there." Some of the
songs, like "Washington Twist," tried to stay abreast of the times. He
even promised, as he put it, "to write a little closer to the book," but
added, "I hate that term 'integrated score.' If you have a great song,
you can always integrate it into any show."

What Berlin did not have was a star like Merman or Astaire he
could tailor his songs to. For the leading man, *Mr. President* had the
nonsinging actor Robert Ryan, perhaps in the hope that he could
talk his way through song lyrics as Rex Harrison had done in *My
Fair Lady* and Robert Preston in *The Music Man*. Nanette Fabray,
the female lead, could sing, but her real strength lay in comedy, and
her resemblance to Jackie Kennedy. Fabray recollects the first cast
gathering where Irving Berlin sat at the piano and played through
the entire score; if they could sing the songs as well as he, she
thought, *Mr. President* would be a hit.

Unfortunately, as Berlin reflected, "We all got off on the wrong
foot." When *Mr. President* opened in Boston, one critic dubbed the
show "Dreadful," then added, "Dreadful is the only word." Berlin
felt "more pressure with this show than any other I've ever done—
but I asked for it." "We have a terrible problem," he told the company, "But we'll fix it, we'll fix it." Going to the well one more time, he

Robert Ryan and Nanette Fabray in the 1962 production of *Mr. President*.

wrote another counterpoint song, "Empty Pockets Filled with Love."
As he said, however, "If you have a bad tune or a bad lyric, you can
do something about it. But when you start off with a bad show or a
bad book it's difficult to fix." When the show moved to Washington,
the Kennedys and their entourage turned out for the premiere, but
the reviews were equally bad. Nothing could save *Mr. President*,
which one critic compared to the voyage of the *Titanic*, with the
cast singing a finale reminiscent of "Nearer My God to Thee." When
it reached New York, in the most scathing review Irving Berlin had
ever received, theater critic Walter Kerr pointed out his most fundamental errors in songwriting, such as rhyming "act" with
"attacked." Kerr lamented that Berlin had lost his lifelong touch for
"the words—which were always simple, but simply evocative," and
he compared the "prosaic" lyrics to "mere wooden soldiers keeping
up with the beat."

Amazingly, Berlin was able to take the collapse of *Mr. President* in
stride. "I thought the show was going to run five years," he reflected,
"but no one appeared interested in an ex-President. I nursed my
wounds and went back to work." To his wife Ellin, he confided,
"Listen, I'd rather be 'unhappy' doing something than really being

unhappy doing nothing." Soon, he was planning an even bigger project. Approaching Arthur Freed at MGM, Berlin proposed a lavish film musical, *Say It With Music*, that would include twenty-five of his greatest songs together with seven new ones he had composed specifically for the project. When Berlin played the new songs from his score, plugging them as passionately as he had his first hits back in 1910, Freed was ecstatic and agreed to produce the picture. Freed had assumed the picture would be a biography of Berlin himself, laced with a chronology of his songs, but Berlin, as always, steadfastly refused a film biography. "There's only been one biographical movie of a songwriter that hasn't made me too embarrassed to sit and watch it," he said, "And that was George M. Cohan's *Yankee Doodle Dandy*. I couldn't take the risk of one about me turning out to be a syrupy tribute." Anyone who has seen *Till the Clouds Roll By*, Jerome Kern's biopic, or Cole Porter's *Night and Day*, could hardly blame Berlin.

But Arthur Freed was worried that, without Berlin's biography, nothing would hold the film and its vast array of songs together:

> In the old days, all you needed was the money to develop the negative and the picture would make a profit. You didn't need a book. You just strung the songs together, threw in a few dance routines and that was a musical. Now you need a script. It's more important than stars. You need choreography. . . . It's tough enough to make a buck with an ordinary movie. And it's even tougher with a musical.

"Who needs a book?" Berlin chided his old friend, "I'll turn out songs without a book."

Despite his concern, Freed began to assemble a stellar cast—the picture would star Frank Sinatra and Judy Garland, and include such show-business veterans as Ethel Merman and Fred Astaire along with newcomers Pat Boone, Connie Francis, and Johnny Mathis. They would sing new numbers like "I Used to Play By Ear," with its autobiographical wink at Berlin's pianistic abilities, and "The Ten Best Undressed Women in the World," which recaptured Berlin's happiest days, when he was writing songs for Ziegfeld's revues as well as his own lavish spectacles at the Music Box Theatre. Although the songs told the story of his life, Berlin adamantly refused to let the script do the same. "What the hell would I do with a handsome leading man impersonating me?" he quipped, "I'm not handsome." When pressed, he turned serious, even defensive of the privacy he had always guarded for himself and his family. "I don't want my life story told," he insisted. "It would be an invasion of my

Irving Berlin, age 75, singing with gusto at an awards ceremony in 1963.

privacy while I'm still alive. When I'm dead, they can tell it all they want." Various writers struggled with the grandiose project, including lyricist-librettists Betty Comden and Adolph Green, who had written with equal success for stage musicals (*On the Town*) as well as for films (*Singin' in the Rain*). Finally, after seven years, enough of a script had emerged that *Say It With Music* was ready to begin filming. By that point, starring roles had shifted, with Frank Sinatra replaced by Robert Goulet and Judy Garland by Julie Andrews.

Just as production was about to get underway, MGM, which had been experiencing economic difficulties, was put under new management that cared little about the studio's great tradition of film musicals. Without even consulting Arthur Freed, the project, with its estimated $4 million price tag, was scrapped. "*Say It With Music*," Berlin reflected bitterly, "was to be Arthur's and my swan song in motion pictures." "Those 'civilians'" as he termed the new executives, "were stupid." A film that might well indeed have been one of the last great original film musicals and a stunning tribute to Irving Berlin's canon of songs was never made.

Irving Berlin's last hurrah fittingly came in a revival of his greatest stage show, *Annie Get Your Gun*, in 1966. The idea for a revival of the twenty-year-old musical came from Richard Rodgers, who arranged for it to be staged at Lincoln Center, New York's new center of musical culture. Once again, it starred Ethel Merman; "she can play it till she's ninety," Berlin said, "And I hope she does." For the revival, Berlin wrote a new counterpoint song, "An Old Fashioned Wedding," as a finale. Berlin wrote the song, not as a tour de force, but to strengthen the romantic tension between the characters. Despite his antipathy toward the term "integrated score," he said, "I always like to write songs that come out of a dramatic situation." Frank Butler, who early in the show sings his idealized version of "The Girl That I Marry," closes the show by singing his half of "An Old Fashioned Wedding." Berlin gives him a sweeping, stepwise melody and a lyric that envisions a homespun traditional ceremony. But then Merman chimes in with a brassy, syncopated tune, full of leaps and turns, and demands a big, modern, and, above all, expensive wedding replete with champagne and caviar. When the two melodies are combined, Frank sings "love and honor and obey," while Merman's perfect counterpoint counters his meaning with the postwar "liberated" woman's "love and honor yes—but not obey." The song, as so many of Berlin's had before, stopped the show. After the fifth encore, Richard Rodgers, standing in the back of the theatre, muttered, "That's not bad for a man 78 years old." The revival was a critical and commercial success that brought Berlin a hard-won satisfaction he had once garnered so easily. "I haven't felt such warmth and affection since *This Is the Army*," he exulted. *Annie Get Your Gun* had been a revival indeed.

It was also, as Berlin must have realized, a swan song. While he remained astute and energetic, the world of popular music, which he had dominated for most of the century, no longer provided an outlet for his talent. For more than twenty years, he would continue to write songs but never tried another Broadway show or film score. The most he did was update a song for the times. He retailored "Alexander's Ragtime Band" for the 1960s by changing the martial

Richard Rodgers, Ethel Merman, Irving Berlin, and Dorothy Fields at the first
rehearsal of the 1966 revival of *Annie Get Your Gun*.

line, "so natural that you want to go to war" to the more neutral "so
natural that you want to hear some more." Still, the times they were
a-changing; at an antiwar rally in 1965, the poet Joel Oppenheimer
shouted down someone who tried to sing "God Bless America" with
"Get out of here! We've been hearing that song too long!"

While Berlin devoted himself to his family and took up painting
again with more dedication, the vacuum created by the end of his

active career as a songwriter made the last years of his life bitter and angry ones. He still oversaw his publishing company and was extremely protective of his precious catalogue of songs. Unlike most songwriters, he owned his copyrights and could refuse permission to anyone who sought to use them in ways he thought demeaning, such as in television commercials. He even sometimes refused scholars permission to quote from his songs he literally considered priceless. "If someone walked in here and offered me $10,000,000 for it," he told a visitor who asked about his catalog of songs, "I'd refuse. What good would it be? It would take from me and give me something I have no need for." While his copyrights gave him control over publication of his songs, he could not prevent how they were performed. Whether Berlin liked it or not, however, his great songs continued to flourish in new performances. Frank Sinatra made "Change Partners" one of the great bossa nova hits of the 1970s, while Dutch rock star "Taco" revived "Puttin' on the Ritz" in all its rhythmic complexity. (When Berlin learned of the latter's success, he said, "I thought 'taco' was a kind of food.")

As his thoughts turned increasingly to memories of his youth, he reflected upon the East River, which he could see from his home on the Upper East Side. "I was once a kid living along another part of the East River," he recalled, "And my mother used to fish me out of a swimming hole at least twice a day." The presence of that body of water, one of the oldest symbols of the course of life, comforted him. Even at ninety-nine years of age, he still visited the Lower East Side. "I've always lived near this river, ever since I came to New York," he mused, "It's like completing a circle." Still, even in his last years, his never-resting mind toyed with the thought of one last, Broadway show:

> I have nursed one idea maybe 10 years just about. I have researched it, used my personal memories, and have written songs, not all of them, but at least half, for a musical I'd like to call *East River*. A turn-of-the-century musical based on the immigrants. The already-established Irish, the incoming Jews and Italians, their problems, triumphs, loves, and disasters.

But memories of *Mr. President* made him wary. "At my age," he confided, "it's hard to go to auditions and rehearsals and the rest. Besides, you get frightened. You can stand success, but you're afraid of failure."

Those notes of vulnerability, loneliness, and insecurity that so often are sounded in his songs, such as "Say It Isn't So" and "What'll I Do?," were now resounding in his life. A man who had lived by expressing his era now found himself silenced by the changing times. He withdrew more deeply into himself, and, much like his otherwise completely different contemporary, the poet Ezra Pound, lived his final days in a morose and secluded silence. For Pound, who had never known popularity among his contemporaries, that silence was his way of leaving his work to the judgment of future generations. For Irving Berlin, it may have been a similar determination to look beyond the current age. "Who cares anymore?" he wondered. "There's a whole new public out there, and they don't even know people like me are still around. . . . We're antiques, museum pieces. Today, it's all kids." Berlin commented that, without an audience, he lost his enthusiasm for composing:

> Few professionals can write well if they know from the start what they write isn't going to be published. I don't think that any kind of creator—songs or stories—can work well if he knows that his stuff is just headed for the trunk in the attic. You have to feel that people are going to see or hear—and buy—what you've done. Talking about dream jobs, maybe the real dream job is being a failure. Then you wouldn't have to worry about maintaining a standard.

It wasn't just the general public Berlin needed to reach with his songs. Like the other great songwriters of his era, the artistic quality of his work was largely due to the fact that he was writing for great performers like Astaire and Merman, literary collaborators like Kaufman and Hart, and, most of all, for the Gershwins, Cole Porter, and the other great songwriters who had been his contemporaries. Knowing his music would be heard by Rodgers and Arlen, his lyrics by Hammerstein and Fields, drove Berlin to the highest standards of songwriting, just as these other composers and lyricists wrote with Irving Berlin in mind. "Our tribe of songsmiths always wrote for our peers," Yip Harburg recalled, "We were very much . . . an artistic community where people took fire from one another." Only when such a community emerges do we have great eras of literary, artistic, and musical culture such as America enjoyed in the first half of the twentieth century.

Without such peers and without a public to write for, Irving Berlin retreated still further into himself. He spurned celebrations, reunions, and tributes. He refused to go out in public, saying, "I don't want people to look at me and say, 'See how old he looks.'"

He communicated almost exclusively with a small circle of old friends over the telephone. When they asked about his health, he would say, "My health is wonderful—from the neck up." Still, some

Irving Berlin, age 86, playing piano at his last photo session in September 1974.

recalled, he would sometimes tell them he was working on songs, even scores for new shows. "I've got an awful lot of unpublished stuff lying around," he said in his 90s, "but at my age it's hard to go to auditions and rehearsals and all the rest." Even these friends were passing away. "Freddy" Astaire's death in 1987 (which took with it a whole world of artistry and elegance) was particularly devastating to Berlin. With the death of his wife Ellin the next year, to whom he had given "Always" as a wedding present, Berlin seems to have lost everything else. By then, Berlin himself had lived to be one hundred years old, a fitting span for a man who had embodied so much of the twentieth century in his life and works. The occasion of his centenary prompted the songwriter to soften a little and sanction—but not attend—a tribute at Carnegie Hall, an appropriate ceremony for a man who had produced the closest thing America has to a body of classical American song.

Even those songs had begun leaving him. Irving Berlin was probably the only modern songwriter who outlived many of his own copyrights. In 1978, a change in the copyright law meant that the copyright on his songs expired after seventy-five years, so that he lived to see such beloved songs as "Alexander's Ragtime Band" pass into public domain, where they no longer earned royalties. Yet art, he knew, survived the brevity of life. A lyric, found among his papers after his death, has him rewriting "Alexander's Ragtime Band" as a heavenly roll call of songs by his brilliant contemporaries:

> Gershwin and Kern, Jerry Herman, many more,
> Romberg, Cole Porter, Rodgers AND Hammerstein!
> The list is long—with every song
> There's a new chance to begin
> AND three or four, or maybe more,
> Written by the great Berlin.

With that balance of modesty and honest recognition of his own talent and achievement that he always maintained, he placed himself in his own songwriting pantheon.

Such fierce creative energy, which apparently drove him, as he had always predicted, to write songs until the day he died, gave out at last. On September 22, 1989, Irving Berlin, né Israel Baline, died, peacefully, in the kind of deep and restful sleep that had eluded him for a lifetime.

Irving Berlin Songography

Compiled by Ken Bloom

All music and lyrics by Irving Berlin unless otherwise indicated.
Date indicates copyright year not year of composition.

C   composer

L   lyricist

1907 *POP SONGS*
Marie from Sunny Italy (C: Nicholson, Nick)

1908 *POP SONGS*
Best of Friends Must Part, The; Queenie (My Own) (C: Abrahams, Maurice)

SHOW SONGS
Boys and Betty, The (Show): She Was a Dear Little Girl

1909 *POP SONGS*
Christmas Time Seems Years and Years Away (C: Snyder, Ted); Do Your Duty, Doctor (C: Snyder, Ted); Dorando; Goodbye Girlie and Remember Me (C: Meyer, George W.); I Didn't Go Home at All (C/L: Berlin, Irving; Leslie, Edgar); I Just Came Back to Say Good-Bye (C: Snyder, Ted); I Wish That You Was My Gal, Molly (C: Snyder, Ted); If I Thought You Wouldn't Tell (C: Snyder, Ted); Just Like the Rose (C: Piantadosi, Al); My Wife's Gone to the Country (Hurrah! Hurrah!) (C: Snyder, Ted; L: Berlin, Irving; Whiting, George); Next to Your Mother, Who Do You Love? (C: Snyder, Ted); No One Could Do It Like My Father (C: Snyder, Ted); Oh! What I Know About You; Oh! Where Is My Wife To-Night? (C: Snyder, Ted; L: Berlin, Irving; Whiting, George); Some Little Something About You (C: Snyder, Ted); Someone Just Like You Dear (C: Snyder, Ted); Someone's Waiting for Me (C/L: Berlin, Irving; Leslie, Edgar); That Mesmerizing Mendelssohn Tune; We'll Wait, Wait, Wait (L: Leslie, Edgar); Wild Cherries, That Cooney Spooney Rag (C: Snyder, Ted)

SHOW SONGS
Girl and the Wizard, The (Show): Oh! How That German Could Love (C: Snyder, Ted)
Jolly Bachelors, The (Show). Music by Ted Snyder: If the Managers Only Thought the Same as Mother; Stop That Boy

1910 *POP SONGS*
Alexander and His Clarinet (C: Snyder, Ted); Angels (C: Snyder, Ted); Before I Go and Marry (I Will Have a Talk with You); Call Me Up Some Rainy Afternoon; Colored Romeo (C: Snyder, Ted); Dat Draggy Rag (C: Snyder, Ted); Dear Mayme, I Love You (C: Snyder, Ted); Dreams, Just Dreams (C: Snyder, Ted); How Can You Love Such a Man?; I Love You More Each Day (C: Snyder, Ted); I'm Going on a Long Vacation (C: Snyder, Ted); I'm a Happy Married Man (C: Snyder, Ted); Innocent Bessie Brown; Is There Anything Else That I Can Do for You? (C: Snyder, Ted); Piano Man (C: Snyder, Ted); Stop! Stop! Stop! (Love Me Some More); Telling Lies (C/L: Belcher, Fred E.; Berlin, Irving; Blank, Henrietta); Thank You Kind Sir, Said She (C: Snyder, Ted); When I Hear You Play That Piano, Bill (C: Snyder, Ted); Yiddisha Eyes; Yiddle on Your Fiddle (Play Some Ragtime)

SHOW SONGS
Getting a Polish (Show): That Opera Rag (C: Snyder, Ted)
Girl in the Kimono, The (Show): Oh, That Beautiful Rag (C: Snyder, Ted)
He Came from Milwaukee (Show): Bring Back My Lena to Me
Jolly Bachelors, The (Show): Stop That Rag (Keep on Playing, Honey); Sweet Marie—Make a Rag-a-Time Dance with Me
Jumping Jupiter (Show): Angelo; It Can't Be Did; Thank You, Kind Sir, Said She
Two Men and a Girl (Show): Herman, Let's Dance That Beautiful Waltz; Wishing
Up and Down Broadway (Show). Music by Ted Snyder: Oh, That Beautiful Rag; Sweet Italian Love; That Beautiful Rag (C: Berlin, Irving)
Ziegfeld Follies of 1910 (Show): Dance of the Grizzly Bear, The (C: Botsford, George); Good-Bye Becky Cohen; Sadie Salome Go Home (C/L: Berlin, Irving; Leslie, Edgar)

1911 *POP SONGS*
After the Honeymoon (C: Snyder, Ted); Bring Back My Lovin' Man; Bring Me a Ring in the Spring; Business Is Business,

Rosey Cohen; Cuddle Up; Dat's-a My Gal; Don't Put Out the Light (L: Leslie, Edgar); Down to the Follies Bergere (C: Snyder, Ted; L: Berlin, Irving; Bryan, Vincent); Dying Rag; Everybody's Doing It Now; He Promised Me; How Do You Do It, Mabel, on Twenty Dollars a Week?; Kiss Me, My Honey, Kiss Me (C: Snyder, Ted); Meet Me To-Night; Molly O! Oh, Molly; My Melody Dream; One O'Clock in the Morning I Get Lonesome (C: Snyder, Ted); Ragtime Violin, The; Real Girl; Run Home and Tell Your Mother; Sombrero Land (C: Snyder, Ted; L: Berlin, Irving; Goetz, E. Ray); That Kazzatsky Dance; That Monkey Tune; That Mysterious Rag (C: Snyder, Ted); Virginia Lou; What Am I Gonna Do?; When I'm Alone I'm Lonesome; When It Rains, Sweetheart, When It Rains; When You Kiss an Italian Girl; When You're in Town; Whistling Rag; Yankee Love (L: Goetz, E. Ray); Yiddisha Nightingale; You've Got Me Hypnotized

SHOW SONGS
Fascinating Widow, The (Show). Music and Lyrics by E. Ray Goetz. Music by Irving Berlin: Don't Take Your Beau to the Seashore; You Built a Fire Down in My Heart
Friars' Frolic of 1911 (Show): Alexander's Ragtime Band
Jardin De Paris/Ziegfeld Follies of 1911 (Show): Doggone That Chilly Man; Ephraham Played Upon the Piano (C/L: Berlin, Irving; Bryan, Vincent); Woodman, Woodman, Spare That Tree (C/L: Berlin, Irving; Bryan, Vincent); You've Built a Fire Down in My Heart
Never Homes, The (Show): There's a Girl in Havana (L: Berlin, Irving; Goetz, E. Ray); You've Built a Fire Down in My Heart (C: Berlin, Irving)
Temptations (Show): Answer Me; Dear Old Broadway (C: Snyder, Ted; L: Berlin, Irving; Bryan, Vincent); I Beg Your Pardon, Dear Old Broadway (C/L: Berlin, Irving; C: Snyder, Ted; L: Bryan, Vincent); Keep a Taxi Waiting, Dear; Spanish Love (C: Snyder, Ted; L: Berlin, Irving; Bryan, Vincent)

1912 *POP SONGS*
Antonio, You'd Better Come Home; At the Devil's Ball; Becky's Got a Job in a Musical Show; Belle of the Barber's Ball (C: Cohan, George M.); Call Again; Come Back to Me—My Melody (C: Snyder, Ted); Do It Again; Don't Leave Your Wife Alone; Down in My Heart; Elevator Man (Going Up—Going Up—Going Up); Father's Beard; Fiddle Dee Dee; Funny Little Melody, The; Goody Goody Goody Goody

Goody Goody; He Played It on His Fid, Fid Fiddle-Dee-Dee
(C/L: Berlin, Irving; Goetz, E. Ray; Sloane, A. Baldwin); I'm
Afraid, Pretty Maid, I'm Afraid; I'm Going Back to Dixie (I
Want to Be in Dixie) (C: Snyder, Ted); I've Got to Have
Some Lovin' Now; Keep Away from the Fellow Who Owns
an Automobile; Lead Me to That Beautiful Band (L: Goetz,
E. Ray); My Sweet Italian Man; Pick, Pick, Pick on the
Mandolin, Antonio; Ragtime Mocking Bird; Ragtime Soldier
Man; Spring and Fall; Take a Little Tip from Father (C:
Snyder, Ted); That's How I Love You; True Born Soldier
Man; Wait Until Your Daddy Comes Home; When I Lost
You; When I'm Thinking of You; When Johnson's Quartette
Harmonize; When the Midnight Choo-Choo Leaves for
Alabam'; Yiddisha Professor

SHOW SONGS
Hanky-Panky (Show): Million Dollar Ball (L: Goetz, E. Ray);
Ragtime Sextette
Hokey-Pokey (Show): Alexander's Bagpipe Band (C/L: Berlin,
Irving; C: Sloane, A. Baldwin; L: Goetz, E. Ray)
My Best Girl (Show): Follow Me Around
Passing Show of 1912, The (Show): Ragtime Jockey Man
Sun Dodgers, The (Show): Hiram's Band (C/L: Berlin, Irving;
Goetz, E. Ray; Sloane, A. Baldwin)
Whirl of Society, The (Show): I Want to Be in Dixie (C:
Snyder, Ted); Ragtime Sextette; That Society Bear
Ziegfeld Follies of 1912 (Show): Little Bit of Everything

1913 *POP SONGS*
Abie Sings an Irish Song; Anna 'Lize's Wedding Day; Apple
Tree and the Bumble Tree, The; Daddy Come Home; Down in
Chattanooga; Happy Little Country Girl; He's So Good to Me;
I Was Aviating Around; If All the Girls I Knew Were Like You;
If You Don't Want Me Why Do You Hang Around?; In My
Harem; International Rag, The; Jake—Jake; Keep on Walking;
Ki-Yi-Yodeling Dog, The; Kiss Your Sailor Boy Good-Bye;
Monkey Doodle Doo; Old Maid's Ball, The; Pullman Porters'
Parade (C: Abrahams, Maurice); Rum Tum Tiddle; San
Francisco Bound; Snookey Ookums; Take Me Back; There's a
Girl in Arizona (L: Clarke, Grant; Leslie, Edgar); They've Got
Me Doin' It Now; Tra, La! La! La!; We Have Much to Be
Thankful For; Welcome Home; You Picked a Bad Day Out to
Say Good-Bye; You've Got Your Mother's Big Blue Eyes

SHOW SONGS
All Aboard (Show): Somebody's Coming to My House
Sun Dodgers, The (Show): At the Picture Show

1914 *POP SONGS*
Along Came Ruth; Always Treat Her Like a Baby; Come to the Land of the Argentine; Furnishing a Home for Two; God Gave You to Me; Haunted House; He's a Devil in His Own Home Town (L: Clarke, Grant; Leslie, Edgar); He's a Rag Picker; I Hate You; I Love to Quarrel with You; I Want to Go Back to Michigan (Down on the Farm); If I Had You; If You Don't Want My Peaches You Better Stop Shaking My Tree; If that's Your Idea of a Wonderful Time (Take Me Home); It Isn't What He Said (It's the Way He Said It); Morning Exercise; Revival Day; Stay Down Here Where You Belong; That's My Idea of Paradise; They're on Their Way to Mexico; This Is the Life; When It's Night-Time in Dixieland

SHOW SONGS
Queen of the Movies (Show): Follow the Crowd
Watch Your Step (Show): Chatter, Chatter; I Love to Have the Boys Around Me; I've Gotta Go Back to Texas; Lead Me to Love; Let's Go Around the Town; Lock Me in Your Harem and Throw Away the Key; Look at Them Doing It!; Metropolitan Nights; Minstrel Parade; Move Over; Office Hours; Opera Burlesque; Play a Simple Melody; Settle Down in a One-Horse Town; Show Me How to Do the Fox Trot; Syncopated Walk; They Always Follow Me Around; Watch Your Step; What Is Love?; When I Discovered You (C/L: Berlin, Irving; Goetz, E. Ray)

1915 *POP SONGS*
Araby; Cohen Owes Me Ninety-Seven Dollars; Homeward Bound; I Love to Stay at Home; I'm Going Back to the Farm; My Bird of Paradise; Once in May; Sailor Song; Si's Been Drinking Cider; Until I Fell in Love with You; Voice of Belgium; When I Leave the World Behind; When You're Down in Louisville (Call on Me); While the Band Played an American Rag

SHOW SONGS
Stop! Look! Listen! (Show): (Why Don't They) Give Us a Chance?; And Father Wanted Me to Learn a Trade; Blow Your Horn; Everything in America Is Ragtime (Ragtime Finale);

Girl on the Magazine Cover, The; I Love a Piano; I Love to
Dance; I'm Coming Home with a Skate On; Law Must Be
Obeyed, The; Pair of Ordinary Coons, A; Stop! Look! Listen!;
Take Off a Little Bit; Teach Me How to Love; That Hula Hula;
When I Get Back to the U.S.A.; When I'm Out with You

1916 *POP SONGS*
By the Sad Luana Shore; Friars' Parade; He's Getting Too
Darn Big for a One-Horse Town; Hurry Back to My Bamboo
Shack; I'm Down in Honolulu Looking Them Over; I'm Not
Prepared; In Florida among the Palms; Just Give Me Ragtime
Please; Someone Else May Be There While I'm Gone; When
the Black Sheep Returns to the Fold; You Ought to Go to
Paris

SHOW SONGS
Century Girl, The (Show): Alice in Wonderland; It Takes an
Irishman to Make Love; Music Lesson, The; On the Train of a
Wedding Gown; That Broadway Chicken Walk; You've Got
Me Doing It Too
Step This Way (Show): I've Got a Sweet Tooth Bothering Me;
Step This Way; When You Drop Off at Cairo, Illinois

1917 *POP SONGS*
For Your Country and My Country; From Here to Shanghai;
How Can I Forget (When There's So Much to Remember)?;
Let's All Be Americans Now (C/L: Berlin, Irving; C: Meyer,
George W.; L: Leslie, Edgar); Mr. Jazz Himself; My Sweetie;
Poor Little Cinderella; Pretty Birdie; Put a Little Letter in My
Letter Box; Road that Leads to Love, The; Smile and Show
Your Dimple; That Goody Melody; There Are Two Eyes in
Dixie; There's Something Nice About the South; Wasn't It
Yesterday; What Did I Ever Do to You That You Should Want
to Do to Me? (C: Meyer, George W.; L: Berlin, Irving; Leslie,
Edgar); Whose Little Heart Are You Breaking Now?

SHOW SONGS
Cohan Revue of 1918, The (Show): Bad Chinaman from
Shanghai, A; Down Where the Jack O' Lanterns Grow; King
of Broadway; Man Is Only a Man, A; Polly, Pretty Polly (Polly
with a Past) (C/L: Berlin, Irving; Cohan, George M.); Show
Me the Way; Wedding of Words and Music
Dance and Grow Thin (Show): Birdie; Cinderella Lost Her
Slipper; Dance and Grow Thin (C: Berlin, Irving; Meyer,
George W.); Letter Boxes; Mary Brown; Way Down South

Jack O' Lantern (Show): I'll Take You Back to Italy
Rambler Rose (Show): Poor Little Rich Girl's Dog

1918 POP SONGS
Devil Has Bought Up All the Coal, The; Dream On, Little Soldier Boy; Good-Bye, France; I Have Just One Heart for Just One Boy; I Wouldn't Give That for the Boy Who Couldn't Dance; Over the Sea, Boys; Send a Lot of Jazz Bands Over There; Sterling Silver Moon; They Were All Out of Step but Jim; When the Curtain Falls; You've Been the Sunshine of My Life

SHOW SONGS
Canary, The (Show): It's the Little Bit of Irish
Everything (Show): Circus Is Coming to Town, The; Come Along to Toy Town
Yip! Yip! Yaphank (Show): Bevo; Ding Dong; God Bless America; Hello, Hello, Hello; I Can Always Find a Little Sunshine in the Y.M.C.A.; Kitchen Police (Poor Little Me); Mandy; Oh! How I Hate to Get Up in the Morning; Ragtime Razor Brigade; Soldier Boy; We're On Our Way to France; What a Difference a Uniform Will Make (Ever Since I Put on A Uniform)
Ziegfeld Follies of 1918 (Show): Blue Devils of France; I'm Gonna Pin My Medal on the Girl I Left Behind Me

1919 POP SONGS
Everything Is Rosy Now for Rosie (L: Berlin, Irving; Clarke, Grant); Eyes of Youth; Hand that Rocked My Cradle Rules My Heart, The; I Left My Door Open and My Daddy Walked Out; I Lost My Heart in Dixieland; I Never Knew (L: Janis, Elsie); I Wonder; I've Got My Captain Working for Me Now; New Moon, The; Nobody Knows (And Nobody Seems to Care); Since Katy the Waitress Became an Aviatress; Sweeter than Sugar (Is My Sweetie); Was There Ever a Pal Like You?

SHOW SONGS
Oh! What a Girl (Show): You'd Be Surprised
Shubert Gaieties of 1919 (Show): You'd Be Surprised
Ziegfeld Follies of 1919 (Show): Bevo; Harem Life; I Want to See a Minstrel Show; I'm the Guy Who Guards the Harem; Look Out for the Bolsheviki Man; Mandy; My Tambourine Girl; Near Future, The; Pretty Girl Is Like a Melody, A; Prohibition; Syncopated Cocktail; We Made the Doughnuts Over There; You Cannot Make Your Shimmy Shake on Tea (L: Berlin, Irving; Woolf, Rennold); You'd Be Surprised

1920 *POP SONGS*
After You Get What You Want You Don't Want It; But She's Just a Little Bit Crazy About Her Husband—That's All; Drowsy Head (C/L: Berlin, Irving; DeLeath, Vaughn); Home Again Blues (C: Akst, Harry); I Know Why; Just Another Kill; Lindy; Relatives; Streak of Blues, A

SHOW SONGS
Broadway Brevities of 1920 (Show): Beautiful Faces (Need Beautiful Clothes)
Ziegfeld Follies of 1920 (Show): Bells; Chinese Firecrackers; Come Along; Girls of My Dreams, The; I Live in Turkey; I'm a Vamp from East Broadway (C/L: Berlin, Irving; Kalmar, Bert; Ruby, Harry); Leg of Nations, The; Syncopated Vamp, The; Tell Me, Little Gypsy
Ziegfeld Girls of 1920 (Show): Metropolitan Ladies
Ziegfeld Midnight Frolic of 1920 (Show): I'll See You in C-U-B-A

1921 *POP SONGS*
All By Myself; At the Court Around the Corner; Passion Flower, The; Pickanniny Mose; There's a Corner Up in Heaven

SHOW SONGS
Music Box Revue (Show): Behind the Fan; Dancing the Seasons Away; Everybody Step; I'm a Dumb-Bell; In a Cozy Kitchenette Apartment; Legend of the Pearls, The; My Ben Ali Haggin Girl; My Little Book of Poetry; Say It With Music; Schoolhouse Blues, The; They Call It Dancing
Ziegfeld's 9 O'Clock Frolic of 1921 (Show). Music by Harry Akst: I'm Gonna Do It If I Like It
Ziegfeld's 9 O'Clock Frolic (Show): (I'm Gonna Do It If I Like It And) I Like It

1922 *POP SONGS*
Funny Feet; Homesick; Little Red Lacquer Cage, The; Mont Marte; Rainy Day Sue; Some Sunny Day

SHOW SONGS
Music Box Revue (Show): Bring on the Pepper; Crinoline Days; Dance Your Troubles Away; I'm Looking for a Daddy Long Legs; Lady of the Evening; My Diamond Horseshoe of Girls; Pack Up Your Sins and Go to the Devil; Porcelain Maid; Take a Little Wife; Three Cheers for the Red, White and

Blue; Too Many Girls; Will She Come from the East (North, West, or South)?

1923 *POP SONGS*
His Royal Shyness; If You Know How to Strut; Tell All the Folks in Kentucky (I'm Comin' Home); Tell Me with a Melody; Um-Um-Da-Da

SHOW SONGS
Music Box Revue (Show): Climbing Up the Scale; Learn to Do the Strut; Little Butterfly; Maid of Mesh; One Girl; Orange Grove in California, An; Tell Me a Bedtime Story; Too Many Sweethearts; Waltz of Long Ago, The; When You Walked Out Someone Else Walked Right In; Yes! We Have No Bananas Parody; Your Hat and My Hat

1924 *POP SONGS*
Lazy; We'll All Go Voting for Al (C: Blake, James; Lawlor, Charles B.); What'll I Do?

SHOW SONGS
Music Box Revue (Show): All Alone; Bandana Ball; Call of the South, The; Come Along with Alice; Couple of Senseless Censors, A; Don't Send Me Back to Petrograd; Happy New Year Blues, The; I Want to Be a Ballet Dancer; In the Shade of a Sheltering Palm; Listening; Rock-A-Bye Baby; Sixteen, Sweet Sixteen; Tell Her in the Springtime; Tokyo Blues; Unlucky in Love; Where Is My Little Old New York?; Who?; Wildcats

1925 *POP SONGS*
Always; Don't Wait Too Long; He Doesn't Know What It's All About; It's a Walk-In with Walker; Tango Melody; They're Blaming the Charleston; Venetian Isles; You Forgot to Remember

SHOW SONGS
Cocoanuts, The (Show): Everyone in the World (Is Doing the Charleston); Family Reputation; Five O'Clock Tea; Florida by the Sea; Gentlemen Prefer Blondes; Little Bungalow, A; Lucky Boy; Minstrel Days; Monkey Doodle Doo; Tale of a Shirt, The; Ting-A-Ling (The Bell's Ring); Too Many Sweethearts; We Should Care; Why Am I a Hit with the Ladies?

1926 *POP SONGS*
Along Came Ruth (2) (L: Britt, Addy; Link, Harry; Walsh, Christy); At Peace with the World; Because I Love You; I'm on My Way Home; Just a Little Longer; My Baby's Come Back to Me; That's a Good Girl; We'll Never Know; Why Do You Want to Know Why?

SHOW SONGS
Betsy (Show): Blue Skies
Time, the Place and the Girl, The (Film): How Many Times?

1927 *POP SONGS*
In Those Good Old Bowery Days; Russian Lullaby; Together, We Two; What Does It Matter?; What Makes Me Love You; Why I Love My Baby; Why Should He Fly at So Much a Week (When He Could Be the Sheik of Paree)?

SHOW SONGS
Ziegfeld Follies of 1927 (Show): I Want to Be Glorified; It All Belongs to Me; It's Up to the Band; Jimmy; Jungle Jingle; Learn to Sing a Love Song; My New York; Ooh! Maybe It's You; Rainbow of Girls; Ribbons and Bows; Shaking the Blues Away; Tickling the Ivories; You Gotta Have IT

1928 *POP SONGS*
Evangeline (C: Jolson, Al); Good Times with Hoover, Better Times with Al; How About Me?; I Can't Do Without You; Roses of Yesterday; Sunshine; To Be Forgotten; Yascha Michaeloffsky's Melody

SHOW SONGS
Awakening, The (Film): Marie
Coquette (Film): Coquette
Lady of the Pavements (Film): Where Is the Song of Songs for Me?

1929 *POP SONGS*
I'm the Head Man; In the Morning

SHOW SONGS
Cocoanuts, The (Film): I Lost My Shirt (C: Bizet, Georges); When My Dreams Come True
Hallelujah (Film): Swanee Shuffle; Waiting at the End of the Road
Puttin' on the Ritz (Film): Puttin' on the Ritz; With You

1930 *POP SONGS*
Broker's Ensemble; Do You Believe Your Eyes—Or Do You Believe Your Baby?; How Much I Love You; If You Believe; It's Yours; Just a Little While; Little Things in Life, The; Toast to Prohibition; What a Lucky Break for Me

SHOW SONGS
Bad One, The (Film): To a Tango Melody
Mammy (Film): (Across the Breakfast Table) Looking at You; Call of the South, The; Here We Are; Knights of the Road; Let Me Sing and I'm Happy; To My Mammy

1931 *POP SONGS*
Any Love Today; Chase All Your Cares (And Go to Sleep, Baby); How Can I Change My Luck?; I Want Your for Myself; I'll Miss You in the Evening; Me!; Nudist Colony; Police of New York; Two Cheers Instead of Three

SHOW SONGS
Reaching for the Moon (Film): Reaching for the Moon; When the Folks High-Up Do that Mean Low-Down
Shoot the Works (Show): Just Begging for Love
Top Speed (Film): Reaching for the Moon

1932 *POP SONGS*
How Deep Is the Ocean? (How High Is the Sky?); I'm Playing with Fire; Say It Isn't So

SHOW SONGS
Face the Music (Show): Dear Old Crinoline Days; I Don't Wanna Be Married (I Just Wanna Be Friends); I Say It's Spinach—And the Hell with It; Let's Have Another Cup O' Coffee; Lunching at the Automat; Manhattan Madness; My Beautiful Rhinestone Girl; On a Roof in Manhattan; Soft Lights and Sweet Music; Torch Song; You Must Be Born with It

1933 *POP SONGS*
Debts; Eighteenth Amendment Repealed (C: Foster, Stephen); I Can't Remember; Maybe I Love You Too Much; Metropolitan Opening; Skate with Me; Society Wedding

SHOW SONGS
As Thousands Cheer (Show): Easter Parade; Funnies, The; Harlem on My Mind; Heat Wave; How's Chances?; Lonely

Heart; Not for All the Rice in China; Our Wedding Day;
Revolt in Cuba; Supper Time; To Be or Not to Be; We'll All
Be in Heaven When the Dollar Goes to Hell

1934 *POP SONGS*
Butterfingers; Get Thee Behind Me, Satan; I Never Had a
Chance; Moon Over Napoli; So Help Me; Wild About You

1935 *POP SONGS*
Moonlight Maneuvers; There's a Smile on My Face

SHOW SONGS
Top Hat (Film): Cheek to Cheek; Isn't This a Lovely Day (to
Be Caught in the Rain)?; No Strings (I'm Fancy Free);
Piccolino, The; Top Hat, White Tie, and Tails

1936 *SHOW SONGS*
Follow the Fleet (Film): But Where Are You?; I'd Rather Lead
a Band; I'm Putting All My Eggs in One Basket; Let Yourself
Go; Let's Face the Music and Dance; We Saw the Sea
Song of Freedom, The (Film): Lonely Road

1937 *POP SONGS*
Let's Make the Most of Our Dream; What the Well-Dressed
Man Will Wear

SHOW SONGS
On the Avenue (Film): Girl on the Police Gazette, The; He
Ain't Got Rhythm; I've Got My Love to Keep Me Warm; On
the Avenue; On the Steps of Grant's Tomb; Slumming on
Park Avenue; Swing Sister; This Year's Kisses; You're
Laughing at Me

1938 *POP SONGS*
Since They Turned Loch Lomond into Swing; You Can Be My
Cave Man

SHOW SONGS
Alexander's Ragtime Band (Film): I'm Marching Along with
Time; My Walking Stick; Now It Can Be Told
Carefree (Film): Care-Free; Change Partners; I Used to Be
Color Blind; Night Is Filled with Music, The; Yam, The

1939 *SHOW SONGS*
Second Fiddle (Film): Back to Back; I Poured My Heart into a

Song; I'm Sorry for Myself; Old Fashioned Tune Always Is New, An; Song of the Metronome, The; When Winter Comes

1940 *POP SONGS*
Everybody Knew but Me

SHOW SONGS
Louisiana Purchase (Show): (Come Along and) Dance with Me (At the Mardi Gras); Fools Fall in Love; I'd Love to Be Shot from a Cannon with You; It'll Come to You; It's a Lovely Day Tomorrow; Latins Know How; Lord Done Fixed Up My Soul, The; Louisiana Purchase; Old Man's Darling, Young Man's Slave; Outside of that I Love You; Sex Marches On; Tonight at the Mardi Gras; What Chance Have I with Love?; You Can't Brush Me Off; You're Lonely and I'm Lonely

1941 *POP SONGS*
Any Bonds Today?; Little Old Church in England, A

SHOW SONGS
Louisiana Purchase (Film): It's New to Us

1942 *POP SONGS*
Angels of Mercy; Arms for the Love of America; I Paid My Income Tax Today; I Threw a Kiss in the Ocean; Me and My Melinda; President's Birthday Ball, The; When This Crazy World Is Sane Again; When That Man Is Dead and Gone

SHOW SONGS
Holiday Inn (Film): Abraham; Be Careful It's My Heart; Easter Parade; I Can't Tell a Lie; I'll Capture Your Heart; I've Got Plenty to Be Thankful For; Let's Start the New Year Right; Say It with Firecrackers (inst.); Song of Freedom; White Christmas; You're Easy to Dance With
This Is the Army (Show): Army's Made a Man Out of Me, The; How About a Cheer for the Navy?; I Left My Heart at the Stage Door Canteen; I'm Getting Tired So I Can Sleep; Ladies of the Chorus; My Sergeant and I; Soldier's Dream, A; That Russian Winter; This Is the Army, Mister Jones; This Time (Is the Last Time); What the Well-Dressed Man in Harlem Will Wear

1943 *SHOW SONGS*
This Is the Army (Show): Kick in the Pants, The; My British Buddy; Ve Don't Like It

1944 *POP SONGS*
All of My Life

SHOW SONGS
This Is the Army (Show): Fifth Army's Where My Heart Is, The; There Are No Wings on a Foxhole; What Are We Going to Do with All the Jeeps?

1945 *POP SONGS*
Heaven Watch the Philippines; I'll Dance Rings Around You; Just a Blue Serge Suit; Oh, to Be Home Again; Race Horse and the Flea, The; Wilhelmina

1946 *SHOW SONGS*
Annie Get Your Gun (Show): (There's No Business Like) Show Business; Anything You Can Do; Ballyhoo; Colonel Buffalo Bill; Doin' What Comes Natur'lly; Girl That I Marry, The; I Got Lost in His Arms; I Got the Sun in the Morning; I'll Share It All with You; I'm a Bad, Bad Man; I'm an Indian Too; Let's Go West Again; Moonshine Lullaby; My Defenses Are Down; Take It in Your Stride; They Say It's Wonderful; Who Do You Love, I Hope?; With Music; You Can't Get a Man with a Gun
Blue Skies (Film): (Running Around in Circles) Getting Nowhere; Couple of Song and Dance Men, A; Serenade to an Old-Fashioned Girl, A; You Keep Coming Back Like a Song

1947 *POP SONGS*
Help Me to Help My Neighbor; Kate (Have I Come Too Early, Too Late); Love and the Weather

1948 *POP SONGS*
Freedom Train, The; I Gave Her My Heart in Acapulco

SHOW SONGS
Easter Parade (Film): Better Luck Next Time; Couple of Swells, A; Drum Crazy; Fella With an Umbrella, A; Happy Easter; It Only Happens When I Dance with You; Mr. Monotony; Steppin' Out with My Baby
Stars on My Shoulders (Show): What Can You Do with a General?

1949 *POP SONGS*
I'm Beginning to Miss You; Man Chases a Girl (Until She Catches Him), A

SHOW SONGS
Miss Liberty (Show): (Just One Way to Say) I Love You; Business for a Good Girl Is Bad; Extra! Extra!; Falling Out of Love Can Be Fun; Follow the Leader Jig; Give Me Your Tired, Your Poor (L: Lazarus, Emma); Homework; Hon'rable Profession of the Fourth Estate, The; I'd Like My Picture Took; Let's Take an Old-Fashioned Walk; Little Fish in a Big Pond; Me an' My Bundle; Miss Liberty; Most Expensive Statue in the World, The; Only for Americans; Paris Wakes Up and Smiles; Policeman's Ball, The; Train, The; You Can Have Him

1950 *SHOW SONGS*
Call Me Madam (Show): (Dance to the Music of) The Ocarina; (I Wonder Why) You're Just in Love; Best Thing for You, The; Can You Use Any Money Today?; Free; Hostess with the Mostes' on the Ball, The; It's a Lovely Day Today; Marrying for Love; Mrs. Sally Adams; Once Upon a Time Today; Something to Dance About; They Like Ike; Washington Square Dance; Welcome to Lichtenburg

1952 *POP SONGS*
Anthem for Presentation Theme; For the Very First Time; I Like Ike; Our Day of Independence

1953 *POP SONGS*
Sayonara, Sayonara; Sittin' in the Sun (Countin' My Money); What Does a Soldier Want for Christmas

1954 *POP SONGS*
I Still Like Ike; I'm Not Afraid (I Believe in America); Is She the Only Girl in the World; When It's Peach Blossom Time in Lichtenburg

SHOW SONGS
There's No Business Like Show Business (Film): But I Ain't Got a Man; I Can Make You Laugh (But I Wish I Could Make You Cry); Sailor's Not a Sailor ('Til a Sailor's Been Tattooed), A
White Christmas (Film): Best Things Happen While You're Dancing, The; Choreography; Count Your Blessings Instead of Sheep; Crooner—A Comic, A; Gee, I Wish I Was Back in the Army; Love, You Didn't Do Right By Me; Old Man, The; Singer—A Dancer, A; Sisters; Snow

1955 *POP SONGS*
Aesop, That Able Fable Man; Most, The; Out of This World Into My Arms; Please Let Me Come Back to You

1956 *POP SONGS*
Anybody Can Write; I Never Want to See You Again; I'm
Gonna Get Him; Ike for Four More Years (C: Traditional); It
Takes More than Love to Keep a Lady Warm; Klondike Kate;
Love Leads to Marriage; Opening the Mizner Story; Smiling
Geisha; When a One Star General's Daughter Meets a Four
Star General's Son; You're a Sentimental Guy; You're a
Sucker for a Dame

1957 *POP SONGS*
(You Can't Lose the Blues with) Colors; I Keep Running
Away from You; I'll Know Better the Next Time; Irving Berlin
Barrett; Silver Platter; Song for Elizabeth Esther Barrett;
When Love Was All

1959 *POP SONGS*
Israel

1960 *POP SONGS*
Sam, Sam (The Man What Am)

1962 *POP SONGS*
If You Haven't Got an Ear for Music; Poor Joe; Popular Song,
The; Who Would Have Thought?

SHOW SONGS
Mr. President (Show): Don't Be Afraid of Romance; Empty
Pockets Filled with Love; First Lady, The; Glad to Be Home;
I've Got to Be Around; In Our Hide-Away; Is He the Only
Man in the World; It Gets Lonely in the White House; Laugh
It Up; Let's Go Back to the Waltz; Meat and Potatoes; Mr.
President; Once Ev'ry Four Years; Only Dance I Know (Song
for Belly Dancer), The; Opening; Pigtails and Freckles; Secret
Service, The; They Love Me; This Is a Great Country;
Washington Twist, The; You Need a Hobby

1963 *POP SONGS*
(It's) Always the Same; Guy on Monday, A; Man to Cook For,
A; One Man Woman; Outside of Loving You, I Like You; P.X.,
The; Ten Best Undressed Women, The; Whisper It

1964 *POP SONGS*
Let Me Sing

1965 *POP SONGS*
I Used to Play by Ear

1966 *POP SONGS*
Long As I Can Take You Home; Wait Until You're Married

SHOW SONGS
Annie Get Your Gun (Show, Lincoln Center revival): (Who Needs) The Birds and Bees?; Old-Fashioned Wedding, An

1967 *POP SONGS*
You've Got to Be Way Out to Be In

1977 *POP SONGS*
All I Bring to You Is Love

Endnotes

Abbreviations for frequently cited sources:

AW Alexander Woollcott, *The Story of Irving Berlin*. New York: G.P. Putnam's Sons, 1925.

LB Laurence Bergreen, *As Thousands Cheer: The Life of Irving Berlin*. New York: Penguin Books, 1990.

MF Michael Freedland, *Irving Berlin*. New York: Stein and Day, 1974.

CH Charles Hamm, *Irving Berlin Songs from the Melting Pot: The Formative Years, 1907–1914*. New York: Oxford University Press, 1997.

IW Ian Whitcomb, *Irving Berlin and Ragtime America*. London: Century Hutchinson, 1987.

IBSLC The Irving Berlin scrapbooks at the Library of Congress.

Unless otherwise indicated, quotations are taken from newspaper clippings in Irving Berlin's scrapbooks in the Irving Berlin Archive of the Library of Congress. Because many clippings are undated and unidentified, I can only refer the reader, generally, to the scrapbooks.

Chapter 1: Russian Lullaby

1 *"I always think of my youth"*: New York *World-Telegram*, November 6, 1941.

1 Although Irving Berlin, for much of his life, could neither read nor write music, late in his career, evidently, he learned enough about musical notation to take down a "lead-sheet"—the melody line for a lyric. As Mary Ellin Barrett notes, her father "was not quite as ignorant, however, as he pretended. . . . Among his papers is a music manuscript with the thirty-two bar melody of 'Soft Lights and Sweet Music' and a line in his hand: '1st lead sheet ever taken down by Irving Berlin, Aug. 16, 1932'" (Mary Ellin Barrett, *Irving Berlin: A Daughter's Memoir*. New York: Simon & Schuster, 1994, pp. 112–13).

1 "the greatest American song composer": Barbara Salsini, *Irving Berlin: Master Composer of Twentieth Century Songs*. Charlotteville, N.Y.: SamHar Press, 1972, p. 21.

1 "the greatest songwriter of all time": *LB*, 418.

1 "Irving Berlin has no 'place'": *AW*, p. 215.

3 "the best writer": Alec Wilder, *American Popular Song: The Great Innovators, 1900–1950*. New York: Oxford University Press, 1972, p. 120.

3 "he had no style": Willam G. Hyland, "The Best Songwriter of Them All," *Commentary* (October 1990), p. 41.

4 "embodies the feelings of the mob": *MF*, p. 152.

4 "The public wants": MF, p. 70.

4 "he honestly absorbs the vibrations": *AW*, p. 215.

6 "We weren't all political prisoners": "The Baline *family* came from the village of Tolochin in Byelorussia. . . . Tolochin was in the township of the larger and better known Mogilev—and Mogilev was what my grandparents wrote on their immigration papers and what my father put on his naturalization papers and his marriage license. Sometime between 1925 and 1942 he must have had confirmation that he himself was indeed born in Siberia, that his father, an itinerant cantor, had migrated to Tyumen." pp. 98*n*–99*n*.

7 "and were conspicuous in our 'Jew clothes'": Kenneth Kanter, *The Jews on Tin Pan Alley*. New York: Ktav Publishing House, Inc., 1982, p. 134.

8 "from a careening building": Stephen Crane, *Maggie: A Girl of the Streets*. New York: Fawcett Premier, 1960, p. 15.

8 "Everyone should have a Lower East Side": *MF*, p. 17.

8 "I never felt poverty": *New York Sun*, February 24, 1947.

8 "I was a little Russian-born kid": *Saturday Evening Post*, January 14, 1944.

10 "I used to sing": "£16,000 a Year from Songwriting": unidentified news clipping, *IBSLC*.

10 "I suppose it was singing": *MF*, p. 19.

10 "when I was a boy": "£16,000 a Year from Songwriting."

10 "just dreams and sings": Ibid., p. 17.

10 "I used to go there": *The New York Sun*, February 24, 1947.

11 "I was scared": *MF*, p. 18. In later life, Berlin told a different version of this famous story to his family—that he'd not fallen into the river but had been pushed by some Irish kids in the neighborhood, who then "saved" him. The same kids then came to his mother routinely for days asking for rewards for their good deed.

11 "sick with a sense": *AW*, p. 21.

11 "You are losing time": "Boy from Depths Won a Big Success," unidentified news clipping, *IBSLC*.

12 "To see the Bowery": Armond Fields and L. Marc Fields, *From the Bowery to Broadway: Lew Fields and the Roots of American Popular Theater*. New York: Oxford University Press, 1993, pp. 4–5.

13 "In the 1890s American popular culture": Lewis Erenberg, *Steppin'
   Out: New York Nightlife and the Transformation of American Culture,
   1890–1930*. Westport, Conn.: Greenwood Press, 1981, p. 61.

14 "it would have resented being called that": *New York Sun*, February 24,
   1947.

14 "I know I didn't sing good": *Washington Post*, September 6, 1942.

15 "the best songs came from the gutter": Edward B. Marks, *They All
   Sang*. New York: Viking, 1935, p. 3.

17 "the Chinese with their white women": *New York Sun*, February 24,
   1947.

18 "claimed the lives": Edgar A. Berlin, *Reflections and Research on
   Ragtime*. Brooklyn, N.Y.: Institute for Studies in American Music,
   1987, p. 42.

18 "aging streetwalkers who no longer": Ibid.

18 "A waiter learns": *Washington Post*, September 6, 1942.

18 "Like it was yesterday, I remember Oiving Berlin": *Liberty Magazine*,
   December 20, 1924.

19 "I got my musical education": "Boy from Depths Won a Big Success."

19 "sort of took to the kid": Ibid.

20 "No, sir, it was my honor": *MF*, p. 24.

23 "went the way of all imitation": *New York World-Telegram*, February 29,
   1936.

24 "Izzy fell asleep at the bar": *IW*, p. 31.

Chapter 2: Ragged Meter Man

25 *"Fourteenth Street was very swell"*: *New York Sun*, February 24, 1947.

29 "We did it . . . get away with it": *IW*, p. 38.

30 "Bing! *There* I had a common place": *IW*, pp. 66–67.

32 "had a profound effect on American music": Berlin, pp. 2–3.

32 "a vocabulary of unadorned passion": Isaac Goldberg, *Tin Pan Alley*.
   New York: John Day Company, 1930, pp. 155–56.

34 "I know rhythm": *Green Book Magazine*, February 1915.

34 "Russians make wonderful dancers": *Portland Oregonian*, October 17,
   1915.

34 "the black keys are right there under your fingers": *New York Press*,
   December 20, 1914.

34 "the key of C": *LB*, p. 57.

36 "They were tolerant but firm": *AW*, p. 80.

36 "I had always loved": *MF*, p. 30.

37 "writing both words and music": *Green Book Magazine*, February 1915.

38 "more money in royalties": *New York Times*, January 2, 1916.

38 "simon-pure inspiration": *CH*, p. 115. Hamm quotes from two maga-zine stories about Berlin, "The Boy Who Revived Rag-time," *Green Book Magazine* 10 (August 1913), and "Irving Berlin—A Restless Success," *Theatre Magazine* 21 (February 1915), to develop an argu-ment that Berlin did not, as has been assumed, compose "Alexander's Ragtime Band" as a purely instrumental number, only to add lyrics (*CH*, pp. 112–17). Professor Hamm's scholarship is always formidable, and his argument also has the force of common sense behind it, since Berlin was a songwriter who almost always thought in terms of music and words. In my research, however, I have come across several inter-views where Berlin himself states that "Alexander's Ragtime Band" was first an instrumental. I quote these statements in the text and cite them below.

39 "'Alexander' was done originally as an instrumental": *New York Sun*, July 30, 1938.

39 "I wrote it without words": *New York Post*, July 14, 1938.

39 "In the history of New York": *CH*, p. 120.

40 "A cabaret show": Ibid.

40 "This is a good song": Ibid., p. 136.

40 "the man who turned down": Ibid.

40 "George M. Cohan was one of the first": "Mr. Berlin Returns to Our Island," unidentified news clipping, *IBSLC*.

40 "encores were as the sands of the sea": *CH*, p. 124.

40 "was jealous of his younger colleague": Ibid., p. 133.

41 "in only a mild pale-pink way": *Green Book Magazine*, February 1915.

41 "cut that band song out": *CH*, p. 130.

41 "the second verse of a song": *MF*, pp. 42–43.

42 "Slavonic and Semitic folk tunes": *New York Daily News*, July 29, 1938.

42 "any composer of standard ballads": Irving Berlin, "Song and Sorrow Are Playmates," unidentified news clipping, *IBSLC*.

42 "simply terrible . . . silly": *Detroit Journal*, December 1, 1914.

43 "Three-fourths of that quality": *Melody Maker*, November 6, 1954.

43 "What *Alexander* succeeded in doing": David Ewen, "The Big Five of American Popular Music," *Theatre Arts*, November 1951.

44 "Youth is gravitating": Erenberg, p. 64.

44 "the rising tide": Ibid., p. 74.

44 "Ragtime isn't music": Edward Jablonski, "Alexander and Irving," *Listen—Music Monthly*, September–October 1961.

44 "its opening words": *LB*, p. 68.

45 "is the music of the hustler": Ibid., p. 89.

Chapter 3: I Love a Piano

47 *"I confess that my knowledge"*: *New York Times*, January 2, 1916.

47 "To see this slim little kid": *Variety*, September 16, 1911.

48 "Gee, Izzy . . . We've been hanging around": *AW*, p. 81.

49 "You know, Irvy, there's a story circulating": *IW*, p.81. For a full discussion of the authorship of "Alexander's Ragtime Band" and the rumors of Berlin's reliance upon black songwriters, see *CH*, pp. 107–12.

49 "Songwriters don't steal": *Green Book Magazine*, April 1916.

50 "The syncopated, shoulder-shaking type of vocal": *IW*, pp. 15–16.

50 "are based on the primitive motive of orgies," Erenberg, p. 81.

50 "brought the nice girl into the café": Ibid., p. 146.

51 "If customers of that joint": Ibid., p. 123.

51 "it seems to me now that the *Folies Bergère*": Erenberg, p. 123.

51 "we seldom serve tea": Edward Berlin, *Reflections on Ragtime*, p. 67.

51 "From the slum to the stage": Erenberg, p. 81.

51 "a presentment condemning the turkey trot": *New York Times*, May 28, 1913.

52 "It was the dance craze": *Green Book Magazine*, February, 1915.

52 "Everybody's Overdoing It": Edward Berlin, *Reflections on Ragtime*, p. 69.

52 "reckless and uncontrolled dances": Erenberg, p. 84.

53 "Everybody is doing it": *New York Telegraph*, April 30, 1912.

53 "another Broadway adorable": *MF*, pp. 38–39.

54 "Well, she's just the finest, sweetest": "Composer Wins Bride Through Friendship with Her Composer Brother," unidentified news clipping, *IBSLC*.

54 "You're a man who writes from your emotions": *MF*, p. 42.

55 "none of the hundred and thirty songs": Wilder, p. 96.

56 "Go where you will": *Daily Express*, June 20, 1913.

57 "until the cylinder choked": *MF*, p. 45.

57 "I hum the songs": *Daily Express*, June 20, 1913.

57 "his ragtime songs with such diffidence": *Times* (London), July 8, 1913.

57 "That night in London": *MF*, p. 43.

58 "the prettiest song I ever heard": *New York Times*, January 2, 1916.

59 "before the 'wisest' crowd in New York": *Variety*, December 25, 1914.

59 "his inspiration, the model, the idol": *MF*, p. 29.

59 "the first time Tin Pan Alley": *New York Herald Tribune*, May 16, 1948.

60 "was a great versifier": *New York Herald Tribune*, June 2, 1922.

60 "Most bards would think it hopeless": Harry Smith, *First Nights and First Editions*. Boston: Little Brown, 1931, pp. 280–81.

62 "We get our new dances from the Barbary Coast": Erenberg, pp. 163–64.

62 "brought to the awkward and vulgar-looking dance forms": Ibid., p. 164.

63 "burlesque of the conventional love song": Smith, p. 282.

64 "the musical part didn't give me much trouble": *Saturday Review*, October 1, 1966.

64 "Irving Berlin stands out like the Times building": *IW*, pp. 172–73.

65 "While the war was going on": Smith, p. 273.

65 "has ever wanted for the good things": *CH*, p. 9.

65 "successful first night": *Variety*, December 25, 1914.

Chapter 4: A Pretty Girl Is Like a Melody

67 *"The reason our American composers"*: *Theatre Magazine* February 1915.

68 "You see, there's a real American opera": Ibid.

69 "I never had a chance": Ibid.

69 "I'm a little bit commercial": Ibid.

69 "The publisher sells his songs": *Green Book Magazine*, April 1916.

70 "If music did not pay": David Ewen, *The Life and Death of Tin Pan Alley*. New York: Funk and Wagnall's, 1964, pp. 209–13.

71 "twiddly little notes": P. G. Wodehouse, *Author! Author!* New York: Simon & Schuster, 1962, p. 15.

75 "Reversing the nineteenth-century's view": Erenberg, p. 166.

77 "Irving . . . You have nothing to worry about": *MF*, p. 51. Berlin clearly renewed his studies by the 1930s, for, as noted above, he had learned enough about musical notation to write his own lead sheet for the melody of "Soft Lights and Sweet Music."

77 "it was apparent as soon as the curtains parted": *LB*, p. 137.

79 "There were a lot of things about army life": *American Heritage*, August 1967.

82 "Do you know how many people?": Max Wilk, *They're Playing Our Song*. New York: Atheneum, 1973, p. 275.

82 "recognizing how much theater was inherent": *LB*, p. 158.

83 "See, there were so many patriotic songs": Wilk, p. 276.

85 "It is extraordinary that such a development": Wilder, p. 99.

86 "nostalgia . . . longing": Charles Hamm, *Yesterdays: Popular Song in America*. New York: Norton, 1979, p. 61.

86 "Look at these costumes": *Cleveland News*, October 14, 1954.

Chapter 5: Say It With Music

87 *"I suppose we all work best"*: *Theatre Magazine*, February 1915.

87 "Talent and business are wedded in him": *Saturday Review*, June 26, 1948.

88 "If you ever want to build a theater": *AW*, pp. 173–74.

88 "The boys think they're building": *New York Times*, September 23, 1971.

88 "I'm in trouble": *MF*, pp. 64–65.

89 "The Music Box would be the first": *LB*, p. 179.

89 "Never mind. It's no more": Ibid., p. 181.

90 "greatest masterpieces of musical art": *AW*, p. 211.

91 "It was no more than being able to recognize": *MF*, p. 69.

92 "We had a terrible time": *LB*, p. 185.

92 "Its bewildering contents confirmed the dark suspicion": *New York Times*, September 23, 1921.

93 "We were living . . . in a time of literate revelry": E.Y. Harburg, "From the Lower East Side to 'Over the Rainbow,'" in *Creators and Disturbers: Reminiscences by Jewish Intellectuals of New York*, eds. Bernard Rosenberg and Ernest Goldstein. New York: Columbia University Press, 1982, pp. 141–42.

96 "read the good books": *Theatre Magazine*, February 1915.

96 "lean, compact heroic couplets": George Frazier, "Irving Berlin," unidentified news clipping, *IBSLC*.

96 "There goes time": Barrett, p. 233.

96 "Pope became his own publisher": Pat Rogers, "Introduction," *Alexander Pope*. New York: Oxford University Press, 1994, p. x.

98 "a sprinkle of theatrical mystery": Wilder, pp. 101–102.

98 "No, they emerge from tree trunks": *New York Herald*, October 24, 1922.

99 "A little man in a tight-fitting suit": *AW*, pp. 204–06.

99 "While we all sat around, celebrating": Wilk, p. 279.

101 "I would not want it said": "Irving Berlin and Modern Ragtime," unidentified news clipping, *IBSLC*.

101 "Just because a man": *MF*, p. 105.

102 "He was no angel, maybe": *LB*, p. 205.

102 "They bore down heavily on Berlin": Ibid.

104 "There is radio music in the air": Frederick Lewis Allen, *Only Yesterday: An Informal History of the 1920s*. New York: Harper & Row, 1931, p. 65.

105 "syntactic surprise": Gerald Mast, *Can't Help Singin': The American Musical on Stage and Screen*. Woodstock, N.Y.: The Overlook Press, 1987, p. 45.

106 "Stick to your own songs, kid": Barrett, p. 155.

106–7 "exercise their credit . . . break down consumer resistance": Allen, pp. 140–42.

107 "I intend to do such a work": *New York Sun*, February 17, 1922.

Chapter 6: Blue Skies

109 *"When I say that jazz"*: *MF*, p. 69.

110 "Oh, Mr. Berlin, I do so like": Barrett, p. 21.

111 "Our Elders criticize": *The New Yorker*, November 28, 1925.

112 "clearly written for my mother": Barrett, p. 31.

113 "the little musical phrase that is coupled": *20th Century*, August 5, 1938.

113 "it's the lyric that makes a song": *New York City PM*, August 9, 1942.

113 "With 'Remember,' I tried to express a feeling": *New York Telegraph*, December 27, 1925.

114 "piled the waters of Biscayne Bay": Allen, pp. 233–34.

115 "I never knew that musical comedy": *New York Telegram*, March 11, 1926.

117 "but not the lyric": *Leader Magazine*, October 5, 1946.

117 "the opening line might be a little more in accord": Malcolm Goldstein, *George S. Kaufman: His Life, His Theater*. New York: Oxford University Press, 1979, p. 130.

117 "editorials, health talks, comic strips": Allen, p. 157.

118 "hurled at one in huge headlines": Ibid., p.158.

118 "over my dead body": *Variety*, January 6, 1926.

118 "knowledge or approval": *New York Times*, January 5, 1926.

118 "'Always' was a love song I wrote": *MF*, p. 84.

120 "lyrical renaissance . . . general run of musical comedies": *Variety*, December 30, 1925.

120 "Irving, I'm opening in a show tomorrow night": Wilk, pp. 281–82.

According to Max Wilk, Baker approached Berlin on December 27, 1926, but Mary Ellin Barrett notes that "Blue Skies" had been registered for copyright the week before Christmas (Barrett, p. 55).

Chapter 7: The Song Is Ended

125   *"You do it piece"*: *LB*, p. 290.

125   "The big horns over which the recordings were played": Richard Barrios, *A Song in the Dark*. New York: Oxford University Press, 1995, p. 14.

127   "The laugh-clown-laugh aria": Ibid., p. 24.

130   "satisfactory simultaneous direct recording": Mast, p. 92.

131   "detailed the exodus": Barrios, p. 108.

132   "In their crassest manifestations": Ibid., p. 111.

132   "Irving Berlin would write a theme song": Ibid., p. 82.

132   "You can find him in Paris": Barrett, p. 76.

133   "the best musical comedy": *LB*, p. 284.

136   "one of the more creative backstagers": Barrios, p. 216.

138   "ever since talking pictures found voice": Ibid., p. 213.

139   "had the hideous distinction": *LB*, p. 296.

Chapter 8: How Deep Is the Ocean?

145   *"I was scared"*: *Saturday Evening Post*, January 9, 1943.

146   "We have become a world of listeners": *MF*, p. 131.

146   "Irving's all washed up": Ibid., pp. 153–54.

147   "I keep taking lines": Ibid.

148   "Those two songs": Barrett, p. 108.

149   "not only the world of the theatre": Moss Hart, *Act One*. New York: Random House, 1959, p. 35.

149   "I do not write musical comedies": Ibid., p. 263.

150   "writing a show with Irving Berlin": *Stage Magazine*, November 1936.

152   "We both agreed that we had no desire": *New York Times*, October 8, 1932.

152   "After I had been": Ibid.

152   "And so, Mr. Berlin and I": Ibid.

153   "There are some persons": *New York Herald Tribune*, October 10, 1933.

153   "Berlin obviously listened": Wilder, p. 107.

155   "sounded terrible . . . It sounded even more terrible": *Time*, April 28, 1952.

157 "I was telling my comfortable, well-fed": Ethel Waters, *His Eye Is on the Sparrow*. New York: Da Capo Press, 1992, p. 222.

158 "refused to take a bow": Barrett, pp. 120–21.

158 "We wanted a big Fifth Avenue number": *New York World Telegraph*, October 1, 1933.

160 "A song is like a marriage": Ibid.

160 "I can never guess a song": *New York World-Telegram*, November 6, 1946.

162 "But we open on Saturday night": Hart, p. 263.

162 "Still a bit shaken": *New York Times*, October 10, 1933.

163 "Radio's most valuable asset": *MF*, p. 124.

163 "Despite Irving's misgivings": *LB*, pp. 338–39.

164 "how in the world": *MF*, p. 124.

Chapter 9: Cheek to Cheek

165 *"I'd rather have Fred Astaire"*: *LB*, p. 347.

165 "hot-shot, ace-high, lowdown": Ethan Mordden, *The Hollywood Musical*. New York: St. Martin's Press, 1981, p. 44.

166 "enormous ears and bad chin line": John Mueller, *Astaire Dancing: The Musical Films*. New York: Wings Books, 1991, p. 7. Mueller notes that Selznick, however, went on to say "his charm is so tremendous that it comes through even on this wretched test." Mueller also discounts the "Can't act" story: "RKO producer Pandro Berman says he never heard it in the early 1930s, and that it emerged only years later."

168 "I did not go into [pictures]": Bob Thomas, *Astaire: The Man, the Dancer*. New York: St. Martin's Press, 1984, p. 105.

168 "I was amazed that the reaction": Mueller, p. 51.

168 "Unless I can do something outstandingly important": Ibid., p. 8.

169 "In the first place—as this book": Bill Adler, *Fred Astaire*. Santa Barbara, Calif.: ABC-CLIO, 1988, p. 122.

170 "holed up in his hotel": *LB*, p. 345.

170 "four to five songs a week": *CH*, p. 3.

171 "If I can, you can": I discovered this fragment of a lyric in one of the early scripts for *Top Hat* in the UCLA Film Scripts Archive. It is not clear whether the lines were written by Irving Berlin himself.

172 "emphasizes the wonder of movement": Mast, p. 151.

172 "Either the camera will dance": Adler, p. 112.

173 "blasted away . . . crawled sheepishly": *American Film Institute Catalog of Motion Pictures Produced in the U.S., 1931–1940*. Berkeley: University of California Press, 1996, p. 2237.

174 "as though he were talking": *LB*, p. 346.

176 "feathers started to fly": Fred Astaire, *Steps in Time*. New York: Harper and Bros., 1959, pp. 208–10.

178 "I hadn't done a tune like that": *New York Times*, November 19, 1974. Berlin considered making the lyric even more absurd. When Hermes Pan observed that "The Piccolino" was about a musical instrument rather than a dance, Berlin suggested revising it to "The Lido" with the line, "Come and do the Lido / It's very good for your libido" (Adler, p. 131).

179 "I love it": Ibid.

180 "was led through the swinging doors": *Variety*, January 29, 1936.

182 "depends on numbers . . . This is a clever frame": Twentieth-Century Fox Collection, Archives of the Performing Arts, University of Southern California L.A.

182 "When I had to write for Fred Astaire": *New York Sunday News*, September 7, 1947.

182 "as far out and as unanticipatable": Wilder, p. 112.

183 "Twentieth-Century Fox spun variations": Mast, p. 227.

184 "Maybe our trouble": Twentieth-Century Fox Collection, Archives of the Performing Arts, University of Southern California.

186 "What keeps the twenty-seven year chronicle together": Mast, pp. 230–31.

186 "wondered how long it would be safe": Astaire, p. 222.

187 "redundant and negative": *Life*, April 15, 1943.

188 "it is *Rogers* who consummates the kiss": Mueller, p. 144.

190 "nothing is so corny": *MF*, p. 129.

Chapter 10: God Bless America

191 "*I'd like to write a great peace song*": *New York Journal American*, September 4, 1938.

192 "I worked for a while on a song": *New York Times*, October 27, 1940. In some accounts of the song's history, Kate Smith, in 1938, asks Berlin for a patriotic song she can sing on the radio, and he recalls "God Bless America" from 1917.

192 "And not casually": Dale Carnegie, "Biography of a Song," typescript essay, *IBSCL*.

192 "the era of the Depression": Ann Douglas, *Terrible Honesty: Mongrel Manhattan in the 1920s*. New York: Alfred A. Knopf, 1996, p. 3.

192 "I had to make one or two changes": *New York Times*, October 27, 1940.

194 "The reason 'God Bless America' caught on": *New York Times*, July 11, 1940.

194 "it could be sung by those": Ibid.

195 "patriotic pretense . . . a specious substitute": *Fort Wayne Sentinel*, October 24, 1940.

195 "One does not 'croon'": Cleve Sallendar. "G-A-W-D- Bless A-M-E-R-I-K-A," unidentified news clipping, *IBSCL*.

195 "because its author": *Altamont, Missouri Times*, August 16, 1940.

195 "The high spot of the evening": *Chicago Times*, June 15, 1941.

195 "the genuine emotion of its lyric": *Variety*, August 14, 1940.

197 "the first song I ever wrote": *New York Times*, July 11, 1940.

197 "would I think be in much better taste": *Variety*, August 14, 1940.

197 "Those who benefited immediately": Tony Palmer, *All You Need Is Love*. New York: Grossman Publishers, 1976, p. 112.

198 "BMI had at least a foot in the door": Hamm, *Yesterdays*, pp. 389–90.

199 "In the face of the threat of war, holidays": *LB*, p. 385.

199 "our very own 'country house'": Barrett, p. 166.

201 "No song . . . is important enough": *Richmond Afro-American*, November 14, 1942.

202 "We working composers all too often": *Saturday Evening Post*, January 14, 1944.

204 "Away down under, this latest hit of Irving Berlin": *Chicago Times*, December 6, 1942.

204 "It became a peace song": *MF*, p. 148.

204 "You don't have to worry about this one": *Liverpool Evening Express*, September 27, 1946.

205 "It was as if he were going to have a baby": *LB*, p. 388.

205 "It was then that I noticed": *MF*, p. 146.

205 "the set that has been used": Mueller, p. 210.

208 "The boys are different": *New York Times*, May 17, 1942.

208 "Parades are out": *Buffalo News*, July 25, 1942.

208 "In his show business milieu": *LB*, pp. 396–97.

211 "We always insisted that the black guys": *LB*, p. 412.

211 "I shall never forget a performance in Rome": *New York Times*, August 20, 1944.

213 "He has set . . . a high standard": *LB*, p. 441.

Chapter 11: Anything You Can Do

215 *"The Hollywood yardstick for success"*: *MF*, p. 171.

215 "to present classic and contemporary works": Amy Henderson and Dwight Blocker Bowers, *Red, Hot, and Blue: The American Musical on Stage and Screen*. Washington: Smithsonian Institution Press, 1996, p. 141.

217 "These were not, contrary to legend": Henderson and Bowers, p. 146.

218 "I'm not out to write popular song hits": Wilk, p. 48.

218 "During the war, my late husband": Ibid., p. 289.

219 "writing the book was a dream": Ibid.

219 "After the funeral, we were all sitting": Ibid.

220 "He wouldn't have to find": *LB*, pp. 450–51.

220 "in the twelve days he agreed": Wilk, p. 290.

221 "I felt the only way": Bob Thomas, *I Got Rhythm! The Ethel Merman Story*. New York: Putnam, 1985, p. 96.

222 "Irving made me a lady": Ibid., p. 99.

224 "Listen, Josh, don't bother Irving": Wilk, pp. 291–92.

224 "Hello, Josh—this is Irving": Ibid., p. 292.

225 "a musical about show business": *LB*, p. 451.

227 "'know' . . . heard as a repetition": Mast, p. 44.

228 "Irving was very proud of it": Wilk, p. 290.

228 "Only by fixing his eyes": *LB*, p. 452.

228 "It wasn't petulance": Wilk, p. 291.

229 "intense, controlled, with a hint of something": Mueller, p. 11.

230 "Never, never": Thomas, *Astaire: The Man, The Dancer*, p. 193.

230 "It took longer to write": *New York Times*, May 11, 1958.

231 "Dear Joe—you and I shook hands": *New York Times*, April 28, 1952.

232 "Dear Louis—why should I ask for one thing": *New York Times*, May 11, 1958.

232 "Sometimes . . . would come in": Hugh Fordin, *MGM's Greatest Musicals: The Arthur Freed Unit*. New York: Da Capo Press, 1996, p. 223.

232 "was eager for their script": *LB*, p. 477.

232 "who privately complained to Freed": Ibid.

233 "You can't put Judy Garland": Fordin, pp. 223–26.

233 "If Kelly had played it": *New York Sun*, June 3, 1948.

234 "Let's have a 'tramps' number": *MF*, p. 174.

Chapter 12: Count Your Blessings

237 *"I've always thought of myself as a songwriter"*: *New York Times*, May 11, 1958.

237 "There was a saloon right there": *New York Sun*, February 24, 1947.

238 "Who is going to tell me": *St. Louis Star-Times*, December 20, 1942.

238 "It had all the qualities": *New York Times*, June 5, 1949.

239 "too distinguished . . . for this kind of show": Martin Gottfried, *Broadway Musicals*. New York: Harry N. Abrams, Inc., 1980, p. 244.

239 "Look, Bob . . . his mother posed": Liner notes, *American Musicals: Irving Berlin's "Annie Get Your Gun," "Miss Liberty," "Call Me Madam."* Chicago: Time-Life Books, 1981, p. 15.

239 "In *Annie Get Your Gun* I had to defer": *LB*, p. 493.

240 "You must have the courage": Fordin, p. 233.

241 "a disappointing musical comedy": *MF*, p. 184.

242 "opened it up—broadening its physical layout": Fordin, p. 272.

243 "Judy was unsure about what to do": Fordin, p. 273.

243 "I've never been in a tougher spot": *MF*, p. 184.

243 "I have been studying her": Lindsay–Crouse Papers, Wisconsin State Historical Society.

244 "I want a good, solid dramatic role": Thomas, *I Got Rhythm!*, p. 105.

244 "When Howard and Buck asked me if I would write the score": *Boston Post*, September 24, 1950.

245 "I've gone along": Thomas, *I Got Rhythm!*, p. 110.

246 "Don't tell Ethel you heard this": *LB*, p. 504.

247 "Give her a song and she'll make it sound good": Thomas, *I Got Rhythm!*, p. 113.

249 "Did you ever try counting your blessings": Barrett, p. 278.

249 "For sone reason . . . Bing": *Philadelphia Inquirer*, August 25, 1966.

251 "I've just eaten the biggest lunch": *Los Angeles Examiner*, February 2, 1954.

251 "I got really sick": *LB*, p. 529.

251 "Do you like them, Irving?": *New York Times*, October 18, 1953.

252 "as if he were heading for a breakdown": *London Daily Express*, September 13, 1963.

254 "No A & R man in his right mind": *New York Daily News*, March 27, 1956.

254 "What are they trying": Ibid.

254 "One 'Sh-Boom' or 'Oop-Shoop'": *New York Times*, October 20, 1954.

255 "A professional songwriter would never have rhymed": *MF*, p. 213.

256 "songs that were once sung or danced": Mast, p. 292.

256 "The divorce of American theater music": Ibid., pp. 292–93.

256 "One day, after five years of it": *Philadelphia Inquirer*, August 25, 1966.

257 "I told them I liked the idea": *New York Herald Tribune*, June 4, 1962.

257 "We all got off on the wrong foot": *LB*, p. 541.

258 "the words—which were always simple": *New York Herald Tribune*, October 22, 1962.

258 "I thought the show was going to run": *MF*, p. 202.

258 "Listen, I'd rather be 'unhappy'": Ibid., p. 203.

259 "There's only been one biographical movie": Ibid., pp. 195–96.

259 "In the old days, all you needed": *New York Times*, June 6, 1963.

259 "What the hell would I do": *LB*, p. 549.

261 *"Say It with Music* was to be Arthur's and my swan song": Fordin, p. 524.

261 "she can play it till she's ninety": *MF*, p. 207.

261 "That's not bad for a man": *Philadelphia Inquirer*, August 25, 1966.

263 "If someone walked in here": *Morning Telegraph*, August 24, 1966.

263 "I've always lived near this river": *MF*, p. 208.

263 "I have nursed one idea": *Philadelphia Inquirer*, August 25, 1966.

263 "At my age": *LB*, p. 572.

264 "Who cares anymore?": Wilk, p. 262.

264 "Few professionals can write well": *Saturday Evening Post*, January 9, 1943.

264 "Our tribe of songsmiths": Harold Meyerson and Ernie Harburg, *Who Put the Rainbow in "The Wizard of Oz"?* Ann Arbor: University of Michigan Press, 1993, p. 77.

Permissions

301

Index

Page numbers in italics refer to illustrations.

A

Abbott, George, 245–46
Abrahams, Maury, 121
Academy Awards, 133, 179, 242
Actor's Equity, 88
Adams, Franklin Pierce (F. P. A.), 93,
    111, 149
Aeolian Hall, 109
African-Americans:
    military service of, 208–9
    music and culture of, 23, 31–34,
        45, 48, 49–51, 52, 74, 134–35,
        135, 198
    stereotypes and caricatures of, 16,
        32–33, 83, 134, 201, 208
    See also racism
Akst, Harry, 153
Alda, Frances, 104
Alexander II, Czar of Russia, 6
Alexander III, Czar of Russia, 6
Alexander's Ragtime Band, 42,
    183–86, *185*, 201, 202, 231, 234
Algonquin Round Table, 93–101, 114,
    115, 117, 189
    IB and, 93–97, 99–101, 102, 111,
        118, 149, 238
Ameche, Don, 183, 185, *185*
American in Paris, An, 235
American Jewish Tercentenary, 249
American Red Cross, 112, 207
American Revolution, 7, 239
American Society of Composers,
    Authors and Publishers (ASCAP),
    70–71, 104, 196–98, 219, 253
Annie Get Your Gun, 3, 63, 73,
    218–30, *226*, 232, 234, 238, 239,
    242–43, 261, *262*
anti-Catholicism, 78, 195
anticommunism, 78
antisemitism, 5–6, 58, 78, 112, 195
Antwerp, 6
Anything Goes, 243
Arkansas, *212*
Arlen, Harold, 148, 152, 163, 264
Armstrong, Louis, 134, 154
Army, U.S., 207–13
    IB's service in, 5, 79–84, *80*, 208

Army Emergency Relief Fund, 207, 211
Art Deco, 88, 105, 176, 189, 190
Astaire, Adele, 105–6, 123, 166, 168
Astaire, Fred, 166–82, 185–90, 201–2,
    229–30, *231*, 232–36, *235*, *236*,
    241–42, 250, 264
    Adele Astaire and, 105–6, 166, 168
    death of, 265
    Ginger Rogers and, 3, 62, 130,
        140–41, 150–51, 167–81, *172*,
        177, *180*, 184, 186–90, 230, 232,
        233–34, 241
    IB on, 150–51
As Thousands Cheer, 107, 152–63,
    156, *161*, 169, 170, 179, 198
Atkinson, Brooks, 240–41
Australian Armed Forces, 207
Awakening, The, 133

B

"Bab Ballads," 28
Babbitt, 95
Babes in Arms, 241
Bach, Johann Sebastian, 64, 90
Baker, Belle, 119–22
Baker, Josephine, 153–54
Baline, Leah "Lena" Lipkin (mother),
    5–8, 10
    death of, 101, 102
    IB and, 65, 128, 192
    motherhood of, 5, 11, 13
Baline, Moses (father), 5–8
    cantorial work of, 6, 10, 13
    illness and death of, 10
    immigration of, 6–8
Baltic Sea, 6
band music, 31, 34, 39
Band Wagon, The, 235–36
Bankhead, Tallulah, 98
Barnum, P. T., 16
barrelhouses, 32
Barrett, Elizabeth Esther
    (granddaughter), 252
Barrett, Irving Berlin (grandson), 252
Barrett, Mary Ellin Berlin (daughter),
    119, 121
    on IB, 112, 158, 199

Barrios, Richard, 127, 132
Barrymore, John, 127
Bartholdi, Frédéric, 239
Baxter, Warner, 166
Beatles, 255
Beethoven, Ludwig van, 48, 64, 90, 91
Behrman, S. N., 252
Bel Geddes, Norman, 105
Bell, J. Franklin, 82
Bell Telephone Laboratories, 126
Belorussia, 6
Benchley, Robert, 83, 93, 97, 98–99, 117
Bennett, Arnold, 45
Bennett, James Gordon, 239
Bennett, Joan, 136, 138
Berenson, Bernard, 112
Bergreen, Laurence, 89, 102, 163–64, 199, 208–9, 220
Berkeley, Busby, 166, 168, 171–72, 178, 181
Berlin, Dorothy Goetz (wife), 53–54, 111, 112
Berlin, Elizabeth Irving (daughter), 119
Berlin, Ellin Mackay (wife), 114, 139–40, 199, *200, 250*
    Catholic faith of, 112, 119
    courtship and marriage of, 54, 110–12, 117–19, *119*
    death of, 265
    literary aspirations of, 111, 252
    motherhood of, 119
    social background and education of, 111, 112
Berlin, Irving:
    all-night working sessions of, 24, 30, 57, 79, 82, 87, 100, 121, 162, 170, 176, 202
    as America's greatest songwriter, 1–5, 109
    art and literature collections of, 65, 68–69, 102
    artistic and cultural aspirations of, 65, 68–69, 74, 96–97, 107
    bachelor lifestyle of, 68–69, 79, 93–96, 99–100, 102
    Bar Mitzvah of, *9*
    biographies of, 6, 11, 89, 110
    birth name of, 5
    birth of, 4, 5
    business and financial acumen of, 48–49, 55, 71, 76, 84, 87–89, 106, 107, 135–36, 139, 169, 179,

231–32
    centenary celebration of, 265
    childhood and adolescence of, 1, 2, 4–5, 6–24, *9*, 212
    Christmas memories of, 8–10, 114
    chutzpah of, 27, 36, 82
    composers admired by, 48, 58, 59, 86, 132–33, 189
    compositional methods of, 24, 30, 56–57, 79, 82, 87, 99–100, 244–45
    Congressional Gold Medal awarded to, *250*
    creative crises and comebacks of, 106, 109–10, 112, 124, 145–48, 165, 228, 238, 243–45, 251–52, 256–60
    dance craze crystallized by, 52–53, 256
    death of, 266
    depressions of, 140, 143, 145, 251–53, 254, 255, 256, 263–64
    early jobs of, 10–24, 31
    early poverty of, 1, 8–14, 192
    East River accident of, 11
    education of, 2, 10, 69, 74
    eight siblings of, 5, 8, 10, 11, 65
    European trips of, 56–58, 98, 118–19, 211–12
    fame and fortune of, 38, 47–48, 56–59, 65, 109, 110, 163, 179–80
    fatherhood and family life of, 65, 119, 252, 262
    first lyric writing of, 20–24
    first published song of, 22–24, 25
    first words and music song of, 36–45
    formal musical education lacked by, 1, 2, 10, 34, 38, 47
    generosity of, 102, 133, 196, 211, 254–55
    grandchildren of, 252
    high musical and perfectionist standards of, 2, 24, 54, 112–14, 135, 150, 164, 264
    immigration of, 6–8, 15, 32, 249
    innate musical talent of, 2, 11, 34–35, 87, 110
    insomnia suffered by, 24, 173, 244
    international acclaim of, 4, 43–45, 56–58
    Jewish immigrant background of, 2, 3, 5–10, 58, 110, 111–12, 195, 212, 249

as "King of Ragtime," 47–48,
   57–58, 77
loneliness and isolation of, 102–3,
   112, 202, 263–64
lyrical vs. narrative bent of, 41
marriages of. *See* Berlin, Dorothy
   Goetz; Berlin, Ellin Mackay
Medal of Merit bestowed on,
   213
military service of, 5, 79–84, *80*,
   208
musical illiteracy of, 22, 35, 38,
   56–57, 77
naturalization of, 78
nickname of, 19, 23, 180
one key piano playing of, 1, 34–35,
   35, 38, 99–100, *123*, 155, 182,
   257, 259, *265*
painting hobby of, 252, 262
as performer, 14, 18, 47–48, 53,
   57–58, 83, 180, 210, 212–13, *212*,
   255, *260*
photographs of, *ii, 9, 35,* 47–48, *80,*
   94, 119, 123, 180, 200, 210, 212,
   236, 240, 253, 265
physical appearance of, 99
privacy guarded by, 54–55, 259–60
producer role of, 82–84, 87–89, 92,
   98–100, 106, 107, 115, 135–43,
   157–58, 169, 179
professional insecurity of, 113–14,
   117, 140, 143, 145–46, 162, 228,
   238, 251–53, 263–64
public vs. private personas of, 54,
   101
publishing interests of, 48–49,
   67–68, 69–71, 76, 84, 85, 87, 104,
   263
retirement of, 252
reviews of, 57–58, 64, 65, 92, 98,
   134, 229, 240–41, 257–58
royalties earned by, 23, 27–28, 30,
   38, 47, 70–71, 87, 103, 104–5,
   118, 196, 265
shyness of, 54, 59, 95
singing voice of, 14, 18, 57, 83,
   155
social life of, 93–97, 99–100, 110
song "plugging" of, 14–17, 31, 197,
   259
staff lyricist position of, 25, 30,
   33–36
street and saloon singing of, 11,
   13–14, 17–24, 25–26, 30, 51, 52,

74, 88, 110, 126, 195, 237–38
synagogue choir singing of, 10
work ethic and temperament of,
   24, 30–31, 41, 47, 54, 79, 82, 87,
   99, 112–14, 150, 176, 205,
   244–45
Yiddish speaking of, 2, 7
youthful ambitions of, 10, 13, 24,
   36
Berlin, Irving, Jr. (son), 119
Berlin, Irving, lyrics of:
American girl celebrated in, 3,
   75–76, 83, 85–86, 97–98, 107
blending of music with, 2, 41–43,
   55–56, 100–101, 105, 120, 148,
   160, 187–88
catch phrases and words in,
   30–31, 52, 84, 105, 146–47
clichés in, 20–21, 55, 150, 227
comic and novelty elements in, 56,
   78–81
common touch and realism in,
   4–5, 26, 27, 30, 78–81, 97, 194
contractions used in, 100, 157, 173
distorted verbal accents in, 138,
   155, 173, 178
ethnicity and dialect in, 20–24,
   27–28, 29–30, 36, 78, 135, *135*
evocative nostalgia of, 160–61,
   192–94, 204
literary allusions in, 95, 97
manipulation of consonants and
   vowels in, 91, 100–101, 105, 113,
   121, 138, 159, 173, 174, 203
"memorable," 37–38, 91, 105
metaphors used in, 74, 97
modern life reflected in, 3, 4–5,
   44–45, 93–94, 150–51
patriotism in, 3, 78, 81, 192–97,
   206–13
rhyming schemes of, 60, 91, 95,
   100, 117, 122, 148, 158, 159–60,
   178–79, 203–4, 227
satire in, 148–53, 163, 178–79
singability of, 21–22, 38, 39, 43,
   105, 174–75, 196
slang and elegance combined in,
   138, 155, 173, 183
"turnaround" phrases and tag lines
   in, 113, 117
vocalization of triplets in, 72, 100,
   148, 188
wartime sentiments in, 3, 4, 5,
   78–84, 206–13

Berlin, Irving (*continued*)
  wit and sophistication in, 28–29,
    85–86, 96, 150–51, 154–55,
    189–90
  Berlin, Irving, popular and show
    songs of:
  artful simplicity of, 31, 43, 117,
    122, 148, 159, 187, 195, 203
  blue notes and chromaticism in,
    10, 42, 156–57, 203
  bridge sections in, 121–22
  collaborations on, 20–24, 28–29,
    30–31, 36, 53, 121
  duets and counterpoint in, 63–64,
    225, 234, *235*, 246–47, *248*, 250
  emotional content of, 3, 4, 42,
    55–56, 101, 113–14, 155–56, 196
  enduring and timeless power of,
    2–4, 86, 160, 163–64, 193–97,
    205
  harmonies of, 35, 55, 98, 151,
    182–83
  as "hits," 2–3, 31, 40–45, 47–49,
    86, 146–48, 160–61
  holidays celebrated in, 3, 10,
    158–61, *161*, 199–206, *206*,
    231–36
  IB's ownership and control of,
    48–49, 71, 84, 87, 135–36, 139,
    263
  IB's publication of, 67, 76, 84, 85,
    263
  inspirations for, 31, 38–39,
    112–13, 140, 202, 224
  jazz elements in, 91, 92, 97, 138
  key changes within, 41, 63, 117,
    148, 151, 156, 203–4
  listening to vs. performing of,
    103–4, 146
  melodic content of, 10, 36, 42, 55,
    85, 98, 113, 117, 121, 134,
    156–57, 160, 164, 193, 203–4
  "Number One" pinnacle reached
    by, 2
  orchestrations of, 65, 109–10
  performer's individual talents
    suited in, 153–57, 174–75, 182
  popularity of, 1, 2–3, 4, 31, 39–45,
    56–58, 163–64, 193–96
  in public domain, 265
  quality of, 2, 148, 163–64
  ragtime elements in, 23, 31, 33–34,
    36–45, 47–50, 52–53, 56–57,
    63–64, 68, 74–75, 76, 89–90, 101

  range and variety of, 2–4, 152
  rapid output and quantity of, 2, 38,
    47, 170
  recordings of, 85, 103, 105
  relationship of verse to chorus in,
    21, 29, 31, 36, 41–42, 155
  retrieval and reworking of, 83,
    120–21, 147, 158, 160, 162, 170,
    171, 176, 184–86, 192–94,
    239–40, 245, 252, 259, 261–62
  romantic ballads as, 3, 55–56, 75,
    85–86, 90–91, 99–101, 103–5,
    112–13, 116–17, 145–48, 182–83
  rumored ghostwriting of, 49–50
  Slavonic and Semitic folk tunes
    reflected in, 42
  as "standards," 2, 3, 86, 160–61,
    184
  storyline integrated with, 3, 59–60,
    73, 150, 221–25
  structure of, 1, 36, 41–42, 68, 76,
    95, 96, 117, 121–22, 135, 146–48,
    156–57, 175, 181, 182, 222, 226
  titles of, 22, 113, 189, 192
  "Top Ten" designation of, 2
  transcription of, 22, 35, 57
  verse section eliminated in, 148,
    156, 175
Berlin, Linda Louise (daughter), 119
Berlin, Mary Ellin. *See* Barrett, Mary
  Ellin Berlin
Berman, Pan, 167–69, 181
Bernhardt, Sarah, 125
Besserer, Eugenie, 129, *129*, 130
Betsy, 120, 122
Big Jerry, 20
Big Red Scare, 78
Billboard, 138, 139
Birth of a Nation, The, 126
Bizet, Georges, 216
"blackface" humor, 16, 32–33, 83,
  201, 209
Black Sea, 6
Black Sox scandal, 147
Blake, Joseph, 112
Blind George, 237
Blind Sol, 14
Blitzstein, Marc, 217
Blore, Eric, 171
*Blue Monday, Opera Ala Afro-
  Amerique*, 68
blues, 102, 105, 153–54
Blue Skies, 229–30, *231*, 232
Bolshevik Revolution, 78

Bolton, Guy, 71, 72
Boone, Pat, 259
Bordoni, Irene, 132
Bornstein, Saul, 113, 114
bossa nova, 263
Boston, Mass., 7, 40, 257
Bowers, Dwight, 217
Boy Scouts of America, 196
Brando, Marlon, 252
Brazzi, Rossanno, 241
Breen Office, 242–43
Brice, Fanny, 29–30
Bringing Up Baby, 170
British Navy, 20
Broadcast Music Incorporated (BMI),
    197–98, 253, 255
Broadway Melody, 128, 136, 137
Broadway musicals, 14–16, 148–64
    "Americanization" of, 59, 65, 67,
        71–73, 123
    "book" shows as, 105–6, 114, 150,
        152, 199, 218–30
    cast albums of, 217–18, 229, 256
    "doctoring" of, 14, 63, 71, 115,
        162, 217, 245–46, 257–58
    film versions of, 128, 132, 133–34,
        241–43
    groundbreaking developments in,
        71–73, 106, 120, 123–24, 215–18,
        255–56
    IB's performances in, 14, 47–48,
        53, 210
    integration of story and song in, 3,
        59–60, 71–73, 105, 109, 120,
        123–24, 132, 215–18, 238–39,
        241, 255–56
    jazz elements in, 105, 152
    out-of-town tryouts of, 14, 71, 158,
        161–62, 217, 257–58
    satirical style in, 148–53, 162, 163,
        244
    separation of popular songs and,
        255–56
    show-stoppers in, 225–29, 247
    touring of, 69–70, 89, 128, 210–13,
        218
    See also musical revues; *specific
        titles*
Broderick, Helen, 171, 175
Brodie, Steve, 237
Brown, Herb Nacio, 230, 235
Bucket of Blood saloon, 13
burlesque, 11, 40, 97
Burns, Robert, 85–86

C
cabarets, 2, 13, 39–40, 50–51, 60–62,
    70, 102, 104, 110–11
Callahan's saloon, 13, 20, 78
Call Me Madam, 243–49, *248*, 251,
    257
Calloway, Cab, 154
Camp Upton, 79, 84, 208
Camelot, 239
Cantor, Eddie, 12, 84–85, *123*, 124
Carefree, 187–89
Carmen Jones, 216
Carnegie Hall, 184, 265
Caron, Leslie, 233
Carousel, 239
Carpenter, John Alden, 90
Carroll, Lewis, 137
Carus, Emma, 41
Case, Anna, 112, 140
"Casey at the Bat," 26
Castle, Irene, 60–62, *61*, 64, 71,
    73–74, 75, 110, 169, 256
Castle, Vernon, 60–62, *61*, 64, 71, 73,
    169, 256
CBS radio, 191
Century Theatre, 77, 82–84
Chamberlain, Neville, 191–92
Chaplin, Charlie, 88, 95
Charisse, Cyd, 233
Charleston, 110
Charlie Chan, 130
Chauve Souris, 97
Chevalier, Maurice, 165, 200
Chez Paree Chicago, 196
Chicago, Ill., 32, 40, 41, 195–96
Chicago World's Fair of 1893, 32,
    41
China, 11, 191
Chinatown Gertie, 18
Chopin, Frédéric, 48, 90, 91, 110
Cinemascope, 251
City Hospital, 219
Civil War, U.S., 140
Clooney, Rosemary, 250
Cobdock Hotel, 14
Cocoanuts, The, 115–17, *116*,
    133–34
Cody, Buffalo Bill, 225–26
Cohan, George M., 5, 34, 40, 58–59,
    65, 78, 87–88, 259
Columbus, Christopher, 32
Comden, Betty, 260
"concert" saloons, 12–14
Congress, U.S., 7, 78, 104

Connecticut Yankee in King Arthur's Court, A, 122
Connelly, Marc, 93
"Conning Tower," 149
Connors, Chuck, 17–18, 48
Conrad, Con, 167
Coolidge, Calvin, 93, 106
"coon" songs, 32–34, 45, 48, 52, 74
Copland, Aaron, 217
copyright law, 103, 104, 108, 265
Coquette, 133
Cotton Club, 135
Coward, Noel, 95, 153
Cradle Will Rock, The, 217
Crane, Stephen, 8
Crawford, Joan, 153, 167
criminal gangs, 17–18
Crosby, Bing, 142, 199–205, *206*, 229, 232, 246, 250, 251
Crosby, Gary, 246
Crouse, Russel, 93, 243–45, 257
Czechoslovakia, 191–92

D

Dailey, Dan, 251
Dale, Virginia, 201
Daly, T. A., 26–27
Damsel in Distress, A, 187
Dancing Lady, 167
Daniels, Bebe, 140–42, *141*
Davies, Marion, 76
DeForest, Lee, 126
Dell, Floyd, 95
Del Rio, Dolores, 126, 167
de Mille, Agnes, 188, 217
democracy, 78
Dempsey, Jack, 104, 119
Depression, Great, 3, 4, 5, 107, 140, 145, 148, 150, 164, 166, 181, 191, 192, 193, 216, 231, 248
Deslys, Gaby, 73–74, 76
De Sylva, Buddy, 159
Diamond Lottie, 237–38
Dietrich, Marlene, 200
Dietz, Howard, 87, 120, 152, 235–36
Dillingham, Charles, 59, 62, 66, 73, 76, 77
Donizetti, Gaetano, 68
Don Juan, 127
Donovan, Biggie, 238
Dorsey, Tommy, 133
Drake, 20
Dubin, Al, 165, 179
Dust Bowl, 191
Dvořák, Antonin, 23

E

Earhart, Amelia, 142
Eastern European Jews, 5–10
    diaspora of, 5–7
    discrimination against, 5–6, 58, 78, 112, 195
    ethnic and religious customs and clothing of, 7, 10
    immigrant experience of, 6–10, 14–15
    success of, 111, 112
    urban congregation of, 7
Easter Parade, 231–36, *235, 236*, 238, 240, 242
Eastman Kodak, 176
Eastmans gang, 18
East River, 11, 263
Edison, Thomas, 106, 125
Edward VII, King of England, 20
Edward VIII, King of England, 111
Einstein, Albert, 44
Eisenhower, Dwight D., 211, 249, *250*
elections:
    of 1920, 104
    of 1924, 249
    of 1940, 195
    of 1954, 249
Eliot, T. S., 103
Ellen, Vera, 250
Ellington, Duke, 134
Ellis Island, 7
England, 7, 28, 73, 192, 238
English music-hall songs, 28–29
Erenberg, Lewis, 13, 75
Etting, Ruth, 124
Etude, 90
Europe, James Reese, 62

F

Fabray, Nanette, 257, *258*
Face the Music, 150–51
Fairbanks, Douglas, Jr., 140–42, *141*, 153
Fascism, 192
Faye, Alice, 182–85
Ferber, Edna, 95, 96, 123, 132, 217
Fiddler John, 22
Fields, Dorothy, 186, 218–20, 225, 228, *262*, 264
Fields, Herbert, 218, 225
Fields, Lew, 12, 218
Fields, W. C., 62
Fifty Million Frenchmen, 133, 142
Fisher, Eddie, 249
Fitzgerald, F. Scott, 50, 95, 111

Five-Pointers gang, 18
Flea Bag saloon, 13
Fleming, Victor, 133
Fletcher, Andrew, 4
"Flying Circus," 81
Flying Down to Rio, 167, 168, 180
Folies Bergere, 39–40, 51
Follow the Fleet, 180–81
Fontaine, Joan, 187
Ford, Henry, 106
Fort McHenry, 194
42nd Street, 128, 165–66, 167
Foster, Stephen, 15, 21, 48, 58, 70,
    86, 135, 197, 219
fox-trot, 110, 256
France, 7, 84, 239
Franco, Francisco, 191
Franklin, Benjamin, 5, 38
Freed, Arthur, 230–35, 242–43,
    259–61
Freud, Sigmund, 44, 91
Friars Club, 40, 47, 88
    IB "roasted" by, 58–59
Friars' Frolic shows, 40
Frisco Joe, 19
From Rags to Riches, 14
Frost, Robert, 204
"Frühlingslied," 36
Fun, 28
Funny Face, 123, 166

G
Gable, Clark, 179
Gandhi, Mohandas K. "Mahatma,"
    153
Garland, Judy, 15–16, 128, 195–96,
    230, 232–34, *235, 236*, 242–43,
    259, 260
Garrick Gaieties, The, 120, 216
Gay Divorce, 166, 167
Gay Divorcée, The, 167–68
Gaynor, Mitzi, 241
George White's Scandals, 68, 89
Germany, Imperial, 7
Germany, Nazi, 191–92, 204
Gershwin, George, 1, 3–4, 73, 91, 96,
    116, 132, 186, 235
    death of, 189
    hit musicals of, 105–6, 107, 112,
        122–23, 148, 163, 166, 221, 241,
        244
    operas and symphonic pieces of,
        68, 107, 110, 156, 189, 216
    piano playing of, 103, 106, 110,
        189

Gershwin, Ira, 2, 21, 22, 93, 163, 207,
    216, 217
    George Gershwin's collaboration
        with, 3–4, 73, 105, 107, 112, 120,
        122–23, 132, 148, 174, 186, 221,
        235, 241, 244
Gilbert, William S.:
    lyrics of, 28–29, 71–73, 120, 132
    and Sullivan, 2, 12, 28, 64, 71, 73,
        90, 107, 120, 132
Girl Crazy, 244
Girl Scouts of America, 196
Glaspell, Susan, 95
Goetz, Ray, 53, 54–55, 56, 132
Goldberg, Isaac, 32–33
Gold Diggers films, 166, 167, 179
Goldwyn, Samuel, 133, 179
Gone With the Wind, 133
Goodrich, Frances, 232
Gordon, Mack, 167
Gorney, Jay, 150
Gouvernor's Hospital, 11
Grange, Red, 118
Grant, Cary, 170
Great Gatsby, The, 95
Green, Adolph, 260
Green Grow the Lilacs, 216
Griffith, D. W., 88, 126, 140
grizzly bear, 40, 50, 60
G. Schirmer Music, 70
"Gunga Din," 26

H
habanera, 21
Hackett, Albert, 232
Haley, Jack, *185*
Hallelujah, 134–35, *135*
Hamlet, 36, 102
Hamm, Charles, 40, 86, 198
Hammerstein, Oscar, II, 123–24, 224,
    225, 239, 264
    Kern and, 123, 132, 215, 216
    Rodgers and, 124, 174, 199,
        216–19, 224, 228, 230, 240, 241,
        245
Hammerstein Victoria Theatre,
    47–48, 53
Harbor Hill, 112
Harburg, E. Y. "Yip," 2, 73, 93, 150,
    152, 218, 264
Harding, Warren Gamaliel, 104, 106
Harlem Renaissance, 134
Harnick, Sheldon, 255–56
Harrigan and Hart, 58, 64
Harris, Charles K., 15, 41, 104, 106

Harris, Sam, 87–89, 92, 115, 149
Harrison, Rex, 257
Hart, Lorenz, 21, 93
    Rodgers and, 2, 3–4, 73, 120, 122,
        132, 165, 189, 216–17, 241
Hart, Moss, 149
    IB's collaboration with, 152–53,
        155, 161, 162–63, *240*, 264
Harvey Girls, The, 199, 230
"Hat-in-the-Ring" flying squadron,
    81
Hayes, Daniel L., *135*
Healey, Dan, 82
Hearst, Mrs. Randolph, 31
Hearst, William Randolph, 11, 76
Hearst newspapers, 117
Hearts in Dixie, 134
Hebrew language, 10
Heifetz, Jascha, 95, 97
Helburn, Theresa, 215, 216, 217
Hemingway, Ernest, 153
Henderson, Amy, 217
Henie, Sonja, 186
Hepburn, Katherine, 170
Herbert, Victor, 58, 59, 70, 77, 104
Hess, Clifford, 47, 65
Hickock, Wild Bill, 225–26
Hilliard, Harriet, 181
Hip Sing Toy gang, 17
Hitler, Adolf, 181, 191–92
H.M.S. Pinafore, 28, 90
Hob-nailed Casey, 19
Hogan, Ernest, 32
Holiday, Billie, 157
Holiday Inn, 199–206, *206*, 209, 229,
    250
Holmes, Oliver Wendell, 70
Homer, Winslow, 23
Hoover, Herbert, 145, 150, 153, 194
Horton, Edward Everett, 141, 171,
    173
Hullo, Ragtime, 57–58
Hutton, Barbara, 153
Hutton, Betty, 243
Hyland, William, 3

I

Imagist poetry, 74
Immigration Act of 1921, 78
Internal Revenue Service, 207
Irish Melodies, 86
Irving Berlin, Inc., 76, 84, 85, 87
Israel, 252

J

Jablonski, Edward, 43–44
Jackson, "Shoeless" Joe, 147
Jakobson, Roman, 249
Japan, 191, 252
jazz, 2, 3, 91, 92, 97, 107, 109–10,
    134, 138, 152, 165
Jazz Age, 50–51, 91, 97, 100, 102–3,
    110, 114, 252
Jazz Singer, The, 3, 16–17, 128–30,
    129, 136
Jerusalem, 6
Jessel, George, 128
Jimmy Kelly's restaurant, 25–26, 30,
    109, 110
Johnston, Arthur, 115–16
John the Barber, 30
Jolson, Al, 3, 16–17, 126, 127, 128–30,
    129, 131, 136, 139, 146, 147, 254,
    255
Jones, Bobby, 118
Jonica, 149
Joplin, Scott, 31–32
Jubilee, 163
Judaism, 10

K

Kahn, Otto, 112
Kaltenborn, H. V., 191
Kaufman, George S., 93, 96, 107, 111,
    114–17, 118, 123, 149–50, 252,
    264
Kaye, Danny, 250
KDKA radio, 104
Keaton, Buster, 16–17
Keeler, Ruby, 167
Keith-Albee Company, 16
Keller, Julius, 51
Kelly, Gene, 141, 230, 232–33, 234
Kelly, Jimmy, 25
Kennedy, Jacqueline, 257, 258
Kennedy, John F., 257, 258
Kern, Jerome, 1, 4, 71–72, 85, 106,
    123, 132, 186, 215, 216, 219, 259
Kerr, Walter, 258
Key, Francis Scott, 194
KFWB radio, 126
Kinetoscope, 125
King and I, The, 239
Kiss Me, Kate, 241
Koehler, Ted, 148
Ku Klux Klan, 78, 195
Kutchinsky, Kutch, 18, 19

L

Lady, Be Good!, 105–6, 112, 166
Lady in the Dark, 163, 216
Lady of the Pavements, 140
Lardner, Ring, 93
Lasky, Jesse, 39, 40, 50–51
Lawrence, Bullhead, 18, 24
Lazarus, Emma, 7, 239
League of Nations, 191
Legion of Decency, 167
Lehar, Franz, 58
Lerner, Alan Jay, 163, 239
Leslie, Edgar, 28–29, 254
Let 'Em Eat Cake, 163, 216
Lewis, Jerry, 200
Lewis, Sinclair, 95
Lieber and Stoller, 255
Lincoln, Abraham, 196, 201
Lincoln Center, 261
Lindbergh, Charles, 118
Linden, Kathy, 255, 257
Lindsay, Howard, 243–45, 247, 257
Liszt, Franz, 48, 91, 110
Little Johnny Jones, 58, 87–88
little magazines, 74
Loewe, Frederick, 163
Logan, Josh, 221–22, 224–25, 228, 252
London, 56–58, 96, 167, 192, 207, 211
London Hippodrome Theatre, 57–58
Longfellow, Henry Wadsworth, 97
Long Island, 95, 111, 112
Louis, Prince of Battenberg, 20
Louisiana Purchase, 63, 162, 216, 245
Love Me Tonight, 165
Loy, Myrna, 189
Lubitsch, Ernst, 165, 170, 175
Luchow's restaurant, 70
Lukas, Paul, 245

M

MacAlear's saloon, 14
McCabe, John, 12
McCormack, John, 104
machine age, 5, 56–57, 91
Mackay, Clarence, 111, 112, 118, 139–40
Mackay, Katherine Duer, 112, 140
McKinney, Nina Mae, *135*
McMein, Neysa, 99, 149
McPherson, Aimee Semple, 153
Maggie: A Girl of the Streets, 8

Magidson, Herb, 167
Mammy, 136, 138, 147
Mamoulian, Rouben, 165, 170, 217
Manson, Alan, 209
March of Dimes, 207
Marks, Edward, 15
Marquis, Don, 93
Marshall, George, 207–8, 211, 213
Martin, Dean, 200
Martin, Mary, 241
Martinelli, Giovanni, 127
Marx, Chico, 115, *116*, 134
Marx, Groucho, 115, *116*, 133–34
Marx, Harpo, 95, 115, *116*, 134
Marx, Zeppo, 115, *116*
Marx Brothers, 115, *116*, 117, 133–34, 200
Mascot lodging house, 14
Mast, Gerald, 105, 130–31, 172, 183, 186, 256
Maxim's, 51
Mayer, Louis B., 231–32
Meet Me in St. Louis, 199, 230, 232
Mencken, H. L., 78, 95
Mendelssohn, Felix, 36, 91
Merman, Ethel, 174, 183, 185, 218, 221–23, 225, *226*, 242, 243–49, *248*, 251, 257, 261, *262*, 264
Merry Whirl, The, 40
Merry Widow, The, 58
Mesta, Perle, 244, 248–49
Metro Goldwyn Mayer (MGM), 126, 131, 134–36, 167, 183, 184, 230–36, 242–43, 259–61
Metropolitan Opera, 63, 68, 112
"Mia Carlotta," 26–27
Michener, James, 252
Middleton, Ray, 221, *226*
Miller, Alice Duer, 111, 149
Miller, Ann, 233–34
Miller, Marilyn, 83, 84, 153, 159, 160, 163
Minnelli, Vincente, 230
minstrel shows, 12, 16, 32–33, 73, 83, 136
Miss Liberty, 7, 163, 238–41, *240*, 244
Mizner, Wilson, 252
Mogilev, 6
Monroe, Marilyn, 251
Monte Carlo, 165
Moore, Clement Clarke, 194
Moore, Grace, 98, 99, 101, 105
Moore, Thomas, 48, 86

More Cheers, 163, 170, 171, 176
Morgan, J. Pierpont, 78
Morgenthau, Henry, 207
movies:
    backstage stories in, 128–30,
      136–39, *139*, 165–66, 168, 169
    censorship in, 242–43
    established hit tunes in, 128–30,
      129, 131, 184, 202, 259
    IB's production involvement in,
      135–43, 169, 179, 231–32
    IB's songs and scores for, 3, 23,
      42, 128–30, *129*, 132–42, *135*,
      139, 165–90, *172*, *177*, *180*, *185*,
      201–6, *206*, 211, 229–36, *231*,
      235, 241–43, 249–51, 259–61
    musical, 128–43, *135*, *139*, 165–90,
      172, *177*, *180*, *185*, 199–206, *206*,
      211, 229–36, *231*, *235*, 241–43
    musical accompaniment to, 17, 45,
      126
    prerecording and sound editing in,
      166, 174, 182, 241–42, 243
    preview showings of, 179
    recorded scores for, 126–32, 140
    "screwball" comedies in, 170, 189
    silent, 5, 13, 16–17, 88, 126–30,
      133, 140
    song slide presentations and, 17,
      126
    sound "shorts" between reels of,
      126–27
    synchronization of sound and
      image in, 125–27, 130–31,
      241–42
    talking, 3, 17, 106, 125, 126, 130,
      131, 132, 133, 138, 149
    technical developments and, 106,
      125–27, 166, 172, 174, 176,
      187–88, 251
    theater chains and, 242
Moviola, 166
Moy, Murty, *226*
Mr. Bones, 136
Mr. President, 257–58, *258*, 263
Mueller, John, 188, 205, 229
musical revues, 3, 58, 60, 68, 73,
    82–84, 89, 97–98
    decline of, 105–6, 112, 151, 198–99
    "little," 151–52
Music Box Revues, The, 136, 178, 179
    of 1921, 89–92
    of 1922, 97–98

    of 1923, 98–101
    of 1924, 105, 106, 137
Music Box Theatre, 3, 88–89, *90*, 95,
    106, 107, 113, 148, 149, 152,
    157, 169, 259
Music Man, The, 218, 257
Mussolini, Benito, 181, 191
Mutiny on the Bounty, 179
My Fair Lady, 163, 218, 239, 252

N

National Association for the
    Advancement of Colored People
    (NAACP), 201
Naughty Marietta, 58
Navy, U.S., 82
NBC radio, 163
Nevada Comstock silver mines, 111
New World Symphony, 23
New York, N.Y:
    Bowery in, 11–14, 16–25, 30, 39,
      48, 65, 88, 109, 133, 228, 237–38
    Bronx in, 65, 128
    Chinatown in, 17–24, *19*, 25, 38,
      52, 65, 88, 109, 180
    entertainment districts in, 11–14,
      16–17, 25–26
    Greenwich Village in, 25, 81, 95,
      110, 111
    immigrant experience in, 7–10,
      12–13
    Lower East Side of, 7–14, 24, 51,
      65, 69, 87–88, 110, 211, 237–38
    prostitution and crime in, 12,
      17–18, *19*, 102
    sweatshops in, 10, 12
    tourism in, 17–18, 20
    Union Square in, 12, 16–17,
      25–27, 70, 109, 110
    Upper East Side of, 263
    Upper West Side of, 54, 95
New York Commission on Amuse-
    ments and Vacation Resources
    for Working Girls, 52
New Yorker, 95, 111, 189
New York Evening Journal, 10–11, 31
New York Mirror, 118
New York *Morning Telegraph*, 39
New York Philharmonic, 127
New York Sun, 50
New York Times, 91, 92, 195, 240–41
New York World, 38, 51, 149
New York World's Fair of 1939, 195

Nicholson, "Professor" Mike "Nick,"
    18, 20–24
nickelodeons, 17, 41, 126
Night and Day, 259
No! No! Nanette!, 132
No Sirree, 97
Nype, Russell, 245–47, *248*

O
Oakley, Annie, 218–30, 243
O'Connor, Donald, 250
Of Thee I Sing, 107, 148, 149, 163,
    216
Oh, Boy!, 71
Oh, Lady! Lady!, 71
O'Hara family, 8–10
Oklahoma!, 124, 188, 199, 216–18,
    241
Oland, Warner, *129*, 130
Olliffe's Drugstore, 17, 23, 88
Olympic Games of 1908, 27
Once and Future King, The, 239
Once in a Lifetime, 149
O'Neal, William, *226*
O'Neill, Eugene, 114
On the Avenue, 182–83
On the Town, 260
opera, 11, 63, 68, 98, 107, 127
operetta, 28, 58, 59, 65, 71, 73, 77,
    107, 123, 127, 165, 169
opium dens, 17–18
Oppenheimer, Joel, 262
Orpheum circuit, 16
Ozzie and Harriet, 181

P
Pagliacci, 127
Pale of Settlement, 5–6
Pal Joey, 216
Palmer, Mitchell, 78
Pan, Hermes, 169, 176–77
Paramount Pictures, 126, 165, 166,
    169, 170, 171, 175, 199–200, 229
Paris, 60, 98, 112, 153
Paris, 132
Parker, Dorothy, 93, 95, 96, 97, 98,
    99, 102, 111, 117
Parsons, Louella, 251
Pelham Café and Dance Hall, 18–24,
    19, 25, 34, 88, 101–2, 179–80
Philadelphia, Pa., 7, 40, 158, 161–62
Phonofilm, 126
phonograph, 103, 106, 125, 126

Photoplay, 131
piano rolls, 103
pianos:
    player, 35, 103
    ragtime and stride styles for, 31,
        34, 36, 74–75
    transposing, 34–35, 41
Piantadosi, Al, 20, 28, 78, 180
Pickford, Mary, 88, 133
Pietri, Dorando, 27
Pinza, Ezio, 241
Pirate, The, 234
pogroms, 6
Poland, 5–6
Polgase, Van Nest, 176
Pong, Jimmy, 17
Pope, Alexander, 96–97, 147
Porgy and Bess, 68, 107, 156, 189,
    216, 217
Porter, Cole, 3–4, 73, 81, 132–33, 142,
    151, 163, 166, 167, 168, 189, 190,
    218, 225, 234, 241, 243, 255, 259
    on IB, 1, 3, 145–46
Pound, Ezra, 264
Powell, Dick, 181–83
Powell, William, 189
Power, Tyrone, 42, 183, 185, *185*
Presley, Elvis, 200, 255
Preston, Robert, 257
Princess Theatre, 71–73, 105, 120
Production Code Administration, 167
Prohibition, 84, 95, 110
P.S. 147, 10
Puccini, Giacomo, 68
Pulitzer, Joseph, 239
Pulitzer Prize, 107, 148
Punch, 28
Puritanism, 95
Puttin' on the Ritz, 137–39, *139*, 174
Pygmalion, 239, 252

R
racism, 78, 124, 157–58, 195–96, 201,
    208–9, 210–11
radio, 3, 5, 70, 104–5, 106, 118, 146,
    184, 185
    ASCAP war with, 196–98, 253
    IB on, 163, 164, 253–54
    payola scandal and, 254
Radio City Music Hall, 179
Radio City Revels, 167
Radio-Keith-Orpheum (RKO),
    166–89, 201, 230–31

ragtime, 2–3, 13, 21, 23, 31–34,
    50–53, 253
    black roots of, 49–50, 51
    brass bands and, 31, 34, 39
    classical melodies in, 36, 63–64, 68
    critical attacks on, 44, 51
    dances spawned by, 2–3, 50,
        51–53, 60–62
    IB's use of, 23, 31, 33–34, 36–45,
        47–50, 52–53, 56–59, 63–64, 68,
        74–75, 76, 89–90, 101
    instrumentals in, 31–32, 33, 34, 39,
        42
    sexual and emotional content of,
        32–34, 36, 37, 52
    structure and syncopated rhythm
        of, 31–32, 34, 36, 50, 52
Ramona, 126
Raye, Johnnie, 251
Raymond, Gene, 167
Razaf, Andy, 49
Reaching for the Moon, 140–43, *141*,
    170, 179
Reagan, Ronald, 211
"Red, Red Rose, A," 86
Report on the Social Evil of 1910, The,
    44
Republican party, 106, 195
"Résumé," 102
Revel, Harry, 167
Reynolds, Marjorie, 201, 202, 205,
    206
Rhapsody in Blue, 110
Rhodes, Eric, 171
Rhynland, 6–7
Richman, Harry, 136–38, *139*, 196,
    229
Richtofen, Baron von, 81
Rickenbacker, Eddie, 81
Riggs, Lynn, 216
Rin-Tin-Tin, 126
Ritz Brothers, 183
Ritz-Carlton Hotel, 111
Roaring Twenties, 4, 139
Robbins Company, 131
Roberta, 168–69
Roberts, Luckey, 34
Rockefeller, John D., 150, 153
rock 'n' roll, 53, 253–55
Rockwell, Norman, 23
Rodeo, 217
Rodgers, Richard, 2, 216–20, 223,
    261, *262*, 264

Lorenz Hart and, 2, 3–4, 73, 120,
    122, 132, 165, 189, 216–17, 241
Oscar Hammerstein and, 124, 174,
    199, 216–19, 224, 228, 230, 240,
    241, 245
Rogers, Ginger, 201
    Fred Astaire and, 3, 62, 130,
        140–41, 150–51, 167–81, *172*,
        177, *180*, 184, 186–90, 230, 232,
        233–34, 241
Rogers, Lela, 176
Roman Catholic Church, 7, 112, 119,
    181, 183, 195
Rooney, Mickey, 128
Roosevelt, Eleanor, 194, 210
Roosevelt, Franklin D., 145, 167, 191,
    207, 210, 213
Roosevelt, Theodore, 17
Ross, Harold, 95, 111
Round the Clock, 39
Royal Air Force, 73
Royal Opera House (Rome), 211–12
Ruby, Harry, 82, 83
Russia, 5–6, 10, 212
Ruth, Babe, 118
Ryan, Robert, 257, *258*
Ryskind, Morrie, 107

S
Sadler, Frank, 65
Salomé, 29
Salter, "Nigger Mike," 18, 20, 23–24,
    25, 88, 101–2, 179–80
Sandburg, Carl, 195, 204
Sandrich, Mark, 169, 171–72, 201
Say It With Music, 136–37, 259–61
Sayonara, 252
Scandal in Budapest, 169
Scandinavia, 7
Scharf, Walter, 205
Schenck, Joseph, 22–23, 88–89, 92,
    133, 134, 181, 230–31, 251
Schubert, Franz, 1
Schwartz, Arthur, 152, 235–36
Scopes "Monkey Trial," 118
Scott, Randolph, 180–81
Scripps-Howard newspapers, 117
Second Fiddle, 186
Selwyn, Edgar, 89
Selznick, David, 166
Seminary Music, 27, 29
Senate Patents Committee, 104
Shakespeare, William, 68, 170

Shall We Dance?, 186
Shanley's restaurant, 70
Shapiro and Bernstein music
    publishers, 14
Shaw, George Bernard, 68, 239, 252
sheet music:
    covers on, 16, 23, 32, 133
    plugging of, 15–17, 40, 53, 69, 70,
        104, 106, 107, 158
    sales and royalties of, 14–17,
        22–23, 27–28, 41, 70–71, 85, 103,
        158, 196–98
    star performances of, 16, 41, 53,
        193, 195, 196
Sheldon, Sidney, 232, 242
Sherwood, Robert, 93, 97, 238–41,
    240
Short, Hassard, 89, 92, 98, 105, 153,
    162
Show Boat, 123–24, 132, 136, 215,
    216, 217
Show Girl, The, 14, 15
Shubert, J. J., 251
Siberia, 6
Sidney, Philip, 55
Sinatra, Frank, 53, 259, 260, 263
Singin' in the Rain, 235, 260
Sixty Club, 92
Smith, Al, 249
Smith, Bessie, 134
Smith, Harry B., 59–60, 62–63, 65,
    71, 73–74, 76
Smith, Kate, 167, 193, 195, 196, *210*
Snapshots of 1921, 89
Snyder, Ted, 30, 31, 33, 36, 40
socialism, 78
Société des Auteurs, Compositeurs
    et Éditeurs de Musique
    (SACÉM), 70
Sondheim, Stephen, 255–56
"Song and Sorrow are Playmates," 42
Sonny Boy, 131
Sousa, John Philip, 103
South Pacific, 239, 241, 242
Soviet Union, 78
Spanish Civil War, 191
speakeasies, 84, 110
spirituals, 23, 134–35
Star is Born, A, 163

Stars on My Shoulder, 257
Statue of Liberty, 7, 238, 239–41
Stein, Gertrude, 153
Stewart, Donald Ogden, 99–100
Stokowski, Leopold, 196
Stop! Look! Listen!, 73–76
"Stopping By Woods on a Snowy
    Evening," 204
Strauss, Richard, 29
Strike Up the Band, 123, 148, 149,
    216, 241
Suicide Hall saloon, 13
Sullivan, Arthur, 2, 12, 28, 64, 71, 73,
    90, 107, 120, 132
Summer Stock, 230, 232
Supreme Court, U.S., 70, 242
Sweet, Jubal, 18–19
swing, 3, 133
Swing Time, 186–87
Swope, Herbert Bayard, 95, 111, 149

T
Taco, 263
tango, 51
Technicolor, 187–88
telegraph, 111
telephone, 44, 104, 105
television, 2, 242, 249
Temple, Shirley, 179
Theatre Guild, 215–16
thé dansants, 51
*There's No Business Like Show
    Business*, 251
Thin Man, The, 189
This Is the Army, 207–13, *210, 212*,
    218, 229, 261
Three Keatons, 16
Till the Clouds Roll By, 259
Time, 163
Times (London), 45
Tin Pan Alley, 14–16, 25–30, 131,
    196–98
    dance craze and, 52–53
    films and, 131
    inroads into legitimate theater by,
        59, 73
    music publishers of, 14–16, 22–23,
        29–30, 32, 49, 52–53, 69–70, 103,
        206, 254

Tin Pan Alley (*continued*)
  preeminence of music over lyrics in, 28, 71
  radio and, 3, 104–5, 146, 163–64, 196–98
  shift from performance to consumption and, 103–4, 146
  shift from urban to rural sentiments in, 198, 220
  song "plugging" in, 15–17, 40, 53, 69, 70, 104, 106, 107, 158
  unisex song lyrics of, 30
  See also sheet music
Titanic, 258
Todd, Mike, 217
Tolochin, 6
Tony Pastor's Music Hall, 16–17, 25, 122
Top Hat, 130, 169–80, *172, 177, 180*, 181, 182, 184, 186, 201, 245
"Treasurer's Report, The," 97, 98
Truman, Harry, 213, 244
Tucker, Sophie, 16
turkey trot, 50, 51, 60
Twain, Mark, 122
Twentieth Century–Fox, 181–86, 231–32, 251
Tyumen, 6

U
United Artists, 23, 133
United States:
  changing social mores in, 44, 95, 102–3, 110–11
  dance craze in, 2–3, 50–53, 60–62, 76, 102, 110, 184, 256
  economic depressions in, 3, 4, 5, 50, 107, 139–40, 145, 148, 150, 164, 166, 181, 191, 192, 193, 216, 231, 248
  economic prosperity in, 106–7, 114–15
  emergence of popular culture in, 11–17, 39–40, 44–45, 50–53
  growth of business and advertising in, 106–7, 158
  immigration patterns in, 6, 7, 44
  isolationism in, 77–78, 195
  new images of women in, 75–77, 103, 110–11, 207
  opportunity and freedom symbolized by, 6–7

  technological development in, 5, 44, 91, 103–6, 125–27, 166
  urbanization and industrialization of, 5, 44, 91, 95, 102–3
Urban, Joseph, 76, 77, 105

V
Valentino, Rudolph, 119
Vallee, Rudy, 146, 167
Variety, 40, 118, 120, 138–39, 180
variety shows, 12, 16
vaudeville, 13, 25, 39, 41, 58, 60, 73, 97, 119, 166, 168
  birth of, 16
  circuits of, 16, 41
  filming of, 126–27
  IB and, 47–48
  poetry recitations in, 26–27
  "singing stooges" of, 15–17, 122
  stars of, 16
Verdi, Giuseppe, 48, 63
Vidor, King, 134, *135*
VistaVision, 251
Vitaphone, 126–28
Vogue, 75
Volstead Act of 1920, 84
Von Tilzer, Harry, 15–16, 25–26, 27, 104
Von Tilzer music publishers, 14–16

W
Waller, Fats, 49
Wall Street Crash of 1929, 11, 107, 139–40, 142, 151, 189
Walters, Charles, 232
waltzes, 3, 28, 32, 50, 68, 100, 101, 113, 115–16, 223, 256
Warner Brothers, 126–28, 131, 136, 142, 165–67, 168, 169, 171, 178, 181, 211
War of 1812, 194
Warren, Harry, 165, 179
Washington, George, 194
Waste Land, The, 103
Watch Your Step, 59–66, *61*, 67, 68, 71, 73–74, 256
Waters, Ethel, 153–58, *156*
Waterson, Berlin & Snyder Company, 49, 52–53, 57, 83, 84, 158
Waterson, Henry, 27–28, 36, 40, 49
Waterson & Snyder Company, 29–30, 33, 36, 40

Webb, Clifton, 153, 159, 162
Weber and Fields, 12
Weill, Kurt, 163, 216
Weser Company, 35
West, Mae, 200
"Westward the Course of Tin Pan
    Alley," 131
Whitcomb, Ian, 64
White, George, 30, 68
White, T. H., 239
White Christmas, 249–51
White House, 104, 257
Whiteman, Paul, 109–10
white slave trade, 17
"Why We Go to Cabarets: A Post-
    Debutante Explains," 111
"Why We Love Band Music," 39
Wilder, Alec, 3, 55, 85, 154, 183
wild west shows, 225–26
Wilk, Max, 121
Williams, Bert, 77, 84
Wilson, Woodrow, 84
Winchell, Walter, 227
Winslow, Max, 25–27, 29, 40, 113–14,
    146
Witmark music publishers, 14, 131
Wizard of Oz, The, 230
Wodehouse, P. G., 71–73
Woolf, Virginia, 44
Woollcott, Alexander, 6, 11, 23, 36,
    92–93, 98, 110, 111
Woolworth's, 15

World's Columbian Exposition, 32
World War I, 3, 5, 77–84, 95, 106,
    112, 185, 191, 206, 207
    armistice signed in, 84, 193
    IB's service in, 5, 79–84, *80*, 208
    outbreak of, 65, 73
World War II, 3, 4, 190, 198, 204,
    206–13, 248

Y
Yankee Doodle Dandy, 259
Yiddish language, 2, 7, 29–30, 36
Yip! Yip! Yaphank, *80*, 82–84, 87, 192,
    207, 209, 210
Youmans, Vincent, 254–55
Young, Joe, 153
"Your Hit Parade," 164, 179, 247, 254

Z
Zanuck, Darryl F., 179, 181–86, 251
Ziegfeld, Florenz, 3, 76–77, 82–83, 84,
    86, 87, 89, 105, 122, *123*, 124,
    132, 151, 160
Ziegfeld Follies, 29–30, 76–77, 87, 89,
    92, 259
    of 1907, 76
    of 1911, 77
    of 1916, 77
    of 1919, 83, 84–86
    of 1924, 105
    of 1927, *123*, 124
    stars of, 29–30, 77, 83, 84–85

About the Author

Philip Furia is the Chair of the Department of English at the University of North Carolina at Wilmington. He is the author of *The Poets of Tin Pan Alley: A History of America's Great Lyricists* and *Ira Gershwin: The Art of the Lyricist*, both published by Oxford University Press. He has also written a book on Ezra Pound. In addition to his books, Professor Furia has written about lyricists and poets in such journals as *American Literature* and *The American Scholar*. A native of Pittsburgh, Pennsylvania, Philip Furia studied at Oberlin College (B.A., 1965), the University of Chicago (M.A., 1966), and the Iowa Writers Workshop (M.F.A., 1970). He received his Ph.D. in 1970 from the University of Iowa and taught at the University of Minnesota (where he was also Chair of the English Department and Associate Dean for Faculty) for twenty-five years. He is a recognized expert in American song lyricists of the "golden age" of popular song (1910–1950) and has been interviewed on "The Larry King Show," "All Things Considered," and other national television and radio programs. He is currently editing two volumes of the *Dictionary of Literary Biography* devoted to American song lyricists and, with his wife, Laurie Patterson, is writing a book about songs in Hollywood musicals.